MEDALS
AND
DECORATIONS
OF THE
BRITISH ARMY AND NAVY

BY

JOHN HORSLEY MAYO

LATE ASSISTANT MILITARY SECRETARY TO THE INDIA OFFICE

WITH NUMEROUS COLOURED PLATES AND ILLUSTRATIONS

VOL. I

Westminster

ARCHIBALD CONSTABLE AND CO.

2 WHITEHALL GARDENS

1897

Printed and bound by Antony Rowe Ltd, Eastbourne

TO

VICTORIA

EMPRESS-QUEEN

WHOSE VIRTUES RICHLY GRACE

THE LONGEST AND MOST GLORIOUS REIGN

OF ENGLAND'S SOVEREIGNS

THIS RECORD OF REWARD

FOR GALLANT DEED AND DEVOTED SERVICE

IS

BY HER MOST GRACIOUS PERMISSION

HUMBLY DEDICATED

PREFACE

ALTHOUGH many of our Naval and Military Medals and Decorations, other than those of Orders of Knighthood, have been described and exemplified in various books, pamphlets, periodicals and catalogues, no attempt has, we believe, been made to compile a complete record of all those which can be traced as having been awarded by the Crown or by Government. It is chiefly with the view of supplying this deficiency that the present work has been undertaken.

The scheme of the work has been to give an account of all the medals of which official evidence has been obtained, accompanied, whenever possible, by illustrations, and to print *in extenso* the General Orders, Royal Warrants, and other papers relating to their issue, many of which have been extracted from manuscript records, and are now printed for the first time. The book will thus be useful not only to those interested in the general subject, but also for official reference.

Several instances of decorations which are not positively known to have been rewards for warlike service, will also be found in the book. Indeed, in respect to many of the earlier medals, it is impossible to determine whether they were intended as military rewards, or merely as tokens of regard. The representations given will, however, serve to illustrate the style of medallic art in the sixteenth and seventeenth centuries.

A few examples of decorations which the author has discovered in the course of his researches among the records of the Hon. East India Company have also been included, although, strictly speaking, they cannot be claimed as being naval or military in character.

It has not been a part of the author's project to give an historical narrative of the operations which occasioned the grant of the various decorations. Accounts of these operations have, in most instances, been published already. Even were such an enormous work as a detailed history of all the events for which medals have been awarded ever to be written, it would be an utterly inadequate record of the wars of England, inasmuch as it would be almost entirely silent in respect to the achievements of our arms ashore and afloat in the eighteenth century.

Our armies which 'swore terribly in Flanders' won no medals there. The conquerors of Plassey and Quebec; the 'unsurpassable six' Minden regiments;[1] Rodney, Hawke, Boscawen and their men;—all these, and many more, never had the gratification of receiving any medallic reward.

In the arrangement of the medals chronological order has as a rule been maintained, this being deemed preferable to a division into classes as Naval, Military or Indian. The decorations for gallantry, long service, and eminence in other directions, are, however, grouped together.

The technical descriptions of the medals have, wherever possible, been taken from the *Medallic Illustrations of the History of Great Britain and Ireland to the death of George II.*; and the author desires to acknowledge most fully the assistance he has thus derived from that valuable work.

Full-size facsimile illustrations of most of the decorations are given.

A photographic process has been adopted in the earlier cases, and there was no occasion in regard to many of them, examples of which in various metals are extant, to indicate in colours any particular metals. Moreover, as in the early days possessors of medals probably did very much as they pleased in respect to mountings and ribbons, there was no necessity to indicate what, after all, might only have been done in a single instance.

In the later cases, however, where there was no doubt about metals, mountings or ribbons, chromo-lithography has been

---

[1] See Carlyle's *Frederick the Great*. The regiments were the 12th, 20th, 23rd, 25th, 37th, and 51st Foot.

employed. Indeed, the ribbon is now so essential a part of the decoration, that not to show its colours accurately would be a serious deficiency.

The illustrations have been executed by Messrs. Maclure and Co., of 97 Queen Victoria Street, London, and it is believed that the coloured examples are the most successful of the kind that have yet been produced. The difficulty to be dealt with was how to produce the effect of relief, and at the same time to obtain a metallic appearance. The method adopted has been to show the flat surface of the medals burnished, and the relief work frosted, the appearance thus produced resembling as nearly as practicable that of medals when newly struck.

The preparation of the book has entailed an extended search, often of a very tedious nature, among old records, in consequence of so-called 'indexes' being little better than caricatures. Indeed, in the old days, the least intelligent clerks would appear to have been selected for the important work of index-making. Certainly the art of indexing was then only imperfectly understood, and the idea was never grasped that the object of an index is to show at a glance whether the book contains information of the description sought.

Much correspondence has been necessary. Inquiries have in most cases received a courteous response, and the author would take this opportunity of sincerely thanking all those who have thus rendered him information and assistance. He desires, however, particularly to record his obligations to the late Mr. R. S. Poole, formerly head of the Medal Department of the British Museum; to Mr. H. A. Grueber, of the same Department; and to Professor J. K. Laughton.

It was originally intended to include in this book the class of medals known as 'Regimental,' and likewise the medals and decorations given by foreign Powers to British officers and men; but it was found that these two classes would of themselves afford sufficient material for a separate volume, and the idea was therefore abandoned.

An Appendix is added in which are printed a number of official and other documents which it was not deemed necessary to insert in the body of the work. Many of these are printed for the first time.

The author is conscious that in some places the text may appear to be overburdened with extracts from official correspondence and regulations, but it would have been difficult to have avoided this. To have put all official documents in the Appendix would have involved the insertion of their substance in the text, when very often the documents themselves tell their own story with sufficient brevity.

A copious index is given, which will enable the information contained in the book to be readily referred to.

Many medals are mentioned the designs of which are not now known; but should any of such medals be extant, the author will feel greatly obliged to their owners if they will kindly communicate with him in regard to them.[1]

Although it is probable that many of the medals of the seventeenth and eighteenth centuries have been melted down, it is doubtless the case that in private hands, as family treasures or heirlooms, there may be several still surviving.

If there could be held a Loan Exhibition of the contents of boxes which for very long periods have been lying unopened in bankers' strong-rooms, a large number of medals would probably be discovered. What a wealth of other objects of value and interest, originally locked up for safety, but now forgotten and therefore practically ownerless, would then be brought to light, can only be left to the imagination to conjecture.

Such an Exhibition would doubtless lead to many objects passing into the hands of those to whom they rightly now belong. At any rate, they would be rescued from the utterly useless, if secure, oblivion to which they are at present consigned.

Of the numerous official documents given in this work, those which have not already been published are now printed with the consent of the Lord President of the Council, the Lords Commissioners of the Admiralty, and the Secretaries of State for War and India.

J. H. M.

---

[1] Such communications may be sent to the Editor, care of the Publishers.

P.S.—Care has been taken to include the grant of medals issued since the author's decease, and many thanks are due to Mr. William Foster of the India Office and to Mr. Alan Duffus of the War Office for assistance given while the work was passing through the press. At p. 603 will be found some Addenda and Corrigenda, which came to light too late for incorporation in the text.

The indulgence of the reader is desired for any blemishes which may appear in the work, which the practised eye of the author would have detected had he been able to supervise its issue from the press.

THE EDITOR.

LIST OF PRINTED BOOKS AND MS. RECORDS CONSULTED DURING THE COMPILATION OF THIS WORK

Admiralty, Minutes of the Board of, now kept at the Public Record Office.
Apsley House, Heirloom Catalogue.
Barrett, Charles Raymond Booth. The Trinity House of Deptford Strond. London, 1893. 4to.
Boulton, Major Charles A. Reminiscences of the North-West Rebellions. Toronto, 1886. 8vo.
Boutell, Charles. Monumental Brasses. London, 1849. 8vo.
British Museum Manuscripts. Additional, Harleian, Sloane, etc.
British Museum, Catalogue of Seals. Department of Manuscripts.
Brown, Richard. History of Cape Breton. London, 1869. 8vo.
Buckle, Captain E. Memoirs of the Bengal Artillery. London, 1852. 8vo.
Bulstrode, Sir R. Memoirs (written 1688). London, 1721. 8vo.
Campbell, John, LL.D. Lives of the Admirals. London, 1750. 8vo.
Carlyle, Thomas. Letters and Speeches of Oliver Cromwell. 1850. 8vo.
Carroll, J. Code of Bengal Military Regulations. Calcutta, 1817.
Carter, Thomas. Medals of the British Army, and How they were Won. London, 1861. 3 vols. 8vo.
Catalogue, East India Company. Loan Collection of Relics. Empire of India Exhibition. 1895.
Catalogue, Exhibition of Miniatures. Burlington Fine Arts Club. 1889.
Catalogue, Guelph Exhibition. 1891.
Catalogue, Royal Military Exhibition. 1890.
Catalogue, Sotheby's. June, 1888.
Chamberlayne, Edward. Present State of England. London, 1687.
Clarendon, Earl of. History of the Great Rebellion. Oxford (Edition 1839).
Clarke, J. S., and M'Arthur, J. Life of Nelson. London, 1809. 4to.
Cochrane, G. E. Staff Corps Rules. London.
Dixon, W. Hepworth. Life of Blake. London, 1852. 8vo.

Duff, James Grant. History of the Mahrattas. London, 1826. 3 vols. 8vo.
East India Company's Records; Court Minutes; Correspondence, etc.
Ellis, Sir Henry, F.R.S. Original Letters, 1686, 1687, 1688. London (Edition of 1829). 8vo.
Evelyn, John, F.R.S. Numismata. London, 1697. Folio.
Favine, Andrew. The Theater of Honour and Knighthood. London, 1623. Folio.
Fontenay, Eugene. Les Bijoux Anciens et Modernes.
Fosbrooke, T. D. Dictionary of Antiquities. London, 1860. 8vo.
Fryer, John, M.D., F.R.S. New Account of East India and Persia. London, 1698. Folio.
General Orders, Army Circulars, etc., issued by the War Office and the Horse Guards.
General Orders by the various Indian Governments and Commanders-in-Chief.
Gentleman's Magazine.
Godwin, George Nelson. The Civil War in Hampshire. London, 1882. 8vo.
Gough, Richard. Sepulchral Monuments. London, 1786. Folio.
Grace, Captain Henry. Code of Military Standing Regulations, Bengal Establishment. Calcutta, 1791–1799. 2 vols.
Haines, Herbert. Manual of Monumental Brasses. London, 1848. 8vo.
Harris, William. Life of Oliver Cromwell. London, 1762. 8vo.
Hartshorne, Albert. On Collars of SS. (Archæological Journal, vol. xxxix.)
Henfrey, Henry William. Numismata Cromwelliana. London, 1877. 4to.
Henley, William. An Abstract of General Orders and Regulations, Hon. East India Co.'s Army, Bengal Establishment. Calcutta, 1812.
House of Commons, Journals of.
Hutchins, Rev. John. History of Dorset. 3rd Edition. 1874. Folio.
India Office Library Tracts.
India Office Records.
Irwin, D. Hastings. War Medals. London, 1890. 8vo.
Laughton, Professor J. K. Memoirs of Richard Griffiths. (Dict. Nat. Biog. London, 1890.)
Low, Charles Rathbone. History of the Indian Navy. London, 1877. 8vo.
Lyde, Robert. A true and exact account of the retaking a ship called the *Friends' Adventure*. London, 1693. 4to.
Macaulay, Thomas Babington, Lord. History of England.
Markham, Clements Roberts. Life of the Great Lord Fairfax. London, 1870. 8vo.
Medallic Illustrations of English History, British Museum. London, 1885. 8vo.
Mint Account, Calcutta.
Moor, Captain Edward. A Compilation of all the Regulations of the Bombay Army, 1750–July 1801. Bombay, 1801. Folio.
Murray, John. Handbook for India. London, 1859.
Naval Chronicle.
New Zealand Gazette.
New Zealand House of Representatives, Journals of.
Nicolas, Sir Nicholas Harris. History of the Orders of Knighthood. London, 1841-42. 4 vols. Folio. (Including History of Medals, etc., for Naval and Military Services.)
Nicolas, Sir Nicholas Harris. Despatches and Letters of Nelson. 1844. 8vo.
Norman, Lieut.-General Sir F. B. Medals and Honorary Distinctions. (United Service Inst. of India, Journal of.)
Numismatic Chronicle. Journal of the Numismatic Society, London. 8vo.
Papworth, John B. Select Views of London. London, 1816. 4to.
Penn, Granville. Memorials of Sir William Penn, Knight. London (Edition 1883). 2 vols. 8vo.
Penruddocke, Charles. Article, Wiltshire Archæological Magazine. Vol. xxvi.

Perry, Francis. A Series of English Medals. London, 1762. 4to.
Pinkerton, T. Medallic History of England. London, 1790. 4to.
Planché, J. R. The Pursuivant of Arms.
Rapin, Paul de Thoyras. The Metallick History of the Reigns of William III. to George I. London, 1747. Folio.
Richter, Rev. G. Manual of Coorg. Mangalore, 1870. 8vo.
Scott, J. R. Memorials of the Family of Scott of Scot's Hall. 1876.
Scott, Sir James Sibbald David, Bart. The British Army. London, 1868. 2 vols. 8vo.
Smith, William. Dictionary of Antiquities. London, 1890. 8vo.
Somerset and Dorset Notes and Queries. Sherborne, 1893. 8vo.
Sprigge, Joshua. Anglia Rediviva. Oxford Edition, 1854. 8vo.
State Papers, Domestic, Treasury, and others, Calendars.
Stothard, C. A. Monumental Effigies of Great Britain. Folio.
Strafforde, Earl of. Letters and Despatches. London, 1739. Folio.
Tancred, Captain George. Historical Record of Medals and Honorary Distinctions. British. London, 1891. 4to.
Van Loon, Gerard. Histoire Metallique des Pays Bas. La Haye, 1732-37. 5 vols. Folio.
Vertue, George. Medals, Coins, Great Seals, Impressions from the Works of T. Simon. London, 1753. 4to.
Vibart, Colonel H. M. Addiscombe: Its Heroes and Men of Note. London, 1894. 8vo.
Walsh, Sir Robert, Knight and Baronet. True Narrative and Manifest. 1679. Folio.
Warburton, Eliot. Prince Rupert and the Cavaliers. London, 1849. 3 vols. 8vo.
Warrants, Royal, not published in the *London Gazette*.
Weiss, Hermann. Kostümkunde. 1880. Stuttgart, 1881-83. 8vo.
Wellington, Duke of. Despatches during his various Campaigns. Edited by Colonel Gurwood. London, 1834–1839. 6 vols.
Wheeler, J. Talboys. Madras in the Olden Time, 1639–1748. Madras, 1861–1862. 3 vols. 4to. Madras, 1882. 1 vol. 4to.
Williams, Captain John. Historical Account of the Rise and Progress of the Bengal Infantry from its formation in 1757 to 1796. London, 1817.
Wilson, Lieut.-Colonel. W. J. History of the Madras Army, 1746–1826. Madras, 1882–1889. 5 vols.
Yule, Sir Henry. Diary of William Hedges. Hakluyt Society. London, 1888.

MEMOIR OF THE AUTHOR

THE writer of this work, the late Mr. JOHN HORSLEY MAYO, was born in London on the 26th November, 1838, being the only son of Mr. John Mayo,[1] for many years in the service of the Hon. East India Company, in the India House, London.

He was educated at Brighton College, and entered the India House on the 28th February, 1855, and from that date, until his retirement from prolonged ill-health in 1895, continued in the service, first of the old Establishment and then of the Government Department in which it was absorbed. From December, 1882, he filled the office of Assistant Military Secretary.

His attention had for many years been called to the subject of Medals and other Decorations issued from time to time to the Naval and Military Forces of the Empire, and the present volumes represent the result of much assiduous labour, careful research, and discriminating selection of materials. Throughout the course of the investigations necessary for the purpose in view, and especially in regard to the preparation of the illustrations which adorn the work, he found an active and sympathetic coadjutor in the person of his wife, who survives him.

The plates of medals had been prepared under the author's superintendence during his lifetime, and the work was practically complete, and the first sheets passing through the press, when he succumbed to a bronchial attack with which, in his delicate state of health, he was unable to cope.

He died on the 29th September, 1895, in his fifty-seventh year, and was buried in the churchyard of Avebury, Wilts, the burial-place of his family.

---

[1] Son of Rev. James Mayo, B.A., Vicar of Avebury, Wilts. See *Genealogical Account of the Mayo and Elton Families*, 1882, p. 58.

He married Apollonia Anne, daughter of the late Vice-Admiral G. S. Reynolds, but left no issue.

Upon Mr. Mayo's decease, the editing of the manuscript was entrusted to his cousin,[1] who has throughout received the invaluable assistance of the widow of the author, already the helper of her husband in the preparation of the work.

C. H. M.

---

[1] Charles Herbert Mayo, M.A., Non-res. Canon of Salisbury, and Vicar of Long Burton with Holnest, Dorset.

ERRATUM.

On page xxiv.—

For "Lord Camoy's Brass, p. xlviii."

Read "Lord Camoy's Brass, facing p. xlviii."

TABLE OF CONTENTS

LIST OF MEDALS

AND OTHER DECORATIONS, AND THE PLATES WITH WHICH THEY ARE ILLUSTRATED

Besides the Plates (55 in number), above mentioned, the following illustrations occur in the text of the work :—

PLATE I.

COLLAR PRESENTED TO THE DUKE OF WELLINGTON,
BY H. R. H. THE PRINCE REGENT.
½ SCALE.

PLATE 2.

PLATE 3.

IACOBVS·D·G·MAG·BRITA·FR·ET·HI·REX

STET·SALVVS·IN·VNDIS

1

IACOBVS·D·G·MAG·BRITA·FR·ET·HI·REX

2

IACOBVS D G MAG BRITA FR ET HI REX
FIDEI DEFENSOR

3

STET·SALVVS·IN·VNDIS

PLATE 4.

1
2
CAROLVS·I·D·G·MAG·BRITANN·FRAN·ET·HIB·REX
NEC·META·MIHI·QVÆ·TERMINVS·ORBI
3
4
CAROLVS·DG·MAG·BRIT·FR·ET·HI·REX
HONI·SOIT·QVI·MAL·Y·PENSE
5

PLATE 5.

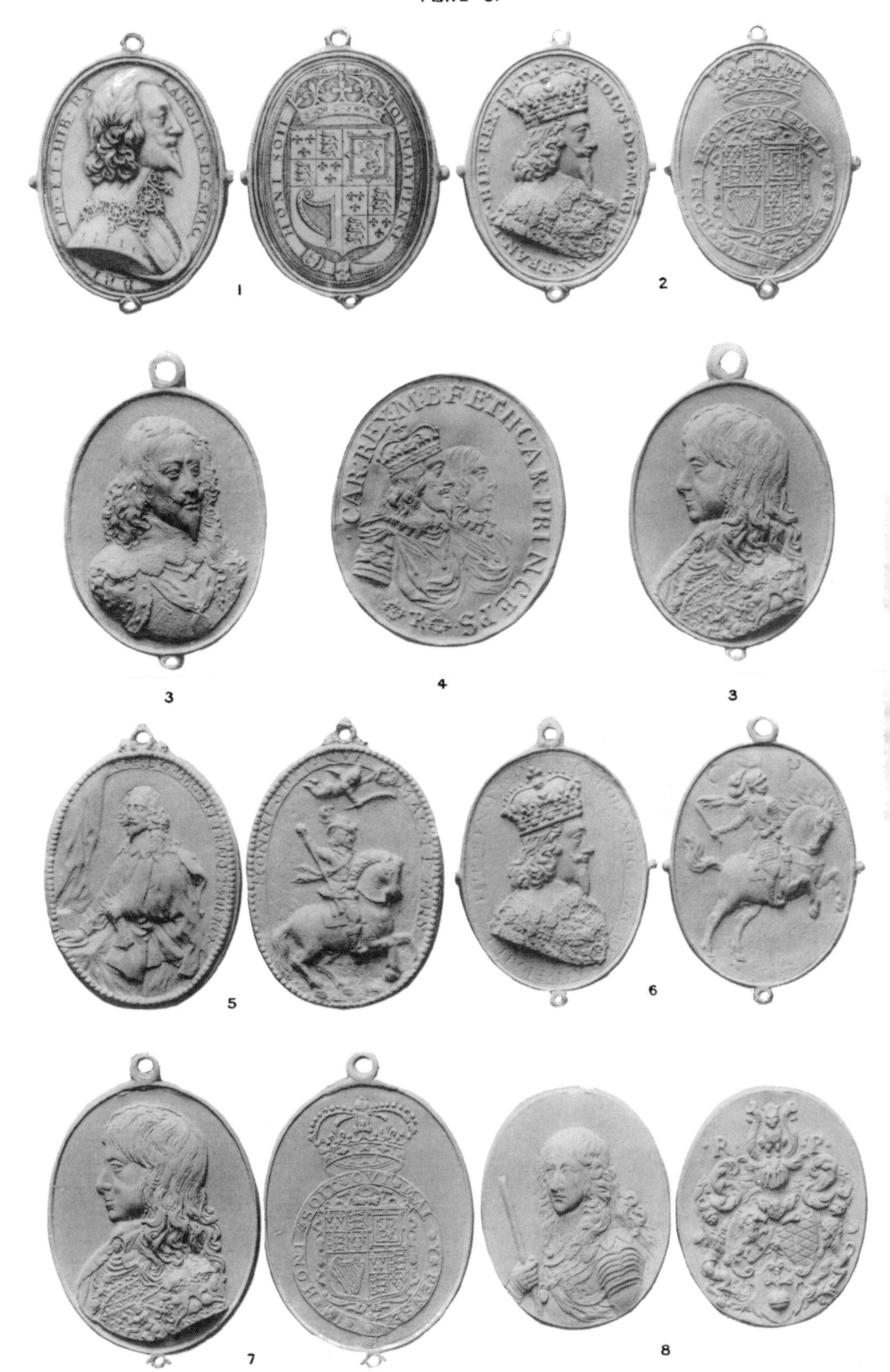

PLATE 6.

(1) CONVEX.

(2) CONVEX.

(3) CONCAVE OF (2)

JEWEL PRESENTED TO SIR THOMAS FAIRFAX,
BY THE HOUSE OF COMMONS.

PLATE 7.

PLATE 8.

1
THE SWORD OF THE LORD AND OF GYDEON
2
3
THE LORD OF HOSTS
4
5
MERUISTI
SERVICE DON AGAINST SIX SHIPS
6

PLATE 9.

PLATE 10.

GEORGE DUKE OF ALBEMARLE
CAROLVS·SECVNDVS·DEI·GRATIA·MAG·BRIT·FRAN·ET·HIBER·REX
·PRO·TALIBVS·
·AVSIS·
CAROLVS·II·D·G·M·BR·FR·ET·HI·REX
NOS·PENES·IMPERIVM
CAROL·II·D·G·ANGL·SCOT·FRAN·ET·HIB·REX
1
2
3
4

PLATE II

IACOBVS·II·ET·MARIA·D·G·MAG·BRI·FRAN·ET·HIB·REX·ET·REGINA·
SEMPER TIBI PENDEAT HAMUS
NAVFRAGA REVERTA
1687
1
IACOBVS·II·DEI·GRA·ANG·SCOT·FRAN·ET·HIB·REX·
GENVS ANTIQVVM
2
GVL·ET·MAR·D·G·M·B·F·ET·H·REX·ET·REGINA·
NOX·NVLLA·SECVTA·EST
3

PLATE 12.

ANNA DEI GRATIA MAG BRITAN FRA ET HIB REGINA
1
IN PIAM MEMORIAM GULIELMI REGIS
2
Her Majties reward
to Capt James Lampriere
for his Zeal to her Service and
his Successfull Conducting ye Squadron
commanded by Rear Admiral Dilkes
who destroyed a considerable number
of ye Enemys Merchant Ships under
Convoy of 3 Men of War
on their own coast
TRUE TO MY TRUST

PLATE 13.

PRO TALIBUS AUSIS

1

CUMBERLAND

2

MDCCXLVI

GEORGIVS·II·DEI·GRATIA·

3

1757.

PLATE 14.

GEORGIUS III DEI GRATIA
PUBLIC REGARD ATTESTIMONY OF
GR
2
By Order of the King with 500 Pound for the Wound Capt. Ewing Recv.d the 17 of June 1775
HONI SOIT QUI MAL Y PENSE
DIEU ET MON DROIT

PLATE 15.

1
2
FOR
SERVICES
IN MYSORE
A.D. 1791 1792
3
FOR
SERVICES
IN MYSORE
A.D. 1791 1792
4

PLATE 16.

FOR SERVICES ON THE ISLAND OF CEYLON A.D. 1795/6.
1
2
IV. MAY. MDCCXCIX.
3
MDCCCI.

PLATE 17

MDCCCX · RODRIGUES VI JULY MDCCCIX · BOURBON VIII JULY & ISLE OF FRANCE III DEC

1

CORNELIS

MDCCCXI. JAVA CONQUERED XXVI AUGUST

2

این تمغا از پیشگاه
نواب گورنر جنرل بهادر
بجلدوی حسن خدمت
و تردد و جان بازی که
در سنه هجری ۱۲۲۹ و ۱۲۳۰
مهم کوهستان بظهور
رسیده عنایت گردید

3

PLATE 18.

REAR-ADMIRAL LORD NELSON OF THE NILE

1

ALMIGHTY GOD HAS BLESSED HIS MAJESTY'S ARMS
VICTORY OF THE NILE
AUGUST 1.1798

HORAT'O. V'SCO'NT NELSON . K · B · DUKE OF BRONTE .

2

ENGLAND EXPECTS EVERY MAN WILL DO HIS DUTY
TRAFALGAR
OCT: 21: 1805

3

CAPTAIN
JAMES WOOLDRIDGE
LED THE
BRITISH FIRE SHIPS
WHEN

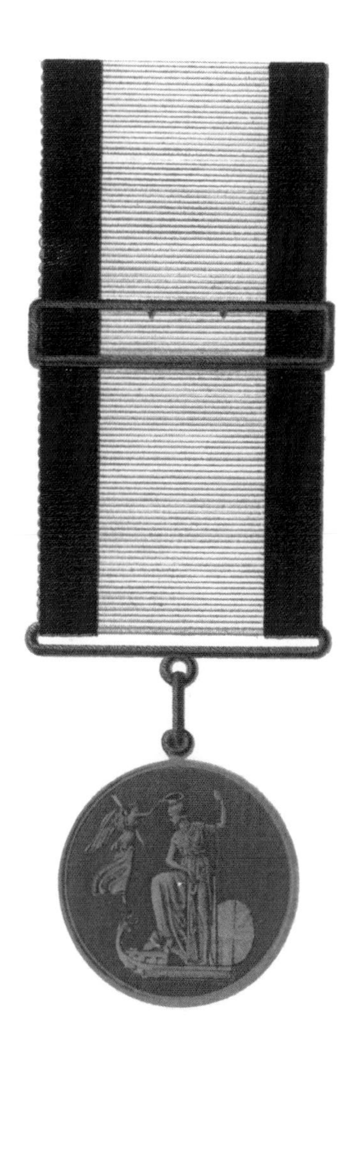

GOLD MEDALS – NAVY.

GOLD MEDALS – ARMY.

CIUDAD RODRIGO
BADAJOZ
SALAMANCA
VITTORIA
VIMIERA
TALAVERA
BUSACO
FUENTES DE ONOR

PLATE 22.

MAIDA. WATERLOO.

1

2

REWARD OF MERIT

3

FOR DISTINGUISHED CONDUCT AND LOYALTY TO THE BRITISH GOVERNMENT
COORG
APRIL 1837

PLATE 24.

GHUZNEE – 1839

KELAT – I – GHILZIE.

PLATE 25.

1ST 2ND

JELLALABAD.

PLATE 26.

AFGHANISTAN — 1842

PLATE 27.

MILITARY COLLEGE ADDISCOMBE
PRESENTED BY
THE BRITISH INHABITANTS
OF CALCUTTA
AND AWARDED BY
THE SECRETARY OF STATE
FOR INDIA
TO THE MOST DISTINGUISHED
CADET
OF THE SEASON
POLLOCK PRIZE

1

2

1 & 2

3

4

PLATE 28.

CHINA.

VICTORIA
REGINA

MEEANEE
1843

HYDERABAD
1843

MEEANEE
HYDERABAD
1843

SINDE 1843.

PLATE 30.

MAHARAJPOOR
PUNNIAR
1843

PLATE 31.

SUTLEJ

PLATE 32.

PUNJAB.

INDIAN MUTINY.

PLATE 33.

GENERAL SERVICE
ARMY.

GENERAL SERVICE
NAVY.

GENERAL SERVICE
INDIA.
1ST

GENERAL SERVICE
INDIA.
2ND

PLATE 35.

ARCTIC.

PLATE 36.

CRIMEA.

BALTIC.

SOUTH AFRICA.

PLATE 38

ABYSSINIA.

ASHANTEE.

PLATE 39.

NEW ZEALAND. CANADA.

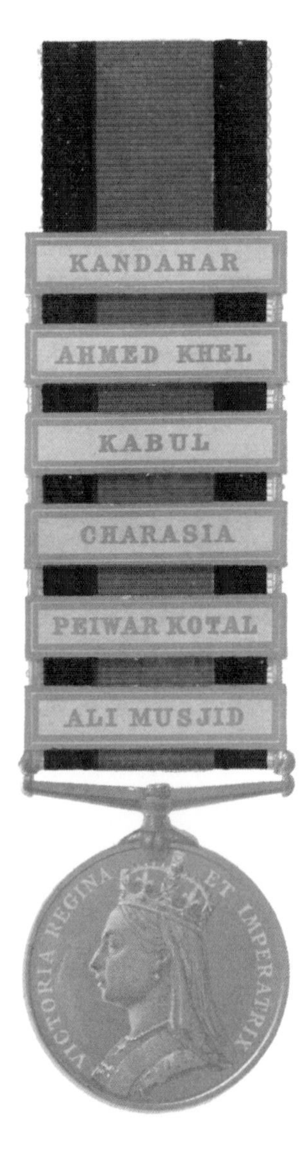

AFGHANISTAN 1878 - 80.

EL-TEB _ TAMAAI
TAMAAI
EL-TEB
SUAKIN 1884
TEL-EL-KEBIR
ALEXANDRIA 11TH JULY
VICTORIA REGINA ET IMPERATRIX
EGYPT
1882

EGYPT 1882

EGYPT

PLATE 42.

PLATE 43.

ORDER OF MERIT

VICTORIA CROSS.

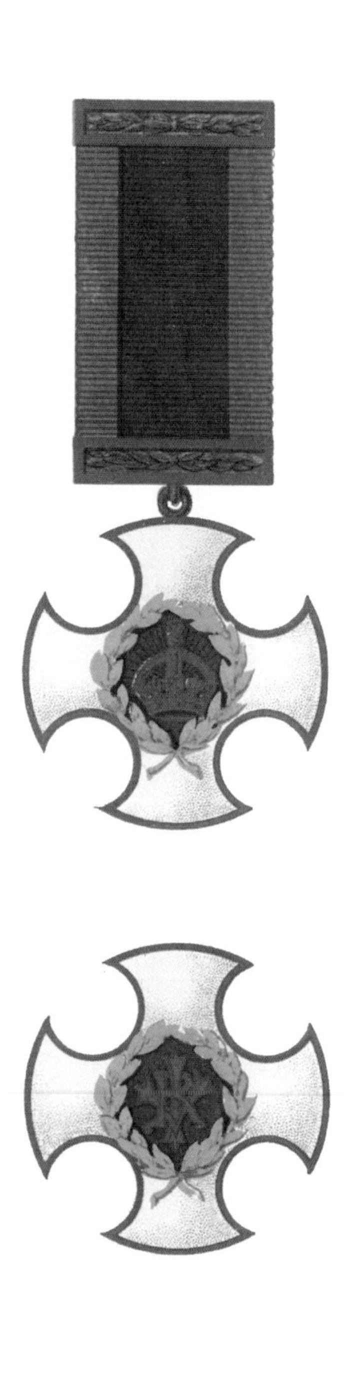

PLATE 45.

ARMY.

NAVY.

PLATE 46.

LONG SERVICE &c. — NAVY.

PLATE 47.

LONG AND MERITORIOUS SERVICE — ARMY.
BRITISH.

PLATE 48.

LONG AND MERITORIOUS SERVICE — ARMY.
INDIA.

PLATE 49.

BEST SHOT.
BRITISH ARMY.

BEST SHOT.
INDIAN ARMY

PLATE 50.

THE MAGDALA MEDALS

PLATE 51.

1300 1500
1860
SIT PERPETUUM

THE NATIONAL
RIFLE
ASSOCIATION
1860.

Presented by the Government of India

BEST SHOT OF THE VOLUNTEERS

PLATE 52.

MISS NIGHTINGALE'S JEWEL.

ROYAL RED CROSS

LIFE·AT·SEA

SAVING·LIFE·ON·LAND

FOR·GALLANTRY·IN·SAVING·LIFE·AT·SEA

SEA

FOR·GALLANTRY·IN·SAVING·LIFE·ON·LAN

LAND

FOREIGN OFFICE MEDALS.

PLATE 55.

EMPRESS OF INDIA.

QUEEN VICTORIA.

INTRODUCTION

THE personal decorations employed amongst the ancients as honorary rewards for military or athletic achievements were crowns or wreaths, and ornaments for the neck and arm. Fillets or ribbons were also worn round the head as emblems of victory.

The following crowns were used by the Romans:—Corona Obsidionalis (grass or wild flowers); Corona Civica (oak); Corona Navalis or Rostrata (gold); Corona Muralis (gold); Corona Castrensis or Vallaris (gold); Corona Triumphalis (laurel or gold); Corona Ovalis (myrtle); Corona Oleagina (olive).

The personal decorations, other than those of Orders of Knighthood, awarded in modern times in recognition of warlike services, consist of collars, chains, medals, crosses, stars, and various kinds of badges and clasps. The sword of honour may likewise be considered as in the nature of a personal decoration.

Although the practice of commemorating important events by medals is of ancient origin, the custom of making the medal serve a double purpose by using it as a decoration is comparatively modern.[1] When or where the custom originated has not been ascertained.

---

[1] The Chinese, however, seem to have been an exception. Military medals are said to have been used during the Han dynasty, A.D. 10 (*English Encyclopædia*, 1860).

It used to be supposed that the circular ornaments on Roman standards had medals in their centres. But there does not seem to be satisfactory evidence that this was the case. Otherwise, the Roman standard might have been cited as the earliest example of the use of the medal in a decorative manner. None of the standards shown on the column of Trajan appear to have anything else in their centres than plain bosses.

The crosses borne on the garments of the Knights Hospitallers and Knights Templars were merely the badges of their Orders, and were not intended as decorations. But this use of the cross doubtless led to its introduction into the decorations of many later Orders of Knighthood, so that what was originally a simple distinctive mark became the basis of an elaborate ornament.

With respect to the army, in some cases a badge conferred on the individual soldiers of a regiment in commemoration of a particular event, as a medal might be, has been retained by the corps as its own distinctive badge, thus losing its character as a personal honorary reward.

The following are some of the earlier decorative medals conferred in Europe and America :—

1622-3—Holland. Medal to Volunteers.
1630—Sweden. Military Medal of Gustavus Adolphus.
1706-7—Austria. Medal for Campaign.
1708—Russia. Medal for Liesna.
1709—Russia. Medal for Pultowa.
1757—Prussia. Cross for Battle of Lissa.
1792—Brunswick. Medal for Royal Swiss Guards.
1793—France. Cross for Siege of Lyons.
1797—Papal States. Medal for Military Service.
1801—Denmark. Medal for Battle of Copenhagen.
1807—Baden. Medal.
1811—Spain. Cross for Albuhera.
1812—S. America. Argentina, Medal.
1814— „ Venezuela, Medal to prisoners of War.
1815— „ New Granada, Medal for Siege of Carthagena.
1815—Oldenburg. Medal for Military Merit.
1830—Belgium. The Iron Medal.

In England, although the wearing of medals was common in the reign of Henry VIII., the earliest instance we know of one commemorative of a particular event being evidently meant to be worn as an ornament, is the Armada Medal.

British naval and military decorations may be classed generally under two heads :—

I. As rewards to particular individuals :—
(*a*) For personal valour.
(*b*) For generally meritorious behaviour.

II As rewards for participation in battles or campaigns :—
(*a*) To commanders and superior officers.
(*b*) To officers and men alike.

Again, the use on some occasion of a particular thing as a badge may lead to its adoption as a national badge. For example, the wearing of the leek by the Welsh soldiers at the battle of Crecy. Captain Fluellyn says :—

'The Welshmen did goot service in a garden where leeks did grow, wearing leeks in their Monmouth caps ; which your Majesty knows to this hour is an honourable badge of the service.'—*Henry V.*, Act iv. Scene 7.

CLASS I. (*a*).

This comprises the Forlorn-Hope Badge of Charles I.; the Medal for Captains of Fireships; the Indian Order of Merit; the Victoria Cross; the Medals for Distinguished Conduct in the Field, and for Conspicuous Gallantry; together with many medals and badges given by officers or private individuals in recognition of signal acts of bravery. In this subdivision may likewise be included the Albert Medal, although it is not a reward for *warlike* service.

CLASS I. (*b*).

The various medals given during the Commonwealth and the five reigns which succeeded it; the Order of British India; the Distinguished Service Order; the Medals for Meritorious Service, and for Long Service and Good Conduct. To these may be added the numerous decorations which were formerly given regimentally as rewards for long or meritorious service.

CLASS II. (*a*).

The Armada Medals; those given by the Parliament to Monk, Blake, and others; and the gold medals and crosses given in the reign of George III.

CLASS II. (*b*).

The Dunbar Medal; the earlier medals given by the Government of India; the medals for the Nile and Trafalgar given by Davison and Boulton. The Waterloo Medal heads the series awarded by the Crown.

The great Napoleon set a high value on military decorations. Lord Nelson greatly appreciated medals, and he was indignant with the Government for not sanctioning one for Copenhagen. Lord Collingwood, also, had a high regard for medals. The Duke of Wellington does not appear to have held any very pronounced views on the subject. But he was not altogether satisfied with the system under which the Peninsular gold medals and crosses were given to general and field officers only; he would have preferred that all ranks of officers should have been eligible, and that the medals should only have been granted for individual services calling for special reward.

Amongst others, General Sir Charles Napier may be cited as placing a very high value on medals, and he has left it on record that he would have preferred a medal to prize-money.

MEDALS AND DECORATIONS.

The following is a brief account of the grants of decorative war medals from the time of Queen Elizabeth to the present day.

QUEEN ELIZABETH, 1558-1603.

The decorative medals of this period are numerous, and often very handsome. Whether any of them were 'war medals,' in our sense of the term, it is not easy to say; but it is a traditional belief that in several instances they were bestowed as rewards for the defeat of the Spanish Armada. Jewels were given by the queen as honorary rewards, and some of them are still in existence.

JAMES I., 1603-1625.

It is very doubtful whether any of the decorative medals of this reign have a distinct reference to war services.

CHARLES I., 1625-1649.

The medals and badges of the reign of Charles I. are very numerous, and, for the first time, we meet with examples manifestly associated with military events.

Although most of these display the portrait of the king, and were probably bestowed by him, several bear the portraits of other persons, and it cannot always be determined whether the medals were in the nature of rewards, or merely tokens of friendship. The practice of wearing medals and badges was very common, and the same badge, which may in one case have served as a reward, may in another have been only a token of regard.

To Charles I. may be attributed the introduction of a definite system in respect to the bestowal of decorations as rewards for military service. By a Royal Warrant, issued at Oxford in 1643 (see p. 9), His Majesty instituted a silver badge, bearing the images of himself and his son, Prince Charles, as a reward to soldiers distinguishing themselves in forlorn-hopes.

PARLIAMENT AND COMMONWEALTH, 1649-1660.

The Parliament and the Commonwealth were somewhat lavish in recognising warlike services by means of medals; and statutory provision was made for their bestowal as naval rewards.

ACTS OF PARLIAMENT IN THE YEAR 1648, *Cap.* 12.

'ACT FOR ENCOURAGEMENT TO MARINERS AND IMPRESSING SEAMEN.

'*Passed 22nd February*, 1648.

'*Section* 7. Provided also, That the Tenths of all Prizes customarily due to the Lord High Admiral shall be paid into the hands of such Treasurer as the Council of State shall appoint for the Profits of the Admiralty; the said Tenths to be disposed by order of the said Council, for Medals or other Rewards, to such Officers and Seamen of the Fleet, as by certificate under the hand and seal of the Commissioners commanding the Fleet at Sea, or any two of them, shall be found to have done any singular, eminent, and extraordinary service therein. And the said Council of State is hereby required to take special care for the observance of this Act, in all points concerning the encouragement of Officers, Mariners and Seamen to engage in this Service, that none may be defrauded of any benefit or advantage growing due unto them by virtue of this Act, or anything therein contained, according to the tenor and true meaning thereof.'

This provision was re-enacted by the Act passed 17th April, 1649, cap. 21, sec. 10. See Appendix A.

COUNCIL OF STATE, *8th May*, 1649.

'The Council of State, on 8th May, 1649, ordered that £1000 out of the tenths of the Admiralty should be laid up for making chains and medals, as rewards to officers and mariners who should do eminent service at sea; and on 29th June following, a Warrant was issued by the Admiralty Committee to the Collectors for Prize goods, to lay up for the above purpose the tenths of the prizes that came to their hands until they amounted to £1000. (See Medal No. 39.) The Proceedings of the Council of 15th November, 1649, furnish evidence as to the designs of these Medals. They were to bear on one side the arms of the Commonwealth, with the word "Meruisti"; and on the other a picture of the House of Commons.' (*Calendar of State Papers—Domestic Series*, 1649-50, pp. 130, 214.)

19*th and* 21*st November*, 1649.

'Thomas Simons, Chief Graver to the Mint, was appointed to make the Medals, and he was allowed to have the use of presses from the Tower for the purpose. He was, however, required to find security to the amount of £500 that the presses were not put to any unlawful use.' (*Calendar of State Papers—Domestic Series*, 1649-50, pp. 401, 555.)

20*th December*, 1652.

'Three years later, the Council of State, in considering certain propositions for the encouragement of seamen, ordered that the Lord Admiral's tenths of all prizes be appointed for defraying the charges of the sick and wounded, and for the relief of the widows and children of those slain in the service at sea; also for Medals and rewards to officers and seamen.' (*Calendar of State Papers—Domestic Series*, 1652-3, p. 43.

Thus the whole of the Lord Admiral's tenths, instead of £1000 of them if they amounted to more than that sum, were set aside for public purposes.

Under the operation of the above Acts and Orders many medals and chains were given as rewards for sea service, the principal event being Blake's victories over the Dutch in 1653.

Although there does not appear to have been any corresponding general provision for the grant of medals to officers and men of the army, several instances of such grants are on record, orders having been issued as the occasions arose; the battle of Dunbar was the most noteworthy.

On a few occasions valuable *jewels* were voted by the Parliament as military rewards.

Decorations usually in the form of gold chains were bestowed on the ministers and agents of foreign states. The Swedish Ambassador, however, received a jewel worth £850.

This practice on the part of the Commonwealth authorities was a compliance with foreign custom. Their attention had been directed to the subject by Sir Oliver Fleming, Master of the Ceremonies, who, in a letter to the Council of State, dated April, 1649, stated that he required instructions in the place the Commonwealth had intrusted to him.[1] He desired to know what titles he was to give the Commonwealth and Council of State in conversing with foreign ministers. He related something of the customs of foreign nations in such matters; and in regard to the Republic of Venice, after describing the manner of receiving ambassadors, ordinary or extraordinary, stated that on departure the extraordinaries had a gold chain worth 2000 ducats, and the ordinaries one worth 1000, and their secretaries chains of less value, presented to them. (*Calendar of State Papers—Domestic Series*, 1649-50, p. 114.)

Most of the medals of this period were the work of Thomas Simon, Master and Chief Graver of the Mint, and they are generally considered to be amongst the best specimens of the medallic art that have been produced in this country. After the victory of Dunbar, he was specially deputed by the Parlia-

---

[1] We do not know whether Sir Oliver Fleming wore any distinctive badge as Master of the Ceremonies. The office of Master of the Ceremonies was instituted by James I., for the more honourable reception of ambassadors and strangers of quality. Sir Charles Cotterel, who held the office in the time of Charles I., and who followed the fortunes of Charles II. while abroad, was reappointed to the office at the latter's restoration. The king, as a mark of his favour, and of the said office, put about his neck (the day before his coronation) a 'Chain of gold, with a Medal under the Crown of England, having on the one side an emblem of Peace, with King James's motto, *Beati Pacifici*; and on the other, an emblem of War, with *Dieu et mon Droit*; which mark is to continue to his successors.' (See *Present State of England*, by Edward Chamberlayne, London, 1687, p. 160.) The chain and badge, as above described, are still worn by Her Majesty's Master of the Ceremonies.

ment to repair to Scotland to take the likeness of the Protector for the medal for that battle.[1]

CHARLES II., 1649-1685.

The medals of this reign are very numerous. Although the nominal duration of the reign was from 1649 to 1685, it is to the latter twenty-five years of the period that most of the medals awarded by the king for warlike services are to be ascribed. Before the Restoration he had, however, bestowed medals on many individuals who had shared his misfortunes.

The only instance in this reign of a regulation bearing on the grant of medals is an Order in Council in 1669 (see p. lx), providing for the issue of medals and chains to captains of fireships burning any of the enemy's vessels. As the medals and chains were to be of the value of £30, they were probably of gold. Instances of the grant of medals for other services, but chiefly by sea, are also met with, but they are not very numerous. We have the testimony of Evelyn that it was the practice of His Majesty to bestow medals and chains as 'gratuities of respect' (see p. 40).

In this reign we first find notices of the grant of medals for services rendered to the East India Company.

It was His Majesty's intention, in commemoration of his restoration, and as a mode of rewarding those who had been faithful to him, to institute an Order of Knighthood to be styled the 'Order of the Royal Oak,' but the intention was never carried out. The badge of the Order was, it is said, to have been the medal by T. Simon, bearing on the *obverse* the bust of Charles II., and on the *reverse* an oak tree, with three crowns in it, and the sun shining above.—(See Vertue, p. 46; and *Medallic Illustrations*, vol. i. p. 476.)

Amongst the petitions addressed to Charles II., there is one by John Madden and Dr. Henry Wyatt, representing that there was no external badge to distinguish baronets from knights

---

[1] Simon does not appear to have always received very prompt payment for his work. On 3rd August, 1658, we find him petitioning the Council for payment of £1160, and complaining that although he had a year before presented to them his account for making coins, public seals for England, Scotland, and Ireland, and divers medals and chains of gold, he had not been paid. He begs the Council to consider that he and his servants had wrought for five years without recompense, and says that the interest he had to pay for gold and silver eat up his profits. (*Calendar of State Papers—Domestic Series*, 1658-9, pp. 105-6.)

bachelors, although Knights of the Garter and the Bath, and Baronets of Nova Scotia had such a badge; and requesting that baronets might wear a gold medal, pendent to a green ribbon, with the effigy of the sovereign who created them, and that the petitioners might be empowered to provide the said medals. No date. (*Calendar of State Papers—Domestic Series*, 1661-2, p. 223.)

This project does not appear ever to have been carried into execution.

JAMES II., 1685-1688.

This short reign does not offer many instances of medals for war services. Some few were given by the East India Company.

WILLIAM III. AND MARY, 1689-1694.

WILLIAM III., 1694-1702.

Several medals were given for sea service during these reigns; none apparently for land service.

In an Act passed in 1692, provision was made for the grant of medals and other rewards for sea service.

'4° GUL: & MAR: Cap. 25, 1692.

'An Act for continuing the Acts for prohibiting all Trade and Commerce with France, and for the encouragement of Privateers.

. . . . . .

'X. Provided always and be it further enacted that in all cases where the said Prize shall not be taken by any private Man-of-War one-tenth part thereof after such sale and deduction of their Majesties Customs as aforesaid (and before any division of the proceed thereof shall be made as aforesaid) shall be paid to the Treasurer of the Navy for the time being, which tenth part shall be separated and kept apart by the said Treasurer of the Navy and shall be disposed of from time to time by Warrant of the Commissioners for executing the Office of Lord High Admiral or Lord High Admiral for the time being for Medals and other Rewards for Officers, Mariners, and Seamen in their Majesties Service at Sea who shall be found to have done any signal or extraordinary service.'

The above provision is practically identical with the provisions comprised in the Acts of 1648 and 1649. Under its authority and that of the Order in Council of Charles II., a large number of gold medals were awarded to individuals for service against the enemy at sea. Except, however, in the case of Captain Jolliffe of Poole in 1695, we are unacquainted with the design made use of. Captain Jolliffe's medal may reasonably be regarded as typical of the series. The *obverse* is the same as that of the medal for La Hogue, namely, the busts of the king and queen; the *reverse* bearing an engraved inscription. After the queen's death the *obverses* would have borne the effigy of the king alone. The *reverses* would have been blank to admit of suitable inscriptions being engraved.

William III. presented Sir Godfrey Kneller with a gold chain of the value of £300, and a medal.

ANNE, 1702-1714.

In the following Royal Declaration, published shortly after the accession of Queen Anne, further provision was made as to medals for sea service:—

'HER MAJESTY'S MOST GRACIOUS DECLARATION.

'FOR THE INCOURAGEMENT OF HER SHIPS OF WAR AND PRIVATEERS.

'ANNE R ,

'Her Majesty, for maintaining the Publick Faith, for Vindicating the Honour of Her Crown, and for Preventing the Mischiefs which all Europe is threatened with, Finding Herself obliged to Declare War against France and Spain, is Resolved, in so Just and Necessary an Undertaking, in Conjunction with Her Allies, Vigorously to Prosecute the same. And being most Graciously Inclined to give all due Encouragement to the Valour and Fidelity of Her Subjects, serving Aboard any of Her Majesties Ships of War or Privateers, hath thought fit, by the Advice of Her Council, to Publish and Declare':

(Here follow regulations regarding prizes captured from the enemy.)

'That there shall be also paid out of Her Majesties Shares of Prizes, all such sum and sums of money as the Lord High Admiral shall, from time to time, Think fit to Direct to be Paid to any Person or Persons for Medals or other Rewards for Officers, Mariners, Seamen or Soldiers, or others, who shall be found to have done any Eminent or Extraordinary Sea Service.

. . . . . .

'Given at Our Court at St. James's the First Day of June, 1702. In the First Year of Our Reign. God save the Queen.'

(*London Gazette*, 1st-4th June 1702, No. 3815.)

This provision differs from the Act of 1692, in that the medals and other rewards are to be paid for out of Her Majesty's share of prizes, whereas that Act directed that they were to be defrayed from a tenth part of the prizes specially set apart for the purpose.

The following Admiralty Minute provided that, as a rule, the capture of prizes by privateers should not be held to call for the grant of medals.

'ADMIRALTY OFFICE, 16 *Nov*r. 1703.

'It was agreed that noe Letters of Mart men, or Privatrs who take Prizes shall have Medalls and Chaines, because of the benefitt they have by the said Prizes, unless they do some signall service, and that then it be consider'd of.'

From the *Journals of the House of Commons* of 7th and 11th November, 1704 (Appendix A.), it appears that the sum of £575 had recently been paid by order of the Lord High Admiral for medals and other rewards for extraordinary service at sea, pursuant to Her Majesty's Declaration.

Medals were granted to several individuals in this reign, but the only one of which we have been able to obtain a description is that presented to Captain Lampriere in 1703.

GEORGE I., 1714-1727.

We have not been able to trace any medals as having been given by George I. in reward for military service.

In several instances medals were awarded by the India authorities.

GEORGE II., 1727-1760.

Exceptional merit seems still to have attached to the burning of an enemy's ships. Charles II.'s plan of giving medals and chains of the value of £30 to the captains of fireships had, however, undergone some modification, since from the *Minutes of the Privy Council* of 16th December, 1742 (see p. lxii), it appears that it was then the established practice of the navy to allow a reward of £100, or a gold medal and chain of that value, for burning a ship of forty guns or more. An Order in Council, of the same date, instituted a reward of £50 to lieutenants of fireships.

On the ground that it had been usual in the wars of William III. and Queen Anne to reward good service done by private ships against the enemy, a gold medal and chain were awarded in 1744 (see p. 92), to Richard Hornby, master of a ship belonging to Sunderland.

There is reason to believe that one or more medals, struck in commemoration of the battle of Culloden, were worn as decorations, but we are not aware whether they were issued by authority of the Government—probably not.

GEORGE III., 1760-1820.

This long reign, embracing as it did so many naval and military services of the first importance, was productive of several medals, although those given by the Crown—viz. the naval and military gold medals, the medal for Maida, and the gold cross and the Waterloo medal—belonged to the latter half of it. The first four were given to officers only; the last was given to all ranks alike, being the first occasion on which such a general distribution had ever taken place under the orders of the Crown.

A distribution of medals to all ranks engaged in the battles of the Nile and Trafalgar was, however, made at the expense respectively of two private individuals—Mr. Davison and Mr. Boulton.

In India the practice of bestowing medals on all ranks of the native army was resorted to by the Government of the East India Company on several occasions—the first being in 1784, in the case of an army which had been operating in the west of India. The other services thus commemorated were campaigns in the Carnatic, the expedition to Ceylon, the capture of Seringapatam, the expeditions to Egypt, Mauritius and Java, and the Nepaul War.

The earliest case we can trace of the bestowal of a medal by George III. is that of Captain Ewing. A wound gratuity of £300 accompanied the medal.

The reconstitution of the Order of the Bath, after the Peninsular War, removed the necessity for rewarding superior officers by means of medals, the several classes of the Order affording suitable rewards for the various ranks. The East India Company had contemplated the application to India of the system in respect to medals and crosses which had obtained in the British service, but in their case also the extension of the Order of the Bath rendered it unnecessary.

GEORGE IV., 1820-30.

The only medals issued during the reign of George IV. were those given by the Government of India to the native troops who took part in the Burmese War of 1824-26, and to certain friendly native chiefs who co-operated with the British forces during that war.

WILLIAM IV., 1830-1837.

To William IV. is to be ascribed the inauguration of a regular system of bestowing medals as rewards for meritorious service and good conduct on the part of soldiers and sailors.

The institution of these medals led to the discontinuance of the practice of medals for long service and good behaviour being given regimentally by the colonel or officers.

In 1837 the East India Company took the important step of instituting two Orders of Distinction for their native troops: the one being the Order of British India, for the reward of general *merit*; the other, denominated the Order of Merit, being the special reward of *bravery*. The latter Order was, in fact, the forerunner of the Victoria Cross.

QUEEN VICTORIA, 20TH JUNE, 1837.

The reign of Her Most Gracious Majesty, although celebrated for the advances made in respect of all affairs which flourish in a time of peace, has been prolific also in decorations commemorative of warlike events.

Commencing with the siege of Ghuznee in 1839, the series of war medals is continued in commemoration of the successes of the British arms in Afghanistan, Sinde, China, the Punjab, South Africa, the Crimea, the Indian Mutiny, the North-West Frontier of India, Abyssinia, New Zealand, Ashantee, Afghanistan, Egypt, and Matabeleland.

For the peaceful expeditions to the Arctic regions, medals were also awarded.

Her Majesty has likewise instituted the Victoria Cross and the Albert Medal as Orders of Distinction for acts of signal bravery, besides medals for exceptional gallantry in both services. She has also founded the Distinguished Service Order for officers of the Army and Navy. The Order of the Royal Red Cross has been established by her as a reward to women for devotion to the sick and wounded.

Excellence in musketry, in both the regular and volunteer forces, has likewise been duly recognised.

Another feature of Her Majesty's reign has been the grant of medals to the survivors of those who participated in services, whether by sea or land, since 1793, which had not previously been so commemorated; and the survivors had therefore the satisfaction of receiving, albeit somewhat late in the day, the coveted reward of their services.

Almost the latest decoration is that for officers of volunteers for long and approved service. If an officer has served the required number of years, and has fulfilled the other prescribed conditions, he is qualified for the decoration. The principle is a novel one in the British service, and, like that which governs the grant of medals for long service and good conduct in the ranks, perhaps somewhat mechanical; but having been introduced into one branch of the public service, and a beginning thus made, it will possibly be extended to others, so that eventually no commissioned officer of twenty years' service in the Army or Navy will remain undecorated.

In 1894 the grant of decorations for Meritorious Service, Distinguished Conduct in the Field, and Long Service and Good Conduct, was extended to the Colonies, and the grant of the Volunteer Officers' Decoration to India and the Colonies, followed in 1896 by the Volunteer Long Service Medal for Indian and Colonial Forces.[1]

MEDALS FOR SERVICE IN INDIA.

As the medals for service in India constitute so large a proportion of our national series, it may be well to devote a few lines to their separate treatment.

The London East India Company early adopted the practice of bestowing medals as honorary rewards for important services performed by those in their employ; and later on the practice was also resorted to by the representatives of the Company in India.

All the earlier medals were bestowed on individuals as rewards for particular services. The earliest appears to be that given by the Company in 1668 to Sir George Oxinden, who, as President of Surat, had rendered considerable civil and military services.

In 1673 the Company awarded gold medals to Mr. Gerald Aungier, President of Surat, and to Mr. Streynsham Master, in reward for their good service in defending the Company's possessions at Surat.

Gold medals and chains were presented in 1687 to the military officers who, with the soldiers under their command, had assisted in defending one of the Company's ships against an attack by pirates; and in the same year a medal was conferred on an officer for his meritorious conduct in the action at

---

[1] Care has been taken to bring the present work up to date, by including an account of those decorations which have been conferred since the author's death, and while the proof sheets were passing through the press.—EDITOR.

Hooghly in 1686. In 1698 the Company gave a gold medal and chain to their broker in Persia.

The following are instances of the bestowal by the Governments in India of medals for individual good service:—

1755. Mahomed Isouf Cawn Bahauder.
1795. Subadar Abdul Cawder, 5th Madras N. I.
1795. Jemadar Boodh Sing, 13th Madras N. I.
1806. Sepoy Mustapha Beg, 1st Madras N. I.
1813. Jemadar Iyaloo, 14th Madras N. I.
1814. Subadar Mookrund Sing.
1817. Subadar Hoolas Pundit.
1818. Subadar Bugwunt Sing, 6th Bengal Light Cavalry.

Other instances of the gift of medals to Europeans and natives will be noticed in their places. There may, indeed, have been further cases, and, if so, they will doubtless come to light whenever the old Indian records are regularly calendared.

The last case in which the East India Company gave a medal to an individual in recognition of eminent service in the field, was that of Major Herbert Edwardes, in 1848.

In 1814 we find the Court of Directors writing to the Government of India that they would be glad to see a more frequent recurrence to the practice of granting medals to native officers and soldiers, who might distinguish themselves otherwise than in regular warfare, since they felt persuaded that such honorary badges had a powerful influence in exciting the zeal of the native soldiery, and attaching them to the service (*Despatch*, 8th Nov. 1814, Appendix I., p. 572).

It may here be mentioned that in 1816 the Court of Directors proposed to confer gold medals and crosses on superior officers of both the royal and Indian armies distinguishing themselves in action in India, under regulations similar to those which had been laid down by the Horse Guards during the Peninsular War. Owing, however, to the discontinuance by the Crown of the practice of bestowing such badges consequent on the extension of the Order of the Bath, in the benefit of which officers of both armies serving in India participated, the intentions of the Court were never carried into effect.

In 1823 the Government of Bombay brought to the notice of the Home Government the desirability of rewarding instances of gallantry and fidelity amongst the native soldiery, and suggested that the Court of Directors should send out a supply of medals with appropriate mottoes and devices of a general character, to be issued as deserving cases might arise. The Court replied, however, that although they would at all times be ready to attend to any specific proposals for the grant of medals, they did not think it necessary to provide a stock in the manner suggested. (See Appendix I., pp. 572-3.)

In the same way that the extension of the Order of the Bath led to the discontinuance of the practice of conferring gold medals on British officers, so the institution, in 1837, of the Order of British India and the Order of Merit, rendered unnecessary the continuance of any system of rewarding individual native soldiers by means of special medals. Since that year the meritorious native officer or soldier has met with an appropriate reward in one or other of these Orders.

The Court shortly afterwards appear to have overlooked their new Orders of distinction since, in 1840, they observed in reference to certain promotions and prospective advantages, which had been awarded by the Madras Government in the cases of some native soldiers, that they would prefer the grant of medals or pecuniary gratuities as rewards for conspicuous merit.

The first occasion of the general distribution of a medal to an army by the Government of India was in 1784, on the return home of a detachment of the Bengal Army from field service in the west of India.

The next occasion happened in the following year, on the return of another detachment of the same army, which had been on service in the Carnatic.

During the succeeding forty years many medals were awarded, namely, for the Mysore War of 1791-92; the expedition to Ceylon in 1795-96; the campaign in Mysore in 1799, including the capture of Seringapatam; the expedition to Egypt under Sir D. Baird in 1801; the capture of the French islands of Rodrigues, Bourbon and Mauritius in 1809-10; the capture of Java in 1811; the Nepaul Campaign of 1814-16; and the Burmese War of 1824-25. Prior to the battle of Waterloo, therefore, the general grant of medals was a well-established practice under the Company's Government. To that Government consequently must be ascribed the revival of a system of honorary reward which had only been adopted once previously in the annals of British arms—viz. for Cromwell's victory at Dunbar.

All of these earlier medals, with the exception of that for Seringapatam, were bestowed on *native* soldiers only.

Subsequently to the Burmese War of 1824-25, medals were granted for the following services:—

1799-1826. General Service.
1839. Capture of Ghuznee.
1842. Afghan Campaigns.
1843. Conquest of Sinde.
1843. Gwalior Campaign.
1846. Sutlej Campaign.
1849. Punjab Campaign.

The remaining medals awarded by the Government of India are those for 'General Service,' given first for the Burmese War of 1852, and subsequently for Persia, the North-West Frontier, and for many other services; and those for the Indian Mutiny, 1857-58, Afghanistan, 1878-80, and the India medal, 1895.

All of the above mentioned medals have been issued alike to European and Native officers and soldiers.

Amongst the Indian medals we have included the 'Pollock Medal,' instituted in commemoration of the eminent services rendered by General Sir George Pollock in Afghanistan in 1842. This medal was originally given at the East India Company's Military College at Addiscombe to the most distinguished cadet of each term. On the abolition of that College the prize was transferred to the Royal Military Academy at Woolwich. It is not, however, a decorative medal.

Up to the time of the Punjab Campaign of 1849, the Government of India had usually assumed the initiative in regard to the grant of medals, although the approval and consent of the Crown had to be obtained for the acceptance of the medals by officers and soldiers of the British service. But in confirming the grant of the Punjab medal, the Court of Directors expressed their desire that this practice should cease, and that the authorities in India should confine their action to *recommending* only, leaving the question of the actual grant to the discretion of the Home authorities. (See p. 322.)

Prior to the Burmese War of 1852, all the medals which were awarded by the Indian Government for campaigns were of a distinctive character, and bore direct reference to the services for which they were granted. On the occasion, however, of the grant of the medal for that war, the Governor-General, Lord Dalhousie, suggested that with the view of avoiding the multiplication of medals, the new issue should be of a general character, to be accompanied by a clasp indicating the service for which it was bestowed. His lordship's suggestion was adopted; and the medal then first given, since known as the 'India Medal of 1854,' has been awarded for numerous services.

As already observed, all the medals for campaigns up to the first Burmese War were, with one exception (Seringapatam), given to native troops only. There were various motives for giving medals to the native soldiery. They were intended primarily as a gratification to men who had undergone the perils and fatigues of war, and as a general incentive to valour and fidelity. But they were also meant to act as a stimulus to recruiting, as it was thought that the sight of such decorations on the breasts of old soldiers would have the effect of inspiring their young relatives and friends with martial ardour. It does not seem to have occurred to the authorities that *European* officers or soldiers could, or would, stand in any need of a similar incentive. There were, however, instances of the presentation to European officers of swords of honour, which, doubtless, were prized as highly as medals.

But prior to any record of medals or swords of honour, the East India Company had adopted the practice of giving presents of plate as honorary rewards. Thus, in acknowledgment of the good service done by their sea-captains William Morris and Wills, in the fight against the Portuguese on shore at Surat on 17th October, 1630, the Court of Committees presented each of those gentlemen with plate, with the Company's arms graven thereon, to the amount of 20 marks or £13, 6s. 8d. (*Court Minutes*, 18th January, 1633, and 7th March, 1634. Also, *Calendar of State Papers—Colonial*, East Indies and Persia, 1630-34. Nos. 87, 383, 544.)

In 1668 the Court had thoughts of presenting a piece of plate to Sir George Oxinden, in acknowledgment of his successful defence of the Company's Factory at Surat in 1664. The gold medal, to which reference has already been made, was, however, given to him instead of it.

We have made no attempt to trace the instances of the presentation of plate. The following may, however, be noted:—

On 7th February, 1766, Captain Thomas Howe was thanked by the Court of Directors, and presented with 100 guineas to purchase a piece of plate, with the Company's arms engraved thereon, for the gallant defence he made in the ship *Winchelsea*, when attacked by a French frigate off the Hooghly River in January, 1763. (*I. O. Court Books*, vol. lxxiv. p. 353.)

In February, 1804, a fleet of the Company's ships, sixteen in number, homeward bound from China under the command of Captain Nathaniel Dance as commodore, had an engagement in the China seas with a French squadron, composed of the *Marengo*, 84 guns, *Belle Poule*, 44 guns, *Semilante*, 36 guns, *Berceau*, 32 guns, and a brig of 18 guns, and commanded by Admiral Linois. The Indiamen succeeded in beating off the French, and continued their voyage. The value of the sixteen ships, with their cargoes and private property, was little short of £8,000,000 sterling.

In order to show their gratitude for the resolute and gallant behaviour of the officers and crews of the several ships in defending their property, the Court of Directors resolved, on 15th August, 1804, to present to the commodore the sum of 2000 guineas, and a piece of plate value 200 guineas; to Captain J. F. Timins, 1000 guineas, and a piece of plate value 100 guineas; to Captain W. Moffat, 500 guineas, and a piece of plate value 100 guineas; and to Captains H. Wilson, R. Torin, W. W. Farrer, W. S. Clarke, J. Farquharson, H. Meriton, J. Wordsworth, J. Kirkpatrick, A. Hamilton, J. Pendergrass, R. H. Brown, T. Larkins, and J. C. Lochner, each 500 guineas, and a piece of plate value 50 guineas. Also Lieut. Fowler, R.N., for the services he rendered to Commodore Dance, was granted 300 guineas for a piece of plate. The other officers and men of the fleet likewise received pecuniary gratuities according to their respective ranks and ratings. The whole of the rewards amounted to nearly £50,000.

The Court further resolved that the Chairman and Deputy-Chairman should express to His Majesty's ministers the high sense the Court entertained of the conduct of the commanders of the above-mentioned fleet, and more particularly of the commodore, and of the captain of the leading ship of the line.

Commodore Dance was knighted, 21st August, 1804, having refused a baronetcy.

Besides the rewards given by the East India Company, the Committee of the Patriotic Fund resolved, on 14th August, 1804, to present Commodore Dance with a sword and a vase of silver, each of the value of £100. To each of the other captains, and likewise to Lieut. Fowler, R.N., the Committee presented swords of the value of £50 each; and to Captain Timins a vase of

£100. (*Court Minutes*, 15th August, 1804. Also, *Register of Ships employed by the East India Company*, 1760-1812: London 1813, App. pp. 137, 138.)

As several of the medals given by the East India Companies bore their arms, it may be as well here to describe them.

ARMS OF THE GOVERNOUR AND COMPANY OF MERCHANTS OF LONDON TRADING TO THE EAST INDIES, 1601-1708.

Azure, three ships, *or*, all under sail, garnished with crosses *gules*; and upon a chief, *or*, between two roses, *gules*, an additionment out of the arms of England—viz. quarterly *azure* and *gules*, in the first and last a fleur-de-lis, *or*, in the second and third a lion passant guardant of the same.

Crest.—Upon a helm, on a wreath, a sphere, or globe celestial, between two standards of St. George.

Mantled *gules*, doubled *argent*.

Supporters.—Two sea lions, *or*, *azure*.

Mottoes.—Above the crest, 'Deus indicat'; below the shield, 'Deo ducente nil nocet.'

ARMS GRANTED TO THE NEW, OR ENGLISH, COMPANY IN 1698.

Argent, a cross *gules*, on a shield in the dexter quarter, the arms of France and England quarterly within a compartment adorned with an imperial crown.

Crest.—Upon a helm on a torse or wreath *argent* and *gules*, a lion rampant guardant, *or*, holding between his paws an imperial crown proper, mantled *gules*, doubled *argent*.

Supporters.—Two lions guardant *or*, and each of them holding a banner *argent*, charged with a cross *gules*.

Motto.—'Auspicio Regis et Senatus Angliæ.'

On the amalgamation of the two Companies in 1709, these arms became the bearings of the United Company.

ARMS OF THE EAST INDIA COLLEGE, HAILEYBURY, 1807-1858.

Argent, a cross *gules*, on a shield in the dexter quarter the arms of France and England quarterly within a compartment adorned with an imperial crown; on a chief of augmentation, *azure*, an olive wreath between two open books proper, bound and clasped, *or*.

Crest.—On a wreath *argent* and *gules*, a lion rampant guardant, on his head an Eastern crown, *or*, holding between the forepaws a scroll, with a seal pendent therefrom proper.

Supporters.—On either side a lion guardant, on the head an Eastern crown, *or*.

Motto.—'Auspicio Regis et Senatus Angliæ.'

These arms were used as the *obverses* of some of the gold medals given as College prizes. The only occasion on which they are mentioned in this book is in the description of the medal given to certain Burmese chiefs for good services in the first Burmese War.

DECORATIONS OTHER THAN MEDALS.

The following are comprised under this heading :—

- CHAINS AND COLLARS.
- CROSSES AND STARS.
- CLASPS.
- JEWELS.
- SWORDS OF HONOUR.
- MISCELLANEOUS.

CHAINS AND COLLARS.

As a symbol of dignity and authority, the chain or collar is of high antiquity, and was from an early period in use among Oriental nations.

In his work entitled *Les Bijoux Anciens et Modernes*, M. Eugene Fontenay, after pleasantly suggesting that the collar as an ornament probably made its appearance soon after the advent of the first woman, says that man adorned himself with it, and that the earliest collars were composed of amulets of stone or bone, of teeth and claws of wild animals, the trophies of man's conquests over Nature. He remarks that the collar was the token of manhood with the Egyptians, amongst whom earrings were seldom met with. In the Assyrian *bas-reliefs* he only found three collars, such collars being composed apparently of threaded grains, the figures they ornamented representing fantastic divinities. Having discovered no other trace of the collar on any of the *bas-reliefs* representing persons of mark, although all have earrings, he concludes that the Assyrians used earrings and not collars, and the Egyptians collars and not earrings.

The *torques* or *torquis* was an ornament of gold, twisted and bent into a circular form, which was worn round the neck by men of distinction amongst the Gauls, the Persians, and other nations.

Torques, whether in the form of collars[1] or bracelets, formed a considerable part of the wealth of those who wore them; they must have been important items in the spoil taken in battle; and they were amongst the rewards of valour bestowed on distinguished victors. It was by taking such a collar from a Gallic warrior that T. Manlius obtained the cognomen of *Torquatus*. The monuments erected to commemorate Roman soldiers often mention the number of torques conferred upon them. Chains and bracelets were likewise given to Roman soldiers as rewards.[2]

Collars of bronze, and less often of silver and gold, have been found round the necks of skeletons in graves in different parts of Russia. These are supposed to date from the eighth to the twelfth century.[3]

In Central Africa at the present day, men wear armlets of ivory as badges of bravery, indicating that the wearer has vanquished a rhinoceros or some other highly dangerous antagonist. Several of such rings may be seen on the arms of some of the natives.[4]

Richard II. and Henry IV. instituted decorations in the form of collars, cognisances and badges; some of the collars having a white hart, the badge of Richard II., appended to them. In the reign of Edward IV. collars made of silver roses with a white lion attached, and collars of suns and roses, were worn. To collars given by Richard III. a white boar was appended. These collars were called 'Collars of the King's Livery'; they were granted to persons of both sexes and of various ranks, and were worn as pledges of loyalty and attachment. Another collar was the celebrated one of SS. In the early part of the sixteenth century, chains with *Tau* crosses were often worn. Chains and badges were commonly worn by retainers. Representations

---

[1] The well-known statue of the Dying Gladiator, or Dying Gaul, affords a good example of the torque as worn round the neck.

[2] Smith's *Dict. Antiq.* *Les Bijoux Anciens et Modernes*, by E. Fontenay.

[3] *Kostümkunde*, by H. Weiss, 1883.

[4] *Pioneer Mail*, 28th May, 1890. Page 702.

of many of the above-mentioned collars and badges are to be seen on monumental effigies and brasses in this country.[1]

The use of chains as marks of royal favour was common under the Tudors, and was continued under the Stuarts. The present of a chain or collar was an ordinary compliment in the case of foreigners of distinction visiting this country. Henry VIII. presented Max Meyer, the commander of the Hanseatic fleet, with a gold chain, and also knighted him. Rubens and Vandyck had gold chains given to them by Charles I., and were knighted. The gold chain appears to have answered in those days the purpose now fulfilled by the insignia of Orders of Knighthood. There was no distinctive pattern in such chains, as was the case with the *livery* collars; they were simply in accordance with the fashion of the day.

It was of old the practice in this country for the king to create an Esquire by the imposition of a collar. The old ballad of 'King Edward IV. and the Tanner of Tamworth' may be cited as a witness on this point. In the time of Charles II., the collar of SS. was used for this purpose.

Under the Commonwealth many gold chains, sometimes with, and sometimes without, appendent medals were given. Those which were rewards for warlike services were usually accompanied by medals, but those given as compliments do not appear to have been so accompanied. The chains were of substantial value. Thus, in 1644, gold chains of the value of £200 and £100 respectively, with medals, were given to Captains Swanley and Smith for their services at sea.

Gold chains of the value of £300 apiece were voted in 1653 to Generals Blake and Monk; chains of £100 to Admirals Penn and Lawson; and of £40 to the four flag-officers of the fleet, in recognition of their services against the Dutch.

Charles II. instituted chains and medals for captains of fireships. He also awarded similar decorations for other services. In his reign we have the first mention of the bestowal of gold chains by the East India Company.

These badges of distinction appear to have been liable to forfeiture in the event of ill-behaviour on the part of the persons on whom they were bestowed. In a letter from Charles II. to the Commander-in-Chief of Barbadoes, dated 1st March, 1665,

[1] Nicolas, *Orders of Knighthood*, vol. i. Introduction. Haines, *Monumental Brasses.*

it is stated that whereas certain Jews—viz. Isaac Israel de Piso, Aaron Israel de Piso, and others, under pretence of ability to discover a gold mine in the West Indies, had fraudulently induced His Majesty to make them free denizens of England, with power to trade everywhere, but had falsified their oaths and promises; His Majesty declared that their patents of denization should be esteemed void, and that they should be banished from Barbadoes: and whereas His Majesty for their encouragement had bestowed a gold chain upon Isaac Israel de Piso, His Majesty ordered that the same should be taken from the said de Piso and returned to Him. (See *Calendar of State Papers—Colonial*, America and West Indies, 1661-68, p. 284. No. 948.)

Several gold chains, with medals, were given as naval rewards in the reigns of William and Mary, and Queen Anne.

To signalise the victory of the glorious 1st of June, George III. presented gold chains to Lord Howe and the five senior officers of the fleet. These officers subsequently received medals likewise, but the fact that in the first instance chains were given alone, shows that the idea of the chain constituting in itself a badge of honour was still in force.

The case of Captain Wooldridge, R.N., in 1809, is the latest of the bestowal of a gold chain for naval service.

A large ornamental collar was presented by George IV. to the Duke of Wellington. A somewhat similar one appears to have been possessed by Field-Marshal Viscount Beresford.

A curious example of a decorative collar of exceptional form is in the possession of the 3rd Hussars. It is of silver engraved, shaped like a dog-collar, and was intended to be worn by the sergeant kettle-drummer of the 3rd King's Own Dragoons, to which regiment it was presented by the wife of Colonel the Hon. Charles Fitzroy, afterwards Lord Southampton, on his being appointed its colonel in 1772. The collar was exhibited in the Royal Military Exhibition at Chelsea in 1890.

Of the use of chains and collars as portions of the insignia of Orders of Knighthood, and as the official badges of public functionaries, it is no part of our purpose to speak. We will only remark that the chain *per se* was originally the mark of distinction, the appendent badge, jewel, or medal being a comparatively modern addition.[1]

[1] The late Mr. Llewellyn Jewitt, a high authority in such matters, informed the author that, in his opinion, the chains *without* badge or pendant, now worn by the Mayors of some boroughs, are older than those with such an appendage.

Chains were usually worn round the neck, but they were sometimes worn over one shoulder and across the breast.[1]

COLLAR OF SS.

Of the various collars which were in use in this country prior to the institution of the Collar of the Order of the Garter by Henry VII., the best known is the Collar of SS., representations of which are seen in many monumental effigies and brasses, usually those of knights. It is also met with on effigies of ladies, and in such cases the lady is nearly always beside her husband.

In its earlier form it consisted of a band or strip of leather or other material, to which the SS. were affixed; at a later time the SS. were linked together, and the band disappeared.

This collar was the *livery* of the Lancastrian kings. It seems to have first made its appearance in this country in the latter half of the fourteenth century.

With the accession of the Yorkists to power in 1461, their Collar of Suns and Roses came into use; but on the accession of Henry VII. in 1485, the Collar of SS. was revived.

In the time of the Tudors their badge of the portcullis, a former badge of the Beauforts, was used in conjunction with the letter S, as was likewise the Union rose—the collars thus combining the Lancastrian, the Yorkist, and the Tudor devices.

In the reign of Henry VIII. the collar appears to have become, to some extent, a badge of civil office, and to have ceased to bear any political significance. At any rate, it is not met with on effigies of knights in armour in that period, and it may therefore be inferred that it had gone out of fashion as a military badge.

---

[1] The following is the most recent authority for the use of a collar and badge :—

'11*th March*, 1897.

'SIR,—The Lord Chamberlain has received the Queen's commands to inform you that Her Majesty has been graciously pleased to permit that you and the future Presidents of the Royal Institute of Painters in Water Colours shall wear the collar and badge which have been submitted to her, and which are herewith returned to you, when attending Her Majesty's levées, and on such other occasions as may be considered fitting.—I am, SIR, Your obedient Servant,

'S. PONSONBY FANE.

'*To* SIR JAMES D. LINTON,
'*President of the Royal Institute of Painters in Water Colours.*'

BRASS OF LORD AND LADY CAMOYS, WITH COLLARS OF SS.

During this reign there seems to have been some danger of the Collar of SS. becoming vulgarised, since it was deemed necessary, in the sumptuary legislation which was then enacted, to impose certain restrictions on the wearing of gold chains and collars in general, and of this collar in particular.

By the Act 6 Henry VIII., Cap. i., it was provided that no man below the rank of a knight should wear a chain of gold or gilt about his neck upon pain of forfeiture thereof; and by an Act of the following year, Cap. vi., it was provided that no one under certain specified degrees, except the sons of knights, and gentlemen having incomes from lands or fees of two hundred marks yearly, should wear any chain or collar of gold or gilt upon pain of forfeiture. An Act passed some years later, 24 Henry VIII., Cap. xiii., ordained that no man, unless he were a knight, should wear any collar of gold named a Collar of S.; and that no man under the degree of a baron's or a knight's son, or unless he had an income of two hundred pounds yearly, should wear any chain at all.

The Collar of SS. in gold differed, therefore, from other gold chains in that the qualification for wearing it was not hereditary or pecuniary, but that the wearer must be a *knight*. On the assumption that the bestowal of knighthood implied acknowledgment of service rendered, it may be inferred that this particular collar bore at that time the nature of an honorary reward.

Knights of the Garter, before they had a distinctive collar of their own, used to wear Collars of SS., or Suns and Roses, according as the party in power was Lancastrian or Yorkist; and they were only distinguishable from other knights wearing similar collars by the Garter on the left leg.

Collars of SS. have been bestowed as compliments on foreign ambassadors and foreigners of distinction visiting this country.

In the time of Charles II., Esquires were created by the king by the imposition of a Collar of SS., and the gift of a pair of silver spurs. (See *Present State of England*, by E. Chamberlayne, London, 1687, p. 312.)

The Collar of SS. has continued in use as a badge of office to the present day. As worn by judges,[1] heralds, or sergeants-at-arms, it is a survival of the royal *livery*.

---

[1] It used to be worn by the Lord Chief Justices of the Queen's Bench and Common Pleas, and by the Lord Chief Baron of the Exchequer. It is only worn now by the Lord Chief Justice of England.

Its use by Mayors, as representatives of the royal authority, may perhaps also be accounted for in the same manner; but we are not aware to what extent it has been so worn.

The use of letters of the alphabet, as links in chains, has not been uncommon. Thus, the collars of some Orders of Knighthood have the initial letters of the titles of the Orders introduced into them. Henry VIII., as shown in his portraits, wore a chain with H links. In such cases as these the signification of a particular letter is apparent.

As regards the first use of the letter S in collars, there is a tradition that the members of a certain religious fraternity, which derived its name from St. Simplicius, an early Christian martyr, wore silver collars composed of SS.[1]

The origin of the collar in this country is a point as to which no satisfactory solution has ever been obtained. It may, of course, very reasonably be surmised that the letter S was used because it was the initial of a particular word; and the question is, *what* word? The following words have been suggested by various authorities:—

Salisbury (Countess of)
Soissons (Martyrs of)
Silentium
Societas
Souvenez
Souverayne
Seneschallus
Sanctus Spiritus
Silver Swan
Swinford.

Mr. Stothard in his *Monumental Effigies of Great Britain*, observes (pp. 82-83), in reference to the effigy of Joan of Navarre, queen of Henry IV., on her tomb in Canterbury Cathedral, that the queen has round her neck a collar of SS., an ornament which is often repeated on other parts of the tomb, as is the king's motto 'Souverayne'; and that it may be therefore inferred that the letter S is used as being the initial of that word. Mr. Stothard believed this to be the earliest example of this collar.

The late Mr. J. G. Nicholls, an eminent antiquary, was of opinion that the fact of the collar having, it is believed, made its first appearance in the time of John of Gaunt, who held the great office of 'Seneschallus,' or Steward of England, might account for the use of the letter.

Mr. J. R. Planché in his *Pursuivant of Arms*, says (p. 188), in reference to the collar of SS. with the Swan of the De Bohuns

[1] Fosbrooke's *Dictionary of Antiquities*.

appendent, on the effigy of the poet Gower in St. Saviour's Church, Southwark, that it is singular that among all the ingenious speculations respecting the origin and meaning of the collar of SS., this pendant of the Swan in one of the earliest examples (1402) should never have been taken into consideration.

Mr. Albert Hartshorne, in a paper on Collars of SS., published in the *Archæological Journal*, vol. xxxix., says there is much to be urged in favour of 'Seneschallus'; not only on account of the office which John of Gaunt held, but also because there is in existence a drawing from a window of Old St. Paul's of the arms of John of Gaunt, within a collar of SS. This is the earliest pictorial example known. John of Gaunt died in 1399, and was buried in St. Paul's. It is noteworthy that the collar should be thus closely connected with him. Mr. Hartshorne observes that the earliest sculptured example of the collar is that at Spratton, Northants, on the effigy of Sir John Swinford, who died in 1371, and that even supposing it were to be proved that the effigy was not executed until many years after his death, the fact would remain that he was entitled to wear the collar, which must therefore have been an established collar of livery when Henry IV. was a boy; and that this would appear to dispose of the conjecture that the collar was first devised by that king in reference to his motto 'Souverayne.' Mr. Hartshorne mentions that the earliest recorded description of a collar of SS. occurs in a wardrobe account of Henry of Lancaster, Earl of Derby, taken in 1391-92.[1]

Having for centuries been styled the collar of SS., some have conjectured that the letters were the initials of two words, such as 'Sanctus Spiritus,' but there does not seem to be any evidence to support such an assumption.[2] In its early days it was called

[1] Mr. Hartshorne observes that a list of the effigies and brasses throughout the kingdom on which the collar of SS. is represented, together with notes on the pendants and the social position of the wearers, would be a valuable contribution to the history of the decoration.

[2] This idea as to the origin of the collar is very prevalent. For example, in an account of a country church, it was recently stated that there was a 'brass of an *armiger* or esquire in full armour, belted and spurred, with a faithful hound at his feet, and round his neck the collar of SS., being the badge of the Guild or Order of the Holy Spirit.' This, of course, is an easy way of explaining the meaning of the collar.

It might reasonably have been expected that the letters would have appeared in the collar of the Order of the Holy Ghost; but the collar of that Order, as founded by Henry III. of France in 1579, was composed of alternate fleurs-de-lis and H's.

a *Collar of Esses*; and in the statute of Henry VIII. a *Collar of S*; from neither of which appellations should we infer that the letter was used otherwise than as the initial of one word.

As to the collar of SS. having been at an early period a *military* decoration, we are justified, from the large number of instances in which it is found on figures in armour, in concluding that it was so regarded

In respect to its use as a *reward* for military service, we may refer to the book entitled *The Theater of Honour and Knighthood*, by Andrew Favine (London, 1623), in which it is stated (vol. ii. book v. p. 67) that Henry V. instituted Knights of the Esses in 1415; and a passage is quoted from the Chronicle of the Ursins to the effect that that king, before the battle of Agincourt, in order to encourage his people, promised to all those of his company who were not noble that he would ennoble them, and give them letters; and would have them thenceforward to enjoy equal franchises with the nobles of England. And, that they should be known, he gave them leave to wear a collar semée with the letters S of his Order.

COLLAR OF SUNS AND ROSES.

As to the origin of this collar there is no doubt. It is composed of the two badges of the House of York—the sun[1] and the white rose—and it would have been the collar of the king's livery during the reigns of Edward IV., Edward V., and Richard III., 1461-85.

Examples appear on brasses at Broxbourne, Herts, 1473; Rougham, Norfolk, 1470; Sawley, Derbyshire, 1478: St. Albans, 1480; Little Easton, Essex, 1483; and Lillingstone Lovell, Oxon., 1471. (See Haines' *Monumental Brasses.*)

Some of these collars are in strap form, imitated evidently from the earlier form of those of SS. Others are in chain form, with the suns and roses linked together.

A good example of the former is on the effigy (brass) of Sir Henry Bourchier, K.G., 1483, at Little Easton, Essex (see Haines and Boutell); and of the latter on the brass of William Yelverton, 1470, at Rougham, Norfolk (figure in armour). (Gough, vol. ii. part 3, p. 230.)

---

[1] 'Now is the winter of our discontent
Made glorious summer by this sun of York.'—*Richard III.*

CROSSES AND STARS.

Under this head are comprised the Gold Cross for services in the Peninsula, the Victoria Cross, the Distinguished Service Order, the Royal Red Cross, and the following stars:—

Order of British India, 1837.
Order of Merit, 1837.
Maharajpore and Punniar, 1843.
Kabul-Kandahar, 1880.
Egypt, 1882—84—84-86—88-89.
Ashanti, 1896.

Amongst the so-called regimental decorations there are many examples of crosses and stars.

CLASPS.

The earliest instance of the use of *clasps* as accessories to medals occurs in connection with the Military Gold Medal and Cross during the Peninsular War. These clasps are large and handsome. The first medal, given alike to officer and soldier, to which clasps were attached, was that for the Sutlej Campaign of 1845-46. The practice previously had been to inscribe on the medal itself the name of the service for which it was given. Thus the Afghanistan, 1842, Medals are inscribed with one or more of the names CANDAHAR, GHUZNEE, CABUL.

In the case of the Sutlej Campaign, in which there were four engagements deemed deserving of medallic commemoration, each man received a medal bearing the name of the first battle at which he was present, with clasps for the others. Thus, a man present at all the battles received a medal inscribed MOODKEE, and clasps inscribed FEROZESHUHUR, ALIWAL, and SOBRAON. A man present only at Sobraon received the medal for that battle, and no clasp.

The system of giving medals for a campaign generally, with clasps added for the principal occurrences, has since been often adopted. In the case of the general service medals for the Army and Navy, 1793-1814, and for services in India, 1799-1826, the name of the campaign or battle is recorded on a clasp only.[1]

[1] There is little doubt that, in respect of these three medals, a good deal of roguery has been practised by cunning people, who, by adding to the medals clasps (taken from other medals) which did not originally belong to them, have given them a fictitious value. Collectors, and especially those living out of England, should therefore be on their guard, although it is somewhat difficult to arrive at the truth in the matter, reference to the Medal Rolls not being always possible.

With regard to the arrangement of clasps there has been no invariable rule; but no doubt the best method is to place the clasp earliest in date *next* to the medal, subsequent clasps being added upwards. This is the plan which has been most often adopted, and it is the most rational and intelligible system. More especially is this the case with general service medals when the clasp next the medal indicates the original service for which the recipient earned the decoration.

The following order was, however, issued in 1892 directing the adoption of the opposite course, on the ground that additional clasps could then be more easily attached. But if ease in the mode of attachment is the main thing to be aimed at, it would be better slightly to alter the construction of the clasps themselves.

STANDING GENERAL ORDER BY H.E. THE COMMANDER-IN-CHIEF, MADRAS, 4th March, 1892. No. 13.

'*Medals.*—It is notified for information that clasps should be attached to medals in order of the dates of campaigns or battles, that is, those for the most recent campaign being placed lowest down. If this is done, no difficulty will be experienced in fitting the clasps, as all that is necessary is to remove the clasp issued with the medal and to attach the new ones in their proper places by means of pins.'

JEWELS.

Valuable jewels were often bestowed as rewards for important services, and there are several now in existence known to have been so given by various sovereigns.

The following are instances of the presentation of jewels of which there is official record:—

In 1645 (see p. 15) the House of Commons presented a jewel, value £800, to Sir Thomas Fairfax.

In 1656 (see p. 37) the Swedish ambassador was presented with a jewel at a cost of £850.

In 1657 (see p. 35) the Parliament voted a jewel worth £500 to Admiral Blake.

In 1659 (see p. 36) the Parliament voted £1000 to Lord Lambert, to buy him a jewel.

In 1660 (see p. 38) Sir John Greenvil, who had been the bearer of the letter in which Charles II. announced to the House of Commons his readiness to be restored to the throne, and who was intrusted with the reply to the king, was presented by the House with £500, for the purchase of a jewel as a badge of honour.

In the same year (see p. 41) the House of Commons voted £1000 to Mrs. Jane Lane, to buy her a jewel. This was the lady who accompanied Charles II. in his flight to Trent, in Somersetshire, after the battle of Worcester.

In 1715 (see p. 88) the East India Company presented a jewel, bearing their arms, to Matthew Martin, one of their sea captains, for his services against the French.

In 1855 (see p. 500) the Queen presented a jewel to Miss Nightingale, in acknowledgment of her services to the sick and wounded in the Crimean War.

The 'Albert Medals' are more in the nature of jewels than of medals.

SWORDS OF HONOUR.

Prominent amongst honorary rewards for warlike services is the sword of honour.

Many such swords have been presented by the Crown and by various public bodies to eminent naval and military officers. One was bestowed upon Sir John Leake, together with jewels and £1000, on his return to England in 1706, after having captured Cartagena, Alicante, Majorca, and Iviza.[1] Another, of the value of 3000 guineas, was given by George III. to Admiral Lord Howe on his return to Portsmouth after the victory of 1st June, 1794.[2] Swords of honour, accompanied usually by the freedom of the city, have frequently been presented by the City of London.

This practice was often resorted to by the East India Company and the Government of India. In 1779 the Company voted swords, of the value of £750 each, to Major-General Sir Hector Munro and Rear-Admiral Sir Edward Vernon, for their services in connection with the reduction of Pondicherry. In later years, in particular, the Company used this means of marking their approbation of services rendered by officers of their navy.[3] In that navy there was no system of promotion for distinguished service, and the officers did not always in other respects receive the rewards that might have fallen to them had they held equivalent positions in the Royal Navy.

---

[1] Barrett's *History of the Trinity House of Deptford Strond*, p. 123.

[2] A picture of the presentation is in the Painted Hall at Greenwich Hospital.

[3] For instance, Captain C. D. Campbell, Captain Rennie, Captain Hewett, Captain Daniell, Commodore Sir Wm. James, Lieutenant Pruen, Commodore Sir John Hayes, Captain Haines, Captain Rogers.—See Low's *History of the Indian Navy*.

A list of the swords of honour presented by the City of London since 1780, communicated by the Town Clerk, is printed in the Appendix.

Mention should not be omitted of the sword given each term at the Royal Military Academy, Woolwich, to the cadet most distinguished for general good conduct.

MISCELLANEOUS.

The following may be mentioned:—

The Badge of the White Horse awarded to the Bombay Grenadiers in 1779 (see p. 100).

The Badge of the Elephant given to the native troops present at the battle of Assaye in 1803 (see p. 151).

The silver and brass armlets given to certain Indian troops who volunteered for foreign service in 1797 (see p. 126, also p. 131).

The silver Badge given to Sepoys of the Bombay Marine Battalion in 1811 (see p. 165).

The silk scarves presented by the Governor of Madras in 1680 to four British officers as rewards for a successful expedition (see p. 54).[1]

Medallions granted by the Colonial Office to certain West African chiefs for assistance in the Ashanti wars of 1874 and 1895-6.

REWARDS FOR BRAVERY.

In the olden time knighthood was the usual reward for bravery in conflict with the enemy.

The earliest *decorative* reward for personal bravery adopted in this country was the badge instituted by Charles I. for those who might distinguish themselves in leading forlorn-hopes; that is to say, it is the earliest for which there is any regular authority for its bestowal as occasion might require.

Medals and other rewards were subsequently given from time to time in recognition of acts of bravery, but there were no rules in regard to them, except in the case of the rewards for captains of fireships (see p. lviii).

In 1837, however, the East India Company instituted an

---

[1] The '*Tasherifs*,' yards of scarlet cloth, given by the Hon. East India Company in 1680 as an 'encouragement' to their principal merchants. (See p. 53.)

'Order of Merit,' for the reward of their native officers and soldiers performing distinguished acts of valour in action.

In 1856, during the Crimean War, the Victoria Cross was established for the reward of British officers and soldiers performing eminent acts of bravery.

With respect to instances of bravery not thought sufficiently distinguished to merit the Victoria Cross, two medals have been instituted—one in 1862, for the army, 'For distinguished conduct in the field'; and the other in 1874, for the navy, 'For conspicuous gallantry.' Officers are not eligible for either of these medals.

The Albert Medal, 'For gallantry in saving life at sea,' was founded in 1866, and the companion medal, 'For gallantry in saving life on land,' in 1877.

One of the medals given by our Foreign Office to foreigners assisting British shipping and subjects, is 'For gallantry and humanity.'

HUMANE SOCIETY'S MEDALS.

'ADMIRALTY, 19*th March*, 1869.

'CIRCULAR NO. 11.—C.

'The Royal Humane Society having made arrangements for reducing the size of their Medals in future—in order to admit of their being worn—and for granting Clasps and Bars for subsequent acts of bravery, in cases where a medal has been already granted, my Lords Commissioners of the Admiralty are hereby pleased to notify to the Officers and Men of Her Majesty's Navy and Marines their permission to Officers and Men to wear such Medals and Clasps when awarded by the Humane Society.

'By Command of their Lordships,

'W. G. ROMAINE.

'To all Commanders-in-Chief, etc.'

PLAGUE MEDAL. HONG KONG, 1894.

The following is the description of a medal given to the troops who helped to combat the Plague in Hong Kong in 1894, viz. six hundred of the Shropshire Light Infantry and several of the Royal Engineers, both officers and men, who volunteered for the work. It was also given to the Nursing Sisters and to several civilians.

The officers received gold medals without ribbons or attachments, the non-commissioned officers and men silver medals with both.

This medal is not placed in the body of the work, as it is not permitted to be worn by soldiers in uniform.

Obv. A sick Chinaman lying on a trestle bed, supported by a European on whose right arm the Chinaman's head reclines, whilst with his left hand the European is pushing away a figure of Death which approaches to strike the Chinaman with a dart. On the other side of the bed stands a European woman, who is ministering to the sick man. On the background, to the left, is the word HONG KONG in Chinese characters. On the ground are a tar-brush and pail, and a whitewasher's brush, significant of the means by which the Plague was fought.

Ex. A representation of the crinkled tiles used in China, on which lies a scroll with the date 1894.

Rev. In the centre are the words 'FOR SERVICES RENDERED DURING THE PLAGUE OF 1894,' surrounded by a band inscribed PRESENTED · BY · THE · HONG · KONG · COMMUNITY.

Circular, 1·5 inch. Gold. Silver.
Artist. Frank Bowcher.
Executed and Struck by A. Wyon, F.S.A.
Mounting. For the Silver Medals only.
Ribbon. 1½ inch wide. Yellow, with one broad and two narrow scarlet stripes.

MEDALS AND CHAINS FOR CAPTAINS OF FIRESHIPS.

The use of fireships for the purpose of destroying an enemy's vessels was always recognised as a hazardous service, and one requiring special inducements to those employed in them.

Fireships were a feature of naval warfare in the seventeenth century, and were very much to the front in the battles with the Dutch.

Having regard to the many naval wars of the eighteenth century, it might have been expected that there would have been numerous cases of the employment of fireships, but as a matter of fact this was not so; and Captain Callis's service in 1742 was perhaps the only instance in the century. (See No. 113.)

The earliest official authorisation of particular rewards for service of this character that we have met with is in the Fighting Instructions issued by H.R.H. the Duke of York, when Lord High Admiral, dated 20th April, 1665.

In these it is provided that in the case of the burning by a fireship of an enemy's vessel of forty guns or more, each person remaining on board till the service was performed was to receive £10, and the captain a gold medal, to remain as a mark of honour to him and his posterity. In the case of an enemy's flagship being burnt, the recompense in money was to be doubled, and the medal for the commander was to be such as should particularly express the eminency of the service.

Finding the above provision in a Code of Fighting Instructions of 1665, we might have expected to meet with something on the same subject in orders issued at an earlier period.

The only Fighting Instructions however, of an earlier date, which have come to the writer's knowledge, are those issued by Sir William Penn at the close of the Dutch War in 1653, and those issued by him in 1655 when in command of the expedition to the West Indies at the beginning of the Spanish War, the latter being an abridgment of the former, and these contain no information.

But although the foregoing is the earliest official regulation which we have been able to trace on the subject, it seems extremely probable that it had at an earlier date been the custom in the Navy for such services to be specially rewarded.

Strong indirect evidence that this was so, is afforded by the following amusing letter from Captain Cranwill to the Admiralty Committee, dated 4th February, 1655 :—

'TO THE ADMIRALTY COMMITTEE.

'RIGHT HON^BLES,

'As for ye Pay yor Hon^rs were please to order mee for my service | in ye Hare Pinke, I returne most humble thankes, and am | ready to serve your Hon^rs and my Country for ye future | . . . For though ye Hare bee mewsed in ye Sand | yet Cranwell at your mercy still doth stand | A Fire Ship now doth hee Crave, And the Fox faine would hee | Have, then has hee had both Fox and Hare, then Spanish | Admirall stand you Cleare, For Cranwell means ye Chaine | of goold to ware; Sett penn to paper it is done, for Cranwell | still will be your man, If yor Hon^rs and fortunes doe not faile | I hope yet to see ye Spaniard Quaile, All which if fortune | bring to pass then shall I bee in your Favour as before I was, | when as I Ranged ye Scottish Shore, wth thundring cannons | made them fly, from towne and Castle to mountaines high | I on the Seas, our forces on ye Land, y^t still wee had these | Rebbles at command, and straite a peace wth them was | made but Cranwell there in his parte hath plaide, I | hope yor Hon^rs will not for-gett, nor cast me out of your | Service yett, thus waiteing on yor Hon^rs pleasures for | to answer my humble request, I take leave to subscrible | my-selfe.

'Yo^r Hon^rs much Oblidged,

'And most humble Servt,

'FRANCIS CRANWILL.

'GREENEWICH *the*
4th *Febru:* 1655.'

(*State Papers—Domestic. Interregnum*, 1655-56, vol. cxxxiii., No. 35. *Calendar*, p. 458.)

It will be seen that the gallant captain desired the command of a fireship, and that he meant, if possible, to burn the Spanish admiral's flagship with the view of earning a chain of gold as a reward.

Had such a reward been mentioned in the Fighting Instructions issued by Sir W. Penn in 1653, Captain Cranwill's reference to it in his letter would have been quite clear.

But, as the matter stands, we think we are justified in inferring that it had not been unusual to bestow gold chains on fireship captains.

The next official announcement is in an Order of the King in Council, dated 12th January, 1669-70, in which the Lord High Admiral is authorised to distribute medals and chains of the value of thirty pounds each, to such captains of fireships as, during the late Dutch War, had burnt any man-of-war, and this is the first authoritative mention we have of a chain in connection with the medal.

How many fireship services may have been rewarded under the operation of the above authorities we have been unable to ascertain. The only instance we have met with is that of Captain John Guy, who blew up his fireship, the *Vesuvius*, under the walls of St. Malo in 1693. (See No. 84, p. 74.) This, as noticed elsewhere, was an exceptional service, and not contemplated by the regulations which only provided rewards in the case of fireships destroying an enemy's ships, and not an enemy's towns.

In 1742, in connection with the case of Captain Smith Callis's service in burning five Spanish galleys at St. Tropez, it was laid down by an Order of the King in Council, dated 16th December, 1742, that lieutenants of fireships should receive a gratuity of fifty pounds.

In 1703 some revised Fighting Instructions were issued by Admiral Sir George Rooke, in which, in respect to the fireship rewards, it was provided that the captain was to have a gratuity of one hundred pounds, or a gold medal and chain of that value, as he should make choice.

The only other case on record is that of Captain James Wooldridge, who burnt four French men-of-war in Aix Roads in 1809.

The direction as to the medal recording the eminency of the service performed was duly observed in respect to those of Captain Callis and Captain Wooldridge, which both bear specially designed representations of the services.

The following instructions, dated March, 1653, are found in

a collection of *Tracts relating to the Navy of England*, in the Sloane MSS. in the British Museum.

'By the Right Honorable the Generalls and Admiralls of the Fleet. Instructions for ye better ordering of ye ffleet in ffighting. Page 158. Instruction 13.

'That the fire shipps in every squadron endeavour to keep ye winde and they with ye small frigetts to bee as near ye great Shipps as they can to attend ye Generalls signall or command in chiefe and to act accordingly if ye General hoyst up a white flagg on ye Mizen Yard Arme or Topmast head all small friggotts in his Squadron are to come under his stern for orders.

. . . .

'Given under our hands at Portsmouth this March 1653.

(Stated in the Index to be given by Generals and Admirals of the late Parliament times.)

(B.M. *Sloane* MSS., xxxii. 32, Part 4.)

'JAMES, DUKE OF YORK AND ALBANY.

'All thought it bee ye Dutys off all persons employed in his Maj^ties fleete Even to ye utmost of hazard of their Lives to Endeavour as well ye Destroying of his Maj^ties Enemies as ye succouring off his Maj^ties Subjects & in most speciall manner to defend & preserve his Majesties Shipps of warre the neglect whereof shalbe at all tymes strictly enquired after and severely punished, nevertheless to the end that no Enducement may be wanting which may oblige all persons serving in his Majesties fleete valiantly and honorably to acquit themselves in their severall Stations, I have thought fitt to publish and declare and doe hereby promise on his Majesties behalfe y^t iff any off ye King's Fire shipps perform ye Service required ofrom them in suik manner y^t any of ye Enemies men of war of 40 gunns or more shall be burned by them Every person Remaining in ye Fire shipp: till ye service be performed shall receave on board ye Admirall imediately after ye service done tenn pounds as a reward for that service over and above his pay due to him: And incase any of them shalbe killd in y^t service itt shalbe paid to his Executor or next relation over & above ye ordinary provisions to be made for ye relations off shuth as are Slaine in ye Kings service, & ye Cap^ts of such fire shipps shall receave a Medall of Gould to remaine as a marke off honour to him and his posterity, and shall receave shuth other future encouragement by preferment & commande as shall be fitt both to reward him & enduce others to perform ye like Service.

'These superior officers shall receive each ten pounds in money and be taken if captured in other shippes before any person whatever.

'In case any of ye Enemies flagg shipps be so fired ye Recompense in money shall be doubled to each man performing itt, and ye medall to ye Commander shall be shuth as shall particularly express ye Eminensye of ye Service, & his with ye other officers preferement shalbe suitable to ye merritt of itt.

'If any of his Majestie's 5th or 6th rate Shipps or any Ketches, Smakes or Hoyes in his Maj^ties service shall bord or destroy any fire-shipps of ye Enemies & soe prevent any of those from coming abord any of ye Kings Shipps above ye 5th rate besides ye preferment that shall begiven to ye comander & officers of shuth shipps performing suth service answerable to their dessarts & merritts ye commander of suth of ye Fire Shipps & vessels or in case they shall be killd in ye service their excecutors or nearest relations shall receave to every man forty shillings as a Reward and suth persons who shall by ye testimony of ye commanders Appeare to have been Eminently instrumentall in shutch service shall receave for their reward according to their merritt.

'Iff ye Mrs off any Ketches Hoyes or those small vessells hired for his Majties service shall Endeavour to perform any of the services aforesaid & shall by shuth his attempt Lose his shippe or vessell ye full vallue thereof shall be paid by ye Treasurer of his Majties Navy upon Certificate of ye Service done signed by ye councell of warr, & ye commanders & men in her service ye same recompense with those serving in his Majties shipps or vessells.

'Given under my hand on board ye Royal Charles ye 20th day of Aprill 1665.

'JAMES.

'A copy of his Riall Highness Command read from his Excellency the Earl of Sandwich.'

(B. M., *Harl. MSS.*, No. 1247, page 52.)

'AT THE COURT AT WHITEHALL,
'*the* 12*th of January*, 1669-70.

'THE KINGS MOST EXCELLENT MATIE.

'It was this day Ordered by his Maty in Councill That his Royall Highness the Duke of York Lord High Admirall of England &ca be, and he is hereby Authorised to Distribute a Medall & Chaine to such Captaines of Fire Shipps as in the last Dutch Warr have burnt any Man of Warr, as also to any of them that shall performe any such service in the present Warr with Algiers. Which Medalls and Chaines are to be of the price of Thirty Pounds each or thereabouts.'

ADMIRALTY MINUTES, Thursday, 29*th July*, 1742.

'*Resolved*, that the Navy Board be directed to pay one hundred Pounds to Captain Smith Callis as an encouragement for his conduct and bravery in burning five Spanish Gallies in the Port of St. Tropez in the Mediterranean.'

'AT THE COURT AT ST. JAMES'S,
'*the* 16*th of December*, 1742.

'*Present*

'THE KING'S MOST EXCELLENT MAJESTY.

'Upon reading at the Board a Memorial from the Lords Commissrs of the Admiralty dated the 8th of this Instant in the words following, vizt.

"The Rules established in the Navy allowing a Reward of one Hundred Pounds or a Medal of Gold with a Chain of the same value to the Captain of a Fireship who shall burn a Ship of War of the Enemy of 40 Guns or more and ten Pounds to every Person remaining in the Fireship till the service be performed and Captain Callis who Commanded Your Majesty's Fireship the *Duke* having lately received the said Reward for his Success in burning five Gallies of the Enemy at St. Tropez: Lieutenant John Greene who was at that time Lieutenant of the said Fireship and performed his Duty as an Officer in that Action has applied to Us that some Consideration be taken of his Service on that Occasion as well as for the Loss of his Cloathes and Chest which were burnt with the Fireship. We do therefore beg leave to represent to Your Majesty that when the aforesaid Rewards were established Fireships had no Lieutenant as they have now, and do humbly propose that Your Majesty may be graciously pleased to Order a Reward of Fifty Pounds to be paid to Lieutenant John Greene for his behaviour in the aforesaid Action: and to establish the like Reward upon all Lieutenants of Fireships for the future in all such Cases where the Captain is entitled to the present reward and that the Conduct of the said Lieutenants therein shall recommend them to the said Allowance."

'His Majesty this day took the said Memorial into Consideration and was pleased with the Advice of His Privy Council to approve of what is therein proposed and to Order as it is hereby Ordered that a Reward of £50 be paid to the said Lieutenant John Greene for his Behaviour in the Action abovementioned. And as an Encouragement for other Lieutenants of Fireships to Distinguish themselves hereafter in the like Service, His Majesty doth hereby further Order that the like Reward of £50 be establisht upon such Lieutenants of Fireships in all Cases where the Captain is entituled to the Reward of £100. Provided that the Conduct of such Lieutenants shall recommend them to the said Allowance. And the said Lords Commissioners of the Admiralty are to give the necessary Directions herein accordingly.'

The above rules continued operative, and in 1809 Captain James Wooldridge was granted a medal and chain 'according to the provision of the ancient fighting instructions regarding fireships.' (See No. 154.)

The rules are possibly still in force although the days of fireships are over. Their place as engines of destruction will in future be taken with greater effectiveness by torpedo boats.

GENERAL NOTES ON MEDALS

MEDAL MOUNTINGS.

By 'mountings' are meant the metal arrangement by which ribbons or chains are attached to medals.

The Naval Gold Medal of 1794 seems to have been the first issued with a mounting of a regulation pattern. Some of the earlier Indian medals had small gold or silver loops through which cords or chains could be passed. The Waterloo Medal had a steel split-ring; and the medals for Afghanistan and Sinde had steel bars for the soldiers, and silver for the officers. The China Medal, 1842, had a German-silver bar. The mountings of all medals issued since 1843 have been of the same metal as the medals.

Throughout this book the term 'bar' is applied to the mounting or ribbon attachment only; the term 'clasp' being used in reference to the tablets bearing dates, or the names of battles and campaigns.

MEDAL RIBBONS.

Although the practice of wearing ribbons as badges of party or gallantry is of considerable antiquity, the use of ribbon as an accessory to metallic decorations is comparatively modern. Shakespeare makes no allusion to ribbon either as a badge in itself, or in connection with any knightly or other badge. He speaks of ribbon 'in the cap of youth,' and ribbon in the shoes, regarding it merely in the way of finery.

Cockades of ribbon seem to have come into fashion in the time of Charles II. The colour of the English military cockade was then red. The black cockade came in with the House of Hanover.

Sir H. Nicolas says that by the Statutes of the Order of the Garter, dated in 1519, permission was given to the knights, on ordinary occasions, to wear the Lesser George suspended either by a chain or lace of silk, but that the lace was soon after abandoned for a ribbon, which was usually, if not always, black.[1]

Medals and pictures of this period afford numerous examples of the custom of wearing medals and badges suspended by narrow ribbons or small cords, which, whatever may have been their colour, were clearly for use only, and did not constitute an essential part of the decoration.

When Claude Melnotte exclaimed, 'What is a riband worth to a soldier? Worth! Everything! Glory is priceless!'[2] he was not, of course, alluding to the *British* soldier of the period, who, although in one sense doubtless 'bien décoré,' was, poor fellow, almost an entire stranger to the 'glory' engendered by the possession of a bit of coloured silk.

As an adjunct to the medal, ribbon may be said to have generally superseded the chain since 1794, in which year the first 'regulation' ribbon was instituted.

More than thirty different ribbons have been used with our various war decorations, the colours being blue—light and dark—yellow, orange, red, crimson, green, brown, grey, white and black.

The list begins with the white, blue-bordered ribbon worn with the gold medals for Lord Howe's victory of 1st June, 1794. This became the naval ribbon of England. It was used with all the naval gold medals, and with the naval general service silver medal given in 1847.

The next in order of date is that directed to be worn with the

---

[1] The ribbon was changed to light blue in 1622, and to dark blue in the reign of George II.

[2] *Lady of Lyons*, i. 3.

gold medal for Maida, which is crimson with blue borders. This was subsequently adopted as the military ribbon of England, and it was used with the gold medals and crosses of 1806-14, with the Waterloo Medal, and with the general service medal of 1847. It was worn by some with the Seringapatam Medal, and the medals of the Madras Army for the first Burmese War were likewise suspended by it. For a number of years it was the only ribbon officially authorised in the British Army. A narrow width of this ribbon was adopted for the 'Distinguished Service Order' instituted in 1886.

The military ribbon of India, red, yellow and blue, was the idea of Lord Ellenborough, when Governor-General, who appears to have thought that as there was but one military ribbon for England, so there should be only one for India. The result was, however, that some soldiers had two or three decorations suspended by similar ribbons. Lord Ellenborough's desire to associate these three colours with the achievements of the Indian Army was also evinced by his presentation of tricoloured flags and standards to the regiment of Kelat-i-Ghilzie and the Sinde Horse. This ribbon was used with the medals for Jellalabad, Kelat-i-Ghilzie, Afghanistan and Sinde, and with the Maharajpore and Punniar Stars; and it has been employed again, nearly forty years later, with the Kabul-Kandahar Star.

With the multiplication of medals the limitation of the number of ribbons almost necessarily ceased, and many new patterns were invented.

Apart from the question of the contrast between the colours of ribbons and of uniforms, a ribbon of one colour bordered by another is, perhaps, the most striking. The borders should be narrower than the centre. The Peninsula, China, and Abyssinia ribbons are good examples. Ribbons with narrow stripes are not generally effective; the Indian Mutiny ribbon is perhaps the best.

There is only one parti-coloured ribbon, namely, the Ghuznee, 1839, red and green: this is a very striking ribbon.

Of tricolours we have the 'Ribbon of India,' composed of the primary colours fading into each other.

Another tricolour is the ribbon issued with the medal granted for services in Eastern and Central Africa in 1895. This is composed of stripes of terra cotta or copper-colour, white and black. (See Nos. 191 and 198.)

On the whole we should be disposed to give the first place

among medal ribbons to the original English 'military ribbon,' and, should a general service medal or decoration ever be instituted, no ribbon could be more suitable than the one which is associated with the famous campaigns and victories of the early part of this century.

It might be well if medal ribbons could carry some special signification. Thus, one or both of the royal colours of England are displayed in several ribbons. It may have been by accident that the China ribbon was red and yellow; but the former would stand for England, whilst the latter is the Chinese imperial or court colour. The ribbon of India has reference to an Oriental sunrise. The Arctic ribbons are white. The Afghanistan, 1878-80, ribbon has red for England, and the colour of the Standard of the Prophet, green.

A new importance has lately been given to ribbon, inasmuch as it has been utilised, in lieu of a clasp, as a means of indicating the service for which a medal was granted.

The medal originally given for Ashantee in 1874, and subsequently in 1892, with distinguishing clasps (dates only) for services in Central Africa, and on the East and West Coasts, has since been given for other operations in Eastern and Central Africa, but without any clasp, the service for which it is granted being indicated by a 'distinctive ribbon' only. The ribbon is tricoloured, as already mentioned.

MODE OF WEARING MEDALS AND ORDERS.

The crosses worn as badges of their Orders by the Knights Hospitallers and Templars, appear to have been sewed or embroidered on the mantle or coat.

As regards medals, contemporary pictures and medals show that in the days of the Tudors they were generally worn suspended round the neck by a chain or ribbon. The only mention which Shakespeare makes of the medal has reference to this mode of wearing it: 'He that wears her like a medal hanging about his neck' (*Winter's Tale*, i. 2). But medals were sometimes worn as ornaments in the hat.

On a medal of the Dutch Admiral, Pieter Heyn (1629), the Admiral is represented wearing a double chain over his left shoulder and under his right arm, a medal being attached to the chain in the centre of the breast. (Van Loon, ii. 183.)

Charles I. directed that the 'Forlorn Hope' Badge which he

instituted should be worn 'on the breast,' presumably suspended round the neck.

Portraits of Charles I. show that it was His Majesty's practice to wear the ribbon by which the George was suspended, sometimes round the neck, and sometimes over the left shoulder, with the badge hanging under the right arm. This latter mode was no doubt for convenience when riding on horseback. But the ordinary mode of wearing it, then and for some time after, was round the neck.[1]

The portrait of Sir Godfrey Kneller, painted by himself for the Kit-Cat Club, represents him wearing a massive gold chain over his left shoulder, with a medal pendent to it under his right arm.[2]

The earliest 'Regulation' relative to the mode of wearing medals appears to have been made on the occasion of the grant of the gold medal for the 1st of June, 1794. It was then directed that the admirals should wear the medal by a ribbon round the neck, and the captains by a ribbon fastened through the third or fourth buttonhole on the left side of the coat. The same fashion was adopted a few years later with the gold medals for the Peninsula: general officers wore them round the neck, and field-officers from a buttonhole in the left breast. It will be borne in mind that the coats worn at this period generally had lapels, in the buttonholes of which ribbons could easily be inserted.

A discussion took place during the Peninsular War as to the manner in which medals should be worn; and the Duke of Wellington expressed the opinion that, although it was very proper for an admiral walking on his quarter-deck to wear his medal round the neck, such practice was unsuitable for officers riding on horseback, and that their medals should be worn at the buttonhole like those for Maida. The Duke's opinion was not, however, adopted by the authorities.

---

[1] At the investiture of the Duke of Norfolk as a Knight of the Garter in 1685, the Sovereign put the blue ribbon, the Lesser George hanging thereat, over the new knight's left shoulder and under his right arm; and this is said to have been the first occasion of a knight being so invested. (Nicolas, i. 265.) The alteration in the style of costume which took place about this period led doubtless to the lengthening of the ribbon, and the relegation of the Lesser George to a less conspicuous and honourable position than on the breast. So that what was originally a mere accessory, became practically the predominant feature of the insignia, and the 'Blue Ribbon' is spoken of rather than the 'George.'

[2] This portrait, together with the other Kit-Cat portraits, is in the possession of Mr. R. W. Baker, of Bayfordbury, Hertford.

The practice of sewing or pinning the medal ribbon on the breast of the coat is probably not earlier in the British service, in point of date, than the Waterloo Medal. The earlier medals given to the Indian native troops used to be worn suspended round the neck, and they were furnished with small rings or loops for the purpose.[1]

The first time that Indian medals were accompanied by ribbon was on the issue of those for Burmah, 1824-25; and it is in connection with this issue that we first find any official indication as to how they were to be worn. An Order by the Commander-in-Chief at Madras in 1831 directed that they were to be worn 'perfectly square upon the centre of the left breast, the upper edge of the ribbon being even with the first button for ranks wearing sword-belts only, and even with the second button for ranks wearing cross belts.'[2] This order may have been based on instructions issued by the Horse Guards in reference to the Waterloo Medal, which we have not, however, been able to trace.

The author has been informed by Colonel J. G. Halliday, late of the Madras Army, that the old 49th Madras Native Infantry had a medal for proficiency in shooting which used to be worn on the right arm, above the elbow, on the sleeve of the coat.

The Bronze Stars for the battles of Maharajpore and Punniar, in 1843, were originally intended to be hooked on to the breast of the coat. They were, however, subsequently worn with ribbons like medals.

The only medal now directed to be worn round the neck is that which was given on the occasion of the proclamation of the Queen as Empress of India. (See p. 512.)

Instructions relative to the wearing of medals and decorations

---

[1] The Regulations for the Military Establishment of Fort St. George, established by Government in General Order, 11th March, 1806 (Section 5, Paragraph 82), contain the following:—'The Gorget to be Gilt with Gold, with the Company's Arms, over the Number of the Regiment only, engraved on the middle, and to be worn with a Ribband, and Tuft or Rosette at each end, of the color of the facing of the Regimental Clothing respectively.' Possibly it may have been the practice for the native troops to wear their medals suspended by ribbons of the colours of the regimental facings.

[2] In an article in the *East Indian United Service Journal* for April, 1837 (Calcutta) the writer states he is not aware of any regulation in reference to the way in which medals should be worn by the native soldiers. He says they generally wore them suspended round their necks by a string. He had evidently not heard of the Madras regulation of 1831.

are promulgated from time to time by the naval and military authorities, and are to be found in the published Regulations. Upon reference to these it will be perceived that decorations are to be worn in full dress only, pieces of ribbons being worn at other times. The reason for this restriction is not very apparent; for why, if a man has earned a decoration, should he not enjoy the privilege of displaying it whenever he may think proper, and not only when he happens to be wearing a particular style of coat? In some cases this rule must operate almost as a denial of the right of ever wearing a decoration at all. In this connection it is curious to note that on the occasion of the first general distribution of a medal to all ranks alike—namely, for Waterloo—it was expressly commanded by the Duke of York, then Commander-in-Chief, that the ribbon issued with the medal should 'never be worn but with the medal suspended to it.'

In regard to Orders of Knighthood, it may be observed that the statutes which contain directions as to how the insignia are to be worn, impose no restrictions as to costume. The statutes would seem to contemplate the not infrequent wearing of the insignia, and certainly they do not, as apparently do the Regulations, regard them as merely in the nature of accessories to full dress uniform. Further, the statutes contain no provision for the wearing of ribbons alone, nor for the wearing of insignia otherwise than in their entirety.

Indeed, military officers have been known to complain of the regulation prohibiting the wearing of anything except ribbons with undress or mess uniform, for the reason that in the case of a possessor of a general service medal with several clasps, his ribbon indicates no more than that worn by another man who has but one clasp.

The grievance, if such it may be called, was not so much felt when *miniature* medals and badges were allowed to be worn in undress. Whilst we cannot express any particular admiration for the miniature medals of the present day, the fact of their existence may perhaps be regarded as an indication that our conventional medal is somewhat cumbersome. If this is the case there would be a valid reason for lessening its size, since there can be no particular virtue in its being the exact shape and weight of a five-shilling piece.

But however this may be, the main object of *decorations* is, or at any rate was originally, to distinguish their possessors in the eyes of the world; and to place any obstacles in the way of their display is materially to defeat that object.

The Regulations direct that decorations are to be worn in one or two horizontal lines suspended from a bar; and that when they cannot, on account of their number, be suspended so as to be fully seen, they may *overlap*. What a fate for a work of art, to have its face ground by its fellow! Here, certainly, is a cogent reason for a reduction in size.

The Regulations permit *miniature* decorations to be worn in evening dress (plain clothes) 'on all public and official occasions,' by officers in the service and likewise by retired officers. It does not appear to be contemplated that they should ever be worn on private occasions.

It is, indeed, a curious feature in connection with the modern decoration hunger, that the more abundant the decorations, the fewer are the opportunities which social usages and official restrictions afford for displaying them. Unless he is on duty, a levée or a city dinner is perhaps the only occasion on which many an officer can display his decorations.

INVESTITURE OF MEDALS.

Although no general rules of investiture have been laid down for medals similar to those governing Orders of Knighthood, it has been the practice, when possible, for the presentation to be accompanied by some amount of ceremony.

In the case of the medals given by the East India Company to the three military officers who assisted in defending the ship *Cæsar* when attacked by pirates in 1686, the Court, in forwarding the medals to the Government of Bombay, desired that they should be delivered to the officers 'with such solemnity as is fit to the honour of such worthy persons.'

When, however, the recipient of a medal happened to be in England, he attended at the East India House in order that the presentation might take place in the presence of the Court of Directors.

From the medal presented by George II. to Captain Callis (see p. 90), we gather that the Captain received it from His Majesty's own hand.

On the occasion of the victory of 1st June, 1794 (see p. 174), George III. proceeded to Portsmouth, and presented to Lord Howe, on the quarter-deck of his flagship, a gold chain and a diamond-hilted sword, and likewise presented gold chains to the other Admirals of the victorious fleet.

In an Admiralty Minute of 13th January, 1812, it was ordered that when officers to whom medals had been awarded were in England, they were to attend the Board in full dress to receive their medals from the hands of the First Lord.

ADMIRALTY MINUTES, January 13th, 1812.

'Capt. Henry Whitby late of H.M.S. *Cerberus* was introduced to the Board and received from the hands of the first Lord the gold medal for his gallant conduct in the action off Lissa in which a superior enemy's force was defeated by His Majesty's Squadron under the orders of Capt. Hoste of the *Amphion*.

'And the Board are of opinion that in future whenever an officer (to whom a medal shall have been awarded) be in England he shall attend the Board in full dress and receive his medal in the form in which it has been this day presented to Capt. Whitby.

'By command,

'J. W. CROKER.'

ADMIRALTY MINUTES, January 13th, 1812.

'Ordered that when the *Briton* Frigate shall be ready to receive men Capt. Henry Whitby late of the *Cerberus* (and who this day received the gold medal for his gallant conduct in that ship) shall have a commission to command her.

'By command,

'J. W. CROKER.

'Appd. 15 April.'

NAVAL CHRONICLE. Vol. xxviii., 1812, p. 276.

'Action with a superior French Naval force off Island of Lissa, 13th March, 1811, under Commodore Hoste.

'Capt. Whitby of the *Cerberus*, 32 guns.

'"Thus much may however be said of the *Cerberus* and her commander, that she went into action 50 men short of her complement which was but 254, and when it ceased, she had 80 of the remainder killed, wounded, or at least rendered unfit for immediate duty."'

Lord Ellenborough and Sir Charles Napier both attributed great importance to the ceremony of presenting medals to soldiers.

Her Majesty has, we believe, made it a point, when practicable, herself to invest those on whom the Victoria Cross and other decorations for distinguished service have been conferred.

Medals for Good Conduct and Meritorious Service are ordered to be presented on parade.

The Royal Red Cross was presented to three ladies of the Indian Nursing Service in 1892. In one case it was presented at a parade of all the troops at the station; in the other two, at evening parties given in honour of the occasion by the officers commanding at the stations.

DESIGNS OF MEDALS.

The designs of our war medals are generally either emblematic, pictorial, or heraldic. Some few bear inscriptions only. The classical figures of Victory, mural and laurel crowns and other devices, frequently occur.

Into the question of the artistic merits of the medals we do not propose to enter. From a popular point of view those medals which are of a *pictorial* character probably afford the most interest.

The examples we give of the medals of Elizabeth and James I. bear their Majesties' effigies, and show them attired according to the fashion of the day. Charles I. is also represented in the costumes which he wore. Those persons, also, who are portrayed on the various medals of his reign and of the succeeding period of the Commonwealth, are shown in ordinary civil or military dress. With the Restoration, however, the classical style came in, with the result that but comparatively few of the medals since struck afford any illustration of the costumes of the periods to which they relate.

The opinion has been held in some quarters that because medals formed a branch of classic art, the classical character should be uniformly maintained. But if this idea had always prevailed, medals would not prove serviceable, as is now frequently the case, in illustrating the persons and events of the periods to which they have reference. If it is desired that medals should be regarded, in a great degree, as illustrations of history, the classic style is certainly unsuitable to the requirements of modern times.

It may, of course, be argued in reference to the modern *war* medal, that as its object is scarcely so much to record events as to constitute a decoration, the design is a matter of minor importance. This may be so; and from this point of view almost any sort of ornament would answer the purpose as well as a medal. But we submit that if a *medal* is used, it should have an intelligible reference to the events for which it was granted. The Naval and Military Gold Medals do not bear the sovereign's effigy, neither do any of the earlier Indian medals. These usually have representations of the operations for which they were awarded, and are consequently of historic interest.

Medals should always bear dates, and these would sufficiently indicate the reigning sovereign at the time.

On the subject of designs for general service medals it may be remarked that the *reverse* of the Silver Military Medal, 1793-1814, does not appear to have been very happily chosen. The crowning of the Duke of Wellington by his sovereign would have been very appropriate for a medal either for the Peninsula or Waterloo, but it has no bearing on the successes of the British arms in Egypt, Sicily, the West Indies or America. Indeed, the designs of the *reverses* of this and the Waterloo Medal might very well change places. The device of the Waterloo Medal, being emblematical of victory generally, would have been applicable to any number of victories in all parts of the world; whilst nothing could have been more eminently suitable for Waterloo than the sovereign crowning the Duke of Wellington.

The general service medal known as the India, 1854, bears no inscription to indicate for what service it was granted. The effigy of Her Majesty shows that it belongs to her reign, but that is all. If the clasp denoting the service happens to become detached from the medal, there is nothing to show for what it was bestowed.

In regard to the shape of medals it will be observed that almost all the earlier examples are oval, and that many of them have ornamental borders, which give them the appearance of badges rather than of medals. With the introduction of the circular form these borders disappear, and the medals consequently lose much of their character as ornaments. There is no question that the oval form is more susceptible of effective treatment for decorative purposes than the round. The idea that the silver war medal should resemble the crown-piece in shape and weight (one ounce) appears to have arisen with the Waterloo Medal, and it has governed the type of almost all our medals since. It may be hoped that the medallists of the future will revert to the earlier form.

In the best period of the art in this country medals were of various sizes, many of them much smaller than modern ones. The earliest medals intended for distribution in large numbers, namely, the Dunbar (No. 35), and the Parliament medal for sea service (No. 39), are very much smaller than any the present generation has been accustomed to see, so that there would be very respectable precedents were it to be determined to adopt a medalet size for future use.

On the question of the most suitable and convenient size for war medals some remarks will be found in the section on the mode of wearing medals.

MODE OF MAKING MEDALS, AND METALS EMPLOYED.

All our earlier medals were cast in moulds, and were frequently worked up with a graving tool. Medals so treated are described as *cast and chased.* Others, as *cast* only.

In the reign of Charles I., Nicholas Briot set up at the Mint his improved balance, which, although it could not be used for striking medals of large size, or in high relief, led to further improvements in the striking machinery which have enabled large medals to be made from dies.

With respect to the medals described in this work, it may be taken for granted that those which are not stated to have been cast were struck.

English war medals have been made in gold, silver gilt, silver, copper, tin, bronze, brass, and gun metal. The earlier issues were doubtless either of gold, silver, or silver gilt.

The medals for the battle of the Nile, presented by Mr. Davison, were of—

Gold for Admirals and Captains
Silver for Lieutenants
Copper gilt for Warrant Officers
Copper bronzed for the Men.

A like system was followed by the East India Company in respect of the Seringapatam Medals. These were issued in gold, silver gilt, silver, copper bronzed, and tin for the various ranks.

The series of medals given by the Crown to officers of superior rank, both naval and military, commencing respectively with the battles of the 1st of June and Maida, were of gold.

For the battle of Waterloo the medals were made in silver only, and this metal has almost invariably been employed since.

The medals given to the Indian Native Troops were usually of gold for the officers, and silver for the men; but since the Burmese War, 1824-25, they have been in silver for all alike. It has, however, been lately decreed that Indian medals for non-combatants shall be of bronze.

Silver medals were formerly made of the pure metal; but as this, on account of its softness, easily became worn and defaced, they are now made of the standard used in the coinage, which is much harder.

MEDALLISTS.

The following particulars are derived mainly from the Introduction to *Medallic Illustrations of British History*.

The names of the artists who executed the medals of the reign of Queen Elizabeth are not known. In the reign of James I., Simon Passe is an artist whose works can be identified by his signature.

In the reign of Charles I., and during the Commonwealth, the brothers Abraham and Thomas Simon, Thomas Rawlins, and two Frenchmen, Nicholas Briot and Jean Varin, were the principal medallic artists in this country. Rawlins and Briot were in the service of the king; the Simons were employed by the Parliament. Of the two Simons, Abraham was the modeller, Thomas the engraver. Thomas was chief engraver to the Mint during the Civil War and the Commonwealth, and produced most of the medals given as military rewards. Rawlins executed almost all the Royalist medals and badges, but his work does not equal Simon's.

With the exception of Briot, who had died during the Civil War, these medallists continued to work in England after the Restoration. Later, the three brothers, John, Joseph and Philip Roettier, who had probably become known to Charles II. in Holland, came over to this country. Another artist of this period was George Bower, but his work is not so good as the Roettiers'.

The medals of the periods of William and Mary, and Anne, were mostly by Dutch artists, the chief being Jan and Martin Smeltzing, Boscam, Hautsch, Luder, and Norbert Roettier, son of John Roettier.

With the accession of the House of Hanover, English medals lose much of their artistic interest. The affairs of England and Holland being no longer so closely allied, the Dutch artists ceased to work for us, and there were but few English medallists. During the reigns of the first two Georges, the principal medallists were James Anthony Dassier, Richard Yeo, Thomas Pingo and John Kirk, but their works are inferior to those of their predecessors. In the second half of the eighteenth century the decadence in the art was still more clearly marked, and this falling off was not confined to England. Of the medallists of the reign of George III. may be mentioned the Westwoods (uncle and nephew), Gosset, Mills, Parkes, Tassie, and Küchler.

In the present century we have the names of Pistrucci and the Wyons. Most of the war medals of Queen Victoria's reign are wholly, or in part, the work of members of the Wyon family.

Daniell, Adams, Boehm, Poynter, and Caldecott, are names also to be mentioned in connection with our war medals.

PRINCIPLES OBSERVED IN THE GRANT OF MEDALS, AND CLASSES OF PERSONS ON WHOM CONFERRED.

So far as we are aware, no definite principles were observed in reference to the bestowal of medals prior to the issue of Charles the First's Warrant of 1643, instituting the badge for soldiers distinguishing themselves in forlorn-hopes. This seems to be the earliest instance of the grant of a decoration as a reward for a particular service, and all ranks would have been eligible for it.

Provision was made by the statutes passed by the Parliament in 1648 and 1649, for the grant of medals or other rewards to such officers and seamen of the fleet as should perform eminent service therein.

No similar provision appears to have been made with respect to the Army, but separate grants were made as occasion arose.

The principle that all ranks were equally eligible for naval rewards is embraced in the statutes above referred to. Similarly, as regarded the Army, when the medal for Dunbar (1650) was granted, all ranks participated.

This principle of equality was preserved in the Acts as to naval rewards passed in the reign of William and Mary, and in the Declaration of Queen Anne. Further, under the operation of these provisions, the issue of medals was not restricted to the Royal Navy, but officers and crews of ships not in the service of the Crown were equally eligible. The principle soon, however, fell into desuetude, and as the eighteenth century advanced medals were few and far between. On the institution of the Naval Gold Medal in 1794, the grant was restricted to admirals and captains. But although the Crown thus restricted its grants, no objection appears to have been taken to the bestowal of medals on all ranks by private individuals. Thus, for the battle of the Nile, medals were given by Nelson's friend, Mr. Davison, to every officer and man present; and, for the battle of Trafalgar, a similar distribution was made by Mr. Boulton.

The precedent of 1794 was followed in regard to the Army in 1806, on the occasion of the battle of Maida, to commemorate which gold medals were given to the general officers and the regimental commanders. The Maida Medal was the forerunner of the gold medals and crosses so frequently awarded, in the years immediately following, to officers of superior rank.

A new departure took place after Waterloo. The Duke of Wellington recommended the grant of a medal to the non-commissioned officers and soldiers. What was his original intention in regard to the officers is not quite clear. He subsequently, however, recommended that officers and men should all have the same medal. This precedent has governed all later grants to both Army and Navy—officers and men having received the same acknowledgment of their services.

The views of the Duke of Wellington as to the principles on which medals should be granted are expressed in his despatches. Writing to Lord Liverpool, on 11th July, 1811 (see p. 198), he says his opinion had always been that the grant of a medal to an individual officer ought to have been founded originally, partly on the importance of the occasion or action which it was intended to commemorate, and partly on the share which the officer had had in the action ; and that medals should be granted for important actions only, and to those engaged in them in a conspicuous manner, whatever might be their rank in the service. The Duke did not concur in the application to the Army of the practice which had been followed in the Navy of giving medals to the superior officers only. He thought that *every* officer should feel that he would receive the mark of distinction if he should be in the place to distinguish himself, and should act in the manner to deserve to be rewarded. It might, his Grace said, be contended by him that the officers of the British Army did not require an honour of this description to stimulate their exertions, and that the grant of the medal was therefore useless. Those, however, who contended for this principle must admit that a selection of those who have had an opportunity of distinguishing themselves in an action is a less objectionable mode of bestowing it than the grant of it by classes, whether the individuals composing those classes had distinguished themselves or not. His clear opinion was that the principle of selection, without reference to ranks, ought to be adopted in every instance of the grant of medals to the Army.

The Duke of Wellington did not consider it to be his duty

to recommend the grant of medals. In a letter to Sir S. Cotton (see p. 201), he says: 'In no one instance has it occurred to me to apply for a medal for any service by the troops. I report the services which they perform, in what I think the clearest and the fairest manner to all concerned; and it rests with Government, and not with me, to notice them as they may think proper.' But, as already stated (see p. 207), after the battle of Waterloo he suggested the expediency of giving a medal to the non-commissioned officers and soldiers engaged, and on this occasion, therefore, he departed from his previous practice.

During the period between the battles of Dunbar and Waterloo no general bestowal of medals for land service under the English Government had taken place. Some thirty years before Waterloo the Indian Government had, however, adopted this method of expressing their appreciation of the services of their *native* troops; whilst for a century earlier it had been their custom to confer medals in recognition of individual merit.

It seems to have been considered at one time that medals and clasps should only be awarded in cases in which the thanks of Parliament had been accorded, but this idea has been long since abandoned. Grants of medals are made by the Sovereign on the recommendation of the Departments of State concerned, and provisions in regard to such grants will be found in the Royal Warrants and Regulations issued from time to time by the authorities.

As regards the grant of medals to other than *regular* combatants, it appears that the War Medal of 1847 was allowed to individuals who had served as volunteers in the Peninsula, on the production of evidence of their having been present in the field as recognised volunteers, and not as mere spectators. (Letter from Office for Military Boards, 22nd August, 1851.)

In respect to the grant to *civilians*, the practice of the Government of India affords, as in other matters connected with war medals, a considerable field of precedents.

In 1845 the Court of Directors, while sanctioning the issue of a medal to a chaplain as an exceptional case, stated that they must prohibit the grant of such distinctions to chaplains in future. There was some controversy on this case, and the Court withdrew the sanction they had given, but afterwards re-awarded it, on learning that it had been the practice of the War Office to allow medals to army chaplains. (Appendix L.)

The Court of Directors having, in 1851, informed the Government of India that certain political officers, volunteers and chaplains, had been granted the medal for the Punjab Campaign, the Governor-General, Lord Dalhousie, took occasion to express some decided views as to the rights of such persons to wear military decorations.

The name of a member of the Civil Service had been returned in an apparently regular manner, but Lord Dalhousie, on hearing of it, wrote to the Court that the name had been submitted without his sanction. He stated that he objected on principle to the grant of military rewards to other than military men; and that he hoped, if the Court disregarded his opinion on the case in question, that he might be permitted to submit the names of other civilians who had accompanied the army in the field. (See despatches of Court of Directors, 9th April, 1851, No. 41; and of Governor-General, 25th June, 1851. Pp. 325-6.)

The Indian Mutiny quite solved the question of the eligibility of civilians to receive medals, as it was then expressly stated that all, whether military or civilians, who had been engaged in its suppression would be entitled to this reward.

On 17th March, 1848, the Government of India published a General Order, No. 115, specifying the classes which would in future be entitled to medals. All the ordinary combatant ranks were included, and likewise certain other grades peculiar to the Army of India. A further General Order by the same Government, dated 4th April, 1871, stated that, subject to certain conditions, non-combatants who might be regularly attached to regiments or departments would be entitled. In connection with the operations in Burma in 1885-87, some additional classes were declared eligible. It was then decided that in future medals for the non-combatant classes should be made of bronze instead of silver. (See p. 359.)

In 1887 the Government of India resolved that efficient members of volunteer corps, when proceeding on any duty with an army in the field, should be entitled to medals. This decision was, it is believed, in accordance with the practice which had been followed by the War Office when awarding medals for campaigns elsewhere than in India; the case chiefly in point being that of the Post Office Volunteers in Egypt. Possibly it was thought that the prospect of medals might encourage civilian clerks and others belonging to Army Departments, who happened to be volunteers, to proceed willingly on active service. (Appendix N., p. 592.)

With regard to claims of 'special correspondents' to medals, although some have been allowed, it has been held by the authorities that civilians who attach themselves to an army in the field for their own purposes are ineligible.

We should not omit to mention that medals have been conferred on female nurses for service with an army in the field. There is also a special decoration, entitled the 'Royal Red Cross,' for the reward of army nurses.

Lastly, ships' dogs and regimental dogs have sometimes been the proud wearers of war medals.

In Appendix P. is an illustration of the collar of 'Bruce,' a Scotch terrier belonging to the captain of H.M.S. *Leopard* during the war with Russia in 1854-55.

POWERS OF COLONIAL GOVERNMENTS TO GRANT DECORATIONS.

The first decoration awarded by a Colonial Government may have been that given by the Legislative Assembly of St. Vincent in the West Indies, in 1773, to the forces which had recently been employed in suppressing an outbreak of the Caribs. (See p. 99).

No authoritative rule in respect to the powers of Colonial Governments to confer honorary decorations was, perhaps, ever laid down before 1869, in which year the Secretary of State for the Colonies, on receiving information from the Governor of New Zealand that the Colonial Government, whilst fully acknowledging the Sovereign as the fountain of honour, had established a decoration, styled the 'New Zealand Cross,' as a reward for valour on the part of individual members of the Colonial forces, acquainted the Governor that he had, in the action taken, overstepped the limits of the authority confided to him. The Secretary of State thought it necessary to point this out in order that no precedent might be established either in New Zealand or any other Colony for taking such a step without the cognisance of Her Majesty's Government, and the personal sanction of the Queen. In the special circumstances of the case in question Her Majesty had, however, been pleased to sanction the establishment of the decoration, and also the regulations issued to govern its award. (See p. 392.)

This ruling seems to settle the question of the incompetency of Colonial Governments to institute decorations of any description as rewards for military service.

On a later occasion, in a debate in the House of Commons on 25th February, 1886, on the subject of the cost of the medals to be given to the Colonial forces of Canada for their services in suppressing the late rebellion, it was admitted that the Colonial Government had no power to grant such decorations. There is, however, no reason why a Colonial Government should not bear the cost of any that may be granted by the Crown, in the same manner as the cost of medals granted for service in India is borne by Indian revenues. The Victoria (Australia) Government instituted a medal for long service some time since, but it had only a local significance.

DISPOSAL OF MEDALS PROHIBITED.

The earliest injunction against soldiers selling their decorations appears to be contained in the Warrant of Charles I., instituting the forlorn-hope badge. The Warrant also forbids any person to buy or wear such badge.

At the present day soldiers and sailors selling or otherwise making away with their medals, and any persons buying or receiving such medals, are liable to punishment.

GENERAL ORDER BY COMMANDER-IN-CHIEF, Jan. 17, 1860.

'The Commander-in-Chief considers it necessary to announce, for general information and guidance, that when a soldier is to be brought to trial for making away with a medal or other honorary decoration, it is essential to state the estimated value of the decoration in the charge, and then to establish that value by evidence, to enable the court-martial adjudicating on the case to sentence the soldier to be put under stoppages, to the amount so established in evidence, according to the provisions of the Mutiny Act.'

THE QUEEN'S REGULATIONS, 1895. *Section* xx. 2.

LOST MEDALS.

'Medals are to be shown at the weekly inspection of necessaries, when officers commanding companies are to ascertain that they are the property of the men shewing them. When a man is unable to produce his medal, a board—to consist of one captain and two subalterns—is to inquire into and record the cause of the loss. If the board be of opinion that the man has designedly made away with his medal, he will be dealt with under the provisions of Section vi. para. 39. If convicted in such a case, the offender may, after five years' absence from the Regimental defaulter's-book, be recommended to the Commander-in-Chief for a new medal, on paying the value thereof. The application will be made on Army Form *B.* 177.'

ROYAL WARRANT, 1896. *Part* I, *Section* 9. No. 1261.

'If a soldier is permitted as required to replace a medal wilfully made away with or lost through carelessness or otherwise, he shall be subjected to a stoppage of 7s. 6d. for the medal, and 1s. 6d. for the clasp.

MINIATURE MEDALS.

These have already been mentioned in the foregoing pages under the section treating of the 'Mode of wearing Medals and Orders.'

Miniature Medals were not made until 1815, at the close of the Waterloo Campaign. The earliest known date from that period. Officers caused them to be made for their wives to wear, and their use was tacitly allowed.

The first reference to them in an official publication is to be found in the 1873 edition of the Queen's Regulations, section 12, para. 6, which says—'Miniature Orders and Medals or ribands of Medals only, are to be worn by officers in undress uniform.'

Further details will be found in Appendix O.

Miniature Medals and Decorations are made at the cost of those on whom the originals have been conferred. See pp. 225, 231.

FORFEITURE OF DECORATIONS.

We have noticed the case of the return of a gold chain being required by Charles II., in consequence of the recipient having proved himself unworthy of it. (See p. xlvi.)

The Statutes of the Victoria Cross, the New Zealand Cross, the Albert Medal, and the Royal Red Cross provide for the expulsion of persons who, by reason of misconduct, become unworthy of the decorations; and the Statutes of the Albert Medal further provide for the return of the decoration which belonged to the expelled person.

Soldiers and sailors are liable to forfeiture of decorations for causes set forth in the Regulations.

GENERAL ORDER, *June* 15, 1854. No. 641.

'The medals granted for service in the field are to be withdrawn from soldiers of the East India Company's service, European or Native, who may be sentenced to transportation, or ordered to be discharged with ignominy, and will be transmitted to the Adjutant-General of the Army for the purpose of being returned to the Military Department.

'This order is applicable to the three presidencies.'

REPLACEMENT OF MEDALS.

GENERAL ORDER BY COMMANDER-IN-CHIEF IN INDIA, Nov. 30, 1854.

'Under instructions from Government, the Commander-in-Chief is pleased to notify for general information that decorations which may be lost in any accidental manner, involving no culpability on the part of the individuals to whom they belong, may, in like manner with those lost by theft or captured by the enemy, be replaced by the issue of fresh ones at the expense of the applicants; the penalty of a fine being added to the cost of the medal in any case in which Government shall deem it necessary to exact the same.'

'ADJUTANT-GENERAL'S OFFICE,
'ALLAHABAD, *January* 21, 1859.

'With reference to G.O.C.C., July 25th, 1858, it is announced for general information that Government has been pleased to sanction the re-issue of medals gratis to all commissioned officers, warrant, and non-commissioned officers and soldiers, to replace decorations lost by the mutiny of native corps.'

GENERAL ORDER BY COMMANDER-IN-CHIEF IN INDIA, March 24, 1864.

'With the sanction of Government the rates of payment for the replacement of lost medals laid down in the following War Office Circular are adopted in the Indian army, and published for general information.

'CIRCULAR No. 833.—(Medals.) Now obsolete.

'WAR OFFICE, *August* 14, 1863.

'Referring to the War Office Circular, No. 616, of the 3rd August, 1860, specifying the amounts which are to be charged to a soldier to replace medals wilfully made away with or lost through carelessness or neglect, Earl De Grey and Ripon has directed that such stoppages should in future be made at the undermentioned rates, viz. :—

	£	s.	d.
For a Crimean or China medal	0	7	0
For each clasp	0	1	0
For a Kaffir war medal, or medal for good conduct or distinguished service	0	7	0
For a medal granted for service in Pegu, Cabul, the Sutlej, Punjaub, and Burmah campaigns	0	9	3
For each clasp	0	1	1½
For a medal granted for service in the campaign in Persia or during the Indian Mutiny	0	7	6
For each clasp	0	1	6
For a Victoria Cross	1	4	0

'It should be clearly understood that Her Majesty's Government cannot replace a medal or decoration granted by a Foreign power.'

MEDALS OF DECEASED OFFICERS AND SOLDIERS TO BE DELIVERED TO THEIR RELATIVES.

In the General Order, dated 9th September, 1810, granting the first gold medal for the Peninsula, it was stated that the medals which would have been conferred upon officers who had fallen, should, as a token of respect for their memories, be delivered to their respective families.[1] (See Medal No. 155.)

This General Order established the rule as regards the British service The following one settled it in respect to the Indian service.

GENERAL ORDER BY THE GOVERNOR-GENERAL OF INDIA, 28th March, 1812.

'His Lordship in Council is pleased to establish it as a rule, that the heirs of deceased men shall be entitled to the medals which their relations would have received, in order that the honorable mark of approbation granted to the deserving soldier may not be lost to his family, to whom under other circumstances it would have descended.' (Code 1845, 673.)

DESPATCH, COURT OF DIRECTORS, Nov. 10, 1852. No. 152 (11); *GENERAL ORDER, Jan.* 13, 1853. No. 44.

'It is our practice, a practice in conformity with that of Her Majesty's Government, to present the medals of deceased officers and soldiers to their next of kin, unless such medals are specifically left by will to some other person.'

GENERAL ORDER, July 22, 1859. No. 1050.

'Her Majesty has been pleased to signify her intention that the practice under which medals granted for service in India have been presented to the representatives of the officers and soldiers who fell in action or died, should be adopted with regard to the medals and clasps, the grant of which Her Majesty has been graciously pleased to sanction in commemoration of the late military operations in India.'

UNCLAIMED MEDALS.

(*Letter to War Office, April* 22, 1864, No. 239.
Reply, May 30, 1864.)

'A great accumulation of unclaimed war medals of both officers and soldiers is taking place in this office, and it seems desirable before removal that some steps should be taken as to their disposal. On receiving a representation from the Government of India, in 1848, regarding the accumulation of medals at Calcutta, the Court of Directors ordered :—

'"Such of these medals as have been unclaimed for upwards of five years, may be sent to the Mint for bullion purposes, with the exception of a few to be retained for re-issue to parties who may lose their medals on duty, and of those enumerated in the enclosed list which we are desirous should be forwarded to us."

'There are now about 2500 medals in the office, these medals are all inscribed with the rank and names of those for whom they were intended.

'The dies for the medals granted for service in India, from 1842 to the present time, are all in this country, and if the medals were melted down, they could be easily replaced if claimed by soldiers or their representatives. It is resolved that after retaining about a dozen of each as specimens, the medals granted for service from the campaigns in Affghanistan, in 1842, to the expedition to Pegu in 1852-3, be sent on the decision of the Government of India thereon being made known, the rolls of those officers and soldiers of Her Majesty's British regiments considered entitled to partici-

[1] The curious notion has been entertained by some people that sons have the right to wear medals granted to their fathers. This idea is, of course, absurd.

pate in the decoration, should be transmitted to the Adjutant-General at the Horse Guards.

'6. The arrangements for the preparation and distribution of medals will be entrusted to the department of Her Majesty's Government, with which, upon a deliberate review of the nature and consequences of the operations performed, the proposal of the grant originated; and by which the cost of the decoration will be defrayed, that department being the best qualified to judge, in each case, whether the service for which the medal is claimed comes properly within the intentions and scope of the royal grant.'

FOREIGN MEDALS.

The following Regulations, regarding the acceptance by British subjects of medals conferred by Foreign Powers, have been issued from time to time by the Foreign Office.

'REGULATIONS RESPECTING FOREIGN MEDALS.

'FOREIGN OFFICE, 24*th January*, 1851.

'The Queen has been pleased to direct that:—

'1st. Application for permission to accept and wear Medals which, not being the decoration of any Foreign Order, are conferred by a Foreign Sovereign on British Subjects in the Army or in the Navy, for military or for naval services, should be addressed, as the case may be, to the Commander-in-Chief, the Master General of the Ordnance, or the Lords of the Admiralty, who, if they see fit, may submit the same to Her Majesty's Principal Secretary of State for Foreign Affairs, for Her Majesty's sanction; upon obtaining which, they may grant such permission without any other formality.

'2nd. Permission to wear a Foreign Medal cannot be granted to a British Subject, unless such Medal is bestowed for military or naval services. But no permission is necessary for accepting a Foreign Medal, if such Medal is not to be worn.

'PALMERSTON.'

'FOREIGN OFFICE, 10*th May*, 1855.

'1. Application for permission to accept and wear Medals which, not being the decoration of any Foreign Order, are conferred by a Foreign Sovereign on British Subjects in the Army or in the Navy, for military or for naval services, should be addressed, as the case may be, to the Commander-in-Chief, the Master General of the Ordnance, or the Lords of the Admiralty, who, if they see fit, may submit the same to Her Majesty's Principal Secretary of State for Foreign Affairs, for Her Majesty's sanction; upon obtaining which, they may grant such permission without any other formality.

'2. Permission to wear a Foreign Medal cannot be granted to a British Subject, unless such Medal is bestowed for military or naval services performed by the command or with the sanction of Her Majesty. But no permission is necessary for accepting a Foreign Medal, if such Medal is not to be worn.

'CLARENDON.'

GENERAL ORDER BY COMMANDER-IN-CHIEF, 30*th January*, 1860.

'Notification has been received from the Horse Guards to the effect that neither the French war medal, nor any other, bestowed by a Foreign power can be replaced when lost.'

'FOREIGN OFFICE, *January*, 1870.

'1. Applications for permission to accept and wear Medals which, not being the decoration of any Foreign Order, are conferred by a Foreign Sovereign on British subjects in the Army or in the Navy, for military or for naval services, should be addressed, as the case may be, to the Commander-in-Chief, or the Lords of the Admiralty, who, if they see fit, may submit the same to Her Majesty's Principal Secretary of State for Foreign Affairs, for Her Majesty's sanction; upon obtaining which they may grant such permission without any other formality.

'2. Any British subject is at liberty to accept and wear a Foreign Medal, not being the Decoration of a Foreign Order, bestowed by competent authority for acts of bravery in saving human life. An officer, soldier, marine, or sailor must, however, first obtain permission from the Commander-in-Chief, or the Lords of the Admiralty, as the case may be.

'3. No permission is necessary for accepting a Foreign Medal, if such Medal is not to be worn.

'CLARENDON.'

'FOREIGN OFFICE, *August*, 1885.

'1. Applications for permission to accept and wear Medals which, not being the decoration of any Foreign Order, are conferred by a Foreign Sovereign on British subjects in the Army or Navy, should be addressed to the Commander-in-Chief or the Lords of the Admiralty, as the case may be, who, if they see fit, may submit the same for Her Majesty's sanction, upon obtaining which they may grant such permission without other formality.

'2. Any other British subject, having obtained Her Majesty's permission, is at liberty to accept and wear a Foreign Medal, not being the decoration of a Foreign Order.

'3. No permission is necessary for accepting a Foreign Medal, if such Medal is not to be worn.

'SALISBURY.'

AN ORDER OF KNIGHTS BANNERET.

In connection with the subject of honorary rewards, it may be remarked that it is strange there should be no Order of Knighthood reserved exclusively for the reward of specially important warlike service, and forming the highest honorary reward attainable in respect of such service.

Whatever may have been the original intention, the military division of the First Class of the Order of the Bath can scarcely be regarded as now fulfilling this condition, inasmuch as it has been not uncommon for G.C.B.'s to be bestowed on officers holding the distinction of K.C.B. for apparently no other reason than seniority in the service coupled with longevity. The principle has seemed to be that, once admitted to the Order, an officer is eligible for advancement in it without performing any further service to the State. The growth of this practice is traceable, perhaps, to the existence of certain established proportions of honour for the respective services, some of the vacancies in which are filled by promotions in the order made, so far as the public are able to discern, in view rather to the maintenance of the numerical proportions than for any other reason.

Such a procedure may gratify those who benefit by it, but it can hardly be deemed an ideal method of awarding distinctions intended primarily as rewards for warlike service. Indeed, if an officer's services are to be gauged by the honours he has received, the system is altogether misleading, because, under it, an officer who obtained a C.B. for, say, commanding a regiment in the Crimea, and whose subsequent service was merely garrison, could, in course of years, be advanced to K.C.B. and G.C.B., thereby being placed on a par with officers who had received those dignities as direct rewards for war service. But if it be possible for a C.B., by effluxion of time, thus to develop into a G.C.B., surely it should be possible for the G.C.B. to attain to some higher dignity. Some day a reformed House of Lords may, perhaps, comprise a class of 'service' life peerages which would be available in such cases.

The practice which has of late been adopted of specifying in the *Gazette* the particular service for which an officer is promoted or decorated, may possibly lead to the discontinuance of the system, since it would be invidious to notify in the same *Gazette* that one K.C.B. had been promoted to G.C.B. for some distinguished warlike service,[1] and that another had been similarly promoted merely 'to complete establishment.' The latter officer might not, under such circumstances, quite appreciate his advancement; and the acceptance of distinctions for having, so to speak, done nothing, may, consequently, become discredited.

The case is altogether different with those Orders of Knighthood which are bestowed exclusively on members of the peerage on account of their position in society or politics. It is not pretended that 'merit,' as usually understood, has very much weight in determining appointments to these. The Duke of Wellington was the last instance of a Knight of the Garter being so created by way of reward for *warlike* service.

With the view of providing a special naval and military

[1] Considerable public feeling was aroused in the days of the Indian Mutiny by two officers, whose service had been in widely different spheres of action, being simultaneously gazetted K.C.B.

honorary reward of the highest nature, to which admission would be obtainable only by eminent warlike service, it is suggested that the Order of Knights Banneret might advantageously be revived in a modified manner.

The Table of Precedence now shows two classes of Bannerets, viz.:—

Those made by the Sovereign, or Prince of Wales, in open war; and

Those not made by the Sovereign in person.

The former rank two degrees above, and the latter next below, Baronets, although above Knights of the Thistle, Grand Crosses of the Bath, and Knights of St. Patrick as such. There is thus only one Order of Knighthood, viz. the Garter, higher than that of Banneret.

But the Crown being now the sole fountain of honour, and it being no longer the practice for our Kings or Princes of Wales to go forth to war, the Order would require a certain amount of reconstruction, and all the Knights would be made by the sovereign. Their precedence might be that of the old higher class, namely, above the younger sons of viscounts and barons, and above baronets.

For such an Order specific eminent service would, as already said, constitute the sole qualification; seniority or longevity would afford no claim. Like the principal Orders of the three kingdoms it should consist of but one class, although there would, of course, be no limit to the number of the Knights. In the restriction to one class the value of a great Order virtually consists. The G.C.B. has never been really equivalent to the old K.B. What would become of the *prestige* of the Garter were the Order to be split up into classes, with hosts of Commanders and Companions?

It would be a pleasing feature in such an Order were it characterised by simplicity, and an avoidance of conventional paraphernalia. The old Knights Banneret had no mark of distinction besides their banneret; and the new Knights might be privileged to have theirs borne before them on occasions of state. And, if a personal distinguishing ornament were deemed necessary, what more appropriate than the mystical Collar of SS., which was doubtless worn by some of their predecessors?

For the rest, St. Paul's might be the temple of the Knights; their bannerets might hang upon its walls!

MEDALS AND DECORATIONS

N.B.—Except when otherwise stated the medals are circular in form.

No. 1.

QUEEN ELIZABETH, 1588.

PLATE 2, No. 1.

Obv. Bust of Elizabeth, *l.*, hair adorned with pearls, ruff very large, gown with lozenge-shaped puffings, and profusion of jewellery.

Leg. ELIZABETH . D . G . ANGLIE . F . ET . HI . REG.

Rev. Ark on waves; above, the rays of the sun.

Leg. SEVAS . TRANQVILLA . PER . VNDAS (Tranquil amid violent waves).

Oval, 2 by 1·75 inches. Silver.
Ring for suspension.

Med. Hist. Pl. vii. 5.
Perry, Pl. v. 1.
Med. Ill. vol. i. p. 148, No. 119.

This is one of the medals supposed to have reference to the defeat of the Spanish Armada, and to have been bestowed as honorary rewards. The significance of the ark riding on the waves is apparent. And there may be a further significance, inasmuch as the ship which carried the flag of the Lord High Admiral, Lord Howard of Effingham, and which had been purchased of Sir Walter Raleigh, was named the *Arke Rawlie*.

No. 2.

QUEEN ELIZABETH, 1589.

PLATE 2, No. 2.

Obv. Bust of Elizabeth, full face, wearing high crown, necklace with pendants, ruff open in front, erect behind, gown and sleeves puffed and jewelled; on shoulders high pointed bows; holds sceptre and orb.

Leg. DITIOR . IN . TOTO . NON . ALTER . CIRCVLVS . ORBE . (No other circle in the whole world more rich).

Rev. A bay tree uninjured by lightning and winds, flourishing upon an island inscribed NON . IPSA . PERICVLA . TANGVNT (Not even dangers affect it). On the island are buildings, and in the sea monsters; three ships in the distance. Floral border.

Oval, 2·3 by 2·1 inches. Gold, silver, copper.
Cast and chased.
Ring for suspension.

Med. Ill. vol. i. p. 154, No. 130.
Num. Chron. N. S. vol. vii. Pl. 2.

This medal is in high relief, and of very fine workmanship. It may have been given as a reward in connection with the defeat of the Spanish Armada.

No. 3.

QUEEN ELIZABETH, 1582.

PLATE 2, No. 3.

Obv. Bust of Elizabeth, *l.*, hair decorated with pearls, large ruff, gown richly jewelled. Bordered with the Garter.

Rev. Royal arms on garnished shield, supported by an angel. Bordered with the the Garter, as on *obverse.*

Oval, 2 by 1·6 inches. Silver, copper.

Med. Hist. Pl. vii. 10.
Perry, Pl. v. 4.
Med. Ill. vol. i. p. 132, No. 85.

No. 4.

SIR JOHN HAWKINS.

GOLD ENAMELLED JEWEL.

This jewel, said to have been presented by Queen Elizabeth to Sir John Hawkins, was exhibited at the Armada Exhibition held at Drury Lane Theatre in December, 1888. It was stated to be the property of the Countess of Rosebery.

No. 5.

SIR FRANCIS DRAKE.

JEWEL AND STAR.

In Tancred's *Historical Record of Medals*, illustrations are given of a jewelled badge and star, said to have been presented by Queen Elizabeth to Sir Francis Drake, which are now at Nutwell Court, Devon, in the possession of his representatives.

The following particulars are quoted from the book in question, p. 23:—

'The Star is in the form of a sun, and has rubies set in the rays, with opals and diamonds interspersed in the border around the inner portion; an orb is engraved in intaglio, emblematical of sovereignty. There are loops fixed to the back of the Star for attaching it to the coat.'

'The Badge or Jewel is richly enamelled in red, yellow, blue and green, and in the border are set diamonds and rubies. A splendid cameo cut in onyx occupies the centre, believed to have been executed by the celebrated Valerio Vincentino. The representation of two heads is the subject of this cameo; one is what might be termed a classical head with regular features, typical of Europe; the other has the features of a negro, and is intended to represent the black races of the world. At the back is an exquisite miniature of Queen Elizabeth by Nicholas Hilliard, and bearing date *Anno Dom.* 1575, *Regni* 20. In a large picture of Sir Francis Drake by Zucchero he is represented wearing this jewel, suspended from the neck by a red and gold cord, over the green silk scarf presented by the Queen with the above-mentioned badge.'

No. 6.

JAMES I.

PLATE 3, *No.* 1.

Obv. Bust of James I., three-quarters, *r.*, hat with jewel and feathers, rich doublet, cloak, lace collar, and the George of the Garter suspended round the neck by a ribbon.

Leg. IACOBVS . D . G . MAG . BRITA . FR . ET . HI . REX.

Rev. An ark upon the sea; above, bright rays bursting from clouds.

Leg. STET . SALVVS . IN . VNDIS (May it stand safe amid the waves).

Oval, 1·9 by 1·6 inch. Gold, copper.

Med. Hist. Pl. xi. 11.
Med. Ill. vol. i. p. 233, No. 96.

No. 7.

JAMES I.

PLATE 3, *No.* 2.

Obv. Bust of James I., three-quarters, *r.*, in hat, with brim fastened up with a jewel; lace ruff, doublet, fur cloak, Collar and George of the Garter.

Leg. IACOBVS . D . G . MAG . BRITA . FR . ET . HI . REX.

There is no *reverse.*
Oval, 2·25 by 1·8 inches. Silver, copper, lead.

Med. Hist. Pl. xi. 10.
Perry, Pl. x. 4.
Med. Ill. vol. i. p. 234, No. 98.

No. 8.

JAMES I.

PLATE 3, *No.* 3.

Obv. Bust of James I., three-quarters, *r.*, head bare, in armour, upright lace collar. Badge of the Garter suspended round neck.

Leg. IACOBVS D . G . MAG . BRITA . FR . ET . HI . REX . FIDEI DEFENSOR.

Rev. An ark upon the sea ; above, bright rays bursting from clouds.

Leg. STET . SALVVS . IN . VNDIS (May it stand safe amid the waves).

Oval, 2·1 by 1·7 inches. Copper.

Med. Hist. Pl. xii. 12.
Perry, Pl. ix. 1.
Med. Ill. vol. i. p. 233, No. 95.

No. 9.

CHARLES I. AND HIS QUEEN.

PLATE 4, *No.* 1.

Obv. Bust of Charles I., *r.*, long hair, lovelock on left shoulder, falling lace collar, ribbon to suspend medal, and scarf across breast.

Rev. Bust of his Queen, Henrietta Maria, *l.*, hair ornamented with beads, lovelock on right shoulder, pearl ear-ring and necklace, with cross. Both sides surrounded by a wreath border.

Oval, 1·85 by 1·6 inch. Silver.
Cast and chased.
Rings for suspension.

Med. Hist. Pl. xiv. 3.
Med. Ill. vol. i. p. 353, No. 213.

No. 10.

CHARLES I.

PLATE 4, *No.* 2.

Obv. Bust of Charles I., *r.*, in falling lace collar, armour, medal suspended by ribbon.

Rev. Royal arms in garnished shield, crowned, within the Garter.

Oval, ·75 by ·6 inch. Silver, silver-gilt.
Cast and chased.
Floral border, within a corded border on both sides.
Rings for suspension.

Num. Chron. vol. xiii. Pl. iv. 28.
Med. Ill. vol. i. p. 363, No. 242.

No. 11.

CHARLES I.

PLATE 4, *No.* 3.

Obv. Bust of Charles I., *r.*, head bare, hair long, lovelock on left shoulder, in plain falling collar; armour with lion's head on shoulder. George of the Garter suspended by ribbon. On truncation, incuse, 1639.

Leg. CAROLVS . I . D . G . MAG . BRITANN . FRAN . ET . HIB . REX. Behind bust, BRIOT.

Rev. A ship in full sail; on left, sea shore with fort.

Leg. NEC . META . MIHI . QVÆ . TERMINVS . ORBI (Nor is that a limit to me which is a boundary to the world).

Circular, 2·35 inches. Silver.
Artist. Nicholas Briot.

Med. Hist. Pl. xvi. 7.
Med. Ill. vol. i. p. 285, No. 97.

No. 12.

CHARLES I.

PLATE 4, *No.* 4.

Obv. Bust of Charles I., *r.*, lovelock on left shoulder, medal suspended by ribbon.

Rev. Royal arms in garnished shield, crowned, within the Garter; all within a beaded border.

Oval, ·85 by ·7 inch. Silver.
Rings for suspension.

Num. Chron. vol. xiii. Pl. iv. 27.
Med. Ill. vol. i. p. 363, No. 241.

No. 13.

CHARLES I.

PLATE 4, *No.* 5.

Obv. Bust of Charles I., *r.*, hair long, plain falling collar, armour with lion's head on shoulder, and George of the Garter suspended by ribbon.

Leg. Incuse. CAROLVS . D . G . MAG . BRIT . FR . ET . HI . REX.

Rev. Incuse. Royal arms, crowned, within the Garter.

Oval, 2·25 by 1·8 inches. Silver.
Cast and chased.
Ring for suspension.

Num. Chron. vol. xiii. Pl. iii. 19.
Med. Ill. vol. i. p. 360, No. 230.

No. 14.

CHARLES I.

PLATE 5, *No.* 1.

Obv. Bust of Charles I., *r.*, hair long, in falling lace collar, doublet buttoned close, ribbon to suspend medal, and scarf across breast.

Leg. Incuse. CAROLVS . D . G . MAG . BRI . FR . ET . HIB . RX.

Rev. Incuse. Royal arms, crowned, within the Garter.

Oval, 1·5 by 1·2 inch. Silver, silver-gilt.
Rings for suspension.

Med. Ill. vol. i. p. 360, No. 231.

No. 15.

CHARLES I.

PLATE 5, *No.* 2.

Obv. Bust of Charles I., *r.*, crowned, hair long, in falling lace collar, ermine robes, and Collar of the Garter.

Leg. CAROLVS . D . G . MAG . BRITAN . FRAN . ET . HIB . REX . FI . D.

Rev. Royal arms within the Garter, crowned.

Oval, 1·5 by 1·2 inch. Silver, silver-gilt.
Rings for suspension.

Med. Ill. vol. i. p. 360, No. 232.

No. 16.

CHARLES I. AND PRINCE CHARLES.

PLATE 5, *No.* 3.

Obv. Bust of Charles I., three-quarters, *r.*, head bare, hair long, lovelock on left shoulder, falling lace collar, armour with lions' heads on shoulders, and medal suspended by ribbon.

Rev. Bust of Prince Charles, *l.*, head bare, hair long, plain falling collar, armour with lion's head on shoulder, and medal suspended by chain.

Oval, 1·7 by 1·3 inch. Silver-gilt.
In high relief, cast and chased.
Rings for suspension.
Artist. Thomas Rawlins.

Num. Chron. vol. xiii. Pl. v. 37.
Med. Ill. vol. i. p. 301, No. 122.

This may be the Badge instituted by Charles I. in his Royal Warrant of 18th May, 1643, as a reward for those taking part in

Forlorn-hopes. (See No. 22.) There are, however, other medals having, on the *obverse* and *reverse* respectively, the effigies of the King and Prince Charles.

No. 17.

CHARLES I. AND PRINCE CHARLES.

PLATE 5, *No.* 4.

Obv. Busts conjoined, *r.*, of Charles I. and his son, Prince Charles, hair long, falling lace collars, armour, scarves festooned upon breasts, and medals suspended round necks by ribbons. The king is crowned, and has a lion's head on his shoulder.

Leg. CAR . REX . M . B . F . ET . H . CAR . PRINCEPS. Below, monogram T . R.

Rev. Same as *obverse.*

Oval, 1·7 by 1·5 inch. Silver-gilt.
Two thin plates soldered together.
Cast and chased.
Artist. Thomas Rawlins.

Num. Chron. vol. xiii. Pl. v. 38.
Med. Ill. vol. i. p. 302, No. 123.

No. 18.

CHARLES I.

PLATE 5, *No.* 5.

Obv. Half-length figure of Charles I., standing, three-quarters, *l.*, dressed in robes of the Order of the Garter; right hand upon hat lying on a table, left hand holding glove.

Leg. Incuse. CAR . D . G . MAG . BRI . FRAN . ET . HIB . REX.

Rev. The King on horseback, *r.*, in armour, plumed hat on his head, right hand resting on his truncheon. Above, a genius with palm and wreath.

Leg. Incuse. HONNI . SOIT . QVI . MAL . LE . PANS.

Oval, 1·65 by 1·25 inch. Silver.
Two thin plates united; cast and chased.
Ring for suspension.

Med. Hist. Pl. xviii. 10.
Med. Ill. vol. i. p. 298, No. 118.

As the palm and wreath have a victorious allusion, this medal may have been executed after the battle of Edgehill, 23rd October, 1642.

No. 19.

CHARLES I. AND PRINCE CHARLES.

PLATE 5, *No.* 6.

Obv. Bust of Charles I., *r.*, crowned, long hair, falling lace collar, ermine robes, Collar of the Garter.

Leg. Incuse. CAROLVS . D . G . MAG . BRITAN . FRAN . ET . HIB . REX . FI . DE.

Rev. Prince Charles on horseback, *r.*, in armour, plumes in helmet, truncheon in hand, scarf floating behind; below, battle scene in the distance; above, C. P. stamped in the field.

Oval, 1·5 by 1·2 inch. Silver-gilt.
Cast, slightly chased.
Rings for suspension.
Artist. Thomas Rawlins.

Num. Jour. vol. i. p. 136.
Med. Ill. vol. i. p. 299, No. 119.

The battle represented on this medal is believed to be that of Edgehill, and the medal was probably executed as a reward for the Royal forces.

No. 20.

PRINCE CHARLES.

PLATE 5, *No.* 7.

Obv. Bust of Prince Charles, *l.*, head bare, hair long, in plain falling collar, armour with lion's head on shoulder, and medal suspended by chain. (Same as No. 16)

Rev. Royal arms within the Garter, crowned.

Oval, 1·7 by 1·3 inch. Silver.
Rings for suspension.

Med. Ill. vol. i. p. 372, No. 263.

No. 21.

PRINCE RUPERT.

PLATE 5, *No.* 8.

Obv. Bust of Prince Rupert, three-quarters, *l.*, head bare, hair long, falling lace collar, armour, scarf across breast, medal suspended by ribbon round neck; truncheon in right hand.

Rev. Armorial bearings of the Prince on three shields, two lions as supporters, helmet and crest; in the field R . P. (Prince Rupert).

Oval, 1·45 by 1·2 inch. Silver.

Med. Hist. Pl. xiv. 9.
Med. Ill. vol. i. p. 323, No. 159.

No. 22.

CHARLES I., 1643.

FORLORN-HOPE SILVER BADGE.

By the following Royal Warrant Charles I. instituted a silver badge as a reward for soldiers distinguishing themselves in Forlorn-hopes.

At this period the term 'Forlorn-hope' was not restricted, as it has been, perhaps, in later times, to the foremost party in the storming of a fortification, but it meant that portion of an army which was intended to lead the attack in battle, and which would have consisted of such numbers of cavalry or infantry as the circumstances of the case required. 'Soldiers' only are specified, and, from the clause of the Warrant forbidding its sale, it was apparently contemplated that the badge would be pretty freely distributed. We have, however, no information as to the extent to which it was issued, nor, indeed, do we know whether it was ever made. None of the records of the Oxford Mint for this period appear to be extant, and it is probable they were all burnt in the fire at Oxford in 1644. The medal No. 16 (Plate 5, No. 3) bears the effigies of the King and Prince Charles, and may be the badge in question.

From a letter addressed by the King to Mr. Thomas Bushell, dated 12th June, 1643, it appears that the idea of this badge originated with him, inasmuch as the King praises him for his 'invention for our better knowing and rewarding the Forlorn Hope with Badges of silver at your own charge.'[1]

ROYAL WARRANT.

'CHARLES R.

'Trusty and well beloved, we greet you well; Whereas we have received information that those soldiers which have been forward to serve us in the Forlorn-hope, are not looked upon according to their merited valour and loyal service. We do therefore require, that from henceforward the Commander-in-Chief, both of Horse and Foot, which lead up the Forlorn-hope, upon whom also we mean to bestow special tokens of our princely favour, do signify in writing the names of those soldiers whom they find most forward in serving us, their King and Country, that care may be taken to reward their deservings, and make them specially known to all our good subjects. For which end we have thought fit to require Sir William Parkhurst, Knight, and Thomas Bushell, Esquire, Wardens of our Mint, to provide from time to time certain Badges of silver, containing our Royal image, and that of our dearest

---

[1] Ellis's *Original Letters*, 2 S., vol. iii. p. 309; Sir Sibbald Scott's *British Army*, vol. ii. p. 476.

son, Prince Charles, to be delivered to wear on the breast of every man who shall be certified under the hands of their Commanders-in-Chief to have done us faithful service in the Forlorn-hope. And we do, therefore, most straitly command, that no soldier at any time do sell, nor any of our subjects presume to buy, or wear, any of those said Badges, other than they to whom we shall give the same, and that under such pain and punishment as our Council of War shall think fit to inflict, if any shall presume to offend against this our Royal command. And we further require the said Commanders, and Wardens of our Mint, to keep several Registers of the names of those and of their country, for whom they shall give their certificate.

'Given at our Court at Oxford, the eighteenth day of May, 1643.

'To Our trusty and well-beloved Sir William Parkhurst and Thomas Bushell, Esquire, Wardens of Our Mint at Oxford.'[1]

No. 23.

CAPTAIN WILLIAM RAINSBOROUGH, 1637.

GOLD CHAIN AND MEDAL.

The following is taken from the *Letters and Despatches of Thomas, Earl of Strafforde*, A.D. 1637, p. 129. 'Letter from Rev. — Garrad to the Lord Deputy in Ireland.' Written from the Strand, Nov. 9, 1637:—

'Here came over with Captain Rainsborough from Sallee an ambassador from the King of Morocco, an English merchant, one Mr. Blague, joined partly in commission with him, some twenty in his train. He fell extream sick of a fever at Gravesend, with some Difficulty he was brought to London, where he is lodged in an Ambassador's house; he is but newly recovered, so that on Sunday last, the 5th of this month, he had his Audience at Court. He rid on horseback through the streets, my Lord of Shrewsbury conducting him with twelve gentlemen of the Privy Chamber, his own Company, and some City Captains. . . . He is come to renew the old League and Amities that have been betwixt the two Crowns, and to render thanks to his Majesty as the chief instrument of restoring Sallee to his obedience by sending his Fleete thither, which, so long as his Master holds it, it shall never again infes any of his Majestie's subjects. The King was very willing and forward to have knighted Captain Rainsborough, but he declined it; so order was given that he should have a gold chain and medal of £300 price.'

No. 24.

CAPTAIN JOHN SMITH, 1642.

GOLD MEDAL.

Obv. Effigy of Charles I.
Rev. The Royal Standard.

At the battle of Edgehill, fought between Charles I. and the Parliamentary Army under the Earl of Essex on 23rd October,

---

[1] In his *History of the Orders of Knighthood*, Sir Nicholas Harris Nicolas states that the Warrant was communicated to him by Mr. Edward Hawkins, of the British Museum. (Vol. iv. Part 2, p. 5.)

1642, the Royal standard was captured by the enemy, the standard-bearer, Sir Edmund Verney, Knight-Marshal, being killed. The standard was, however, rescued by Captain John Smith, of Lord Grandison's regiment of horse.[1]

Captain John Smith, of Lord Bernard Stuart's troop of the King's Guards, with three others, disguised with orange scarves (the colours of Essex), mingled with the enemy, and took the standard out of the hands of Mr. Chambers, Cromwell's Secretary. Captain Smith was knighted the same evening under the standard he had so gallantly recovered, and was the first knight-banneret that had been made for a century. The King afterwards gave him a gold medal, which he is said to have worn by a green watered ribbon across his shoulders.[2]

In Sir R. Bulstrode's *Memoirs* (1688), p. 83, it is stated that 'the King's Royal Regiment of Foot Guards lost eleven of thirteen Colours. The King's Standard-bearer, Sir Edmund Verney, was killed, and the Royal Standard taken, which was presently retaken by Captain John Smith, who was knighted for it that night by the King under the Standard Royal, and made a Baronet with the usual ceremonies; and had afterwards a large medal of gold given him, with the King's picture on the one side, and the Banner on the other, which he always wore to his dying day in a large green watered ribband cross his shoulders. He was afterwards killed at the battle of Alresford in Hampshire, in the year 1644, which was called Cheriton Fight, with the Lord Bernard Stuart, brother to the Duke of Richmond, and several others.'

No. 25.

SIR ROBERT WELCH, 1643.

GOLD MEDAL.

Obv. Busts of Charles I. and Prince Charles.

Rev. The Royal Standard, with the inscription: PER REGALE MANDATVM CAROLI REGIS HOC ASSIGNATVR ROBERTO WELCH MILITI (By the Royal mandate of King Charles this medal is conferred upon Robert Welch, Knight).

Num. Chron. vol. xv. p. 80.
Med. Ill. vol. i. p. 302, No. 124.

---

[1] Clarendon's *History*, Book vi. p. 328. New edition, 1839.

[2] Eliot Warburton's *Prince Rupert and the Cavaliers*, p. 125; Godwin's *Civil War in Hampshire*, p. 132.

It is not known whether this medal is in existence.

At the battle of Edgehill, 23rd October, 1642, Robert Welch or Walsh, an Irish gentleman, in command of a troop of horse, distinguished himself by recovering the standards of the King's Own Regiment, which had been taken by the rebels, and by capturing two pieces of cannon and the Earl of Essex's carriage. On the morning after the battle, Prince Rupert presented Welch and his trophies to his Majesty, who conferred the honour of knighthood upon him; and on the 1st June, 1643, a Royal Warrant was issued to the graver of the King's Seals, to make a gold medal for Sir Robert Welch.

The Royal Warrant of 1st June, 1643, addressed to Thomas Rawlins, Graver of Seals and Medals, and the Earl Marshal's Warrant of 14th August, 1685, for recording the same at the College of Arms, are given below. They are copied from the records at the College of Arms (MS. i. 26, fol. 90). At the foot of the Royal Warrant are drawings of the *obverse* and *reverse* of the medal. These are here reproduced. The *obverse* is the same as No. 17. (Plate 5, No. 4.)

ROYAL WARRANT.

'CHARLES R.

'OUR will and Pleasure is that you make a Medal in Gold for our Trusty and Welbelovd Sr Robert Welch Knight, with our own Figure and that of our dearest Sonne Prince Charles: And on the Reverse thereof to Insculp ye form of our Royal Banner used at the Battail of Edge-hill, where he did us acceptable service, and received the dignity of Knighthood from us; and to inscribe about it Per Regale Mandatum Caroli Regis hoc assignatur Roberto Welch Militi: And for so doing this shall be your sufficient Warrant.—Given at our Court at Oxford this first of June 1643.

'To our trusty and Welbelovd
Thomas Rawlins, our Graver
of Seals, Stamps, and Medals.'

EARL MARSHAL'S WARRANT.

'WHEREAS Sir Robert Walch Knight has produced a warrant under the Royal Sign Manual of King Charles the first of ever blessed memory, whereby the said King granted unto the said Sir Robert a medal of Gold with the Figure of the said King and of his Son (then Prince Charles) with such Motto as in the said Warrant mentioned which he has prayed may be Entred on Record in ye College of Arms, together with such other papers and Warrants as relate thereto: These are to authorise and require you, or any of you to whom these presents shall come, to cause entry to be made of the said Badge, granted as aforesaid to the said Sir Robert Walch, on Record in the said Office of Arms; and for so doing this shall be your Warrant; Given under my hand and the Seal of my Office of Earl Marshall of England the 14th day of August 1685, Anno RR Jacobi Scdi nunc Angliæ etc^a primo.

'To the King's Heralds and Pursuivants
of Arms, or to the Regist^ers of the
College of Arms.

Signed thus 'NORFOLKE & MARSHALL.'

Sir R. Bulstrode in his *Memoirs*, p. 83, says: 'Sir Robert Walsh, an Irishman, who also pretended that he was very instrumental in regaining the [Royal] Standard, did also in the same manner wear a green ribband with a Medal, but whether it was given him by Order, or how he came by it, I do not know, though I have often seen him wear it.'—(See No. 24, Captain John Smith.)

As above stated, it was for recovering the 'Standards of the King's Own Regiment,' and for capturing two pieces of cannon, and the Earl of Essex's carriage, that Sir Robert Welch was knighted, and afterwards received a Medal. The recapture of the 'Royal Standard' by Captain John Smith was a separate incident in the battle. But from the fact of the King's Warrant ordering that on the *reverse* of the Medal should be insculped 'the form of our Royal Banner used at the Battail of Edge-hill where he did us acceptable service,' it would seem possible that Welch had assisted in the affair.

In a book entitled *True Narrative and Manifest set forth by Sir Robert Walsh, Knight and Bart.*, printed for himself in 1679, he says 'he hath the privilege of wearing His Majesty's of blessed memory's effigies, and that of his dearest son Prince Charles, of the one side of his golden Medal; and the form of His Majesty's Royal Banner of the reverse, for the acceptable service he hath rendered at the battle of Edge-hill in the year '43, as his commission for wearing the same from His Majesty of blessed memory now extant can witness, he having received the dignity and honour of Knighthood upon the top of Edge-hill. . . . Though many more deservedly than I might on the day of battle have attained to the dignity of the mark of honour I carry at my breast, I am confident that there is not many who can shew as ample a commission of His Majesty's of blessed memory for the like, as I have now extant; which in this particular it hath profited me in, whereas all Noblemen and Knights are liable to pay Poll money, I having sent my Badge, Title and Commission unto those worthy Commissioners, who were intrusted in the assessment of the Poll money, they then sitting at Hicks' Hall in May, 1678, they were civilly pleased to discharge me from the payment for my dignity, and that I should pay only a shilling for my Poll, signed by two of the Commissioners, and sealed, whom I yet never to my knowledge did see, Sir Ed. Abney and William Beversham, Commissioners, the 29 May, 1678, so in paying a shilling I was quit.'—(See Sir H. Nicolas's *History of Honorary Medals*, pp. 6, 7.)

The following fragment is preserved in the Public Record Office. It is written on half a sheet of paper, and is without either signature or date. As the description of the Medal tallies with that given in the Royal Warrant quoted above, it is not improbable that the writer, who was in difficulties, apparently abroad, was Sir Robert Welch.

STATE PAPERS—DOMESTIC, INTERREGNUM.

Vol. xxiii. No. 127. (1651-52.)

'S^r^, If by yor meanes Mr Fox, or Mr Thamson, may come heather, yo^v^ will Lay a very great obligation Uppo^n^ mee; for I may chance soe Contriv wth them as to procure mee some present releefe, of wch I assuer yo^v^ I have neede I having in the lombard, to the Vallue of 2000 guilders—wch Lye not for 300, and are Uppo^n^ beeing forfeted. I not having eather the principall or Interest to pay them; and y^t^ wch Trobles mee more ten tymes then all y^t^ Ther Lyeth a goolden meadaiele, The late King of Blessed memory gave mee, his owne pictuer and this Kings of one syde, and his standard Royalle of the other syde.'

In the account given by Captain Richard Symonds of the regiments of the army of Charles I. mustered at Aldbourne Chace on 10th April, 1644, occurs the following:—

'Colonel Bennett's Brigade of Horse consisted of these Regiments:—

. . . .

'2d Reg., Sr Geo. Vaughan, Colonel, Sr Robt. Welsh, Lieut.-Colonel, but 2 Troopes 80.

['2 flags—1 blue, 2 blue—with on a scroll argent "Experto crede Robto, for ye lieut.-Colonel."']

. . . .

(*Harl. MS.*, No. 986; *Wilts Archæological Magazine*, vol. xxiii. p. 267.)

No. 26.

SIR THOMAS FAIRFAX, 1645.

JEWEL.

PLATE 6.

In acknowledgment of his services at the battle of Naseby, the House of Commons awarded a valuable Jewel to Sir Thomas Fairfax. The Jewel cost £800, and was presented to Fairfax in November, 1645, at Ottery St. Mary, by a deputation of members of Parliament.

JOURNALS OF THE HOUSE OF COMMONS.

16*th June*, 1645.

'*Resolved, &c.*, That Sir Henry Mildmay, Mr. Lisle, Sir Robert Harley, and Mr. Jennour, do forthwith provide a Jewel of Five hundred Pounds value, to be sent from this House to Sir Thomas Fairfax, as a Testimony of their Affections to him, and of the Esteem they have of his Services.'

24*th October*, 1645.

'Sir Robert Harley presented to the House the Jewel to be bestowed upon Sir Thomas Fairefaxe, with the value or estimate of it, amounting unto Eight hundred Pounds: And

'*It is Resolved, &c.*, That this House doth approve of this value of the said Jewel.

'*Ordered, &c.*, That Mr. John Ashe do present this Jewel from the House to Sir Thomas Fairefaxe.

'*Resolved, &c.*, That the Eight hundred Pounds for the paying for this Jewel shall be paid out of the Fine of the first Delinquent not yet disposed of: And that the said Eight hundred Pounds be paid unto Mr. Francis Allen, or his Assigns: whose Acquittance, together with this Order, shall be a sufficient Discharge for the payment thereof.'

4*th November*, 1645.

'*Ordered, &c.*, That the Committee of Goldsmiths Hall do take care of the Payment of the Eight hundred Pounds assigned to be paid to Mr. Francis Allen, for the Jewel given by this House to Sir Thomas Fairefaxe, General of the Parliament's Forces.'

19*th November*, 1645.

'A Letter from the General Sir Thomas Fairfaxe, from St. Mary-Awtry, of Novembris 14, 1645; together with divers Propositions for carrying on the War, and disposing the Forces to the best Advantage of the Service this Winter, and next Summer; was this Day read.

'A Letter from the General of Novembris 14, 1645, returning his humble Thanks for the Jewel he received from the House, in Testimony of their Respects unto him, was this Day read.'

As regards the actual delivery of the Jewel to Sir Thomas Fairfax, the following is a quotation from *England's Recovery*, *or Anglia Rediviva*, by Joshua Sprigge, 1648 (new edition, Oxford, 1854, p. 164):—

'In the interim, a fair Jewel set with rich diamonds of very great value was presented unto the General, by Mr. Ash, and some other members of Parliament, in the name of both Houses, as a signal of that great honour which God had done him, in the great service which, by God's assistance, he performed for this kingdom at Naseby battle; and, according to the commands of the Parliament, they tied it in a blue ribbon, and put it about his neck.'

The Jewel was in the form of a gold enamelled locket or watch-case, set with diamonds round the border. The artist was Pierre Bordier. The portions of the Jewel now existing are the two sides, known as the 'Naseby enamels,' one of which has pictorial representations on both its surfaces, and the other on the convex surface only, the concave being blank, giving the impression that the original idea was that the jewel should contain a watch. The sides are 1·5 inch in diameter. They are somewhat flat, and that on which the House of Commons is represented is rather flatter than the other.

Convex, No. 1. The House of Commons sitting. All the members are covered, whilst the Sergeant-at-Arms, with the mace on his left shoulder, stands in front of the Bar, behind which stands a man with his head uncovered.[1]

Concave of No. 1. Plain light green enamel.

Convex, No. 2. Sir Thomas Fairfax on his chestnut mare, head bare, in armour, with blue scarf over left shoulder. On the left is a portion of a stone column and its base. On the right, a tree; overhead, a blue curtain; in the background, a battle. On a scroll in the sky on the left, SIC RADIANT FIDELES. On the ground below the horse's foot, P.B. FECIT.

Concave of No. 2. Representation of the battle of Naseby; on a scroll in the sky, NON NOBIS. The flags carried are very large.

The jewel was worn suspended round the neck by a blue ribbon.

The enamels are now in the possession of Lord Hastings, by whose kind permission the present illustrations were executed. They are set in a handsome gilt frame, chased and jewelled, and surmounted by the following inscription:—

'These enamels, painted by P. Bordier, were given by the Parliament to General Fairfax on his victory at Naseby, were purchased of his executors by Mr. Ralph Thoresby, and at his sale by Mr. Horace Walpole, 1764.'

In Markham's *Life of the Great Lord Fairfax* the following account is given of the jewel (App. B, p. 435):—

'*The Naseby Enamels.* The sum of £700 was voted by the Parliament for "the

[1] There is a brownish blur on the right side of this surface, having the appearance of a scorch.

jewel," as it was called, which was presented to Sir T. Fairfax after the Battle of Naseby. Sprigge mentions its presentation at Ottery in November, 1645. Its execution was entrusted to Pierre Bordier, the famous painter on enamel. Petitot and Bordier, brothers-in-law, have never been equalled in enamel painting. They worked at Geneva, went thence to Italy, and afterwards to England. Petitot is said to have executed the heads and hands, and Bordier the hair and draperies of their portraits. But Petitot went to France at the breaking out of the Civil War, so that the Naseby enamels must have been the entire work of Bordier. The "jewel" was a locket, consisting of two enamel plates, with the intervening sides set with diamonds.

'On the death of Lord Fairfax the enamel plates were sold to his old companion-in-arms, John Thoresby, whose son was the famous Leeds antiquary. In 1764 Thoresby's museum was sold by auction in London, and the enamels were bought by Horace Walpole for £10, 10s. At the Strawberry Hill sale (eleventh day, lot 41) they were bought by John P. Beavan for £21. They are now at Melton Constable in Norfolk, and belong to Lord Hastings. They are gold, and one and a half inches in diameter; both concave, but one more so than the other. Walpole took them to be the case of a watch, but this is evidently a mistake, or the fact would have been mentioned by Sprigge. They were simply the two sides of a locket, to be worn round the neck by a blue ribbon. On the outside of the more concave one is the portrait of Fairfax on his famous chestnut mare, in enamel, with men engaging in the distance. Walpole says "the figure and horse are after Vandyck, but with a freedom and richness of colour perhaps surpassing that great master." Under the horse is P. B. FECIT; on a scroll, SIC RADIANT FIDELES. On the outside of the less concave plate is the House of Commons, in enamel, as on the great seals of Simon. Walpole says "nothing can be more perfect than the figures, in some even the countenances are distinguishable." On the inside is the Battle of Naseby, and NON NOBIS on a scroll. Thoresby says of these enamels, "The metal, though gold, is but as dross compared with the workmanship."'

It appears from Markham, pp. 430 and 433, that the under-mentioned portraits of Lord Fairfax showed him as wearing the jewel:—

Portrait painted by Bower in 1646. Figure in armour, head bare, sash round waist, medal set in diamonds hanging round neck.

Portrait, artist not known. Figure half-length, in leathern doublet, sash, gorget, and falling collar, jewel round neck.

It is not known whether either of the above portraits exists.

The enamels were included in the Exhibition of Miniatures at the Burlington Fine Arts' Club, 1889.—(*Catalogue*, p. 136.)

No. 27.

FERDINAND, LORD FAIRFAX, 1643.

PLATE 7, *No.* 1.

Obv. Bust of Ferdinand, Lord Fairfax, full face, in plain falling collar, armour, and scarf across body.

Rev. Arms of Fairfax in garnished shield.

Oval, 1·5 by 1·05 inch. Silver.
Cast and chased, in very high relief.
Ring for suspension.

Med. Ill. vol. i. p. 304, No. 126.

No. 28.

SIR THOMAS FAIRFAX, 1645.

PLATE 7, No. 2.

Obv. Bust of Sir Thomas Fairfax, *l.*, hair long, plain falling collar, armour, and mantle fastened on left shoulder.

Leg. THO : FAIRFAX . MILES . MILIT : PARL : DVX . GEN : (Thomas Fairfax, Knight, General-in-Chief of the Parliamentary Army).

Rev. Inscription. MERVISTI (Thou hast merited).

Leg. POST . HAC . MELIORA . 1645 (Better things hereafter).

Oval, 1·3 by 1·1 inch. Silver, silver-gilt.
Cast and chased.
Ring for suspension.
Artist. T. Simon.

Med. Hist. Pl. xxi. 13.
Van Loon, vol. ii. 323.
Evelyn, p. 116, Fig. 38.
Vertue, xi. Fig. 1.
Med. Ill. vol. i. p. 317, No. 150.

No. 29.

SIR THOMAS FAIRFAX.

PLATE 7, No. 3.

Obv. Bust of Sir T. Fairfax, three-quarters, *r.*, hair long, plain falling collar, and armour.

Rev. Arms of Fairfax in garnished shield, between branches of palm and laurel.

Oval, 1·7 by 1·5 inch. Silver.
Cast and chased.
Wreath border on both sides.
Ring for suspension.

Med. Hist. Pl. xxi. 12.
Vertue, xi. Fig. F.
Med. Ill. vol. i. p. 319, No. 153.

No. 30.

EARL OF MANCHESTER, 1643.

PLATE 7, No. 4.

Obv. Half-length figure of the Earl of Manchester, three-quarters, *l.*, head bare, hair long, in falling lace collar, armour, and sash round body.

Leg. Incuse. *Pro Religione Lege Rege et Parliamento.*

Rev. The two Houses of Parliament, with the King and Speaker.

Oval, 1·7 by 1·45 inch. Silver, silver-gilt.
Cast and chased.
Wreath border on both sides.
Ring for suspension.

Med. Ill. vol. i. p. 310, No. 139.

No. 31.

EARL OF WARWICK.

PLATE 7, *No.* 5.

Obv. Half-length figure of Robert Rich, Earl of Warwick, full face, long hair, plain falling collar, armour, scarf across right shoulder, and truncheon in right hand.

Rev. Garnished shield with arms of Rich; above, an Earl's coronet.

Oval, 1·7 by 1·3 inch. Silver.
In high relief, cast and chased.
Floral border on both sides.
Ring for suspension.

Med. Ill. vol. i. p. 424, No. 66.

The Earl of Warwick was appointed by the Parliament, in 1642, Lord High Admiral of England. He died in 1658. This medal was, possibly, a naval reward.

No. 32.

EARL OF ESSEX, 1642.

PLATE 8, *No.* 1.

Obv. The Earl of Essex on horseback, *r.*, in armour, plumes in helmet, truncheon in hand, scarf floating behind; below, battle-scene in the distance.

Leg. ROBERTVS COMES ESSEXIÆ.

Rev. Arms of Essex, in garnished shield, Earl's coronet above; below, his motto, BASIS VIRTVTVM CONSTANTIA (Constancy the basis of the virtues).

Oval, 1·85 by 1·6 inch. Silver-gilt.
Cast and chased. The legends on both sides are pounced in, and are almost illegible.
Wreath border on both sides.
Ring for suspension.
Artist. T. Rawlins.

Med. Ill. vol. i. p. 300, No. 120.

The *obverse* of this medal is the same as the *reverse* of No. 19 (Plate 5, No. 6), in which the mounted figure is intended for Prince Charles. If the battle portrayed is that of Edgehill, the *obverse* was probably used by Lord Essex to commemorate victory for the Parliamentary Forces, and the design was thus made to serve the purposes of both sides.

No. 33.

EARL OF ESSEX, 1642.

PLATE 8, *No.* 2.

Obv. Bust of the Earl of Essex, nearly full face, in armour, plain falling collar, and scarf over right shoulder, sword in hand, and over his head a hand issuing from clouds brandishing a sword.

Leg. Incuse. THE SWORD OF THE LORD AND OF GYDEON.

Rev. The two Houses of Parliament, with the King and Speaker. (Same as No. 4 on Plate 7.)

Leg. Incuse. IN THE MVLTITVDE OF COVNCELLORS THERE IS PEACE.

Oval, 1·55 by 1·2 inch. Silver-gilt.
Cast and chased.
Rings for suspension.

Med. Hist. Pl. xxi. 6.
Vertue, x. Fig. B.
Evelyn, p. 116, Fig. 37.
Med. Ill. vol. i. p. 297, No. 115.

No. 34.

EARL OF ESSEX, 1642.

PLATE 8, *No.* 3.

Obv. Bust of the Earl of Essex, full face, plain falling collar, armour, and scarf over right shoulder.

Rev. Garnished shield of Essex, surmounted by a Marquis's coronet;[1] below, a plain scroll.

Oval, 1·4 by 1·1 inch. Silver.
Cast and chased.
Ring for suspension.

Med. Ill. vol. i. p. 297, No. 116.

No. 35 (A).

BATTLE OF DUNBAR, 1650.

PLATE 8, *No.* 4.

Obv. Bust of Oliver Cromwell, *l.*, hair long, plain falling collar, armour, and scarf festooned upon the breast; in the distance, a battle.

Leg. THE LORD OF HOSTS . WORD . AT DVNBAR . SEPTEM : Y . 3 . 1650.

On truncation, THO. SIMON . FE.

[1] This is a mistake on the part of the medallist. The coronet should have been an Earl's, as in No. 32 (Plate 8, No. 1).

Rev. The Parliament assembled in one House with the Speaker. On the left, a member standing, addressing the House.

Oval, 1·35 by 1·15 inch. Silver, copper, lead.
Artist. Thomas Simon.
Dies with Messrs. Wyon of Regent Street.

Van Loon, vol. ii. p. 356.
Med. Hist. Pl. xxii. 3.
Vertue, xii. A.
Evelyn, p. 117, Fig. 39.
Med. Ill. vol. i. p. 392, No. 14.
Henfrey, Pl. I, No. 1.

No. 35 (B).

BATTLE OF DUNBAR, 1650.

PLATE 8, *No.* 5.

Obv. Bust of Oliver Cromwell, *l.*, hair long, plain falling collar, armour, and scarf festooned upon the breast; in the distance, a battle.

Leg. THE LORD OF HOSTS . WORD . AT DVNBAR . SEPTEM : Y . 3 . 1650.

On truncation, T. SIMON . F.

Rev. The Parliament assembled in one House with the Speaker.

Oval, 1 by ·85 inch. Gold, silver, copper.
Ring for suspension.
Artist. Thomas Simon.

Med. Hist. Pl. xxii. 4.
Vertue, xii. A.
Med. Ill. vol. i. p. 391, No 13.
Henfrey, Pl. I, No. 2.

These two medals were struck to commemorate the Battle of Dunbar on 3rd September, 1650.

JOURNALS OF THE HOUSE OF COMMONS.

10th September, 1650.

'A letter from Dunbarre, 3° Septembris 1650, from Mr. Rushworth: A letter from the Lord General Cromwell, from Dunbarre, 4° September 1650: with a List of the names of the Scotts officers taken prisoners: Another letter from the Lord General Cromwell, from Dunbarre, of the Fourth of September 1650.

'Which were all this day read.

. . . .

'*Ordered*, that there be a letter written to the Lord General, from the Parliament, taking notice of his eminent services, with the special acknowledgment and Thanks of this House: And that the Lord General be desired to let the Officers and Soldiers of the Army know, that the Parliamen hath taken notice of their good services in this great Battle: And to give them Thanks from the House.

. . . .

'*Ordered*, that it be referred to the Committee of the Army, to consider what Medals may be prepared, both for Officers and Soldiers, that were in this Service in Scotland; and set the Proportions and Values of them, and their number; and present the Estimate of them to the House.' (Vol. vi. pp. 464-465.)

From the following letter of Oliver Cromwell to the Committee of the Army, it appears that in the execution of their instructions they sent Mr. Simon to Scotland for the purpose of taking the Lord General's likeness.

'FOR THE HONOURABLE THE COMMITTEE OF THE ARMY 'AT LONDON': THESE:

'EDINBURGH, 4 *February*, 1650-1.

'GENTLEMEN,

'It was not a little wonder to me to see that you should send Mr. Symonds so great a journey, about a business importinge so little, as far as it relates to me; when as if my poor opinion may not be rejected by you, I have to offer to that which I think the most noble end, to witt, The Commemoracon of that great Mercie att Dunbar, and the Gratuitie to the Army, which might be better expressed upon the Meddal, by engraving, as on the one side the Parliament, which I heare was intended and will do singularly well, so on the other side an Army, with this Inscription over the head of it, *The Lord of Hosts*, which was our Word that day. Wherefore, if I may begg it as a favor from you, I most earnestly beseech you, if I may doe it without offence, that it may be soe. And if you thinke not fitt to have it as I offer, you may alter it as you see cause; only I doe thinke I may truly say, it will be verie thankfully acknowledged by me, if you will spare the having my Effigies in it.

'The gentleman's paynes and trouble hither have been verie great, and I shall make it my second suite unto you that you will please to conferr upon him that imployment which Nicholas Briot had before him: indeed the man is ingenious, and worthie of encouragement. I may not presume much; but if, at my request, and for my sake, he may obteyne this favor, I shall putt it upon the accompt of my obligacons, which are not few; and, I hope, shall be found readie gratefully to acknowledge, and to approve myself,

'Gentlemen,

'Your most reall servant,

'OLIVER CROMWELL.'[1]

Cromwell's desire that his 'Effigies' should not appear on the medal was not acceded to. But his suggestion respecting the representation of the Parliament on one side of the medal was adopted; as was likewise his further suggestion as to the representation on the other side of an army, with the 'word' on the day of the battle. The representation of the 'Army' was, however, subordinated to the General's 'Effigies.'

If all those engaged on Cromwell's side received the medal,

[1] *Life of Oliver Cromwell*, by W. Harris, 1762, pp. 538-539.

a large number must have been prepared, since it appears from Cromwell's despatch to the Speaker of the House of Commons that his army amounted to about 11,000—3500 horse and 7500 foot.

The medal was made in two sizes, but whether the larger size was intended for officers and the smaller for the men, or the larger in gold and the smaller in silver, are points as to which we have found no evidence.

Whether any except combatants received the medal is not known; nor is it known whether during the interval from 1650 to 1660 the medals were worn as decorations. After the latter date they would scarcely have been displayed.

This is the first occasion of medals being distributed to officers and soldiers alike.

No. 36.

CAPTAIN ROBERT WYARD AND HIS CREW, 1650.

PLATE 8, *No.* 6.

Obv. An anchor, from the stock of which are suspended two shields; one bearing the Cross of St. George for England, the other a harp for Ireland; the whole encircled by the cable of the anchor. Above, MERUISTI (Thou hast merited).

Rev. A ship closely engaged between two frigates. Four other ships in the distance.

Leg. SERVICE . DON . AGAINST . SIX . SHIPS . IVLY . Y . XXXI . & AVGVST . Y . I . 1650.

Oval, 1·6 by 1·35 inch. Gold, silver.

Med. Hist. Pl. xxiii. 3.
Vertue, xvi.
Med. Ill. vol. i. p. 390, No. 11.

Under the operation of the Acts passed in 1648 and 1649, a gold medal, of the value of £50, was presented to Captain Robert Wyard, who, whilst in command of a ship of twenty-two guns, was attacked in the North Sea, on the night of 31st July, 1650, by six Royalist frigates, which he engaged until the following afternoon, when he proceeded to Yarmouth.

The master of the ship was awarded a medal of £5; the mates, medals of £4; the boatswain, gunner, and carpenter, medals of £3; the inferior officers, medals of 10 shillings; and the common men, medals of 5 shillings each—of a similar design to the captain's. The medals of 10s. and 5s. were probably struck in silver.

JOURNALS OF THE HOUSE OF COMMONS.

9th August, 1650.

'Sir Henry Vane, junior, reports from the Council of State, A Letter from Robert Wyard, from Yarmouth, of the Fifth of August 1650: Which was this Day read.

'*Ordered*, That it be referred to the Council of State, to consider what Reward and Recompense shall be thought fit to be given to Captain Robert Wyard for his good service; and to the Master and Owner of the Ship, in respect of the damage done to the Ship: And that the said Council be, and are impowered and authorized to give such Rewards and Allowances to them, as they shall think fit, accordingly.' (Vol. vi. p. 454.)

COUNCIL OF STATE.

8th August, 1650.

'5. Sir Henry Vane to report to Parliament Capt. Wyard's letter, containing a relation of the fight which he maintained at sea with several of the enemy's ships.

'6. The Admiralty Committee to consider the good service of Capt. Wyard and his company, and to order such rewards to them as are allowed by Act of Parliament, and care is to be taken of the wounded.

'7. To write Colonel Deane enclosing the letter from the bailiffs of Yarmouth, concerning Capt. Wyard maintaining a fight at sea with his own ship, while Butler and Jones lay still within ken, and came not to his assistance, and to desire him to call those captains to account before a Council of War.' (*Calendar of State Papers—Domestic Series*, 1650, p. 277.)

ADMIRALTY COMMITTEE.

16th August, 1650.

'Order upon conference with Colonel Deane, as to rewarding Captain Wyard and his company:—That Capt. Wyard should have a Gold Medal of £50, with his service against five ships engraved on the one side, and the arms of the Commonwealth on the other, and £100 towards repairing of his ship; the master, a medal of £5; the mates, medals of £4 each; the boatswain, gunner and carpenter, of £3 apiece; the inferior officers, medals of 10s. each; and the common men, of 5s. apiece, with the arms and inscription aforesaid, and that this be reported to the Council of State as the opinion of the Committee.' (*Calendar of State Papers—Domestic Series*, 1650, p. 291.)

COUNCIL OF STATE.

21st September, 1650.

'(21.) Order that Capt. Wyard and his company be allowed medals for good service, as recommended by the Admiralty Committee [see above, 16th August, 1650], which is to issue warrants to the collectors for prize goods to pay for them.' (*Calendar of State Papers—Domestic Series*, 1650, p. 351.)

COUNCIL OF STATE.

5th September, 1650.

'(2) As there has been very good service lately done by Capt. Robert Wyard, commander of a ship belonging to the Commonwealth, wherein he very gallantly acquitted himself and vindicated the honor of this nation, by maintaining a long and well-managed fight against five or six of the enemy, Council, besides a reward and mark of special favour bestowed upon him and his company, remit and pass by his offence in disputing the searching of his ship by the Customs' officers of the port of Hull, about some French wines then on board his ship.' (*Calendar of State Papers—Domestic Series*, 1650, p. 327.)

ADMIRALTY COMMITTEE.

24th September, 1650.

'Order that the collectors for prize goods cause medals to be prepared in pursuance of the Council's order of 21st instant, for Captain Wyard and his company, for their good services, and keep them in their hands until further order.' (*Calendar of State Papers—Domestic Series*, 1650, p. 355.)

No. 37 (A).

VICTORIES OVER THE DUTCH. 1653.

PLATE 9, *No.* 2.

Obv. An anchor, from the stock of which are suspended three shields, bearing St. George's Cross for England, St. Andrew's for Scotland, and a harp for Ireland ; the whole encircled by the cable. Near the ring of the anchor, the monogram T. S.

Rev. A naval battle: in the foreground is a ship sinking, on the stern of which is the artist's name, SIMON, and on the prow of another, T. S.

On both sides a broad border of naval trophies, with, on the *obverse*, the shields of Holland and Zealand.

Oval, 2·2 by 2 inches. Gold.
Ring for suspension.
Artist. Thomas Simon.
Die of *reverse* in British Museum.

Med. Hist. Pl. xxiii. 1.
Van Loon, vol. ii. 366.
Vertue, xvi.
Med. Ill. vol. i. p. 398, No. 26.

No. 37 (B).

PLATE 9, *No.* 1.

The *obverse* and *reverse* are, with the exception of the border, the same as the preceding. The borders on both sides are of laurel.

Oval, 2 by 1·8 inches. Gold.
Ring for suspension.
Med. Ill. vol. i. p. 399, No. 27.

No. 37 (C).

PLATE 9, *No.* 3.

The same medal as the preceding, but without any border. The inscription shown in the plate on the *reverse* was not on the medals issued to the officers of the Fleet generally, but only on those of the officers of the *Triumph.*

Oval, 1·6 by 1·4 inches. Gold.
Ring for suspension.

Med. Hist. Pl. xxiii. 2.
Vertue, xvi.
Med. Ill. vol. i. p. 400, No. 28.

This is the medal which was struck to commemorate Admiral Blake's victories over the Dutch in 1653.

As will be seen from the following documents, the Parliament awarded gold chains of the value of £300 to Admirals Blake and Monk; of the value of £100 to Vice-Admiral Penn and Rear-Admiral Lawson; and of the value of £40 to the four flag officers. It likewise appears that the sum of £960 allowed for the chains was augmented to £2000, in view to the provision of medals for the Admirals and other Fleet officers. The sum of £1040 was therefore allotted for all the medals. Thomas Simon received in all £2011, 18s. 6d. for making the chains and medals.

It will be noticed that the gold chain was the principal token of the good acceptance of the service performed in the cases of the senior officers.

COUNCIL OF STATE.

6th August, 1653.

'(24) Moyer and Courtney to report to Parliament that two Gold chains worth £300 each be given to Colonel Blake and General Monk; and Chains worth £100 each to Vice-Admiral Penn and Rear-Admiral Lawson, as a mark of favor for their services against the Dutch.' (*Calendar of State Papers—Domestic Series*, 1653-54, p. 77. *Papers*, vol. xxxix.)

8th August, 1653.

'(23) Mr. Moyer to report to Parliament that four gold chains of £40 be given to the four flag officers for service in the late engagement, and that the money to be laid out in these chains, and in those to the generals and vice and rear-admirals, be raised to £2000, to be given in Medals amongst the other fleet officers, by advice of the Generals.' (*Calendar of State Papers—Domestic Series*, 1653-54, p. 79. *Papers*, vol. xxxix.)

JOURNALS OF THE HOUSE OF COMMONS.

8th August, 1653.

'Mr. Moyer reports from the Council of State:

'That it be humbly reported to the Parliament, from this Council, that Two Gold Chains, to the value of Three hundred Pounds apiece, may be made and given to General Blake and General Monck, as a Mark of Favour from the Parliament, and a Token of their good Acceptance of the eminent services performed by them against the Dutch:

'And that a Chain, to the value of One hundred Pounds, may be made and given to Vice-Admiral Penn; and one of the same value to Rear-Admiral Lawson; upon the same consideration.

'That it be also humbly presented to the Parliament, That the Four Flag Officers have Chains given them, of Forty Pounds apiece: And that, if the Parliament shall so please, the former sum of Nine hundred and sixty Pounds be made up Two thousand Pounds, to be given in Medals amongst the Officers of the Fleet, as a mark of the Parliament's Favour, and good Acceptance of their service, in such manner as the Commissioners of the Admiralty, by Advice with the Generals of the Fleet, shall think fit.

'*Resolved*, by the Parliament, That Two Gold Chains (to the value of Three hundred Pounds apiece) be made and given to General Blake and General Monck, as a Mark of Favour from the Parliament, and a Token of their good Acceptance of the eminent services performed by them against the Dutch: And that a Chain to the value of One hundred Pounds, be made and given to Vice-Admiral Penn, and one of the same value to Rear-Admiral Lawson; upon the same consideration.

'*Resolved*, by the Parliament, That the Four Flag Officers have Chains given them of Forty Pounds apiece: And that the former sum of Nine hundred and sixty Pounds be made up Two thousand Pounds, to be given in Medals amongst the Officers of the Fleet, as a Mark of the Parliament's Favour, and good acceptance of their service, in such manner as the Commissioners of the Admiralty, by Advice with the Generals of the Fleet, shall think fit.

'*Resolved*, by the Parliament, That it be referred to the Council of State, to see the same done accordingly.

. . . .

'*Ordered*, that the Resolutions of this House this day, be communicated to the Generals, and other Officers of the Navy, by the Commissioners for ordering and managing the Affairs of the Admiralty and Navy.' (Vol. vii. pp. 296, 297.)

LETTER FROM ADMIRALTY COMMITTEE TO THE NAVY COMMISSIONERS.

23*rd August*, 1656.

'Order to make out a Bill for the balance of £11, 18s. 6d., due to Thos. Simons for making Gold medals and chains for the fleet, he having received £2000 from the Prize Office—With Simons' accounts.' (*Calendar of State Papers—Domestic Series*, 1656-57, p. 416. *Papers*, vols. lxvi-viii.)

MEDAL (A).

There would appear to have been only four medals of this pattern, viz. those given to Blake, Monk, Penn, and Lawson, to be suspended to their gold chains. Of these four, three are now in existence, viz. in the collection of Her Majesty the Queen, at Windsor Castle; Colonel William Stuart, of Tempsford House, Beds; and at Wadham College, Oxford. That in possession of Colonel Stuart, with its chain, is the one which belonged to his ancestor, Admiral Penn; but it is not known to which of the other three Admirals the remaining two medals belonged. The third specimen was formerly in the collection of the late Captain John Hamilton, which collection was purchased by Mr. James Sanders, by whom it was sold by auction at Sotheby's in May, 1882. The medal fetched £305, but the name of the person for whom it was bought did not transpire. It was, however, exhibited at the Royal Naval Exhibition at Chelsea in 1891 (*Catalogue*, No. 2584), when it appeared that it was lent by the Warden and Fellows of Wadham College, Oxford, to which Society, it is presumed, it still belongs. Blake was a member of Wadham College, and his portrait hangs in the Hall.

Imitations of this medal have been made, but they may be easily distinguished (*a*) by the omission of the monogram 'T. S.' on the anchor on the *obverse*; and (*b*) by 'A. Simon' instead of 'Simon' only on the stern of the sinking ship on the *reverse*.

The illustration, No. 2, Plate 9, is from a cast of the medal at Windsor Castle, taken, by Her Majesty's gracious permission, for the purposes of this work.

MEDAL (B).

This variety of the medal is probably that which was given to the four 'Flag Officers,' who received chains of £40 apiece. These officers were in all likelihood the Captains of the Admirals' ships, later on designated Flag Captains. The one which belonged to Captain Haddock is still in existence.

MEDAL (C).

This is probably the one given to the Captains and other officers of the Fleet, although, of course, without the engraved inscription on the *reverse* shown in the Plate, regarding which see No. 38.

No. 38.

FOR SAVING THE *TRIUMPH*, 1653.

PLATE 9, No. 3.

This is the same medal as No. 37 (C), but with the following inscription engraved on the *reverse*: FOR EMINENT SERVICE IN SAVING Y TRIVMPH FIERED IN FIGHT WH Y DVCH IN JVLY 1653.

Oval, 1·6 by 1·4 inches. Gold.

Med. Hist. Pl. xxiii. 2.
Vertue, xvi.
Med. Ill. vol. i. p. 400, No. 29.

During the fight with the Dutch, in July, 1653, the British ship *Triumph* took fire, and most of her crew threw themselves into the sea. Those who remained on board extinguished the fire, and the medals, inscribed as above, were, it is presumed, those given to them.

This medal would have been given under the Resolution of Parliament of 8th August, 1653.

No. 39.

MEDAL OF THE PARLIAMENT.

FOR SEA SERVICE, 1649.

PLATE 9, *No.* 4.

Obv. An anchor, from the stock of which are suspended two shields, one bearing the Cross of St. George for England, the other a harp for Ireland; the whole encircled by the cable of the anchor. Above, MERVISTI. (Thou hast merited.) On the stock, T.S.

Rev. The House of Commons, with the Speaker in the chair.

Oval, ·95 by ·85 inch. Gold, silver.
Ring for suspension.
Artist. Thomas Simon.

Med. Hist. Pl. xxiii. 4.
Vertue, Pl. xvi.
Med. Ill. vol. i. p. 390, No. 12.

The following Minute of the Council of State has reference to this medal:

MINUTE OF THE COUNCIL OF STATE.
15*th November*, 1649 (No. 5).

(*State Papers—Domestic*, *Interregnum*, vol. i. No. 63.)

'DIE JOVIS, 15° *November* 1649.

Lo. Presid^t Bradshaw.	Sr William Constable.
Sr William Armyne.	Mr Heveningham.
Col: Wauton.	E. of Pembrooke.
Lord Grey.	E. of Salisbury.
Colonel Jones.	Mr Bond.
Mr Scot.	Sr Henry Mildmay.
Col: Purefoy.	Col: Ludlow.
Lo: Lisle.	

'(5) That the Formes of the medalls which are now brought in to be given to the severall Mariners who have done good service this last Sum̃er be approved off, vizt: the Armes of the Com̃on wealth on one side with *Meruisti* written above it, and the picture of the House of Com̃ons on the other.

No. 40.

MEDAL OF THE PARLIAMENT.

FOR LAND SERVICE.

That there was a 'Medal of the Parliament' for land service seems clear from the way it is mentioned in the Resolution of the House of Commons of 27th August, 1651, granting it, with a Gold Chain, to Colonel Humphry Mackworth, as a reward for his defence of Shrewsbury. (See No. 44.) This is the only mention we have met with of such a medal. There is no doubt as to the medal of the same designation for sea service. (See No. 39.) 'Medal of the Parliament' meant not merely that the medal was given by Parliament, but that it bore a representation of the House of Commons. We know, consequently, what must have been on one side of it; the question is, what was on the other?

At page 117 of Evelyn's *Numismata*, on which the larger Dunbar Medal is figured, is an engraving of another medal of the same size and general appearance, but without any inscription. The engraving is not numbered; it is placed between Nos. 39 and 40; and there is nothing in the text relating to it; but the medal must have been in existence in Evelyn's time, otherwise he could not have given a representation of it. There is no example of it at the British Museum. Since no device could have been more appropriate for a medal for land service generally than the effigy of the Protector and a representation of the Parliament, it seems quite possible that the medal figured by Evelyn may have been the one in question. A reproduction of Evelyn's engraving is given below.

The representation of the Parliament on the *obverse* differs in certain details from that on the Dunbar Medal; whilst, on the *reverse,* the treatment of the armour and collar, together with the disposition of the troops in the background, are not the same as in the Dunbar Medal, showing that the dies of that medal were not utilised in producing this.

No. 41.

CAPTAIN ROBERT SWANLEY AND CAPTAIN SMITH, 1644.

GOLD CHAINS AND MEDALS.

We have no information as to the designs of these two medals. They appear to have been the earliest given by the Parliament.

JOURNALS OF THE HOUSE OF COMMONS.

4th June, 1644.

'A letter from the Gentlemen of Pembrokeshire, dated at Carmarthen the Fourth of May 1644, was read; and also a Relation of the Fight near Carmarthen, with a List of the Enemy's Commanders then engaged.

'*Ordered,* That Captain Swanley[1] have the Thanks of this House returned unto him, for his faithful services, and valiant actions, performed by him, for the good of the Publick, both at the Isle of Wight, Pembrokeshire, and Carmarthenshire: And that a Chain of Gold, of Two hundred Pounds Price, with a Medal annexed unto it, be bestowed upon him: And a Chain, of One hundred Pounds Value, of Gold, be bestowed on Captain Smith, with a Medal, in a Token of the good services done by him for the Publick.

'*Ordered,* That the Committee of the Navy do take care, that a Chain of Gold, of Two hundred Pounds value, with some Medal unto it, be provided and bestowed on Captain Swanley; and a Chain, of One hundred Pounds value, in Gold, with a Medal, to be bestowed on Captain Smith: And it is specially recommended to Sir Henry Mildmay and Mr. Jenner, to see these Chains provided accordingly.

'Captain Swanley was called in: And Mr. Speaker returned him the Thanks of the House; taking notice of the special services done by him; and acquainted him with the Resolution of the House, to bestow a Chain of Gold upon him: And that, in due time, they will take him into further consideration.

'The like was expressed to Captain Smith, after he was called in, upon Captain Swanley's withdrawing. (Vol. vii. p. 517.)

No. 42.

LIEUT. STEPHEN ROSE, JAMES PARKER, VOLUNTEER, THOMAS TULLEY, CORPORAL, 1649.

GOLD MEDALS.

ADMIRALTY COMMITTEE.

27th October, 1649.

'Report to the Council of State, on the petition of Lieut. Stephen Rose and the rest of the seamen of the *Happy Entrance,* that for destroying the *Antelope,* Lieut.

[1] It appears from the *Journals of the House of Commons* for 17th August, 1644, that Captain Swanley's Christian name was 'Robert.'

Rose deserves a gratuity of £50, whereof 40s. is to be in a Gold Medal. James Parker, a volunteer, and Thos. Tulley, corporal, £10, 20s. to be in a Gold Medal; and each of the mariners £5; to be paid by the Collectors for Prize Goods, out of the tenths of the prizes, which, by an Order of the Council of State of June last, were to be reserved, to the sum of £1000, to be disposed of in Medals or rewards to such mariners as have been active in the service of the State.'

. . . .

COUNCIL OF STATE.

29th October, 1649.

'Order to the above effect. A warrant to be issued to the Collectors of Prize Goods to pay the money and provide the Medals.' (*Calendar of State Papers—Domestic Series*, 1649-50, pp. 367 and 368.)

From their small value it seems probable that these three medals were the 'Medal of the Parliament for sea service,' No. 39. Lieutenant Rose's may have been twice the thickness of the others.

No. 43.

CAPTAIN RICHARD STAYNER, LIEUTENANT THOMAS AXTELL, 1650.

MEDALS.

ADMIRALTY COMMITTEE.

13th April, 1650.

'Order:—In pursuance of the reference by the Council of State of the good services done by Capt. Richard Stayner, and Lieut. Thos. Axtell, last year, and as to what may be done for their encouragement according to the Act, recommending that Capt. Stayner be allowed £20, and £5 for a gold medal, and Lieut. Axtell £10, and 40s. for a medal, to be paid by the collectors for prize goods, as rewards and encouragements.

'Also, considering the good service of Andrew Rogers, assistant to the carpenter of the *Triumph*, that £6 be allowed him by the same collectors, as an addition to his wages.' (*Calendar of State Papers—Domestic Series*, 1650, p. 102.)

Captain Stayner appears to have been commander of the *Elizabeth* prize.

No. 44.

COLONEL HUMPHRY MACKWORTH, 1651.

GOLD CHAIN AND MEDAL.

For his defence of Shrewsbury, the House of Commons voted Colonel Humphry Mackworth a Gold Chain, with the *Medal of the Parliament*, to the value of one hundred pounds.

From the Minutes of the Council of State of 2nd June and 30th July, 1652, there seems to be no doubt that the Chain and

Medal were duly made and delivered to Colonel Mackworth. His descendant, Colonel Sir Arthur W. Mackworth, Bart., Royal Engineers, states, however, that he knows nothing of them.

As to the possible design of this Medal see No. 40.

JOURNALS OF THE HOUSE OF COMMONS.

27th August, 1651.

'A letter from Humfry Mackworth, Esquire, Governor of Shrewsbury, the twenty-third of August 1651, from Shrewsbury; together with a Summons and a Letter directed to the said Colonel Mackworth, signed *Charles R.*, for the surrender of the said Garrison and Castle; and the Answer returned by him thereunto: Which were all this day read.

'*Resolved*, That Notice be taken by the Parliament of the great Fidelity and Courage of Colonel Mackworth, upon the Summons and Letter sent to him for surrendering the Garrison and Castle of Shrewsbury; and that a Letter be written, taking Notice of the good Acceptance of the Parliament of his Fidelity, and returning the Thanks of the Parliament for the same: And that the Lord Commissioner Whitelock do prepare the Letter; and that Mr. Speaker do sign the same.

'*Resolved*, That a Chain of Gold, with the Medal of the Parliament, to the Value of One hundred Pounds, be sent to Colonel Mackworth, Governor of Shrewsbury, as a mark of the Parliament's Favour, and good acceptance of his fidelity: And that the Council of State do take care for the providing the same, and sending it forthwith.' (Vol. vii. pp. 6, 7.)

COUNCIL OF STATE.

27th August, 1651.

'That the Council of State make provision for Colonel Mackworth, Governor of Shrewsbury, for making up the works there according to his desire.

'That a Chain of Gold, with a Medal of the Parliament, value £100, be sent to Colonel Mackworth, as a mark of the Parliament's favor and good acceptance of his fidelity, the Council of State to take care for providing and sending the same.

. . . .

'Alderman Allein to prepare a Chain of Gold and a Medal, value £100, for Colonel Mackworth, in pursuance of an Order of Parliament.' (*Calendar of State Papers—Domestic Series*, 1651, pp. 373, 374. *Papers*, vol. xvi.)

COUNCIL OF STATE.

2nd June, 1652.

'(4) Mr. Thurloe to deliver to Mr. Lathrop the Medal and Chain to be given to Colonel Mackworth by order of Parliament, as a mark of favour for special services.' (*Calendar of State Papers—Domestic Series*, 1651-52, p. 273. *Papers*, vol. xxiv.)

COUNCIL OF STATE.

30th July, 1652.

'(13) The Medal given by Parliament to Colonel Mackworth to be paid for out of the contingent monies of Council, according to the bill given in to the Council, and signed John Borrodale.' (*Calendar of State Papers—Domestic Series*, 1651-52, p. 352. *Papers*, vol. xxiv.)

No. 45.

CAPTAIN YOUNG, 1651.

CHAIN AND MEDAL.

COUNCIL OF STATE.

15*th November*, 1651.

'(12) The Irish and Scotch Committee to consider how the ship commanded by Captain Young near the Isle of Man may be disposed of, and in case they order that ship to some other service, they are to consider what other ship shall be appointed thither.

'(13) The Admiralty Committee to give order for providing a Chain and Medal for Captain Young, not exceeding £50 value, to be given him in token of Council's acceptance of his good service.' (*Calendar of State Papers—Domestic Series*, 1651-52, p. 19. *Papers*, vol. xvi.)

No. 46.

MAJOR BOURNE, 1651.

MEDAL.

COUNCIL OF STATE.

21*st November*, 1651.

'(6) The Order of Council made yesterday on a report from the Admiralty Committee, for giving £50 to Major Bourne for his services, vacated, and instead thereof a Medal, value £60, to be bestowed upon him, and the Admiralty Committee to provide the same.' (*Calendar of State Papers—Domestic Series*, 1651-52, pp. 27 and 29. Vol. xvi. of *Papers*.)

This was probably Major Nehemiah Bourne, Commander of the *Speaker*, frigate. He afterwards served as Rear-Admiral in the *St. Andrew*, in the fight with the Dutch in May, 1652; and in the Kentish Knock fight. (*Memorials of Sir W. Penn, Kt.*, by Granville Penn, London, 1833, vol. ii. p. 614.)

No. 47.

CAPTAIN JEREMIAH SMITH, 1654.

MEDAL.

'Captain Jeremiah Smith, Hull, writes to the Admiralty Committee, 3 Nov., 1654, that as they have given Medals to several Captains for services against the Dutch, and have one for him, he desires it may be delivered to Captain John Northend.' (*Calendar of State Papers—Domestic Series*, 1654, p. 567.)

No. 48.

MAJOR REDMAN, 1655.

MEDAL AND CHAIN.

COUNCIL, 10*th August*, 1655.

'(2) Thomas Simons, Medal maker to his Highness, to prepare a Medal and Chain for Major Redman, according to an order of August 1.' (*Calendar of State Papers—Domestic Series*, 1655, p. 278. *Papers*, vol. c.)

No. 49.

COLONEL THOMAS SADLER, 1655.

GOLD MEDAL AND CHAIN.

COUNCIL, 18th September, 1655.

'(9) A Gold Medal and Chain worth £50 to be prepared by Thomas Simons for Colonel Thomas Sadler, as a gratuity for his faithful service. Approved 21 Sept.' (*Calendar of State Papers—Domestic Series*, 1655, p. 340. *Papers*, vol. c.)

No. 50.

ADMIRAL ROBERT BLAKE, 1657.

JEWEL.

The House of Commons, in recognition of Admiral Blake's services in destroying the Spanish fleet at Teneriffe in April, 1657, voted him a jewel of the value of £500. The jewel was sent to Blake by the Lord Protector, with a letter dated 10th June, 1657. Blake died on 7th August following within sight of Plymouth; he may therefore have received the letter and jewel some time previously. In Hepworth Dixon's *Life of Blake* it is stated (p. 360) that the letter of Cromwell, the thanks of Parliament, and the jewelled ring sent him by an admiring country, all reached him together out at sea. The authority for the statement as to the *jewel* being in the form of a *ring* is not, however, given.[1] Cromwell in his letter forwarding it calls it a 'small jewel.' As this letter is dated 10th June, 1657, and as the jewel was only voted on 28th May, it must have been of a sort that was quickly obtainable.

JOURNALS OF THE HOUSE OF COMMONS.

28th May, 1657.

'Mr. Secretary acquaints the House with the good success the Lord hath been pleased to vouchsafe to the Fleet of this Nation, under the command of General Blake, at the Port of Santa Cruse, on the Island of Teneriffe, on Monday the 20th of April last; at which time the said Fleet fell in among five or six Galleons; whereof were Admiral, Vice Admiral, and Rear Admiral, with their Standard and Flag aloft; and other considerable Ships, making up the number of sixteen; some having goods brought from the Indies still on board them; others had taken in goods and provisions to carry back again; most of them furnished with brass ordnance; and their full companies of seamen and soldiers kept continually on board them; where all the said ships were sunk, blown up, or destroyed: The particulars whereof are contained in a Narrative now delivered in by Mr. Secretary, which was read.

. . . .

---

[1] The author is informed by Dr. C. Paget Blake that he believes that nothing is now known in the Blake family regarding the ring.

'*Resolved*, that it be offered to His Highness, as the desire of the Parliament, That His Highness will be pleased to appoint a Jewel, of the value of Five hundred Pounds, to be provided and bestowed on General Blake, as a mark of honor, and a testimony of His Highness' and the Parliament's Retentment of his eminent and faithful services for this Commonwealth.

'*Resolved*, That a hundred Pounds be given to Captain Story as a Reward for his good news brought from the Fleet.'

JOURNALS OF THE HOUSE OF COMMONS.

29*th May*, 1657.

'Sir Richard Onsloe reports from the Committee appointed to attend His Highness with the votes of this House made yesterday, appointing a Day to be set apart for Thanksgiving, and a Jewel of Five hundred Pounds to be given to General Blake, and One hundred Pounds to be given to Captain Story, That His Highness doth consent to them all.'

'TO GENERAL BLAKE, AT SEA.[1]

'WHITEHALL, 10*th June*, 1657.

'SIR,

'I have received yours of ——, and thereby the account of the good success it hath pleased God to give you at the Canaries, in your attempt upon the King of Spain's Ships in the Bay of Santa Cruz.

'The mercy therein, to us and this Commonwealth, is very signal; both in the loss the Enemy hath received, and also in the preservation of our own ships and men; which indeed was very wonderful; and according to the goodness and loving-kindness of the Lord, wherewith His People hath been followed in all these late revolutions; and doth call on our part, That we should fear before Him, and still hope in His mercy.

'We cannot but take notice also how eminently it hath pleased God to make use of you in this service; assisting you with wisdom in the conduct, and courage in the execution thereof; and have sent you a small Jewel, as a testimony of our own and the Parliament's good acceptance of your courage in this Action. We are also informed that the Officers of the Fleet, and the Seamen, carried themselves with much honesty and courage; and we are considering of a way to shew our acceptance thereof. In the meantime, we desire you to return our hearty thanks and acknowledgments to them.

'Thus, beseeching the Lord to continue His presence with you, I remain,

'Your very affectionate friend,

'OLIVER P.'

No. 51.

LORD LAMBERT, 1659.

JEWEL.

On 23rd August, 1659, the House of Commons voted a thousand pounds to Lord Lambert, to buy him a *Jewel*, in recognition of his eminent services in retaking Chester. What form the *Jewel* took, if it was ever purchased, is not known.

---

[1] Carlyle: *Letters and Speeches of Oliver Cromwell*, Letter 152.

JOURNALS OF THE HOUSE OF COMMONS.

23rd August, 1659.

'A letter from the Lord Lambert, from Chester, the 21st of August 1659, touching the surrendering of Chester to the Parliament, was this day read.

. . . .

'Another letter from the Lord Lambert, directed "To the President of the Council of State," from Chester, of the 21st of August 1659, was also read.

'*Resolved*, That the sum of One thousand Pounds be conferred on the Lord Lambert, to buy him a *Jewel*, as a Mark of the Favour of the Parliament, for his signal service.

'*Ordered*, That it be referred to the Council of State, to see the said sum of One Thousand Pounds forthwith paid unto him accordingly.' (Vol. vii. p. 766.)

(See also *Calendar of State Papers—Domestic Series*, 1659-60, p. 147. *Papers*, vol. ccii., No. 14.)

A portrait of General Lambert, by R. Walker, shows him in armour, with a gold chain and medal, but the picture is very dark, and no medallic design can be discerned. The medal may, possibly, be the Jewel. It is oval, about 2 by 1½ inches, and the chain is composed of oval links an inch in length.

This picture was formerly in the Earl of Hardwicke's collection at Wimpole; and at the sale of that collection at Christie's, in June, 1888, it was purchased by Mr. S. M. Milne, of Calverley House, Leeds, who has kindly supplied the above particulars of it.

No. 52.

GOLD CHAIN FOR THE SWISS MINISTER, 1653.

COUNCIL OF STATE, *28th September*, 1653.

'(6) A Gold Chain worth £100 to be provided for the public minister sent to the Commonwealth from the Cantons of Switzerland.' (*Calendar of State Papers—Domestic Series*, 1653-54, p. 171. *Papers*, vol. xl.)

No. 53.

JEWEL TO THE SWEDISH AMBASSADOR. GOLD CHAIN TO HIS SECRETARY.

COUNCIL, *3rd September*, 1656.

'(7) To advise an order to the Treasury Commissioners to pay to Thomas Simons, graver of the Mint and Seals, £850 in full satisfaction for a Jewel he provided to be presented to the ambassador from Sweden. Approved in person.

'(8) A Gold Chain of £100 value to be bestowed in His Highness's name on Mr. Barkman, the ambassador's secretary, and Jones and Strickland to see to it. Approved in person.' (*Calendar of State Papers—Domestic Series*, 1656-57, p. 95. *Papers*, vol. cxxx.)

Cromwell cultivated friendly relations with Sweden, and there are at the present day portraits of him in some of the Swedish royal palaces.

No. 54.

THE ENVOY OF THE PRINCE PALATINE OF THE RHINE, AND THE RESIDENT OF THE KING OF PORTUGAL, 1658.

GOLD CHAINS.

From the *Proceedings of the Council* of 9th March, 1657-8, and 6th May, 1658, it appears that these two functionaries were presented with gold chains, and that the Treasury Commissioners were ordered to pay Edward Blackwell the sum of £202, 15s. on account of the same.

WARRANTS OF THE PROTECTOR AND COUNCIL FOR PAYMENT OF MONEY.

9th March, 1657-8.

'For two gold chains for the Envoy of the Prince Palatine of the Rhine, and the Resident of the King of Portugal, £202, 15s.' (*Calendar of State Papers—Domestic Series*, 1657-58, p. 558.)

COUNCIL, *6th May*, 1658.

'Order on Treasury Commissioners to pay Edward Blackwell the above amount.' (*Calendar of State Papers—Domestic Series*, 1658-59, p. 10.)

No. 55.

GOLD CHAINS TO FOREIGNERS, 1658-9.

PROCEEDINGS IN COUNCIL.

24th February, 1658-9.

'Gold chains to the agents from Bremen and Dantzig.' (*Calendar of State Papers—Domestic Series*, 1658-59, p. 287.)

No. 56.

SIR JOHN GREENVIL, 1660.

JEWEL.

Sir J. Greenvil (or Granvil, son of Sir Bevil Greenville, who was slain at the battle of Lansdown for the King), was the bearer of the letter which Charles II. wrote from Breda, in April, 1660, to the Speaker of the House of Commons, professing his readiness to be restored to the throne. Sir J. Greenvil was entrusted with the reply of the House of Commons, and in order that he should not return to His Majesty without some testimony of their respect to himself, the House 'ordered Five hundred Pounds to be delivered to him, to buy a jewel to wear, as an honour for being the messenger of so gracious a message.' (Clarendon's *History*, Book xvi. p. 959.)

JOURNALS OF THE HOUSE OF COMMONS.

Wednesday, 2nd May, 1660.

'*Resolved*, That Sir John Greenville, who brought His Majesty's letter to this House, be called into the Bar of this House to receive the Thanks of this House.

'*Resolved*, That Five hundred pounds be bestowed by this House on Sir John Greenville, who brought so gracious a letter from the King's Majesty to this House, to buy him a *Jewel*, as a Testimony of the Respects of this House to him, and a Badge of Honour, which this House thinks fit to place upon him.

'*Ordered*, That the Council of State do take care that the Five hundred pounds be forthwith paid to Sir John Greenville, out of the contingencies of the Council.'

No. 57.

GEORGE MONK, DUKE OF ALBEMARLE, 1660.

PLATE 10, *No.* 1.

Obv. Bust of Monk, *l.*, head bare, hair long, plain falling collar, armour, and mantle fastened with brooch on the shoulder.

Leg. Incuse. GEORGE DVKE OF ALBEMARLE.

Rev. Arms of Monk within the Garter, and surmounted by the ducal coronet.

Oval, 1·45 by 1·2 inch. Silver, silver-gilt.
Laurel border on both sides.
Ring for suspension.

Med. Ill. vol. i. p. 466, No. 65.

No. 58.

CHARLES II., 1665.

PLATE 10, *No.* 2.

Obv. Bust of Charles II., *r.*, laureate, hair long, fringed mantle round the shoulders.

Leg. CAROLVS . SECVNDVS . DEI . GRATIA . MAG . BRIT . FRAN . ET . HIBER . REX.

Rev. Charles II., habited as a Roman general, standing on the seashore under a rock, viewing a naval engagement.

Exergue. PRO . TALIBVS . AVSIS . (For such enterprises).

Circular, 2 inches. Silver.
Artist. John Roettier.
Dies in British Museum.

Med. Hist., Ob. Pl. xxxi. 1; *Rev.* Pl. xxix. 5.
Med. Ill. vol. i. p. 503, No. 140.

No. 59.

CHARLES II., 1665.

PLATE 10, *No.* 3.

Obv. Bust of Charles II., *l.*, laureate, hair long, richly figured armour ornamented with a lion's head, mantle over shoulders.

Leg. CAROLVS . II . D : G : M : BR : FR : ET . H : REX. On truncation, T . R.

Rev. A ship in full sail, on the flag at the main mast head, C . R.

Leg. NOS . PENES . IMPERIVM . (The empire is with us).

Oval, 1·6 by 1·5 inch. Gold, silver, copper.
Floral border on both sides.
Artist. Thomas Rawlins.

Med. Hist. Pl. xxix. 3.
Evelyn, p. 130, Fig. 59.
Van Loon, vol. ii. p. 507.
Med. Ill. vol. i. p. 506, No. 144.

No. 60.

CHARLES II.

PLATE 10, *No.* 4.

Obv. Bust of Charles II., *r.*, hair long, falling over right shoulder, armour and mantle.

Leg. CAROL . II . D . G . ANGL . SCOT . FRAN . ET . HIB . REX. On truncation, monogram J . R.

Rev. Royal Arms, supporters, crowned helmet with crest. Below, on a scroll, DIEV . ET . MON . DROIT.

Circular, 2·1 inches. Silver, silver-gilt, copper.
Artist. John Roettier.
Dies in British Museum.

Med. Hist. Pl. xxxii. 6.
Evelyn, p. 142, Fig. 75.
Med. Ill. vol. i. p. 595, No. 277.

Evelyn says, in reference to this medal (*Numismata*, p. 142), that such like medals, with chains of gold, were sometimes given as 'Gratuities of Respect.'

No. 61.

MRS. JANE LANE, 1660.

JEWEL.

Although not a reward for *warlike* service, this grant may properly be regarded as one for personal bravery, seeing that in assisting to save the life of the King, the lady certainly imperilled her own.

Mistress Jane Lane, one of the daughters of Thomas Lane, Esquire, of Bentley, Staffordshire, accompanied Charles II. in his flight after the battle of Worcester, in September, 1651, from Bentley to Trent in Somersetshire. His Majesty was disguised as a servant, and she rode on a pillion behind him. The escape is commemorated by a medal bearing the names of the persons who assisted in it. (Vide *Med. Ill.* vol. i. p. 394, No. 19.)

It is presumed that Mistress Lane duly received the £1000 presented to her by Parliament, but whether she devoted it to the purchase of a Jewel is a point on which we have no evidence.

She married, 8th December, 1662, Sir Clement Fisher, of Great Packington, Warwickshire. She died 9th September, 1689, and was buried at Great Packington.[1]

JOURNALS OF THE HOUSE OF COMMONS.

Wednesday, 19*th December*, 1660.

'*Resolved*, That, as a Mark of Respect to Mrs. Lane, and in Testimony of the high Retentment and Value of her Service, in being so signally instrumental to the Preservation and Security of the Person of his Royal Majesty, there be conferred upon the said Mrs. Lane the sum of One Thousand Pounds, to buy her a Jewel; and that the same be and hereby stands charged on the Arrears of the Grand Excise; and paid to her or her Assigns, in course, after the other sums shall be satisfied, which are charged on the Grand Excise, by former Orders of this Parliament: And the Commissioners of the Excise, for the time being, are hereby impowered and required, to satisfy and pay the same accordingly: And this Order, together with the Acquittance of the said Mrs. Lane, or her Assigns, testifying the Receipt thereof, shall be to the Commissioners of Excise a sufficient Warrant and Discharge.

'The Lords' Concurrence is desired herein: And Sir Clement Throgmorton is to carry it to the Lords.'

JOURNALS OF THE HOUSE OF COMMONS.

Friday, 21*st December*, 1660.

'Sir Clement Throgmorton reports, that he had delivered to the Lords the Orders of this House, for charging the Excise with One Thousand Pounds for Mrs. Lane; and with One Thousand Four Hundred Pounds for the Hospitals of the Savoy and Ely House: And the Lords gave Answer, that they concurred therein.'

---

[1] *Wilts Archæological Magazine*, vol. xxvi. pp. 26-33. Paper by Charles Penruddocke.

No. 62.

SIR GEORGE OXINDEN, 1668.

GOLD MEDAL.

Sir George Oxinden was President at Surat, 1662-1669. In acknowledgment of his valuable services in defending their possessions at that place against Sivajee and the Mahrattas in 1664, the East India Company presented him with two hundred pounds, and a Gold Medal of the value of twenty pounds. Sir George died at Surat on 14th July, 1669, in the fiftieth year of his age. The medal was despatched in April, 1668, and it would therefore, in ordinary course, have been received at Surat some months before his death. What became of it is not known, and Sir P. D. N. Dixwell Oxenden, Bart., of Broome Park, Kent, can give no information regarding it.

No description of the medal is officially recorded, but we derive the following from a book entitled, *A new Account of East India and Persia, in eight letters, being nine years' travels. Begun* 1672, *and finished* 1681. By John Fryer, M.D., F.R.S., London, 1698:—

Speaking of the succession of the Company's Agents, or Presidents, at Surat, the author, in a letter dated Surat, 15th January, 1675, says (page 87):

> 'Sir George Oxendine held it [the agency] till his death, in whose time Seva Gi plunder'd Surat; but he defended himself and the Merchants so bravely, that he had a *Collat* or *Serpaw*, a Robe of Honour from Head to Foot, offered him from the Great Mogul, with an abatement of customs to Two and a half per cent. granted to the Company: for which his Masters, as a token of the high sense they had of his valour, presented him a Medal of Gold with this Device:
>
> '*Non minor est virtus quam quærere parta tueri.*
>
> 'After whose decease, the Honorable Gerald Aungier took the Chair, and encounter'd that bold Mountaineer a second time, with as great applause: when the Governor of the Town and Province durst neither of them shew their heads.'

The die of a medal bearing the Company's motto, and that above mentioned, is preserved at the India Office. An illustration of it is given under No. 70, page 55. In view of the services rendered by Sir George, the motto would be very appropriate.

Regarding Sir George Oxinden's tomb at Surat, Dr. Fryer says (page 100):—'The Ground the English dead are inhumed in is stocked not with so many Tombs as the Dutch; though in one of Sir George Oxinden's it excels the proudest.'

As this statement was made in 1675, it is evident that the tomb must have been erected not very long after Sir George's decease.

In Murray's *Handbook for India, Part II., Bombay*, London, 1859, it is stated (p. 443) that in the English cemetery at Surat is the superb mausoleum of Sir George Oxindon or Oxinden. The tomb of his brother Christopher is close by. The mausoleum is a square pile 40 feet high, and 25 in diameter, with columns at each angle. At the east side are stairs which lead to a terrace at the top. Over this springs a skeleton dome of masonry in the form of a Maltese Cross rendered convex, which is intended to commemorate Sir George, and a lower dome is to the memory of his brother.

There is a long and eulogistic Latin epitaph, but it contains no reference to the defence of the Factory against Sevagee or the gift of the Medal.

A COURT OF COMMITTEES holden the 23rd March, 1665-6.

. . . .

'The Company being now a writeing another letter to Suratt by the Returne the Court was reminded of the eminent service of Sr George Oxinden in the defence of their Estates, the saving halfe the Companyes Custome at Suratt[1] and procureing other previledges, and moved to consider his deserts in that and other matters, and according to their former promise to give him a suitable encouragement; and that there are severall others alsoe that have deserved very well and have binne promised they should be considered, the Court did thereupon seeme very apprehensive of the same, and inclinable to make him and the rest some proportionall returne for their good service. Yett least it might in this time of Warr streighten the Company's hand, they thought it more convenient to deferr it at present, hoping there may be peace ere long, which wilbe a fitter time for this purpose, but however they agreed not to [defer] their resolutions herein longer then the next advices to Suratt, and therefore directed that the Secretary doe mind them hereof after the next election to appoint a Comittee to examine this busines, to prepare the Court for a full conclusion herein.' (*I. O. Records, Court Book*, vol. xxv. fol. 61.)

A COURT OF COMMITTEES holden the 11th day of March, 1667-8.

'The Com^tee for writing of Lres were desired to lay out y^e £20—ordered to bee given ye President of Surratt [Sir George Oxinden] in providing either a Meddall or a piece of Plate, as they shall think fitt.'

FROM THE COURT OF COMMITTEES TO THE PRESIDENT AND COUNCIL IN SURAT, dated 27th March, 1668.

'Wee have taken into our consideration, your great care and courage, in the defence and preservation of our Estates, in the time of Sevagee's invasion (although

[1] The 'saving half the Company's Custom at Surat' doubtless refers to the abatement of Customs to two and a half per cent., granted to the Company by the Great Mogul, mentioned by Dr. Fryer. See page 42.

you did it in the discharge of your trust). And as an acknowledgment of our sense thereof, and your good service therein, Wee have now sent to Sr George Oxinden, the value of £200 in Gold, with a Medall of Gold, put up in a Box, delivered Capt. Whitehorne, wherein is alsoe twoe Seales for Bombay. To Mr John Goodier £100, to Mr Henry Garie, who was then with you in counsell, £60. To Mr Gerald Aungier £60, made up severally and directed to each respective person. And we hereby order for your disposure 400 p^ds to be distributed amongst such persons as you know were active in that service, amongst whom in perticular wee preferr Mr John Pettitt.'

A COURT OF COMMITTEES holden on the 27th day of March, 1668.

'It was Ordered that the golden Meddall provided for Sr George Oxinden, and the 2 silver seales p^rpared for Bombay, bee sent to Captaine Whitehorne, to bee by him delivered to Sr George Oxinden upon his arrival at Surratt.' (*I. O. Records, Court Book*, vol. xxvi. fol. 119.)

'LONDON, 4th *Aprill*, 1668.

'CAP^T W^M WHITEHORNE,

'Hereinclosed wee send you a small Packett, directed to our President and Counsell in Surratt, of wch wee desire your care, And require you to use all possible expedition in the prosecution of your voyage, Wee leave you to the Almighty and remaine,

'Your very loving friends,

'ANDREW RICCARD,
'*Govr.*'

(*I. O. Records, Letter Book*, vol. iv. page 170.)

No. 63.

MR. GERALD AUNGIER

AND

MR. STREINSHAM MASTER,

1671.

GOLD MEDALS.

The grant of these medals by the East India Company is recorded in the following entries in the Court Minutes:—

A COURT OF COMMITTEES holden the 26th day of January, 1671—*Afternoon.*

. . . .

'2 Medals of Gold, to be made for
Mr. Aungier, etc.

'*Resolved*, That a Medal of Gold to ye value of xx £ be provided and sent to the President at Surrat [Mr. Gerald Aungier], as a remembrance of his good service ag^t Sevagee ye last year; And that ye like be provided to be given Mr Streinsham Masters at his arrival in England.' (*I. O. Records, Court Book*, vol. xxvii. fol. 206.)

A COURT OF COMMITTEES holden the Tenth day of December, 1673.

. . . .

'A Golden Medal was now delivered to Mr. Streinsham Masters for his good service performed against Sevagee at Surrat.' (*I. O. Records, Court Book*, vol. xxviii. fol. 177.)

Mr. Gerald Aungier was President of Surat 1669-1677, having succeeded Sir George Oxinden.

Mr. Streinsham Master was a member of the Council at Surat. He was a nephew of Sir George Oxinden, to which circumstance he, doubtless, in some measure, owed his position.[1]

The particulars of the service for which these medals were granted may be gathered from a despatch from the Surat Council to the Court of Committees, dated 20th November, 1670, the Council being then, with the bulk of the Company's merchandise, at Swally Marine[2] for safety.

It appears that at the beginning of October, 1670, news arrived of Sevagee's near approach to Surat with 15,000 horse and foot, on which President Aungier proposed to go up to Surat at once with a guard of men taken out of the ships to defend the Factory, leaving the rest of the Council at Swally to protect the Company's interests there. But the Council, for several reasons, strongly protested against their President thus hazarding his person; and it was determined instead to send up thirty seamen under the command of Mr. Master, 'who cheerfully undertook the charge,' and who was advised that he should

[1] Mr. Master returned to England in 1672. He was appointed Governor of Fort St. George, Madras, by commission dated 16th December, 1675. He assumed the office in 1677, and held it until 1681. On his retirement from India he appears to have lived in England, acquiring property in different parts of the country. His London residence was in Red Lion Square. On the formation of the *New* Company he became one of its Directors, and it was in his capacity as Chairman of the Court (then a weekly office) that he, on 14th December, 1698, received the honour of knighthood on presenting an address to King William on His Majesty's return from the Continent. His knighthood was not, therefore, in recognition of his services in India. He founded the first English church in India, St. Mary's, Madras, so dedicated because the foundations were laid on Lady Day, 1678. He was very instrumental in procuring the erection of the church of St. George the Martyr, Bloomsbury; and it was in regard to his having been Governor of Fort St. George, that the church received that name. (See *Select Viewes of London*, by John B. Papworth, London, 1816, p. 57.) Sir S. Master died at New Hall, Lancashire, on 28th April, 1724, aged 85, and was buried at Macclesfield. A memoir of him is given in vol. ii. of the *Diary of William Hedges*, by Sir H. Yule, Hakluyt Society, 1888.

[2] Swally was the familiar name of the roadstead and beach north of the Taptee river mouth, where ships for Surat usually anchored.

keep his men close to the Factory, and not discharge a gun or fight with the enemy unless he was first assaulted. On the night of 2nd October Mr. Master accordingly proceeded to Surat. What followed is best given in the words of the despatch. It will be seen that Mr. Master acted with great courage and tact under trying conditions in actual contact with the enemy at Surat; and that Governor Aungier[1] probably did all that was possible under the circumstances for the protection of the position at Swally.

'The 3d October Sevagy's army approached the walls, and after a slight assault the Defendants fled under shelter of the Castle Guns, and they possest them selfes of the whole towne, some few houses excepted which stood on their defence, to witt the English house, the Dutch, and Ffrench, and the two Serays or Seraglias, one whereof was maintayned by Persian and Turkish Merchants, the other by a Tartar King called the King of Cascar (who being of kin to the Mogull, and beaten out of his countrey by his owne sonne, desired leave last yeare to go on Pillgrimage to Mecha, from whence he returned two months since). Part of the army the same day assaulted the Tartar's Quarter and the English House; But the Ffrench made a private peace for them selfes, on what tearmes wee cannot Learne; and so never shott off a Gunn, though at first being strong in menn they Vapoured as if they would have fought the whole army them selfes. The enemy found such hott service from our house, having lost severall menn, that they left us and fell on the Tartar Quarter feircely, which lay between the Ffrench house and ours. At first they made a stout resistance, but the Ffrench suffering the enemy to possess some Avenues next their house, and as 'tis affirmed furnishing them with powder and shott, the Tartars could keep their house no longer, but in the night having conveighed away their King to the Castle left their house a prey to Sevagy, where he found a vast treasure in gould, silver, rich plate, a Gould Bedd and other rich furniture. The new Seray also defended by the Turks, they assaulted, but were beaten off with Losse. But the Dutch house lying out of the way, was never attempted by them. The enemy having taken the Tartar Seray, could from thence more safely ply their shott at our house, for which they prepared them selfs; but finding our menn resolute on their defence they held up their hands desiring a Parley, and the Captain of that Brigade calling to speake with Mr. Master from the wall he appeared to them. Many expostulations passed touching our good correspondence at Bombay and our coming at Surratt. The Captain tould Mr. Master the Raja, or Sevagy, was much enraged that wee had killed soe many of his menn, and was resolved on revenge. Mr. Master answered they assaulted and wounded severall of our menn before they shott a gunn, and that if his menn did not assault the English, they would not offend him. But if they offered violence they were resolved to defend the house to the last mann, and would sell their Lives deare. The Captain answered that he would keep his menn in, and desired allso that he would send some understanding person to discourse with him. This being agreed on both sides our house was quiett in two days. In the interim the army ransacked the great houses at leasure, and found therein vast treasure, and with goodes, sett fire to severall places, destroying neare halfe the Towne to the ground. They approached the Castle threatening to storme it, but they were not, it seems prepared for it, for they did not venture near. The third day they appeared

[1] Dr. John Fryer, in his *New Account of East India and Persia*, speaks highly of Mr. Aungier. See page 42, *supra*.

again before our house, notwithstanding our overtures of Treaties before, casting out threatening speeches, that they would take or burne it to the ground. But Mr. Master stood in soe resolute a posture that the Captain not willing to hazard his menn, with much a doo kept them back and sent a mann into the house to advise Mr. Master what was fitt to be done. This person told him the Rajah was much offended for the Loss of his menn and therefore advised he would send some person to him, but he must not goe empty handed, but with a present, though to no great vallue. Mr. Master thought it not imprudent to Secure your goodes together with soe many menn's lives at soe reasonable a rate, and therefore by advice of those with him resolved to prepare and send a present to Sevagy to the amount of rups (*blank*) in Scarlett, Sword blades, knives, & ca., which while he was getting ready, the person that was sent to him being a merchant of Rajapore fell into discourse with him touching our leaving the ffactory, asking the reason why wee did not send our people to trade there as formerly. Mr. Master answered That it was Sevagy's ffault and not ours, for he had plundered the Company's house, imprisoned their servants, and whereas since that time he had given sattisfaction to severall persons whom he had robbed, yet he had not taken care to satisfy the English the Losse they had sustayned, to which he answered that Sevagy did much desire our return to Rajapore and would doe very much to give us satisfaction. Mr. Master told him that In regard the President was at Swally he would say but little, but he would acquaint him therewith and there was no doubt but that he would trade againe in his Port, if Sevagy would restore what he had taken from us, and secure us from such violence in the future. This gratefull discourse bein over the Present was sent by two of your servants who were conveighed to Sevagy's Tent without the Towne. He sent for them and received them with the Piscash, in a very kind manner, telling them that the English and he were good ffriends, and putting his hand into their hands he told them that he would doe the English no wrong, and that this giving his hand was better than any Cowle [written pledge] to oblige him thereunto. Before your Servants were returned to your house Sevagy had called his army out of the Towne to the wonder of all menn, In regard no enemy was near, nor the noyse of any army to appoze him. But he had gott plunder enough and thought it prudent to secure himself and that. When he marched away he sent a letter to the Officers and Cheife Merchants, the substance whereof was that if they did not pay him twelve Lacks of rupees yearly tribute he would returne the next yeare and burn down the remayning part of the Towne.

'Noe sooner Sevagy was gone but the poore people of Suratt fell on plundering what was left, insomuch that there was not a house great or small, excepting those which Stood on their Guard, which were not ransacked.

'In the first dayes ffight one Englishman was shott through the Body, and is since dead of his wound. He was not your servant, but belonged to the King of Bantam's ship called the *Blessing*, only arrived from Mocha, of whome wee advised you last yeare, whose Commander, Capt. Anderson, hath been very Assistant to us, and was himselfe in person with 20 of his menn, English and Javas, to defend the house. He has lost about 8000 rupees in Pepper and other goodes consumed in the great ffire, what losse you have sustayned Wee shall hereafter acquaint you.

'While things passed thus at Suratt, Wee at Swally were not free from danger, being kept in continuall Allarums of the enemy's coming downe, and there was great reason to expect him in regard the Shawbunder, Cozzy [Kazi], with most of the eminent Merchants, Moores, Armenians, Cuttarees, and Banians were fled hither under our protection. And there is no doubt but Sevagy would have sent parte of his army downe had it not beene spring tides that he could not foard over the river.

'Wee prepared the best Wee could to defend your estate, which was very great, having by the help of the Ship's Carpenters, built a Small Platforme at one end of the Marine yard, and mounted thereon 8 gunns which 'tis sayd some of Sevagy's spyes that were at Swally advised him off, and Wee doubted not by God's assistance to preserve your goods from plunder. But Wee feered ffire more than the enemy, against which Wee kept a constant watch.' (*I. O. Records, O.C.* 3575.)

As Mr. Aungier held the post which Sir George Oxinden had occupied, and as his good service was similar to Sir George's, it might be conjectured that the medal now presented to him resembled that given to Sir George, especially as it was to be of the same value, viz., £20. In this case, supposing our speculations in respect to Medal No. 70 to be correct, it would have been circular and three inches in diameter.

On the other hand, having regard to the Court's resolution granting the medal to Mr. Aungier, and directing that 'the like be provided to be given Mr. Streinsham Masters,' we are led to conclude that the two medals were, as far as possible, like each other, and in this case neither of them would have been of the pattern of No. 70. And, presuming such a general similarity, they would have borne on their *obverses* the Company's arms, and on their respective *reverses* the arms of Aungier and Master. This, at least, is the conclusion arrived at on the following evidence.

In the possession of Mr. Master's descendant, the Rev. George Streynsham Master, of Bourton Grange, Gloucestershire, there is at the present time an oval ivory box, 3¾ by 2½ inches, and ½ inch deep, mounted in silver, having inside the lid a picture of Cleopatra, in which box has been preserved the following memorandum in Sir Streinsham's handwriting on an oval piece of paper :—

'This is the case of a Gold Medall given me by the East India Company when I came into England 1672. Upon one side was the Armes of the Company, with this inscription, *Pro meritis contra Sevageum apud Suratt* 1670. Oz. 3½.

'Upon the other side was the Armes of the Family of the Masters, with this inscription, *Non minor est virtus quam quærere parta tueri.* And about it was *Virtutis comes Invidia*' [*i.e.* in the circumference].

Upon a separate piece of paper is written: 'This Medall was delivered to Sir Richard Hoare.'

(*Vide* pp. ccxxv-ccxxvi and ccxxx of vol. ii., *Diary of Sir William Hedges*, by Sir H. Yule. Hakluyt Society, 1888.)

If, as may be inferred from the shape of the box, Mr. Master's medal was *oval*, it could not have been like No. 70; nor, indeed, could any medal, whether oval or circular, of more than 2½ inches in diameter have gone into the box.

Apart, also, from size and shape, an apparently conclusive reason against the similarity of the medals to No. 70 is that the motto *Non minor*, etc., was on the *reverse* of Mr. Master's, the motto, *Pro meritis contra Sevageum apud Suratt*, 1670, being, with the Company's Arms, on the *obverse.*

With respect to the medal having been oval in shape, it may be remarked that the Common Seal of the East India Company at this period was oval, 2 by 1$\frac{3}{4}$ inches, and that it may have afforded the idea for the medal.

No. 64.

CAPTAIN JOHN BADDISSON, 1671.

GOLD CHAIN AND MEDAL.

'WHITEHALL, *October 28th*, 1671.

'The 25 instant safely arrived in the Downes, the *Swallow*, a Merchant man English built, of 180 Tuns, Captain John Baddisson Commander, who, as hath been said, had been engaged with an Argiers Man of War in her voyage from Port O Port, of which rencounter we have these particulars; That about the second instant, the said *Swallow* came out of Port O Port, in company with a small vessel bound for Plymouth, and a Flyboat bound for Bristol; two days after they came out, off of the Isles of Bayon, they were chased by an Argier Man of War of 38 guns, and esteemed to be manned with about 220 Men; the Flyboat sayling heavily, Captain Baddisson feared he might fall into the hands of the Turks first, and therefore towed him about two Leagues, but the Algerine approaching, he cast him off, and prepared to receive him, and by this means gave the two small vessels an opportunity to escape; The Turk after having given Captain Baddisson a broad side, and a Volly of small shot, came to rights on board him and grapled him, putting several Men on board him, but was bravely repulsed, and forced to cut his grapples, leaving six of his Men behind him; in the mean time Captain Baddisson had so well placed his great shot in the Enemies Hull, that he forced him to lye quiet for half an hour; soon after the Turk came up again and boarded him the second time, but was presently forced to fall off again, without being able to recover the six men he had before left on bord (who had got upon the Shrowds, and had cut most of the Rigging and Sayls (two of which were killed, the other four Captain Baddisson gave quarter to, and hath brought home with him) when the night coming on and a fresh gale they parted, and with great difficulty the *Swallow*, her Hull being much torn with great shot, and having onely a Mainsayl and Spritsayl left, the others being burnt in the fight, performed her voyage; in the Rencounter the Captain behaved himself, as did all the Ships Company, with extraordinary courage, the Captain was shot through the cheek, his Boatswain, a stout seaman, with two others were killed out right, the carpenter and about fourteen more (having had in all on board 26 men) dangerously wounded, who are since pretty well recovered.

'This evening the Captain (being come to Town) was presented to his Royal Highness, and by his Royal Highness to his Majesty, who received him very gratiously, and as a reward of so stout and memorable an action, was pleased to order him a Gold Chain and a Medal.' (*London Gazette*, From Thursday, October 26th, to Monday, October 30th, 1671, Numb. 621.)

No. 65.

DANIEL PARSONS, 1677.

GOLD CHAIN AND MEDAL.

'AT THE COURT AT WHITE HALL,
February the 7th, 167$\frac{6}{7}$,
Present
THE KING'S MOST EXCELLENT MAJ^{TE}.

'Upon the Petition of Daniel Parsons representing that his Maj^{te} in August 1675 was graciously pleased to Order that a Chaine, and Medall of gold should be given the Pet^{r} in consideration of his good service in an engagement against two Algier Men of Warr, and for the defence he made against a Salley Man of War, which he hath not yet received, and praying his Maj^{te} will give further Order for the providing and delivering the said Chain and Medall to him. It is this day Ordered by his Maj^{te} in Councill That Samuel Pepys Esqre do take care to see that the Pet^{r} be furnished with such an Order from the R^{t} Honble the Lords of the Admiralty, as may make his Maj^{tes} promise and Bounty of a Chain and Medall of Gold effectuall to him.'

No. 66.

CAPTAIN ROBERT BENNETT, 1677.

MEDAL AND CHAIN.

'AT THE COURT AT WHITEHALL,
the 7th day of December, 1677.
Present
THE KING'S MOST EXCELENT MA^{TY}.

'There being this Day presented to the Board, from the Lords Com^{rs} for executeing the office of Lord High Admirall of England, an Estimate Signed by y^{eir} Ldps: & the Principall Officers of ye Navye, of ye charge of a Medall, & Chaine, to be given to Captain Robert Bennett, Master of the *William and George*, a Merchant man of Poole, in consideration of his great Courage & Valour in defending himselfe against the *Sunn* of Sally, Captain Austeele Comander, the 20th of June, 1676, vizt for ye Medall & Chaine to be provided by Henry Slingsby Esqre Master of his Ma^{tyes} Mint for the use above sayd, the sume of fivety pounds. Which being read at the Board, his Ma^{ty} was pleased to approve thereof, & did order that Henry Slingsby Esqre Master of his Ma^{tyes} Mint, doe cause the same to be provided, & delivered for the above sayd use.'

No. 67.

SIR THOMAS GRANTHAM, 1678, 1685.

GOLD MEDAL AND CHAIN.

A medal and chain, which are said to have been of great value, were presented by Charles II. to Sir Thomas Grantham, in recognition of his distinguished gallantry in command of the ship *Concord*, on the voyage from England to Virginia. On 25th October, 1678, when about 120 leagues from the Land's End, he was attacked by a Spanish renegade and Admiral of the King of Algiers, named Canary, in a Frigate of 48 guns, called the *Rose*, carrying upwards of 600 men. The *Concord*, which had but 22 guns, and only 80 men, including passengers, made such a stout fight, that although she got set on fire, the enemy the next morning stood away, leaving her to pursue her course. (B.M. Add. MS. No. 26,516, F. 72.)

In consequence of the gallantry shown by Sir T. Grantham on the above occasion, the King recommended him to the East India Company, who gave him a commission, and he was employed in an important manner in the East during the next few years.

On his return from India in 1685, Sir Thomas Grantham received from James II. a valuable gold chain and medal, as evidence of his favourable acceptance of his services. He likewise received a considerable present from the East India Company.

A memoir of Sir T. Grantham is given in vol. ii. of the *Diary of Sir W. Hedges*, by Sir H. Yule, Hakluyt Society, 1888, from which the above information is taken.

No. 68.

CASSA VERONA, 1679.

GOLD MEDAL AND CHAIN.

Cassa Verona was an influential merchant at Madras, who had extensive dealings with the East India Company's Establishment there during the period 1670-80. His position as regards the Company seems to have been that of Agent and Broker. He died 1680.[1] He had a claim on the Company for 9000 pagodas, which the Court refused to admit; but in consideration of his useful services they ordered a gold medal and chain to be presented to him. He died, however, before these reached Madras, and the medal and chain, after having been dangled before the eyes of his successor, in view to his good behaviour, a proceeding of which the Court do not appear to

[1] *Madras in the Olden Time.* By J. Talboys Wheeler. Vol. i.

have approved, were eventually, in accordance with the Court's desire, 'turned into pagodas.' In this case, therefore, the history of the medal is fully traced.

The medal and chain cost a hundred pounds. The medal had the arms of the East India Company and an inscription, which was probably engraved on the *reverse.* It seems very likely that this medal was struck from the same die as that from which the medal for Aga Doud, the Company's Linguist in Persia, was struck in 1698, since in that case the medal and chain were ordered to be of the same value as Cassa Verona's. The order for the medal was passed on 4th November, 1679, and the medal was, apparently, ready on 3rd December; and it therefore seems not improbable that the die was already in existence, and had not to be specially prepared for the occasion.

For further remarks on this subject, see No. 70, pp. 55-58.

A COURT OF COMMITTEES holden 4th November, 1679.

'On reading the draught of a letter prepared by the Com^{tees} for the Coast and Bay, it was ordered that a Meddal of Gold with the Comp$^{a's}$ Arms, & a gold chayn to the value of £100, be provided & sent to Cassa Verona, as a testimony of the Comp$^{a's}$ acceptance of his good service in managing their affairs: And the Com^{tees} for the Coast and Bay are to direct the making thereof accordingly.' (*I. O. Records, Court Book*, vol. xxxi., p. 165.)

LETTER FROM THE COURT OF COMMITTEES OF THE EAST INDIA COMPANY TO THEIR AGENT, GOVERNOR, AND COUNCIL AT FORT ST GEORGE, dated 3rd December, 1679.

. . . .

(53) 'As to Cassa Verona's demand of 9000 pagodas upon us, wee have so often and fully given our answer thereto, to which wee shall abide, that wee think it needless to make any further repeticõn thereof. However, as a marke of our Favor unto him for those good services which he hath already performed under your Agency, and on our expectancy of his continuance therein, wee have herewith sent him a Chaine of Gold, and a Gold Meddall with our armes and inscription thereon, which upon its arrivall wee would have you in our names to give unto him.' (*I. O. Records, Letter Book*, vol. vi. p. 124.)

PUBLIC CONSULTATIONS.

FORT ST. GEORGE, *28th March*, 1680.

'In the morning about 3 o'clock, Cassa Verona dyed, having been taken sick the 13th of a malignant feavor, and being not aprehensive that his end was soe neare, made noe settlement of his Estate and family. Thirty guns were fired in the ffort and outworks at his funeralls. And as his body was carrying out of towne to be burned by the Gentues, some Moors, Fackeers and others put a stop to it, saying he ought to be buryed as a Moor for he was a Mussleman and built a Musseer in the towne to be buryed in, whereof notice being brought to the Govr he advised with the

Councell thereabout, and sent order that the body should be burned as a Gentue and not buryed by the Moors, it being aprehended to be of dangerous consequence to admit the Moors such pretences in the towne. Verona left one only child, a daughter by his wife, which dyed in August, 1678; she is about 11 years old and marryed to a kinsman of his said wife's. By his last wife which he marryed at Condore now living he hath noe child, and therefore she would have burnt with him but the Governour would not suffer it. A son of his eldest brother's he adopted for his owne son, a boy now about 10 years old.' (Page 38.)

Monday, 5th April, 1680.

'It being necessary to appoint one as the Company's Chief Marchant (Verona being deceased) that the business may be carryed on in good order; It is thought fit and Resolved that Bera Pedda Vincatadry doe succeed in the said place and imployment, and That Tasherifs be given to him and to the rest of the Principal Marchants as usuall for their encouragement upon this occasion, viz.:—

To Bera Pedda Vincatadry, ...	3 yards Scarlet.
To Verona's adopted son, ...	2½ yards.
To Chena Vincatadry, ...	2½ yards.
To Allinga Pella, ...	2½ yards.
To Kery Narran, ...	2½ yards.

the rest of the Marchants to be sent for into the Councell Chamber, and for the better grace the ceremony performed before them, which was done accordingly, and to Verona's adopted son was given the name of Muddoo Verona, and a Rundell to be carryed over him in respect to the memory of Verona, who hath done many eminent services for the Company and for this Towne, and at thir goeing out of the ffort 11 Canon fired that the towne and country might take notice of the honour done them.' (Page 40.)

6th April, 1680.

'Amongst the Marchants which received Tasherifs yesterday, Vincatry, Verona's son-in-law not receiving one, his wife, Verona's young daughter, was melancholly upon it and would not eate, whereof the Marchants acquainting the Governour this morning when they came to the ffort he was alsoe Tasherifd with 2½ yards Scarlet Cloth, wherewith the young man and his wife were well pleased.' (Page 41.)

It would appear, however, that affairs did not work quite smoothly in regard to the new chief merchant, because in the Consultations for Sunday the 4th July, 1680, it is stated that Pedda Vincatadry had absented himself from the Fort since the previous Wednesday, 'upon disgust that the business of the investments is to be put into a new way.' The Agent (the Governor) and Council, taking the affair into consideration, sent a message to Vincatadry and his brother to the effect that they were resolved that the Company's investments should be done by a Company of Merchants in Joint Stock, and if he would come into the Stock and be one of them he might, and they were willing he should, be the first and Chief of them, but if he would not he might choose, they neither feared nor cared what he did; but being one of the Company's old Merchants they thought good to give him this notice out of friendship. To this he returned answer that he wholly submitted himself to the Agent and Council, and would come to the Fort the following morning, and would do as they would have him.

PUBLIC CONSULTATIONS.

'FORT ST. GEORGE, *Sunday, 4th July*, 1680.

'There was also some intimation given Pedda Vincatadry of a Gold Chaine and a Medall sent out for Verona, which would be given to him if he behaved himself well in this business.' (Page 82.)

LETTERS TO THE AGENT AND COUNCIL AT FORT ST. GEORGE.

'LONDON, *this* 18*th day of Novem.*, 1681.

'(1) By the *Sampson*, which is the onely ship we have yet from the Fort, we recd our late Agent Master and Councill's letters of the 13th of September and 20th of December . . . .'

. . . .

'(10) We would have you keep the Gold Chaine intended [for] Verona untill our further order to dispose thereof.' (*I. O. Letter Book*, vol. vi. page 400.)

'LONDON, 20*th September*, 1682.

'(1) We have now before us yo's of 20th October; The 5th, 12th, 19th Jan., 6th, 8th, 10th February, 1681, which we shall answer in order, and send you with this the copies of all we have writ you this year overland.'

. . . .

'(25) We approve of yor granting Pedda Vincatadry's Peticon.'

. . . .

'(28) Turn Verona's Gold Chain and Medal into Pags.' (*I. O. Letter Book*, vol. vii. page 50.)

PUBLIC CONSULTATIONS.

FORT ST. GEORGE, *22nd November*, 1683.

'The Honble Compa having order'd the melting downe the Gold Chain and Medall, which they formerly sent hether to be given to Verona (who was deceased before itt arrived), was broak and weighed off to the Shroffer of the Mint the 20th instant, by Mr Elihu Yale and Mr John Nicks, who report the weight to bee oz. 25, dwt. 06, which is to be coyned into Pagodas.' (Page 143.)

No. 69.

SCARVES GIVEN BY THE MADRAS GOVERNMENT TO FOUR BRITISH OFFICERS, 1680.

In December, 1680, one Lieutenant Richardson, with a small native force, proceeded from Madras to Poonamallee, for the purpose of recovering property belonging to the British Factory at the former place, which had been detained at the latter by Lingopa, the Naick of Poonamallee. The expedition was successful, and, as a reward, the Governor of Madras, Mr.

Streynsham Master, presented each of the four British officers who accompanied the expedition with a silk scarf. Suitable rewards were likewise given to the natives.[1]

PUBLIC CONSULTATIONS.

FORT ST. GEORGE, *Thursday*, 30*th December*, 1680.

'The Soldyers and Peons having performed a good piece of service in bringing the goods from Pullimelee which were carryed thither by the Mutineers, it is thought fit to gratify them, to the foure Commission Officers each a silke scarf, and a hh[d] Arrack to the Garrison, to the Chief Peon 2½ yards Broad Cloth, and 5 Pag[s] amongst the Peons for a feast.' (Page 153.)

No. 70.

EAST INDIA COMPANY.

Obv. Arms of the Governor and Company of Merchants of London trading to the East Indies, with crest, supporters, and mottoes.

Leg. NON MINOR EST VIRTVS QVAM QVÆRERE PARTA TVERI (To guard a treasure hath no less a merit than to acquire it).

Rev. Probably blank, to admit of an engraved inscription.

Circular, 3 inches. Gold.
Die of *obverse* at India Office.

[1] See *Madras in the Olden Time*, by J. Talboys Wheeler, vol. i. pp. 115, 116.

The period of the existence of the London East India Company was from 1600 to 1708, and this fine medal may from its style be referred to the reign of Charles II. What was the occasion for its being first struck we do not know; but it seems probable that it is the one which was presented to Sir George Oxinden in 1668 (No. 62), and not unlikely to have been that presented to Cassa Verona in 1679 (No. 68), and Aga Doud in 1698 (No. 99).

There is no description in the official records of the medal given to Sir George Oxinden. All that can be gathered from them is that it was of gold, and of the value of twenty pounds.

It is, however, stated in Dr. John Fryer's *New Account of East India and Persia*, 1672-1681 (London, 1698), p. 87, that the Company presented Sir George with a gold medal with the motto, *Non minor est virtus quam quærere parta tueri*, in acknowledgment of his eminent services in defending their property at Surat against Sevagee in 1664. This statement was made by Dr. Fryer in a letter dated at Surat on 15th January, 1675, a few years only after Sir George's death.

Here, then, is a medal of the period, and bearing the motto in question, and there is therefore every reasonable probability that it was the one given to Sir G. Oxinden.

With regard to this medal being similar to that prepared and sent to Madras for Cassa Verona, whose services had been of a commercial nature only, there is, at first sight, no evidence; but the motto, if taken to refer to the preservation of the esteem in which the Company held him, would not have been unsuitable; and the medal, we know, had the Company's Arms and an inscription, the latter in reference probably to Cassa Verona's services.

The order for Cassa Verona's medal was given on 4th November, 1679, and the medal was apparently ready on 3rd December. That it should have been prepared so quickly would rather indicate that the die already existed, and if this was so, it may have been the one used for Sir George Oxinden.

In 1698 we find the Company ordering a gold medal and chain for one Aga Doud, their linguist in Persia, 'of the same value as was done to Cassa Verona at Fort St. George'; and from the letter forwarding the medal to Ispahan we learn that it bore the Company's Arms. It would, therefore, not be unlikely that it was struck from the same die as Cassa Verona's. The provision of the medal and chain was entrusted to Sir

Jeremy Sambrooke, a member of the Court of Committees. They were ready in less than two months, which makes it seem probable, as in the previous case, that the die was already in existence, and not made specially for the occasion.

On the other hand, the Court Minutes of 8th April, 1698, record that it was referred to Sir Jeremy Sambrooke, 'to consider of the bill of parcels, produced in Court, for the die, medal, and chain, bought and provided by Sir Stephen Evance.'[1] And, on the 15th of the same month, it was ordered that the medal and chain should be sent out by the ship *Mary*; 'and that the die by which the said medal was stampt be delivered to the Committee of the Treasury, to be locked up in the Company's Chest under their charge.'

From these passages it might be inferred that the die had been specially prepared for the occasion, or that, if in existence previously, it had been retained in the custody of Sir Stephen Evance, but that the Court now desired to have it in their own possession. The reason for ordering it to be kept in the Company's Treasury Chest may have been that there were already other medal dies deposited there. At any rate, this is the only instance we have met with of instructions being given for the preservation of a medal die.

In how many cases the die may have been used we have no means of knowing; but it is, of course, possible that it may have served for some of the medals bestowed by the old Company of which we have given such particulars as are available.

It is possible that the Company's seals were deposited in the Treasury Chest, and it may have been owing to its being placed with them that this particular medal die came to be taken care of. We know from an entry in the minutes of the first meeting of the Court of Directors of the *United* Company, held on 23rd March, 1708, that both the large seal and the smaller or common seal of the London (the *Old*) Company were then broken up, and it would not have been surprising had the medal die, as it had become obsolete, ceased to be specially cared for, and shared the fate of the numerous interesting

---

[1] Sir Stephen Evance was a Goldsmith and Jeweller, and a man of influence in the City. He became Jeweller to Queen Anne. He was a holder of stock in the London Company, and was afterwards a member of the United Company. It was to him that Governor Pitt consigned his celebrated diamond in 1702. (See *Diary of William Hedges*, by Sir H. Yule. Hakluyt Society, 1889.)

objects which, in course of years, have disappeared from so many places, owing to lack of knowledge or intelligence on the part of their custodians.

But, fortunately, this was not the case, and whether or not there were other medal dies in the Treasury Chest, it is now evident that this one remained there or in some other place of security. Its general resemblance to a seal may have led to its being regarded as one, and to its being kept in the same box as the seals of the successive East India Companies, the last of which became obsolete in 1858 on the transfer of the Government of India to the Crown.

In the Accountant-General's strong-room at the India Office (the modern equivalent of the Company's Treasury Chest), there is a tin box with three locks which contains this latest seal. This box, which it is understood had remained unopened since 1858, was opened on 10th April, 1895, when there were found in it the last-named seal, which was not defaced on becoming obsolete; the defaced seal of the English East India Company (obsolete in 1709); the defaced seal of the United East India Company (obsolete in 1834); and this medal die, thus preserved for a couple of centuries, but at length rescued from oblivion.

A sulphur cast of this medal has been for many years in the British Museum, and was supposed to be an impression of the Company's seal. In the Catalogue of Seals in the Department of MSS., vol. iii. p. 709, it is thus described:—

> Asia—Hindostan—Old E. India Company, 14715 (17 Cent.), Sulphur cast from the matrix, 2⅞ inch. Ref. No. (lxviii. 67).

The survival of the die uninjured may, however, be regarded as the best evidence of its not being a seal, because, if it had been, it would have been destroyed or defaced on becoming obsolete, as were the older seals to which reference has above been made. Further, the block of steel forming the die has some cracks in it, caused, apparently, by blows given in striking a metal impression. Any such amount of force would have been unnecessary for making an impression on a soft substance such as wax.

No. 71.

JAMES II. AND QUEEN, 1687.

PLATE 11, *No.* 1.

Obv. Busts conjoined, *r.*, of James II. and Mary. He, laureate, hair long, wears scale armour and mantle: She, with pearls in her hair, and lovelock, wears mantle.

Leg. IACOBVS . II . ET . MARIA . D . G . MAG . BRI . FRAN . ET . HIB . REX . ET . REGINA.
Below, G . B.

Rev. A ship, the boats of which are engaged in fishing up treasure from a wreck.

Leg. SEMPER TIBI PENDEAT HAMVS (Always let your hook be hanging).

Ex. NAVFRAGA REPERTA. 1687. (Wreck recovered.)

Circular, 2·15 inches.
Artist. George Bower.

Evelyn, p. 151, Fig. 87. Silver.
Med. Hist. Pl. xxxviii. 1.
Gent. Mag. 1792, pp. 17 and 19.
Med. Ill. vol. i. p. 619, No. 33.

This medal was struck in 1687 to commemorate the recovery by William Phipps of treasure to the amount of £300,000, lost forty-four years before in a Spanish ship in the West Indies, off Hispaniola. The medal was presented to the officers of the ship and to the promoters of the undertaking. Phipps was knighted. His share of the treasure amounted to £16,000.

In the *Gentleman's Magazine* for 1792, p. 19, a correspondent, under the signature 'Lico,' sends a drawing of this medal with a chain for suspension, which he states was presented in silver gilt to his ancestor, Admiral Strong, by James II.

The precise spot appears to have been thirty miles north of Cape Français, in the island of St. Domingo.

No. 72.

JAMES II., 1685.

PLATE II, *No.* 2.

Obv. Bust of James II., *r.*, head bare, hair long, shoulders clothed with an ample mantle.

Leg. IACOBVS . II . DEI . GRA . ANG . SCOT . FRAN . ET . HIB . REX.
Below, monogram J . R.

Rev. An antique trophy ; distant naval engagement.

Leg. GENVS . ANTIQVVM (An ancient race).

Circular, 2·5 inches. Silver, gold.
Artist. John Roettier.
Die of *obverse* at British Museum.

Med. Hist. Pl. xxxvii. 6.
Evelyn, p. 149, Fig. 84.
Med. Ill. vol. i. p. 617, No. 29.

No. 73.

PETER MEW, BISHOP OF WINCHESTER, 1685.

MEDAL FOR BATTLE OF SEDGEMOOR.

Dr. Peter Mew was Bishop of Bath and Wells, 1672; he was translated to Winchester, 1684, and died, 1706. The following is extracted from Hutchins' *History of Dorset*, 3rd Edit. vol. iv., p. 149.

'On the death of Bishop Morley, he [Bishop Mew] was translated to Winchester, November 22, 1684; and next year was commanded by the King, in compliance with the request of the gentry of Somerset, to go against Monmouth, and did eminent service at the battle of Sedgemoor, where he managed the artillery; for which he was rewarded with a rich medal.'

Macaulay, in his *History of England*, states that the Bishop accompanied the King's army. He had in his youth borne arms for Charles I. against the Parliament, and neither his years nor his profession had extinguished his martial ardour; and he probably thought that his appearance in the King's camp might confirm the loyalty of some honest men who were wavering between their horror of Popery and their horror of rebellion. Macaulay also says that so defective were then the appointments of an English army that there would have been much difficulty in dragging the great guns to the place where the battle was raging, had not the Bishop of Winchester offered his coach-horses and traces for the purpose.

No. 74.

SIR JOHN CHILD, BARONET, 1685.

GOLD CHAIN AND MEDAL.

Sir John Child was the East India Company's President and General at Surat from 1681 to 1687. It was at the instance of the Company that Charles II. conferred a Baronetcy on him.

A COURT OF COMMITTEES.

30th September, 1685.

GRATUITY FOR GENERAL AT SURAT.

'The Court taking into consideraċon ye eminent service performed by the General at Suratt in ye transaction of their affayrs there, have thought fit that ye sum of £500 sterling be given unto him for a gratuity: one part thereof to be disbursed for defraying ye charge of his patent for Baron^t, which honor his late Ma^ty of ever glorious memory was graciously pleased to confer upon him at the desire of this Comp^a: And ye remainder of ye said £500 is to be in a Gold Chain and Medal: And it is referred to Mr Herne and Mr Goodere to give direcċon for making thereof accordingly.' [*N.B.*—Mr. Herne and Mr. Goodere were members of the Court.]

No. 75.

CAPTAIN ARTHBURNET, 1687.

GOLD CHAIN AND MEDAL.

In *London Gazette* of 18th-22nd August, 1687 (No. 2270), it is stated that the East India Company had presented a gold chain and medal to Captain Archburnett for his services at the action at Hooghly in November, 1686, of which action the *Gazette* contains an account abridged from the original despatch of the Company's officials at Hooghly to Sir John Child, the Company's General at Surat, under date 24th November, 1686. (See paper 5533, *I. O. Original Correspondence*, vol. xlvi. The greater part of this paper is printed at pp. 54-57 of vol. ii. of the *Diary of Sir W. Hedges*, edited by Colonel H. Yule. Hakluyt Soc. 1888.)

No resolution or order regarding the grant of this medal appears in the Court Minutes of the period. The medal is, however, referred to in the following letter from the Court to the President at Fort St. George, but there is no mention of a chain.

'OUR GENERALL OF INDIA AND PRESIDENT AND COUNCIL OF FORT ST. GEORGE.

'LONDON, *the* 25*th* *January*, 168⅞.

. . . .

'In what Package the Sword and Mace to be carryed before our Generall and President, and the Silver Oar to be carryed before the Chief Judge of the Admiralty, and the two City Maces to be carryed before the Mayor, and Medall for Capt Arthburnet, are, you will find at the foot of our Invoice, in a large wooden chest being marked J. R.' (*I. O. Records, Letter Book*, vol. viii. page 483.)

In the old records the name of the recipient is spelt variously, Archburnett, Arthburtnot, and Arthburnet.

The medal was probably similar to No. 76, *i.e.* having on one side the Royal Arms, and on the other the Arms of the Company.

No. 76.

CAPTAIN RICHARD CLIFTON, LIEUTENANT ARTHUR NANGLE, ENSIGN ELISHA BASSETT, 1687.

CAPTAIN EDMOND WRIGHT and OFFICERS OF THE *CÆSAR*, 1691.

Obv. Arms of King James II.

Rev. Arms of the [London] East India Company.

The above would be the correct description of the three medals given in 1687. Probably those issued in 1691 were similar, although they would have borne on the *obverse* the arms of William and Mary instead of those of James II.

On 31st October, 1686, an engagement took place between the East India Company's Ship *Cæsar* and five Pirates, off the Island of St. Jago, Cape de Verdes. In acknowledgment of their gallant conduct on this occasion, the Company presented gold medals and chains to the captain of the ship and three military officers who were on board, and gold medals to the other officers of the ship.

It should be mentioned that the *Cæsar* had on board a company of 100 English soldiers of the Lord Viscount Montgomery's regiment, who were permitted by the King to proceed to Bombay in the Company's service. By commissions under the Common Seal of 'The Governor and Company of Merchants of London trading into the East Indies,' bearing date 20th August, 1686, Captain Richard Clifton was appointed Captain, Arthur Nangle, Lieutenant, and Elisha Bassett, Ensign of this Company. These, therefore, were the military officers who received the medals. (*I. O. Records*, *Letter Book*, vol. viii. pp. 169-170; *Court Book*, 25th August, 1686. Also *London Gazette*, 13th-16th July, 1687, No. 2251, and 18th-22nd August, 1687, No. 2270.)

A COURT OF COMMITTEES holden 10th June, 1687.

'This Court having received a relation of the valiant defence of the Ship *Cæsar* from the assault of five Buccaneers or private ships of war near St. Jago, in which action it is confessed that Captain Clifton, his officers and soldiers behaved themselves very well, as did also Captain Wright, his officers and seamen, which latter, viz. Captain Wright, his officers and seamen may ('tis hoped) in a short time return home to us, and then we shall acknowledge and reward their extraordinary merit. In the meantime it is ordered that three Medals and Chains of Gold be prepared for Captain Clifton, his Lieutenant and Ensign, to be sent to them on the Ship *Royal James and Mary*, in acknowledgment of their faithful service; the said Medals to have on the one side His Majesty's Arms, and on the Reverse the East India Company's, and to be to the values following, viz. £70 for the Captain, £50 for the Lieutenant, and £30 for the Ensign, or thereabouts. And it is also ordered that a gratuity of one month's pay be given to the Sergeants, Corporals, and Private Soldiers of the said Company by the General at Bombay, and be preferred by him as opportunity is offered: And that the letter drawn up to be sent to the General and Council, now read in Court, be signed and dispatched away accordingly.' (*Court Book*, vol. xxxv. f. 13.)

LETTER FROM THE COURT, dated 3rd August, 1687.

'OUR GENERAL AND COUNCIL OF INDIA RESIDING AT BOMBAY.

'LONDON, 3d *August*, 1687.

. . . .

'The promised Medals and Chains of Gold to Captain Clifton and his two commission officers, we have sent by Captain Cooke in a box sealed up with the Companies Seal, and directed to our General who will deliver them with such solemnity as is fit to the honor of such worthy persons, whose future deportment we hope will answer such good beginning, and give our General cause to advise of the increase of their merit.' (*I. O. Records, Letter Book*, vol. viii. p. 329.)

LIST OF THE COMPANY'S PACQUET TO BOMBAY BY THE ROYAL JAMES AND MARY, *dated 8th August*, 1687.

Item 25. 'Medalls and Chaines, in the Box, for Capt. Clifton and officers.' (*I. O. Records, Letter Book*, vol. viii. p. 340.)

From the following entry in the *Court Minutes* of July, 1690, it seems probable that Captain Clifton was then dead.

A COURT OF COMMITTEES, 4th July, 1690.

'It is ordered that the Medall of Gold formerly sent to Captain Clifton being returned on the Ship *Charles the second*, be delivered to such as have power to receive the same free of charge, they giving up the Bill of Loading.' (*I. O. Records, Court Book*, vol. xxxvi. f. 6.)

A COURT OF COMMITTEES, 9th January, 1690-1.

'The Court taking into consideration the good service performed by Captain Wright and his officers and seamen in their outward bound voyage for India in defending the Compa's Estate against five Pyrates or Buckaneers Ships with whom they had a sharp engagement off St. Jago, It is ordered that a Chain and Medall to the value of one hundred Pounds be provided and given to Captain Wright: that three months' pay be given to the rest of the officers, and one month's pay to the Seamen belonging to the said Ship who were actually in that engagement according to the list of their severall wages at which they were entertained at their going out. And it is referred to the Committee for Shipping to consider what is fit to be given to Francis Stephens who lost his arm in the said fight.' (*I. O. Records, Court Book*, vol. xxxvi. f. 40.)

A COURT OF COMMITTEES, 19th January, 1690-1.

'On reading the Court of the 9th instant wherein (among other things) It was ordered that three months' pay should be given to the Mates and other Officers of the ship *Cæsar* for their good service performed in an engagement with five Pyrates or Buckaneers off the Island St. Iago, a Motion being made that each of the said Officers might have a Medall given them of the value of their said three months' wages, the Court agreed thereunto, and ordered that the same be provided accordingly.' (*I. O. Records, Court Book*, vol. xxxvi. f. 41.)

The original report, written presumably by the commander of the *Cæsar*, Captain Edmond Wright, is so graphic and quaint that we give it *in extenso.* An abridgment of it was printed in the *London Gazette* of 13th-16th June, 1687, No. 2251.

'*A True & Exact account of an Engagement maintained by the Ship* Cæsar, *Capt. Edm*$^{d.}$ *Wright Comand*$^{r.}$ *against Five Shipps* (*being Pyrates*) *in sight of y*^{e} *Isleand St. Iago on Sunday, The Last Day of Octob*^{r} 1686. (*I. O. Records, Original Correspondence*, vol. xlvi. No. 5537.)

'Wee presume yor Hon^{rs} were advised of o^{r} safe tho' late arriveall at St. Iago y^{e} 26 Octo^{b} where haveing refresht o^{r} men as usually, on Sunday following being ye Last day of ye month by sun riseing we were gott under saile, and had scarse open'd ye weathermost of ye Road, when we had sight of five ships lying by und^{r} theire Topsailes (waiteing o^{r} comeing out as we found afterwards) for they no sooner espied us, but gave chase Crowding all ye saile they could possible make after us, wereupon imageing the worst wee likewise made saile for ye gaineing time to put o^{r} selves in ye best posture we could for o^{r} Defence, wch we did by staving down, & heaving overboard every thing we imagined might be ye least hinderance to us. Wee lin'd o^{r} quart^{r} wth o^{r} mens bedding, slung o^{r} yards & distributed all o^{r} small armes to ye Shouldiers, sending some in o^{r} topps, we then visited each severall Posts to see all things fitted & contrived for o^{r} utmost advantage, omitting nothing wee could imagine in ye least requisite on so pressing an occasion and now percieving they gained on us apace and that we had allready done all y^{t} men in o^{r} conditions could possibly doe both for defending o^{r} selves & offending ye Enimy, Our Capt^{t} by ye advice & consent of us all comanded o^{r} small sailes to be handed, & o^{r} maine saile & mizell to be furld puting o^{r} ship right afore ye wind (concluding it absolutly ye best man^{r} soe to ingage) & then exhorting o^{r} men to be of good courage, telling them what an Eternall Credit we should gaine to o^{r} selves & nation by baffling ye designes & attempts of soe many & such subtill enemys and on ye contrary what a miserable life would be ye consequence of falling into ye hands of such Desperate, Pyraticall Villains wth such like exhortations all were dismissed to there severall quart^{rs}.

'And by this time (being about 10 in ye morninge) two of ye nimblest were come up wth us, haveing (as ye rest had) French Colo^{rs}, the headmost fireing 3 or 4 shott at us & finding we slighted him, changed his French to bloody colo^{rs}, & then streching to windeward they lay peckeing at us whilest his Companion was doing ye same asterne, whome o^{r} chase gunns, from ye great cabbin, soone brought upon ye cairne [careen] wch we had scarce done, when ye other 3 Ships had got o^{r} length (haveing change their French to blody Colo^{rs}) fireing on us amaine, They were Ships of Burthern & could not have lesse than between 20 & 30 gunns each and full of men, ye Admirall & Vice Admirall on o^{r} larboard side designing to lay us on board, wch ye former did on o^{r} quart^{r} but we plyed him so warmly wth o^{r} small shott wch we showred on him like Haile from o^{r} tops, Poop, & other Posts y^{t} we heard indeed a voice crying to us in ye french Tongue to surrend^{r} but say none bold enough to try for possetion, but were glad to gett cleare of us againe & falling asterne sunk & cutt away all o^{r} boats wch he paid for by ye losse of his Boltsplite, & abundance of his men, his Hull at ye same time not being impenitrable to o^{r} great shot we plaid in & thro' him. The Vice Admirall on ye Bowe had a shortt entertainem^{t} & noe better successe, for we spoake some much terrour to him from o^{r} fore Castle, wast & other quarters (he haveing likewise o^{r} frequents cheers & huzahs) bore away in a ffright, & by that means had ye luck to recieve both o^{r} broadsides wch carried away his foreyard & mizin masts whilest o^{r} stern chase (for we now had got o^{r} gun roome guns out) so gave ye rest a sterne that after five hours sharpe ingagement they began to beare away to amend and repaier ye damage recieved from us.

'Which questionless was very considerable there men at first comeing up being bold & dareing lay open to o^{r} small shott wch continued fireing for 3 hours together wth out ye least intermission, and their men ladeing their great guns wth out board[1] (as is ye custom of these West India Gunn^{r} Pyrates) were cut of as fast as they appeared to doe their duty, and this was ye reason they fired but few great guns when they bore downe upon us for wch wee are beholden unto o^{r} small firearmes, & indeed all o^{r} men in generall behavied themselves like Englishmen & shew'd much Courage & Bravery. But o^{r} small armes (we mean y^{r} Hon^{rs} disciplin'd shouldiers & their officers, whose example they soe well imitated, we cannot forbeare to mention in p'ticular, who fired soe nimbley, & wth soe much skill & caution of placeing their shott to purpose, that we must acknowledge as their due & meritt a large share of ye Glory & Hon^{r} of this day's action.

'Wee now bro^{t} too to see if wee could save o^{r} Barge wch wee toed asterne full of water, but finding it not worth o^{r} [? while] put her adrift after ye rest of o^{r} boats and than continued o^{r} course with an easie saile imageing nothing else but they would have the other bout with us. But they were all bussie upon ye carine, likeing themselves whole as well as they could.

'Finding we were to have noe more of it, we now began to examine into ye damage already sustain'd by them and found (as hath been already hinted) all o^{r} boats lost, 3000 w^{t} of Bread hove overboard to cleare o^{r} gun roome guns, (and we had been happy and they unfortunate could we have plaid our whole gunn deck Fyre, but being so deep we derst beat open never a port between deck save o^{r} sterne chase, wch however did us no small kindness) a great shot thro' o^{r} Boltsprit, four of o^{r} main shrowes cut and much of o^{r} running riging, Our sailes full of holes, a shott or two through o^{r} Hull and many sticking in our sides. They were eager to strike our ancient with their guns seeing they could not doe itt otherwayes and make severall shott for that purpose but wee knoweing there custome, had ordered itt to be seized to ye head of ye Stafe mistrusting should they by any means strike our Colours it might by encourageing them add to their advantage. We found but one man killed, by name In^{o} Stiffe, a shouldier, & eight wounded, a wonderful deliverance wee conclude ye day wth offerings of thanks and prays to him who had so miraculously preserved us in ye midst of so great a danger. This being a moderate acco^{t} of ye day's actions wee have nothing else worth yor Hon^{rs} notice save assurances of o^{r} continuall care and circumspection for the discharge of that great trust reposed in us, & we hope this plaine acco^{tt} will be a lasting testimony and Demonstration of ye Fidelity of

'Yo^{r} Hon^{rs}

'Most Faithful & obedient servant,'

. . . . .

(This is a copy of what was sent home to 'ye Comp^{a} ye 3^{d} day of ye foll. December by a Dutch vessell,' etc.)

---

[1] In regard to loading guns 'without board,' the following note has been communicated by Professor J. K. Laughton :—

'Till the end of the old guns, that is, to about 1860, many ships, in both English and French navies, had carronades fitted on the non-recoil system, and were loaded out-board. In some French ships there was a step under each non-recoil port, on which the two loading numbers put each one foot, and were, of course, quite exposed. The principle of non-recoil, as far as I know, was first adopted for carronades; that is, after 1780; but I can easily conceive that its partial use was much older.'

The instructions given by the East India Company to the captains of their ships about this period usually contained a caution in respect to pirates. In this particular instance the captain of the *Cæsar* was directed to steer 'at least 30 or 40 leagues to the westward of the Maderas, Keeping the same westerly distance from the Palm, for your better security lest the Turks' men of war should be abroad. You must therefore be cautious how you fall in with the Island St Jago, lest the pirates hearing it to be a place we usually refresh at, should lie there in wait to surprise any ship that comes thither' (*I. O. Records, Letter Book*, vol. viii. p. 184). The falling amongst pirates in the manner narrated cannot therefore have been altogether a surprise to Captain Wright.

No. 77.

WILLIAM AND MARY.

BATTLE OF LA HOGUE, 1692.

PLATE 11, *No.* 3.

Obv. Busts conjoined, *r.*, of William and Mary. He, hair long, wears armour with straps on the shoulder, and mantle round the breast; she is draped.

Leg. GVL : ET . MAR : D : G : M : B : F : ET . H : REX . ET . REGINA.

Rev. Sea-fight. The French ship *Le Soleil Royal* in flames.

Leg . NOX . NVLLA . SECVTA . EST . (No night followed).

Exergue. PVGN : NAV : INT : ANG : ET . FR : 21 . MAY . 1692 . (Naval action between England and France, 21 May, 1692).

Circular, 1·95 inch. Gold, silver.
Artist. James Roettier?

Rapin, xiii. 2.
Van Loon, vol. iv. p. 98.
Med. Ill. vol. ii. p. 64, No. 266.

This is one of the series of medals struck to commemorate the battle of La Hogue in 1692. To what extent it was worn as a decoration is unknown, but it was given in gold, with a gold chain, together of the value of £50, to Captain Tupper of Guernsey. (See No. 86.)

The *obverse* was probably used for many of the medals bestowed on individuals about this period for sea service.

No. 78.

WILLIAM III.

PLATE 12, *No.* 2.

Obv. Bust of William III., *r.*, laureate, hair long, in decorated armour with straps on the shoulder, and mantle fastened with brooch on the shoulder.

Leg. IN . PIAM . MEMORIAM GVLIELMI . REGIS . 3 (In dutiful memory of King William III.).

Rev. The harp of Ireland crowned, and surrounded by a deep border of flags, drums, cannon, and other implements of war.

Oval, 2.45 by 1.95 inches. Gold, Unique.
Ring for suspension.
The Medal is in the British Museum.
Méd. Ill. vol. ii. p. 219, No. 545.

This, as a memorial medal, does not come strictly within the scope of this work. It is, however, of a distinctly military character, and was evidently intended for a decoration. The following is a quotation from *Medallic Illustrations*, vol. ii. p. 220:—

'This piece consists of two plates united by a rim, and suspended to a ring. The obverse, probably by Jan Luder, is cast and chased, and the reverse is engraved. This badge formerly belonged to John James Scott, Esq., who was descended from Jeremiah Scott of Ballingarry, co. Tipperary, himself a descendant of the Scotts of Scot's-Hall, Kent. Jeremiah Scott accompanied William III. to Ireland, and for services rendered at the Battle of the Boyne received a grant of land in Ireland. In the *Memorials of the Family of Scott of Scot's-Hall*, 1876, p. 261, it is stated "that Jeremiah Scott received a gold medal from King William III., now in the possession of J. J. Scott." This badge is supposed by the Scott family to be the medal referred to: but this cannot well be, as it is dedicated to the pious memory of William, and therefore could not have been executed before the King's death.'

No. 79.

MR. ROBERT CASON, 1689.

CHAIN AND MEDAL.

'ADMIRALTY OFFICE (YORK BUILDINGS), *Monday morning*, 15*th* *July*, 1689.

'That a letter be writ to the Lords of the Treãry to give the Usuall Orders. That the Chaine & Meddall wch his Maty is pleas'd to give to Mr Robt Cason Mar of a

Collyer called the *Richards Advice* of Ipswich, as a marke of his Mats Favour, & Reward for the said Cason's makeing a stout defence against two French Privateers and protecting the other Collyers in his Company, may be Delivd to the said Mr Cason.'

'YORK BUILDINGS, *Fryday Post Meridian*, 26*th* *July*, '89.

'A letter writ to the Navy Board for Payment of Fifty pounds to Thomas Neal Esqr Master of the Mint, being for a Chaine and Medall for Mr Robt Cason Mar of the *Richards Advice* of Ipswich, which his Maty is pleased to order him as a mark of his Favour for the brave Defence he made against two French Privateers. That they the Navy Board alsoe make an Estimate in due forme of the charge of the said Chaine and Medall, for the regular provideing money for it.

'A letter writ to Thomas Neal Esqr Master of the Mint for provideing a Chaine and Medall for Mr Robert Cason as aforesaid, signifying that Order is sent to the Navy Board for makeing out Bills for payment of 50li for the service aforesaid, and hat the said Chaine and Medall be sent to Us for delivering it according to his Mats pleasure.'

'ADMIRALTY OFFICE, *Monday the* 5*th* *of August*, 1689.

'Upon reading the Navy Boards letter of the date hereof bringing an Estimate of the charge of a Meddall and Chaine Amounting to £50 to be given Mr Robt Cason Commander of the *Richards Advice* of Ipswich in consideration of his courage and valour in defending himself and other Collyers from two French privateers—*Ordered*, That the said Estimate (signed by this Board) be transmitted by the Navy Board for soliciting the money from the Treãry.'

'ADMIRALTY OFFICE, *Munday*, 17 *February*, 1689 (16$\frac{89}{90}$).

'Protection for Robert Cason Mar of the *Richard's Advice* with 16 men for 6 months in consideration of his haveing defended himselfe & severall other Colliers from two French Privateers.'

No. 80.

MR. LEECH, 1689.

CHAIN AND MEDAL.

'AT THE ROBES CHAMBER AT WHITEHALL
Sunday the 19*th* *Janry*, 16$\frac{89}{90}$ *Evening*.

'*Present*.

'The King's Most Excellent Majesty (& 4 Lords or others of the Admiralty).

'*Resolved* That a Medall be given to one —— Leech, Mar of a Merchant Ship which came from Jamaica for his well defending his Ship from a French Privateer.'

'ADMIRALTY OFFICE, *Friday*, 28*th* *of March*, 1690.

'Order for a Chaine & medall to be given to Mr Leech, Mar of a Merchant Ship that came from Jamaica, who well defended his Ship against the French.'

No. 81.

RICHARD GRIFFITH, JOHN CODNELL OR CODNER,	Ship *Tryall.*
ROBERT LYDE OR LOYDE, JOHN WRIGHT,	Ship *Friends' Adventure.*
JOHN YOUNG, RICHARD NICHOLLS OR NICHOLAS, DAVID HINDS, ROGER HUGHS,	Ship *Rose.*

1692.

GOLD MEDALS.

The following extracts from the *Admiralty Minutes* show that for the several services referred to, Griffith,[1] Lyde,[2] Young, Nicholls, and Hinds received Gold Medals and Chains; and Codnell, Wright and Hughs, Gold Medals. The medals appear to have been of £20 value, and the chains of from £30 to £10.

---

[1] In the *Dictionary of National Biography*, 1890, p. 326, there is a Memoir of Richard Griffith, by Professor J. K. Laughton, in which it is stated that he was a Captain in the Navy, and died 1719. In 1691 he was commander of a small merchantman, or pink, the *Tryall*, which was captured by a French privateer, and which he recaptured in the night by the aid of a boy named Codnell or Codner, clapping on the hatches, and overpowering and throwing overboard the sleeping watch. For this exploit he was ordered by their Majesties a gold chain and medal, and appointed Captain of the *Mary* galley, 22nd April, 1692. The boy also received a medal [Griffith to Burchett, 14th June, 1701; *Admiralty Minutes*, 2nd December, 1692]. At La Hogue the *Mary* galley was tender to the Admiral, and was sent the first express to the Queen with the news of beating and burning the enemy's ships, 'for which,' wrote Griffith nine years afterwards, 'her Majesty ordered me a Royal Bounty of £300, which as yet I have not received.'

[2] There is a Pamphlet by Robert Lyde (B. M., E 1972 [9]) entitled 'A True and exact account of the retaking of a ship called the *Friends' Adventure* of Topsham from the French; After She had been Taken Six Days, and they were upon the Coasts of France with it Four Days. When one Englishman and a Boy set upon seven Frenchmen, killed two of them and brought the Ship and them safe to England. Their Majesties' customs of the said Ship amounted to 1000£ and upwards. Performed and written by Robert Lyde mate of the same Ship. London, 1693.'

This pamphlet gives a very minute account of the voyage, capture and retaking of the *Friends' Adventure*. Lyde's mind was much inflamed against the French by reason of having on the previous voyage been captured by them with his ship, a pink of Topsham, and most cruelly treated at St. Malo.

On the present occasion he sailed on 30th September, 1691, for Oporto, and on the return voyage, February 29th, 1692, was overtaken by a French privateer. They took out all the crew and the master, leaving only Lyde and the boy on board, and putting seven Frenchmen in their places. Lyde tried to get the boy to help him for

From the Minute of 17th March, 1696, it is gathered that Codnell or Codner, whose appointment as a volunteer in a royal ship was ordered in a Minute of 18th March, 1692, had given satisfaction, and was deemed worthy of a gratuity of a hundred pounds, and promotion to the rank of Lieutenant. The same Minute also lends colour to the statement in Robert Lyde's pamphlet (see footnote below) that Codner was the leading spirit in the recapture of the *Tryall.*

'ADMIRALTY OFFICE, *Wednesday Evening,* 16 *March,* 169½.

'A lre to be writt to Com^{r} Greenhill to use meanes for examining the French Prisoners now at Falmouth, about the retakeing the *Tryall* of London from O Porto John Codnell the Boy belonging to the said Ship prest on board one of their Ma^{ts} Ships.'

'ADMIRALTY OFFICE, *Fryday Evening,* 18th *March,* 169½.

'R^{d} Griffiths Ma^{r} of the *Tryall* of London from O Porto, & John Codnell his boy attending were called in. Ord^{d} that the Ma^{r} be appointed a Lieuten^{t} in one of their Ma^{ts} Ships, & the Boy a Volunt^{r} & £10 to buy him Cloaths &c. & their further reward for their good service to be laid before the Queen.'

'ADMIRALTY OFFICE, *Monday Evening,* 28th *March,* 1692.

'The Captn & Boy wch retook ye Pinck [*Tryall*] from the French to be here Friday in ye evening.'

'ADMIRALTY OFFICE, *Fryday Evening,* 1st *Aprill,* 1692.

'The matter concerning Captn Gillam & Mr. Battine to be reported to ye Cabinett Councill.

'As also ye Acco^{t} rec^{d} from Plym^{o} of the ffrench Prison^{rs} that were taken in ye Ship *Tryall* wch was retaken by the Ma^{r} & Boy.'

---

some time without effect, for the lad seems to have been of a timid disposition, but at last he got him up to the mark, and they fought the Frenchmen with vigour, and got them at last all below except one, whom they set at the helm with the boy over him armed with a blunderbuss, and, after various adventures, got safe to Topsham. The story ends with :—'By the favor of an Honorable Person I was introduced to the Right Noble the Marquis of Carmarthen who recommended my Case to her Majesty, who was pleased as a token of Her extraordinary Favor to Order me a Gold Medal and a Chain and recommended me to the Right Honorable the Lords of the Admiralty for preferment in the Fleet which I am now attending the Honorable Board for . . .'

. . . .

Advertisement on the last leaf of the pamphlet :—

'Whereas there has been a report industriously spread abroad that it was the Boy that persuaded me to retrieve ourselves; This is to satisfie the Reader, that that Report was maliciously Reported of me, and was not true; for it was the Boy of another ship called the *Trial* of 50 tons that did drive his master to fall upon five Frenchmen, and accordingly they did, and overcame them and brought their ship into Falmouth; for which the master was immediately made Commander of the *Mary* gally; and I that had used the sea thirteen years, did but desire the command of a Fire Ship.'

'ADMIRALTY OFFICE, *Wednesday Evening*, 20*th* *Aprill*, 1692.

'Memdum: to Speake at the Cabinett Councill about the Meddall & Chaine for the Master & Boy who retook their Ship from the French.'

'ADMIRALTY OFFICE, *Thursday Morning*, 21*st* *April*, 1692.

'Mr Griffith to be Captn of ye *Mary* Gally. Jno Codnell to be a Volunteer aboard the *Mary* Gally.'

'ADMIRALTY OFFICE, *Wednesday Evening*, 30 *November*, 1692.

'Mr. Harris to be directed to be here on ffriday next in ye evening & to bring the Meddalls for Captn Griffiths, & Codnell his Boy.'

'ADMIRALTY OFFICE, *Friday Evening*, 2*d* *Xber*, 1692.

'Captn Griffith Commandr of ye *Mary* Gally, and Codnell yo Boy attended, & had the Medalls delivered them wch their Mats Ordd for their Service in retaking ye Pinck from ye ffrench.'

'ADMIRALTY OFFICE, *Wednesday Evening*, 4*th* *May*, 1692.

'Robt Loyde Mate of the *Friends Adventr* & John Wright a Boy belonging to the sd Ship wch they retook from the French were called in & examined—Ordd that enquiry be made of the truth of this mattr from the Prisoners at Plymo and the Mate & Boy to attend the Board this day fortnts & that they have Protection for 3 Months.

'To speak to the Cabbinett Councill about the Meddall & Chaine for the former Master & Boy that retook their Ship' [the *Tryall*?].

'ADMIRALTY OFFICE, *Monday Evening*, 9*th* *May*, 1692.

'Protections to be granted for—

John Young Mate Rd Nicholas Boatsn Davd Hinds Carpentr Rogr Hughs Boy	} belongg to ye *Rose* of Chester for 6 mo: in consideration of retakeing ye sd Ship from ye French.'

'ADMIRALTY OFFICE, *Friday Morning*, 13 *May*, 1692.

'John Young Mate of the *Rose* of Chester taken by a ffrench Privatr & Retaken by him & three Men & a Boy to be appoind a Gunr in one of their Mats Ships.'

'ADMIRALTY OFFICE, *Wednesday Evening*, 18*th* *May*, 1692.

'Orders to be given to the Navy Board to pay £10 to each of the two Boys wch were concerned in the retakeing the Mercht Ships, vizt:—

John Codnell in ye *Tryall* of Londn from O Porto.
John Wright in *ffriends Adventurers* of Topsham from O Porto.

'And that Meddalls be given to the Mar & Mates who were Principally concerned in the retakeing their Ships, vizt:

Rd Griffith Mar of the *Tryall*.
John Young Mate of ye *Rose* of Chestr.
Robt Lyde Mate of ye *Friends Adventr*.'

'ADMIRALTY OFFICE, *Wednesday Evening*, 1*st* *June*, 1692.

'Ordrs to be given to the Navy Board to signe Bills of Imprest for paying to the Mar of the Mint ye sevll sum̃es follo provideing of Meddalls & Chaines for the persons undermencond for Retakeing their Ships from the ffrench & to send Estimates thereof to the Board.

Ship	Name	£
Tryall of Lond^{n} from O Porto.	R^{d} Griffith Ma^{r},	50 Med^{ll} & Chain.
	Jno Codnell Boy,	20 Medall.
Friends Advent^{r} from O Porto.	Robt Lyde Mate,	30 Med^{ll} & Chain.
	Jno Wright Boy,	20 Medall.
Rose of Chest^{r}.	Jno Young Mate,	30 Medalls & Chaines.
	R^{d} Nich^{lls} Boats^{n},	30 Medalls & Chaines.
	Dav^{d} Hinds Carp^{r},	30 Medalls & Chaines.
	Rog^{r} Hughs Boy,	20 Medall.'

'ADMIRALTY OFFICE, *Monday Evening*, 6 *June*, 1692.

'An Estimates of the Meddalls & Chaines for the Men & Boys who retook their Ships from the ffrench, Confirmed.'

'ADMIRALTY OFFICE, *Wednesday Afternoone*, 6 *July*, 92.

'Send to Mr Neale to hasten the dispatch of y^{e} Meddalls & Chaines Ord$^{d.}$'

'ADMIRALTY OFFICE, *Monday Evening*, 18 *July*, 1692.

'Mr Neale to be wrote to, to hasten hither the Medalls he was ordered to make.'

'ADMIRALTY OFFICE, *Wednesday Morning*, 3rd *Aug^{t}*, 1692.

'To speak to the Cabinett Councill about the dispatch of the Meddalls in Mr Neale's hands.'

'ADMIRALTY OFFICE, *Friday Evening*, 12th *Aug^{t}*, 1692.

'John Young to be Gun^{r} of the *Unity* hired Ship.

A Meddall & Chaine delivered to the said Young, late Mate of y^{e} *Rose*, for his service in retaking the s^{d} ship from the French.' (*Vide* Minute of 1st June, 1692.)

'ADMIRALTY OFFICE, *Monday Evening*, 29th *Aug^{t}*, 1692.

'The Medalls & Chaines for sev^{ll} Persons at Chester to be sent to the Mayor of that Place, & a lre to be writt to him to deliver them to the Persons therein named, and take their rec^{ts} for them.'

'ADM^{TY} OFFICE, 29th *August*, 1692.

'S^{R}

'Their Ma^{ts} haveing been graciously pleased to Order Medalls of Gold for the four persons here under named, which belonged to the ship *Rose* of Chester, as a Reward for their Service in retaking the s^{d} ship from the French vizt:—

To John Young the Mate	A Medall and Chaine to Each.
Richd Nicholls Boatsw^{n}	A Medall and Chaine to Each.
Dav^{d} Hinds Carpenter	A Medall and Chaine to Each.
Roger Hughes ye Boy	A Medall wthout a Chaine.

'We have deliver'd to the said John Young that wch was appointed for him; But the other three Persons being, as Wee are Informed, at Chester, We send you here with, their Medalls and Chaines, And do desire you will give Us an Account of your receipt thereof, and forthwith send for the said persons, and deliver unto them the Medalls and Chaines appointed for them respectively, wch you will be Informed of by their names ingraven thereon. And that you will take their Receipts for the same, and send them up to us.

'So we remaine,

'Your affectionate Friends,

'C. : H. P. : F.'

'MAYOR OF CHESTER.'[1]

[CORNWALLIS.
H. PRIESTMAN.
FALKLAND.]

'ADMIRALTY OFFICE, *Monday Evening*, 7th *November*, 1692.

'John Wright one of them concerned in retaking the *Rose*[2] of Chester from the French attended, & had his Meddall delivered to him.' (*Vide* Minute of 1st June.)

'ADMIRALTY OFFICE, *Tuesday Morning*, 17th *March*, 169⅚.

'John Codner to be Paid a hundred Pounds for his former good services against the Enemy with Capt Griffith, out of the Tenths of Prizes. And the Navy Board to order the Treãr of the Navy to putt it out to use for him. The said Codner to be made youngest Lieut of a great ship, and the Captaine to be directed to take care that hee be taught navigation.'

No. 82.

CAPTAIN STOCKER, 1692.

MEDAL AND CHAIN.

'ADMIRALTY OFFICE, *Monday Evening*, 4th *Janry*, 1691-2.

'To speak to the King on Sunday next about a Medall for the *Cloudisly* Gally.'

'ADMIRALTY OFFICE, *Wednesday Evening*, 20th *Janry*, 1691-2.

'Orders to be given for providing a Meddall & Chaine for Capt Stocker Comandr of ye *Cloudisly* Gally for the Couragious fight made by him in takeing a French Privatr of 26 Guñs called the *Mercury* of Dunkirk. The sd Meddall & Chaine to be of the value of £50.'

No. 83.

CAPTAIN ROBERT STEPHENS, 1693.

MEDAL AND CHAIN.

'ADMIRALTY OFFICE, *Monday Afternoon*, 6th 9ber, 1693.

'Upon reading a ľre from the Post Mars Genll wherein they recoñend Captn Robt Stephens, late Coñandr of ye *Vine* Packet Boate to Coñand ye *Advice*, in the room of Captn Jno Chenhall, who they desire may be removed; Resolved that he have a Comn for ye said Boate, & that for his good behaviour agt ye enemy in ye *Vine*, he have a Medall & Chaine to ye value of £60.'

---

[1] There does not appear to be any record of the presentation of the Medals in the *Chester Corporation Records*.

[2] This is an error, as Wright belonged to the *Friends Adventurers*.

No. 84.

CAPTAIN JOHN GUY, 1693.

GOLD CHAIN AND MEDAL.

This is a case of Fireship Service.

'AT THE COURT AT WHITEHALL,
the 28th *of December*, 1693.

'*Present.*

'THE KING'S MOST EXCELLENT MA$^{TY.}$

'Upon reading the Petition annexed of Captain John Guy late Com^{dr} of their Ma^{ts} fireship the *Vesuvius* blown up under the Walls of St. Mallo in the last Expedition, praying His Ma^{ts} Royall bounty, both to himselfe his Officers and Company: His Ma^{ty} in Councill is pleased to Referre the same to the R^{t} hon^{ble} the Lords Comm^{rs} of the Admiralty for their Consideration and to Report what his Ma^{ty} may fitly doe in the matter for the Petitioners gratification.'

'AT THE COURT AT WHITEHALL,
the 4th *of January*, 169$\frac{3}{4}$.

'*Present.*

'THE KING'S MOST EXCELLENT MA$^{TY.}$

'Upon reading a Report from the Lords Comm^{rs} of the Admiralty in the words following:

"ADMIRALTY OFFICE, 10° *January*, 169$\frac{3}{4}$.

"In obedience to His Ma^{tys} Order in Council, dated the 28th day of the last month on the Petition of Captain John Guy, Commander of Their Ma^{tys} late Fire Ship the *Vesuvius* wherein he prays an allowance for himself, officers, and Company for their Service in blowing up the said Ship under the Walls of St. Malo. Wee have considered of the same, and do humbly Report our opinion, that the said Commander and the Officers and Company which did belong to the said Ship when she was blown up, as aforesaid, do deserve the like Reward which by the practice of the Navy is allowed to those who do service in Fireships, by burning any of the Enemies Ships.

"FALKLAND. H. PRIESTMAN.
J. LOWTHER. R. RICH."

'His Ma^{ty} in Councill approving the said Report, Is this day pleased to Order, as it is hereby Ordered, That the Lords Comm^{rs} of the Admiralty do cause the said Captain Guy to have the like Reward for himself, Officers and Company for their said Service, as by the practice of the Navy is allowed to those who do service in Fire Ships, by burning any of the Enemies Ships.'

This order therefore directs that Captain Guy should have a Gold Chain and Medal of £30 value, and the officers and crew pecuniary rewards, as provided in the Fighting Instructions for the Royal Navy issued in 1665, and the Order in Council of 12th January, 1669-70. (See the section on Rewards for Fireship Services in the Introduction.)

This is a rather curious case, inasmuch as the regulations only provided rewards in respect of Fireships burning an enemy's *ships*, whereas Captain Guy apparently attempted to burn a *town*. Happily, the authorities recognised that the risk had been the same, and did not take a red-tape view of the business.

No. 85.

CAPTAIN CYPRIAN SOUTHACK, 1694.

GOLD CHAIN.

'AT THE COURT AT WHITEHALL,
the First of February, 1693 ($169\frac{3}{4}$).

'*Present.*

'THE KING'S MOST EXCELLENT MA$^{TY.}$

'Whereas Captain Cyprian Southack who has been for severall years employed by the Governm^{t} of New England at Sea, and has performed divers Signall Services in severall Expeditions against y^{e} French in those parts, having this day had y^{e} Honour to kisse his Ma^{ts} Hand, Hath presented to His Ma^{ty} a Draft of Newfoundland, Nova Scotia, the River of Canada, and the Seas and Territorys thereunto adjoyning, made by himself in the said severall Expeditions, His Ma^{ty} taking into his gracious Consideration ye Services of ye said Cyprian Southack and for his further Encouragm^{t} is pleased to Order, as it is hereby Ordered, That ye Sum̃e of Fifty pounds be paid to him for y^{e} buying of a Gold chain, as a mark of his Ma^{ts} Royall Favour, and that the R^{t} Hono^{ble} y^{e} Lords Commissioners of y^{e} Admiralty do give all necessary Directions for y^{e} speedy payment of the said Summe.'

'ADMIRALTY OFFICE, *Fryday Morning*, 18th *Jan^{y}*, 94 ($169\frac{4}{5}$).

'Upon reading his Ma^{tys} Order in Council of y^{e} 1st Febr^{ry} directing Capt Cyprian Southack to be allowed £50 for buying him a Gold Chain, Resolved that Ord^{rs} be given to the Navy Board for paying y^{e} same.'

No. 86.

CAPTAIN JOHN TUPPER, 1694.

GOLD MEDAL AND CHAIN.

'ADMIRALTY OFFICE, *Wednesday Morning*, 17th *October*, 1694.

'Upon a L^{re} now read from Capt Tupper, Com̃ander of a Privateer, Resolved that Orders be given for his having a Medall and Chain to ye Vallue of Fifty pound for the good services performed by him.' (See No. 77.)

This is the medal for La Hogue, presented to Captain John Tupper of Guernsey, who, when in command of a privateer, sailed unperceived through the French fleet during a thick fog, and brought the first intelligence of the enemy's presence to England. The action was fought soon after. The decoration is in the possession of his descendant, Colonel Tupper, late R.A.

No. 87.

CAPTAIN STEPHEN ELLIOT, 1694.

MEDAL AND CHAIN.

'AT THE COURT AT WHITEHALL,
the 15th *of Nov*^{r}, 1694.

'*Present.*

'THE KING'S MOST EXCELLENT MAJESTY.

'The R^{t} Hono^{ble} the Lords of the Committee of Trade and Plantations having this day Reported it as their Opinion that Capt: Elliot who escaped from Petit Guaves with two others in a small canoe, and gave notice of the designe of the French upon Jamaica may deserve from His Ma^{tys} Bounty a Medall and Chaine, and the Summ of Five hundred Pounds as a Reward for the said service. And that the Two men who came with him, may in like manner deserve a Reward of Fifty pounds to each of them. His Ma^{ty} in Councill approving the same, is this day pleased to Order, as it is hereby Ordered that the R^{t} Hono^{ble} the Lords Commissioners of the Treasury do cause the summ of five hundred pounds to be paid unto the said Capt: Elliot and fifty pounds a piece to the two men who came over with him from Petit Guaves accordingly.

'The R^{t} Hono^{ble} the Lords of the Committee of Trade and Plantations having this day Reported it as Their opinion that Capt Elliot who escaped from Petit Guaves with two others in a small canoe, and gave notice of the Designe of the French upon Jamaica may deserve from His Ma^{tys} Bounty a Medall and Chaine, and the summ of five hundred Pounds as a Reward for the said Service, And that the two men who came with him, may in like manner deserve a Reward of fifty Pounds to each of them. His Ma^{ty} in Councill approving the same, is this day pleased to order, as it is hereby Ordered that the said Capt Elliot have a Medall and Chaine of the value of one hundred Pounds; And the Lords Comm^{rs} of the Admiralty are to give the necessary directions accordingly. As also to consider of the ability of the said Capt Elliot in Reference to the Command of one of Their Ma^{tys} Ships of War and to Confer the same upon him, if They shall so think fitt.'

'ADMIRALTY OFFICE, *Monday Evening*, 24th *Dec*^{r}, 1694.

'Upon an Order in Councill of the 15th Novr last Resolved that Orders be given for examining Capt: Stephen Elliott as to his qualification for a master of Their Ma^{tys} Ships as also for providing a Medall and Chain for him of the value of one hundred pounds.'

A notice in the sense of the above orders was published in the *London Gazette*, December 24th to December 27th, 1694, No. 3039.

'ADMIRALTY OFFICE, *Tuesday Morning*, 4th *June*, '95.

'Capt: Elliot to be acquainted that the Medall and Chain for him will be delivered to such person as he shall direct to receive the same.'

No. 88.

CAPTAIN STEVENS, 1695.

MEDAL AND CHAIN.

'ADMIRALTY OFFICE, *Wednesday Morning*, 24 *April*, '95.

'Resolved a Medall and Chaine of the value of £50 be given to Capt: Stevens of Guernsey, Comand^{r} of a Privateer for his good services done this War against the Enemy and that Orders be given accordingly to the Navy Board and M^{r} of the Mint.'

No. 89.

JOHN GRESHY OR GRUCHY, 1694, 1695.

MEDAL AND CHAIN.

'AT THE COURT AT WHITEHALL,
the 26th of July, 1694.

'Upon reading the annexed Petition of John Greshy of Guernzey Mariner concerning his taking and destroying some French Privateers, and retaking a Vessell laden with stone for the Buildings at Hampton Court, And praying a Recompense for his said Service. It is this day Ordered in Councill, that it be and it is hereby Referred to the Lords Commissioners of the Admiralty to consider of the matter of the said Petition, and to Report to the Board what they conceive fitt for Her Maty to do therein.'

'AT THE COURT AT WHITEHALL,
the 9th of August, 1694.

'*Present.*

'THE QUEEN'S MOST EXCELLENT MAJESTY.

'Upon reading a Report from the Lords Commrs of the Admiralty upon the Petition of John Greshy of Guernzey, Mariner, in the words following:—

"In pursuance of an Order of the Lords of their Mats most Honble Privy Councill dated the 26th of the last month on the Peticon of John Greshy of Guernzey mariner concerning his taking and Destroying some French Privateers and rescuing a vessell laden with Stone for the Buildings of Hampton Court. Wee have considered of the same, and doe Report it as our Opinion, That in consideration of the good service performed by him, the said Greshy should be allowed a Medall and Chaine to the value of Thirty pounds, as also that the severall Persons which went with him in Capt Rowland's Privateer on the aforesaid service have an allowance of Twenty Shillings each: And that the said Rewards be paid to them by their Mats Commrs for Prizes. Dated at the Admiralty Office this 3rd day of Aug: 1694."

'It is this day Ordered by Her Maty in Councill that the said Lords Commrs give Order for a Medall and Chaine to the value of Thirty Pounds to be given to the said John Greshy, and also for the paying to each of those persons being twenty five in number wch went with him in Capt Rowland's Privateer on the aforesaid service twenty shillings, to bee paid to the said John Greshy by the Treasurer of the Navy out of the tenth part appointed by Act of Parliament.'

'ADMIRALTY OFFICE, *Tuesday Evening*, 14*th Augt.* 1694.

'Upon reading Her Mats Order in Councill of the 9th instt—Resolved that Ordrs be given for providing a Medall and Chaine for Mr Greshy and paying 20s each to several men as is therein directed.'

'ADMIRALTY OFFICE, *Munday Morning*, 21*st Octobr.* 1695.

'Capt Gruchy who cōmands a Guernsey Privatier to send up the Governrs Certifycate, that he has brought in the Prize mentioned in his letter and then he is to have a Meddall and Chaine of the same vallue as yt given to Capt Steevens for his good service [see No. 88], and an extract of the news in ye sd Letter to bee sent to Mr Yard.'

'ADMIRALTY OFFICE, *the* 25*th Octobr.* 1695. *Evening.*

'Capt Gruchy of a Guernsey Privatier to have a Chaine to the vallue of £20 in consideration of his late good service in retakeing a Rich Merchant Ship, notwithstanding hee had formerly a Medall and Chaine of £30 for past service.'

No. 90.

WILLIAM THOMPSON.
WILLIAM WILLIAMS.

1695.

MEDALS AND CHAINS.

'POOLE, *June* 2. On the 30th of the last month, a French Privateer Ship, belonging to *Cherbourg*, gave Chace to a small Hoy of this place, of which *William Thompson* is Master, who was Fishing near the Island of *Purbeck*, having with him only one Man and a Boy; As soon as the said *Thompson* perceived the Privateer bear down upon him, he made ready to defend himself the best he could, with two small Guns he had mounted, and some small Arms, which he employed with such good success, that in a little time the Captain, and Lieutenant of the Sloop, with 6 more of the French Mariners were wounded, and this so discouraged the rest, that they bore away; Whereupon *Thompson* gave chace to the Privateer, and fired upon her for the space of two hours, till at last the French struck, and crying out for Quarter, surrendered to him; And *Thompson* brought the Sloop in, with 14 Prisoners; whereof the Captain is one; and two of the French Men he left at *Corfe* Castle; The said Privateer, had two Pattereroes, several small Arms and Grenadoes, and 16 men.

'The Lords Commissioners of the Admiralty have ordered a Gold Chain and Medal to the value of £50 to be given to the said *William Thompson*, as a Reward for his taking the said Privateer: And the Lords Commissioners have also given a Chain and Medal of the like value to *William Williams*, Master of a Fisher Boat of *Whitsand* Bay, as a Reward for his having retaken from the Enemy several Coasting vessels.' (*The London Gazette*, from Monday, June 3rd, to Thursday, June 6th, 1695, No. 3085.)

In an Admiralty notice dated 17th June, 1695, published in the *London Gazette* of 17th-20th June, 1695, it is stated that 'the Lords Commissioners, for the further encouragement of William Thompson of Poole, have given him the sloop which he took lately from the French.'

'ADMIRALTY OFFICE, *Tuesday Morning*, 4 *June*, 1695.

'Resolved that care bee taken for the Fishers off Poole &c. and that Wm Thompson an Inhabitant of Poole who took a French Privateer with a Hoy with 2 men and a Boy have a Meddall and Chaine to the value of £50.'

'ADMIRALTY OFFICE, *Monday Morning*, 17 *June*, '95.

'A Lre of Mart to be granted to Wm Thompson Master of Fishing Vessell of Poole 30 Tuns 5 Guns and men with liberty to use the Coasting Trade and catch Fish on the English coast in consideration of his good services against the Enemy.'

'ADMIRALTY OFFICE, *Monday Evening*, 3rd *June*, '95.

'Upon the recomendation of severall Gentlemen of the West Country of Wm Williams Master of a Fisher Boat of Whitsand Bay burthen about 8 Tuns with 30 men for his good services against the Enemy and in retaking severall merchant Vessells Resolved that he have a Lre of Mart for the said Vessell and a Medall and Chaine of the value of £50.'

No. 91.

CAPTAIN PETER JOLLIFFE, 1695.

GOLD MEDAL AND CHAIN.

Obv. Busts of William and Mary. Same as No. 77.

Rev. Ins. engraved, 'His Maties' Gift as a Reward to *Peter Jollif*, of Poole, for his good Service ag^{t} the Enemy in retaking a Ketch of Weymouth from a French Privateer, and chaceing the said Privateer on Shoar near Lulworth in ye Isle of Purbeck, where shee was broken in peeces. 1694.'

Circular, 1.95 inch.
Weight 2 oz. 17 dwts.

The chain which was given with the medal is not known to be in existence; but the medal is in the possession of Captain Jolliffe's descendant, Mr. W. A. Jolliffe.

Many medals were awarded during this reign to individuals for sea service, but that given to Captain Jolliffe is the only one we have yet discovered. It may, perhaps, be regarded as a type of those given for services performed before the Queen's death. The *reverses* of the medals probably bore engraved inscriptions relative to the services for which the medals were granted.

'ADMIRALTY OFFICE, *Monday Evening*, 17 *June*, 1695.

'Resolved that a Medall and Chaine be given to Peter Jollife of Poole for his good services against the Enemy, to the value of £50, & that he have a Lr̃e of Mart for a Vessel of his with 25 men, 4 Guñs, and 2 Patereroes.'

'ADMIRALTY OFFICE, *Tuesday Morning*, 2 *July*, 1695.

'Capt Peter Jolliffe of Poole prays his case may be recomended to Sr Cha: Hedges touching the Admiralty Fees for his Commission which amount to £10. Refer'd to Sr Cha: Hedges who is to give a particular Account of the Fees for a Lr̃e of Mart.'

'Whitehall, June 17. The Lords Commissioners of the Admiralty have given a Gold Medal and Chain to Mr *Peter Jolliffe* of *Poole*, Master of the *Sea-Adventure* Hoy of about 25 Tuns, for his good Service, and particularly in retaking, some time since, a Ketch of *Weymouth* from a French Privateer, and chasing the said Privateer on shore near *Lulworth* in the Isle of Purbeck, where she was broken in pieces.' (*The London Gazette*, from Monday, June 17, to Thursday, June 20, 1695, No. 3089.)

On the south wall of the Church of St. James, Poole, Dorset, is a white marble monument bearing the arms of Jolliffe, with the following inscription:

'Near this Place, Lies the Body of Peter Jolliff, who in the late wars Signaliz'd himself against the French with uncommon Courage, And frequently reveng'd their Insolencies towards the English, By Captivity or Death. William the Third, In justice to the merit of so brave a man, Rewarded his Services with a Commission, and a Medal of Gold. George the First, at his Accession to the Throne, Gave him the command of this Town in all military Affairs. Thus having been distinguish'd by these two great Kings, He dy'd in the 72d year of his Age on the 12th day of November 1730. He left several Children, William the youngest, caus'd this monument to be erected to his Memory on the 19th Octobr 1737.'

In *Notes and Queries for Somerset and Dorset*, vol. iii. p. 173, is printed a copy of a contemporary street ballad entitled 'The courageous captain, or a brief account of the several nobele attempts and valliant exploits perform'd by the honoured captain Peter Jolliff over the French privateers to his unspeakable praise, and the honor of the Kingdom.' The ballad consists of twenty-one verses, four of which are given below:

'Right valliant Thomson,[1] brave and bold,
A medel had and chain of gold
For taking a french privateer;
But now anither captain hear

'Hath sins receiv'd the same reword,
For nobel actions don one bord,
Deserving more then common fame,
Stout Peter Jolleff col'd by name.

'He more than onc or twice did fight,
And put french priviteers to flight,
As by the sequel you shall find,
Wich shos his bold undanted mind.

. . . . .

'For this brave valliant act, behold,
He has receiv'd a chain of gold,
A medel and commission too,
That he the french may still pursue.'

. . . . .

No. 92.

CAPTAIN WILLIAM HOLLMAN, 1695.

MEDAL AND CHAIN.

'ADMIRALTY OFFICE, *Monday Evening*, 1st *July*, '95.

'Resolved that Capt Wm Hollman have a Medall and Chain of £100 value given for his good services against the Enemy at Newfoundland.'

No. 93.

JOHN WHITE, 1695.

MEDAL.

'ADMIRALTY OFFICE, *Thursday Morning*, 15 *Aug:* 1695.

'A Medall to be given to Jno. White of the value of £30 for bringing in a Merchant Ship after she was in possession of the Enemy.'

[1] See No. 90.

No. 94.

MR. NORWOOD, 1696.

MEDAL AND CHAIN.

'ADMIRALTY OFFICE, *Wednesday Post Meridian*, 29*th* *Janry*, 169$\frac{5}{6}$.

'Mr Norwood Mar of a Tender who behaved himselfe well in the Service, and lost the use of his arme, to have a Meddall and Chaine of £60.'

No. 95.

JOHN YEAMES, 1697.

MEDAL AND CHAIN.

'ADMIRALTY OFFICE, *Munday Post Meridian*, 9° *Novr*, 1696.

'A Reference read from Sir Wm Trumbull Secy of State, on the Petition of John Yeames, Resolved that he bee acquainted, that if ye said Yeames can make out what is alleadged he will deserve a Meddall.'

'ADMIRALTY OFFICE, *Wednesday Morning*, 14° *Aprill*, 1697.

'The Executr of John Yeames Marrr to have a Meddall and Chaine of £50 :— Upon reading a Letter from Mr Secretary Trumbull for some service hee has signalized himselfe in.'

No. 96.

CHARLES BARRELL, 1697.

CHAIN AND MEDAL.

'ADMIRALTY OFFICE, *Fryday Evening*, 22° *Janry*, 169$\frac{6}{7}$.

'Charles Barrell Mar of a Merchant Vessell to have a Chaine & Meddall of £50 for takeing a French Privatier.'

No. 97.

MR. ALEXANDER CUMBERBATCH.

CHAIN AND MEDAL.

MR. RALPH BEAMES.

MEDAL.

1697.

'ADMIRALTY OFFICE, *Thursday Morning*, 4° *Novr*, 1697.

'Mr Cumberbatch, who writ Capt Norris a Letter att Newfoundland giveing him an account of Monsr Poyntz's Squadron, Attended the Board this morning, & the Board acquainted him that hee had done very good service therein, & that for the present they had Resolved to give him a Chaine & Meddall, & they would Consider how to mak him a further Reward. Hee was asked severall questions relateing to the proceedings of Poyntz, & of our Ships commanded by Capt Harlow, and was bid to put the same in writeing. As was Allsoe his Mate y^t^ attended the Board with him and to come to ye Board to-morrow night.

'*Resolved* that Orders be given for a Chaine and Meddall to ye said Mr Cumberbatch as a Reward to him for hazarding his life when he was sent on Shoare by Mouns^r^ Poyntz (by whom hee was taken) for procureing water and Provĩcons in Newfoundland, by sending a Letter to Capt Norris Commander in Cheife of Our Ships giving him an Account of Monsr Poyntz's Squadron.'

'ADMIRALTY OFFICE, *Fryday, Post Meridian*, 5° *Nov^r^*, 1697.

'Ralph Beames who was Mate to Mr Cumberbatch and taken with him by Monsr Poyntz, with whom the said Cumberbatch conferred with about giveing Capt Norris an account of Poyntz's Squadron att Newfoundland to have a Meddall of £30 for keeping the said Designe private.'

'ADMIRALTY OFFICE, *Monday, Post Meridian* 8° *Nov^r^*, 1697.

'The Ma^r^ of the Mint to be hastened in makeing the Meddall for Mr Cumberbatch and his Mate.'

'ADMIRALTY OFFICE, *Wednesday Evening*, 1st *Dec^r^*, 1697.

'*Resolved* that Mr Alexander Cumberbatch, as a further Reward for his good Service in giveing Capt Norris advice of Monsr Poyntz's Squadron in Newfoundland, have £500; and his Mate £50.'

No. 98.

CAPTAIN ROUNCEVALL, 1699.

MEDAL AND CHAIN.

'ADMIRALTY OFFICE, 21° *June*, 1699, *Wednesday Morning*.

'Some Canary Merchants attended ye Board in favour of Capt Rouncevall and produced an Affidavit of his haveing Behaved himself very well in fighting a Sally Man of War in December last—*Resolved* y^t^ for his encouragement he have a Medall and Chaine to the value of £80.'

No. 99.

AGA DOUD, 1698.

GOLD MEDAL AND CHAIN.

The following extracts from the records of the India Office show that Aga Doud, the East India Company's Linguist in Persia, was presented by them with a gold medal and chain in the year 1698. The medal bore the (London) Company's arms, and, with the chain, was to be of the same value (£100) as that presented to Cassa Verona, the Company's broker at Madras, in 1679. (See Nos. 68 and 70.)

Sir Jeremy Sambrooke, to whom the provision of the medal was entrusted, was a member of the Court of Committees. As the medal was ready in less than two months from the date of the order, it is not improbable that the die was the same as that used for Cassa Verona's medal. One die only is mentioned, and it is possible, therefore, that the *reverse* was merely a blank on which an inscription was engraved. If the die of the Company's arms which served in 1679 was thus available in 1698, it would have been a good reason for the Court ordering, as they did, that it should be locked up and taken care of in view to its use on any future occasion, although, as things happened, it would not have served for many years longer, because, on the union of this, the old Company with the new Company, in 1709, the arms which were granted to the latter in 1698 were adopted as the arms of the United Company, and those of the old Company became obsolete.

The die in question is probably that of the Medal No. 70. The order that it should be locked up in the Company's Treasury Chest was carried out, and in the Treasuries of successive Home Governments of India down to the present time it, or a die of the same period, has been carefully preserved.

A COURT OF COMMITTEES, holden 11 *February*, 169$\frac{7}{8}$.

'*It is ordered*, That Sr Jeremy Sambrooke be desired to provide a Medall & Chain of Gold, to be given to Aga Doud, the Company's Linguist in Persia, of the same value as was done to Cassa Verona, at Fort St George.' [See No. 68.]

A COURT OF COMMITTEES, 8 *April*, 1698.

'*It is ordered*, That it be referred unto Sr Jer: Sambrooke to consider of the Bill of parcells, produced in Court, for the Dye, Medall & Chain, bought & provided by Sr Stephen Evance, & upon examination thereof, to give direction for payment of what shall be found due thereon.'

A COURT OF COMMITTEES, 15 *Aprill*, 1698.

'*It is ordered*, That the Chain and Medall of Gold, prepared for Senior Auga Doud, the Comp^as^ Linguist in Persia, be sent on the Ship *Mary*; And that the Dye, by which the said Medall was stampt, be delivered to the Cōmittee of the Treasury, to be lockt up, in the Comp^as^ Chest, under their charge.'

'*OUR CHIEFE AND COUNCILL OF ISPAHAUN.*

'LONDON, *the* 15*^th^ Aprill*, 1698.

'1. We have received your overland Lr̃e dat. the 4th November last wherein we understand you have disposed of our whole Cargo of Cloth sent you on the *Charles*, and do well approve of what you have done therein; and take particular notice of the care and industry of our Linguist Aga Doude in his assisting you therein, and of his former services in procuring our Phirmaunds. We shall by our Ships more particularly answer your Lr̃e, and what Requests made by Aga Doud to us, which we shall willingly gratify him in as far as may consist with our Interest, and not to the disadvantage of our Affairs, and only now advise you as a more particular Mark of our favour to him, We have caused a Gold Medall (with our Arms) and Chain to be made, which we shall send unto him by the first opportunity, and do intend out of hand to goe on wth Provision of Cloth this summer, and to send it with a Ship directly to Persia as soon as we can.' (*I. O. Records*, *Letter Book*, vol. x.)

No. 100.

CAPTAIN FULLER, 1700.

'ADMIRALTY, 11 *December*, 1700.

'Capt. Fuller who commanded the *Cloudesley* Galley attended the Board and pray'd a Reward of a Meddall and Chaine for takeing a French Man-of-War in the Archipellago.

'He was informed that by taking this Shipp and others, he received the benifitt thereof, and that the Board had noe money for such services.' (*Minute Book*, vol. xvi.)

The terms of the refusal to Captain Fuller of the reward commonly given in cases of the kind (see particularly the case of Captain Stocker, of the same galley, or one of the same name, in 1691, No. 82), may mean that the ships taken by him had not been treated as *prizes* in the regular manner, and that consequently the Admiralty had not received the one-tenth share which should have been paid to them towards the fund out of which rewards were provided. Otherwise, it is not apparent why the application should have been rejected.

It appears, however, to have been decided a few years later that no medals or chains should be given in the cases of capture of prizes by *Privateers* because of the benefit they had by them; although special cases were still to be considered on their merits. (See *Admiralty Minute*, 16th November, 1703; Introduction, Reign of Queen Anne.)

No. 101.

CAPTAIN EVERTON, 1701.

GOLD MEDAL AND CHAIN.

'To provide a Medal and Chain valued £80, to Captain Everton, of the Ship *Tenerife*, Gally of London, carrying six guns and ten men, as a reward to him for his good service in engaging with and defending his ship from a Sally man-of-war of 24 guns, and 200 men. (*Admiralty*, *Lords Letters to the Secretary of State*, vol. ii. fol. 49, Dec. 3, 1701.)

No. 102.

CAPTAIN JAMES LAMPRIERE, 1703.

PLATE 12, *No.* 1.

Obv. Bust of Queen Anne, *l.*, wearing Crown, and Collar and Star of the Order of the Garter.

Leg. ANNA . DEI . GRATIA . MAG : BRITAN : FRA : ET . HIB : REGINA.

Rev. Inscription engraved. 'Her Maj^{ties} reward to Capt James Lampriere for his Zeal to her Service and his Succesful Conducting ye Squadron commanded by Rear Admiral Dilkes who destroyed a considerable number of ye Enemy's Merchant Ships under Convoy of 3 Men of War on their own coast.'

Below, the arms of Lampriere (three eagles displayed), with the motto, 'TRUE . TO . MY . TRUST.'

Circular, 2.75 inches. Gold.
Ring for suspension.

Captain Lampriere may have been one of the two Guernsey Pilots referred to in the Admiralty Minute of 10th August, 1703. (See No. 106.)

No. 103.

HENRY GILBERT, MASTER; ELISHA DANN, BOATSWAIN; BENJAMIN BRYER, GUNNER — of the Ship *Torbay*.

1702-3.

GOLD MEDALS AND CHAINS.

Medals and Chains were awarded to the above, in reward for their good service in extinguishing the fire on board the *Torbay* at Vigo, when the Captain was blown overboard. The *Torbay* was the flagship of Vice-Admiral Hobson, in Sir George Rooke's action in Vigo Bay, on 11th October, 1702.

'ADMIRALTY OFFICE, 22^{d} *Dec^{r}*, 1702.
At night.

'The Gun̄er of the *Torbay* to have a Medall and Chaine to the value of £120, and to be made Gun̄er of the next 1st Rate Ship [the *Barfleur*?] upon account of his good service in extinguishing the Fire on board her at Vigo, when the Capt was blowne overboard.'

'ADMIRALTY OFFICE, 12 *March*, 170$\frac{2}{3}$.

'Upon a Letter now read from the Marquiss of Carmarthen—The Master of the *Torbay* to have a Medall and Chaine to the value of One hundred and twenty Pounds, and the Boats^{ne} the like—The Cooper to have six monthes, and each of the Thirty Seamen three monthes Pay in consideration of their good services in extinguishing the Fire aboard the said Ship at Viego.'

There is printed in Nicolas's *History of Honorary Medals*, pp. 13-14, a letter dated Admiralty Office, 15th March, 1702-3, desiring that a Bill might be signed on the Treasurer of the Navy,

'for paying £240 to Isaac Newton Esq., Master of the Mint, for enabling him to provide two Medals and two Chains, one for Henry Gilbert the Master, and the other for Elisha Dann the Boatswain of the *Torbay*, in the like manner as he has been directed to do for Benjamin Bryer, Gunner of the said Ship, as a reward to them for their good service in extinguishing the fire on board the *Torbay* at Vigo, when the Captain of her was blown overboard; the said Bill to be paid out of money received by the Treasurer of the Navy, for the tenths of Prizes appointed by a late Act of Parliament, for Medals and other rewards for Officers, Marines and Seamen in Her Majesty's service.'

'ADMIRALTY OFFICE, 13 *April*, 1703.

'The Guñer of the *Barfleur* [Benjamin Bryer ?] to come to Towne that he may receive his Medall and Chaine for his good service in assisting in preserving the *Torbay* at Viego.'

'ADMIRALTY OFFICE, 25*th* *Jañry.*, 170$\frac{4}{5}$.

'Upon a Letter now read from Capt: Martin, David Hartley Boatsne of the *Prince George* to be in the *Neptune*, and Elisha Dann late Boatsne of the *Torbay* to be in his room in ye *Prince George.*'

No. 104.

ADMIRAL DILKES AND OTHER OFFICERS, 1703.

GOLD MEDALS.

Gold Medals are said to have been presented to Rear-Admiral Dilkes and his officers for capturing several French vessels near Granville [Cancale Road] in Normandy, in July, 1703. (See *Naval Chronicle*, iv. 469; Campbell's *Lives of the Admirals*, iii. 376; *Nicolas*, iv. Medals, p. 14.)

There is no mention of these medals in the Admiralty Minutes. They were similar, possibly, to that presented to Captain Lampriere. (See No. 102.)

No. 105.

CAPTAIN THOMAS LEGGE, 1703.

GOLD MEDAL.

Captain Thomas Legge, after the accession of Queen Anne, conspicuously distinguished himself under the command of Rear-Admiral Dilkes, in an attack upon some French ships in Cancale Bay. His gallantry on that occasion was rewarded by a gold medal, which was struck purposely to perpetuate the event. (*Naval Chronicle*, vol. xxviii. p. 189.)

No. 106.

TWO GUERNSEY PILOTS, 1703.

MEDALS AND CHAINS.

'ADMIRALTY OFFICE, 10th *August*, 1703.

'Orders to be given for preparing Medalls and Chaines of one hundred pounds for each of the two Guernsey Pylotts who voluntarily went on board the Squadron comãnded by Rr Admll Dylkes, and Pylotted him to Concall Road where he destroy'd severall of the French Ships.' (See No. 104.)

No. 107.

MASTER OF THE SHIP *GOOD LUCK*, 1706.

MEDAL AND CHAIN.

'ADMIRALTY OFFICE, *Thursday*, 13 *June*, 1706.

'Doctor Bramston's Report of the 13th Janry last on the Petition of the Owners of the Guernsey Privateer called the *Good Luck* read and consider'd. Resolved that they bee acquainted that this Ship was not the first that gave the Intelligence of the French Ships to Sir Tho: Dilkes, notwithstanding which the Prince gave her Master a Medall and Chaine, and that his Royll Highness don't think fit to make any further allowance to the Owners.'

No. 108.

THOMAS HEDGES.
JOHN PIMBLE.
PHILIP DEVONSHIRE.
DANIEL LAWLEY.
THOMAS STUBBS.

1703.

MEDALS.

'ADMIRALTY OFFICE, 16 *Novr*, 1703.

'*Resolved* that a Medall of £20 value be allowed to Thomas Hedges Mar of the ship *Leonora*; John Pimble, Philp Devonshire, Danl Lawley Marinr, and Tho: Stubbs to have Medalls also, vizt: the three men of £10 each and the Boy of £5 value, in consideration of their courage and Resolution, in driving the French men then aboard her off from the Quarter Deck, and bringing the said Shipp into England.'

TREASURY PAPERS.

'Letter of the Commissioners of Prizes to Mr. Lowndes as to the distribution of Medals to the value of £55, to the master, three mariners, and a boy, belonging to the *Leonora*, a merchant ship taken by the French, for their extraordinary courage on that occasion. Dated 22 November, 1703.

'Enclosing the order from the Lord High Admiral, which states that after they were taken by the French and made prisoners in the Ship, they set upon 13 Frenchmen which were ordered to sail her to France, whom they obliged to surrender the ship.' (*State Papers—Calendar of Treasury Papers*, 1702-1707, vol. lxxxvii. No. 133.)

'Letter signed Geo. Clarke (Admiralty) to William Lowndes Esq[r], as to the money to be paid by the Prize Office to the Treasurer of the Navy, for Medals to be given to the Master, Mariners, and a boy, belonging to the *Leonora*, about which His Royal Highness had issued an order, which he was not inclined to alter. Dated 25 November, 1703.

'*Minuted.*—Send a copy to the Com[rs] of Prizes. My Lord is of the same opinion as in y[e] letter.' (*State Papers—Calendar of Treasury Papers*, 1702-1707, vol. lxxxvii. No. 145.)

No. 109.

CAPTAIN JOSEPH TAYLOR, 1704.

MEDAL AND CHAIN.

ACCOUNTS OF COMMISSIONERS OF PRIZES for the year 1704-5.

'Sir Tho: Littleton Bart: Treasr. of Her Ma[ty] Navy, for so much paid into his hands in Order to his paying £200 in Specie to Capt: Joseph Taylor Comd[r] of the *Charles* Galley, and £100 to y[e] Ma[r] of Her Ma[ty] Mint for a Meddall and Chaine for y[e] said Capt: in Reward to him for his good Service and gallant behaviour in defending y[e] said Ship when attackt by four y[e] Enemies Gallies at his going into Nice, by virtue of an Order of His Royal Highness Prince George of Denmarke, Lord High Admirall of England, and a like Warrant dated y[e] 22nd of August, 1704. (Total) £300.

'More unto him, being Imprested to him, pursuant to a like Order to be by him paid to y[e] Master and Worker of her Ma[ty] Mint, for y[e] Fashion and Waste in making y[e] Meddall and Chain given to y[e] above named Capt[t] Joseph Taylor, by a like Warrant dated 24th of Novb[r], 1704—£7, 10s. 6d.'

(*Audit Office*, Roll 467, Bundle 1817.)

No. 110.

DR. DON SANCHES, 1715.

MEDAL.

'James Stanhope to the Lords of the Treasury. Signifies His Majesty's pleasure that they pay £100 to Dr. Don Sanches, Assessor of Minorca, who is going to return thither in a few days, and also that they provide him with a Medal, not exceeding £30 in value. Whitehall, 27th August, 1715.' (*State Papers—Calendar of Treasury Papers*, vol. cxci. No. 65.)

Minorca was occupied by the British, 1708-56.

No. 111.

CAPTAIN MATTHEW MARTIN, 1715.

JEWEL.

Obv. Arms of the East India Company, enamelled and set in diamonds.

Rev. Ins. 'The English United East India Company rewarded Capt. Matthew Martin, Commander of The Ship *Marlborough*, with this Jewell and One Thousand Pounds Sterling, for defending his Ship in India three days successively against three French Ships of War, and bringing her safe to Fort St. George, *Anno* 1712.'

This handsome enamelled Jewel was an exceptional sort of decoration. It is presumed it cost the 100 guineas mentioned in the Court's Resolution of 22nd December, 1714. It would be interesting to know if it is still in existence. The fight with the French ships took place in the Bay of Bengal, near Gaujam.

AT A COURT OF DIRECTORS, 10th September, 1714.

'Captain Matthew Martin, Commander of the *Marlborough*, attending the Court, the Chairman returned him the Court's Thanks for his brave defence of the Ship in India, against three French Ships of War, And acquainted him they would take the same into further consideration.'

AT A COURT OF DIRECTORS, 10th December, 1714.

'*Resolved*, That this Court will at their next meeting take into consideration the Advices received by them from India, touching Captain Martin's brave defence of the Ship *Marlborough*, near the Bay of Bengall, against three French ships; And that the said Advices, and all Minutes of this Court relating thereto, be then laid before the Court.'

AT A COURT OF DIRECTORS, 15th December, 1714.

'*Resolved*, That this Court will on Wednesday the 22d December next, take into consideration the case of Captain Matthew Martin's defence of the *Marlborough* against three French ships in India; And that in the meantime, Sir Robert Child, the Deputy-Chairman, be desired to discourse him of some matters wherein as is alleged he deserves the Court's further favour on account of his particular losses, And that Sir Robert do give such account thereof as he thinks proper.'

AT A COURT OF DIRECTORS, 22nd December, 1714.

'The Court taking into consideration the case of Captain Martin, on the promise made him the 10th of September last; And the 221st paragraph of the Generall Letter from Fort St. George, dated the 24th October, 1712, being read relating thereto; And also the Narrative entered in the Consultation Book of Fort St. George, the 6th October, about his defending the *Marlborough* in the East Indies, off Gaujam, against three French Ships of War for three dayes together, and getting clear of them, And thereby saving a very great Estate of the Company's on board, being read; And it appearing to the Court that the Captain was a great sufferer, by his throwing overboard a considerable value of his own Estate; And this Court being deeply sensible of the Captain's extraordinary conduct in defence of the said Ship, wherein the Company had seventy-two chests of Treasure in Rupees, besides goods and merchandizes to a large value.

'*Resolved*, That a Warrant be made out to Captain Matthew Martin for One thousand Pounds, in consideration of his said losses and conduct; And that the value of One hundred guineas more be given him in a Medall, or some other lasting remembrance of his said conduct; And be prepared by the Committee of the Treasury.

'*Resolved*, That a month's pay be given to the Mates and other officers and Mariners that were on board the *Marlborough* at the time of action.'

AT A COURT OF DIRECTORS, 20th December, 1715.

'Sir Robert Child representing that in pursuance of the Order of this Court, the Committee of the Treasury had caused a Jewell to be made for Captain Martin, which was now laid before the Court, and appeared to be this Companyes Arms finely enamell'd, and emblazoned in the proper colours, with the Supporters all set round with Diamonds, in Gold, And on the back of it was the following Inscription:—

> "The English United East India Company rewarded Capt. Matthew Martin, Commander of The Ship *Marlborough*, with this Jewell and One Thousand Pounds Sterling, for defending his Ship in India three dayes successively against three French Ships of War, and bringing her safe to Fort St. George. *Anno* 1712."

'And Capt. Martin being called into Court, Sir Robert Child presented him therewith.'

No. 112.

MAJOR JOHN ROACH, 1717.

GOLD MEDAL.

Obv. The arms of the East India Company set round with diamond sparks.

Rev. An inscription.

Lieutenant Roach had been sent from Madras, with 150 men of the garrison, to obtain possession of the neighbouring village or town of Trivadore, which had been ceded to the East India Company.[1] In reward for his good service, the Madras Government made him a Major, and presented him with a Gold Medal.

FORT ST. GEORGE, PUBLIC CONSULTATIONS, 21st October, 1717.

'*Agreed*, That in consideration of Lieut. John Roach's former services at Fort St. David, for which the Honorable Company have in their letters ordered him a gratuity, which has never yet been given; and also in consideration of his eminent service at Trivadore on 19 instant, in defeating the enemy, with so much loss on their side and without the loss of one man on ours:—That the President by his commission constitute Lieut. John Roach Major of all the Honorable Company's forces on the coast of Coromandel and Island of Sumatra; and that a Gold Medal with the Honorable Company's Arms set round with diamonds sparks, with an inscription on the *reverse* suitable to the occasion (the value about three hundred pagados) be given him.' (*I. O. Records*, 1717.)

No. 113.

CAPTAIN SMITH CALLIS, R.N., 1742.

GOLD MEDAL AND CHAIN.

PLATE 13, *No.* 1.

Obv. George II. habited as a Roman Emperor, presents a medal to a kneeling Officer.

Leg. PRO TALIBUS AUSIS (For such enterprises).
Exergue. T. PINGO F.

---

[1] *Madras in the Olden Time*, by J. Talboys Wheeler, vol. ii. p. 289.

Rev. A squadron of ships preparing to attack five galleys at anchor near the shore.

Exergue. OB . V . TRIREM . HISPAN . A . S . CALLIS . COMBVST . V . IVLII . MDCCXLII (On account of five Spanish galleys burnt by S. Callis, 5th July, 1742.)

Circular, 2·1 inches. Gold.
Artist. T. Pingo.
Med. Ill. vol. ii. p. 568, No. 203.

Captain Callis, in his fireship, the *Duke*, destroyed five Spanish galleys which had put into St. Tropez, in Provence. On 5th July, 1742, he personally reported his proceedings at the Admiralty, and a few days afterwards was ordered a reward of one hundred pounds.

The regulation reward for captains of fireships appears at this period to have been a gratuity of £100, *or* a gold medal and chain of that value. We may infer, therefore, that the sum awarded to Captain Callis was devoted to the provision of his medal and chain.

The date on the medal is a mistake, being that of Callis's report to the Admiralty and not that of the action, which took place before 14th June, 1742. It is said that the medal in silver was given to other officers who were present. (*Med. Ill.* vol. ii. p. 568, No. 203.)

Captain Callis's medal was formerly in the collection of Captain John Hamilton.

ADMIRALTY MINUTES.

'MUNDAY, 5 *July*, 1742.

'Captain Callis and Captain Osborne attending were called in, and Captain Callis gave an account of his having left Vice-Admiral Mathews 19 days ago at Villa Franca, and of his having burnt his own Fireship in setting 5 Gallies on Fire at St. Tropez in Provence; he also informed the Lords that he saw a Privatier at Helvoet Sluys, whose Officers and Crew were all French.'

'THURSDAY, 29 *July*, 1742.

'*Resolved* that the Navy Board be directed to pay one hundred Pounds to Captain Smith Callis as an encouragement for his Conduct and Bravery in burning five Spanish Gallies in the Port of St. Tropez in the Mediterranean.'

An order of the King in Council, dated 16th December, 1742,[1] recites a Memorial from the Lords of the Admiralty of the 8th idem, to the effect that the rules established in the Navy allowed a reward of £100, or a medal of gold with a chain of the same value, to the Captain of a Fireship who should burn a

[1] See Section of Introduction relative to Rewards for Captains of Fireships.

ship of war of the enemy of 40 guns or more, and £10 to every person remaining in the Fireship till the service was performed; and Captain Callis, who commanded the Fireship *Duke*, having lately received the said reward for burning five galleys of the enemy at St. Tropez; Lieutenant John Greene of the said Fireship had applied for some consideration; their Lordships represented that when the aforesaid rewards were established, Fireships had no Lieutenants, and they proposed that a reward of £50 should be paid to Lieutenant Greene, and that a like reward should be established for all Lieutenants of Fireships for the future. The Order states that His Majesty was pleased to approve of the said rewards, and that the Lords Commissioners were to give directions accordingly.[1]

No. 114.

RICHARD HORNBY, 1744.

GOLD MEDAL AND CHAIN.

AT THE COURT AT KENSINGTON, the 18th day of September, 1744.

'*Present.*

'THE KING'S MOST EXCELLENT MAJESTY.

'Upon reading at the Board a Report from the Lords Commissioners of the Admiralty, dated the 17th of this Instant in the words following, vizt.—

"Having read a Petition from Richard Hornby Master of the Ship *Wrightson and Isabella* of Sunderland, Setting forth That the said Ship being loaded with Malt and Barley, Mann'd with five Men and three Boys besides the Petitioner and mounted with four Carriage and two Swivel Guns was on the 13th of June last N:S: attacked by a French Privateer of Ten Carriage and Eight Swivel Guns, and Seventy five men about four Leagues from Gravesand in Holland: That he engaged the said Privateer about Six Hours in which time he was boarded by her three times, and Defended his Ship so well with his Small Crew, that, after having killed a number of the Privateers Men (without having lost any of his own Crew or any one wounded except himself) he obliged her to Sheer off and by a Shott he fired in at the stern of the said Privateer at the

---

[1] MEDALS TO CAPTAINS TALBOT AND MORECOCK ON CAPTURE OF SPANISH SHIPS, 1745.

See *Med. Ill.* vol. ii. p. 597, No. 246.

There is no apparent evidence that this medal was presented to the two captains by the Crown or any other high authority. It seems to have been purely a 'commemorative' medal.

'Another Medal on the Capture of the Spanish ships, the *Marquis d'Antin* and the *Lewis Erasmus*, by Captains Talbot and Morecock, 1745, *s.* 1·45, *both very fine and rare.*' (See Lot 250—Catalogue, Leycester's sale at Sotheby's, June, 1888.)

Distance of about One hundred Yards, blew her up and all her crew Perished; And praying that as by destroying the said Privateer, he has done his Country a real Service and prevented several Captures she might probably have made of the ships of your Majesty's Subjects he may have a suitable Reward. And the credit of the above Action being Attested by Several of the Principal Merchants of the City of London We humbly take leave to lay before your Majesty a Copy of the aforesaid Petition and to represent to your Majesty that it hath been usual both in King William's and Queen Anne's Wars to reward Good Services done by your Majesty's Subjects in Private Ships against the Enemy by Gold Medals and Chains or Bounty in Money; And therefore We do humbly recommend the Petitioner and his crew to your Majesty's Royal Favour; and most humbly propose that your Majesty will be graciously pleased to Empower Us to Order a Gold Medal and Chain of the value of one hundred Pounds to be given to the said Richard Hornby, and a Bounty of five pounds to each of his men and Forty Shillings to the three Boys as a Reward of their Bravery and to encourage others under the like circumstances to exert themselves in the Defence of their Ships and the Destruction of the Enemy."

'His Majesty in Council this day took the said Report into consideration, and is pleased in regard to the good service performed by the Master and Crew of the said Ship *Wrightson and Isabella* in Sinking the said Privateer, and as an encouragement to others under the like circumstances to exert themselves in the Defence of their Ships and the Destruction of the Enemy, to Order, as it is hereby Ordered, that a Gold Medal and Chain of the Value of one hundred pounds be given to the said Master Richard Hornby, and a Bounty of five pounds to each of his Men, and Forty Shillings to each of the three Boys. And the Lords Commissioners of the Admiralty are to give the necessary Directions for paying the same to them accordingly.'

No. 115.

DUKE OF CUMBERLAND.

CULLODEN, 16TH APRIL, 1746.

PLATE 13, *No.* 2.

Obv. Bust of the Duke of Cumberland, *r.*, hair short, no drapery.

Leg. CUMBERLAND. Below, YEO . F (Richard Yeo, *fecit*).

Rev. Apollo, laureate, leaning upon his bow, points to the dragon wounded by his arrow.

Leg. ACTUM . EST . ILICET . PERIIT (The deed is done; it is all over; he has perished).

Exergue. PRŒL . COLOD . AP . XVI . MDCCXLVI (The battle of Culloden, 16th April, 1746).

Oval, 1·75 by 1·45 inch. Gold, silver, copper.
Ornament at border, with ring for suspension.
Artist. Richard Yeo.

Med. Ill. vol. ii. p. 615, No. 283.
Scott. Med. xv. 3.

No. 116.

SUBADAR MEER MUNSOOR, 1753.

GOLD CHAIN AND MEDAL.

Obv. The arms of the East Indian Company.

Leg. 'The gift of the Honorable United East India Company.'

Rev. Effigies of Subadar Meer Munsoor, with a drawn sword in his hand.

The following, purporting to be an extract from the *Proceedings* of the Madras Government, is taken from Wilson's *History of the Madras Army*, vol. i. p. 73. The entry does not appear in the copy of the *Madras Public Proceedings* for 5th November, 1753, amongst the India Office Records.

'FORT ST. GEORGE, 5 *Nov.*, 1753.

'Meer Munsoor, a Subadar of Sepoys, having on many occasions behaved with remarkable bravery, and received many desperate wounds without having ever had any particular reward, it is agreed that he be presented with a Gold Chain and Medal, with the Company's arms on one side, and this legend: "The gift of the Honorable United East India Company," and on the *reverse*, his own effigies with a drawn sword in his hand.'

No. 117.

MAHOMED ISOUF CAWN BAHAUDER, 1755.

GOLD MEDAL.

Obv. The arms and motto of the East India Company.

Rev. 'To Mahomed Isouf Cawn Bahauder, Commander of the Honorable English Company's Sepoys, this Medal is given by the Honorable the Governor and Council of Fort Saint George, as a reward to courage, and to preserve to posterity the name of a brave soldier, a skilful officer and a faithful servant.'

The above description is taken from Wilson's *History of the Madras Army* (vol. i. p. 183), from which also are derived the following particulars regarding the individual on whom the medal was conferred.

Mahomed Yusuff Khan enlisted under Clive in 1752, and distinguished himself on several occasions. In 1754 he was made Commandant of all the Company's Sepoys as a reward for his services against the French. He appears to have remained a favourite of the Government, and to have been for some years employed in important civil and military capacities. His prosperity and ambition tempted him, however, to raise the standard of rebellion against the Government. His forces numbered several thousands, and in 1763 he seized the town of

Madura, where he successfully resisted one siege by the British force sent against him. A second siege was begun in April of the following year, and lasted until October, when, after a blockade of several months, provisions getting scarce, and discontent consequently arising, Mahomed Yusuff was seized by some of the French in his employ, who surrendered the town and delivered him to the English, by whom he was promptly hanged. The latter part of his career did not therefore verify the closing words of the inscription on the medal.

No. 118.

CAPTAIN ANDREW BUCHANAN, 1756.

GOLD MEDAL.

In the *History of the Mahrattas*, by James Grant Duff, it is stated (ii. 91) that Captain Andrew Buchanan was presented with a gold medal by the Government of Bombay as a reward for having refused a bribe to allow the enemy admission to the Fort of Gheriah, which was being besieged by the British. The author observes that Ramajee Pant 'made secret overtures to Captain Andrew Buchanan, the officer on picket, offering him a Bill on Bombay for Rs. 80,000, if he would permit him and a few of his people to pass into the fort, an offer which was rejected as became a British officer; but it is a circumstance worthy of notice, as elucidating the character of the times, that the Bombay Government thought common honesty so rare, as to present Captain Buchanan with a Gold Medal, in consideration of his his extraordinary good behaviour.'

No. 119.

AMERICAN INDIAN CHIEFS, 1757.

PLATE 13, *No.* 3.

Obv. Bust of George II., *l.*, laureate, hair long, in armour and mantle.

Leg. GEORGIVS . II . DEI . GRATIA.

Rev. A European seated under a tree holds out the pipe of peace to an Indian who, seated opposite to him, points to the meridian sun; a fire between them.

Leg. LET US LOOK TO THE MOST HIGH WHO BLESSED OUR FATHERS WITH PEACE.

Exergue. 1757.

Circular, 1·75 inch. Silver.

Med. Ill. vol. ii. p. 682, No. 399.

This medal was given to American Indian Chiefs.

No. 120.

SIR ALEXANDER SCHOMBERG,
GEORGE YOUNG, MIDSHIPMAN, } 1758.

GOLD MEDAL.

Obv. A sailor and a soldier supporting a globe inscribed CANADA AMERICA, above supporters PARITER . IN . BELLA (*sic*), under globe prostrate figure of France.
Rev. Fort firing on the *Prudent* and the *Bienfaisant*.

Leg. LOVISBOURG . TAKEN . MDCCLVIII.

Circular, 1.7 inch.
Struck.
Ring for suspension.
Blue and yellow ribbon.
Artist. Thomas Pingo.

This medal was presented to Sir Alexander Schomberg for his distinguished services at the second siege of Louisbourg, in command of the *Diana* frigate, 36 guns. The medal is in the possession of his great-grandson, Lieutenant-Colonel Schomberg, Royal Marine Light Infantry.

It was also awarded to Senior Midshipman George Young, afterwards Sir George Young. He was serving on board the *York*, under Captain, afterwards Sir Hugh Pigot, and was in charge of one of the boats 'which carrying in all 600 men, started at midnight on 26th July, 1758, and divided into two squadrons, one of which, led by Laforey, attacked the *Prudent*, the other under Balfour surrounded the *Bienfaisant*. Giving three hearty cheers in reply to the fire of the sentinels, on the order being given, the crews seizing their arms with the most intrepid activity followed their brave leaders and boarded the ships on each bow, quarter, and gangway. Both ships were taken, with the loss to us of one officer and three or four seamen.'[1]

This notable exploit, performed under the batteries of Louisbourg, is the subject of a contemporary oil-painting in the possession of the present Baronet, Sir George Young, who says in a letter to *The Times*, 2nd July, 1895: 'The story is told that long after, when the Revolution had driven many naval officers from their country, one of them was brought by a neighbour to luncheon with Sir George Young at Formosa, who, entering the dining-room threw up his hands, exclaiming, "Ah, voilà mon pauvre *Prudent*!" He had been a midshipman on the ship that was destroyed.' The picture was painted by Swaine, from a sketch by Sir George Young. The medal is in the possession of his descendants.

[1] Brown's *History of Cape Breton*, p. 314. Two other specimens of this medal in gold are known, one is in the Montague Collection, and one was sold at Sotheby's, 27th June, 1895. The celebrated navigator Captain Cook won his first laurels at Louisbourg, as petty officer on board one of our ships of war.

No. 121.

BULWAN SING, 1760.

GOLD MEDAL.

On 5th March, 1760, a force under Colonel Eyre Coote captured the Fort of Permacoil in the Carnatic. In his report to Government Colonel Coote wrote: 'The good behaviour of the Sepoys was more remarkable than anything I could conceive. I have ordered a gold medal to be made for Bulwan Sing, a Commandant of Sepoys, who led the attack the night we took possession of the hill.'

See Wilson's *History of the Madras Army*, i. 135, and *Medals and Honorary Distinctions*, by Colonel F. B. Norman. *Journal of the United Service Institution of India*, xii. 145.

There does not appear to be anything on the subject in the *Madras Public Consultations* for 1760.

No. 122.

CAPTAIN WILLIAM WILSON, 1760.

GOLD MEDAL.

Obv. Neptune, seated, *r.*, upon a rock, points out to Mercury (Commerce) a new route to China amidst a cluster of islands.

Leg. ITERARE CVRSVS RELICTOS (To renew abandoned courses).

Ex. MDCCLX. R . YEO . F.

Rev. Ins. THE . GIFT . OF . THE . ENG . EAST . INDIA . COMP . TO . CAPTAIN . WILLIAM . WILSON . COMMANDER . OF . THE . SHIP . PITT . AS . AN . ACKNOWLEDGEMENT . OF . HIS . SERVICES . IN . HAVING . MADE . HIS . PASSAGE . TO . AND . FROM . CHINA . BY . AN . UNUSUAL . COURSE . AND . THEREBY . EVINCING . THAT . NAVIGATION . TO . BE . PRACTICABLE . AT . ANY . SEASON . OF . THE . YEAR.

Circular, 2·7 inches.
Artist. Richard Yeo.
Med. Ill. vol. ii. p. 709, No. 446.

The grant of this medal by the East India Company is recorded in the subjoined Resolution of the Court of Directors. As there is no mention of a chain, it seems doubtful whether, having regard to its large size, the medal was intended to be worn as a decoration.

AT A COURT OF DIRECTORS, Thursday, 26th June, 1760.

'On reading two Reports from the Committee of Shipping, dated the 20th and 25th Instant,

'*Resolved by the Ballott*, That Captain William Wilson be appointed to succeed Captain Francis Cheyne resigned, as Assistant to the Master Attendant, at the Salary of £100 p. annum, to commence from the 24th Instant.

'It was then on a Motion,

'*Ordered*, That the Thanks of this Court be given to Captain Wilson for his valuable services in gaining his passage from Fort St. George to China in the ship *Pitt* at an uncommon season and by a new track greatly to the advantage of the Company, and

'That it be referred to the Committee of Treasury to provide a Medal of One hundred Guineas value, with a suitable inscription thereon, to be presented to him in token of the Court's sense of his merits.

'Captain Wilson being then called in the Chairman gave him the Court's Thanks accordingly, acquainted him with the Present voted him, and with his appointment of Assistant to the Master Attendant, whereupon he was sworn as such.'

No. 123.

AMERICAN INDIAN CHIEFS.

PLATE 14, *No.* 1.

Obv. Bust of George III., *r.*, hair long, in armour, ribbon across breast over left shoulder.

Leg. GEORGIUS III DEI GRATIA.

Rev. The Royal arms, with crown and supporters.

Circular, 3 inches. Silver, pewter.

This is one variety of the large medals made for issue to North American Indian Chiefs. It does not appear to have been struck at the Royal Mint.[1] (See No. 119.)

[1] In connection with the Indian Chief Medals the following extracts from *The Times* are of interest:—

'A correspondent writes:—The death is recorded of Wa-Bun-ah-Kee, chief of the Mansea tribe of Delaware Indians and of the "Six Nations," in his 77th year. This remarkable man was a native of Orford, Ontario, Canada, and was of distinguished Indian ancestry. He was descended from the original owners and occupiers of Canadian territory, a race of people who had had hard times since their country was overrun by European settlers, many of them braving all risks and dangers, even to extermination, rather than submit to a foreign yoke. Wanbuno, as his name was pronounced for brevity, was a trophy of Christian civilisation, becoming an eloquent preacher, and doing a large amount of good amongst his own people by dissuading them from the use of the "fire-water" imported by Europeans. He was a prominent official in the Good Templars' Grand Lodge of Canada. He recently visited England, and was present at the Crystal Palace temperance *fête* in his native costume. His cap and feathers were worn by his father in the celebrated battle of 1812; the medal on his right breast was presented to his father by General Brock after peace was proclaimed, and that on his left breast was given to his grandfather by command of George III. for his services in the war of 1796. The tomahawk, as a peace token, was given to Wanbuno's father by the great warrior Tecumseh, who fought in the same battle with him, and whose doings are chronicled in every history of America. Wanbuno was, indeed, a celebrated man, and his later days were devoted to the advocacy of temperance and peace principles. He used to boast that the tribe to which he belonged was one of the tribes that signed the celebrated Penn Treaty, and that they had never broken it.'—(*7th June*, 1892.)

'Mr. Duncan Milligan, F.R.A.S., writing with reference to Wau-bun-o, Delaware Indian, a notice of whose death appeared in *The Times* a few days ago, says he

No. 124.

CARIB REBELLION, 1773.

Obv. Bust of George III., *r.*, in armour, with ribbon over left shoulder.

Leg. GEORGIVS . III . MB . REX.

Rev. Britannia standing, having her right hand on the Union Shield, and holding out in her left hand a branch of olive to a Carib, who, in token of submission, has placed at her feet his musket, bow and arrows.

Leg. PEACE AND PROSPERITY TO ST. VINCENTS.

Ex. MDCCLXXIII.

Circular, 2·2 inches. Silver.
Mounted with ring for suspension.

This medal is said to have been awarded by the Legislative Assembly of the Island of St. Vincent to the militia and volunteers, as a reward for their services in suppressing the rebellion of the Caribs in that island in 1772-3.[1]

No. 125.

CAPTAIN EWING, 1775.

STAR.

PLATE 14, *No.* 2.

A star, 2 inches diameter, four pointed, with flames between the points.

Obv. The monogram G. R., surmounted by a crown, and surrounded by the words, A TESTIMONY OF PUBLIC REGARD.

---

was born at Muncey town, Ontario, Canada, in 1815. He was hereditary chief of the Delawares there, but of late he resided with his wife on his Indian farm at Moravian town, another Indian reserve. Waubuno is a distinct Indian name, and means morning. He belonged to the Waubuno Kie, or Eastern nations, who lived in Waubun or East. He, all his life, spoke against the "fire-water" amongst his people, who are simple, industrious, and successful farmers. He had nothing in common with the six nation confederacy, which consists of Mohawk, Senecas, Onandagas, Cayugas, Tuscaroras, and Oneidas, who have their own reserves at Brantford, and elect their own council chiefs annually. Being a Delaware, he never could have been a six nation chief. The medal given to his father by General Brock was destroyed by fire when his house was burned out years ago. He wore not only the George III. medal, given to his grandfather in 1796, but also the medal given to his great-grandfather by William Penn as being a signatory to the famous treaty. He was not descended from the Indians who originally owned Canada or any part of it, but from those who owned that part of the United States where William Penn settled. Waubuno visited England five years ago, when Mr. Milligan organised his mission for him. During that time he travelled 6000 miles, opened six bazaars, addressed 200 meetings, collected £300 to build a mission school for Munceyo, and £200 to rebuild his burnt house. As a Christian total abstainer he was a remarkable Indian and was all one could say of him, but he was almost the only Indian who, visiting these shores, was proof against English customs and kept his pledge inviolate.'—(*9th June*, 1892.)

[1] See Tancred's *Historical Record of Medals*, pp. 47, 48. In the engraving of the medal there given, the date shown in the *exergue* of the *reverse* is MDCLLXXIII., a mistake for MDCCLXXIII.

Rev. Ins. 'By Order of the King with 300 Pound for the Wound Capt Ewing Recvd the 17 of June, 1775.'

This is an unusual style of decoration. Who Captain Ewing was, or where he received his wound, is not stated. The 17th June, 1775, is the date of the battle of Bunker's Hill, but the name of Ewing does not appear in the list of officers (army and marines) who were killed or wounded. The list is appended to the despatch of Lieutenant-General the Hon. Thomas Gage, who commanded the British force, published in the *London Gazette*, 22-25 July, 1775.

This badge was formerly in the Collection of Captain John Hamilton.

No. 126.

BOMBAY GRENADIER SEPOYS, 1779.

BADGES.

In November, 1778, a force was despatched from Bombay to Poona, under the command of Colonel Egerton, for the purpose of supporting the pretensions of Rugonath Row as Peishwa. Owing to mismanagement the expedition was a failure, and on 11th January, 1779, a retreat was ordered. In the retreat the six companies of native grenadiers, referred to in the following extract of a General Order by the Bombay Select Committee, behaved with great gallantry:—

GENERAL ORDER OF THE BOMBAY SELECT COMMITTEE,
3rd February, 1779.

. . . .

'The Governor and the Select Committee do, in general, return their thanks to the whole of the officers, whose behaviour has been commended in the above Orders; and if any instance of particular good behaviour has escaped their notice, they will with great pleasure rectify the omission.

'The Governor and the Select Committee also order, that their thanks be returned to the Six Companies of Grenadier Sepoys that composed Captain Hartley's Division, for their gallant behaviour on the 12th ultimo, and that badges be given them to commemorate the honor they gained on that occasion.' (See p. 22 of Journal of the march of the Bombay Detachment in 1778 under Colonel Goddard; and the proceedings of the Bombay Army in their march towards Poona under Colonel Egerton. I. O. Library, *Tracts*, vol. 389.)

What form the badges took, or whether they were ever issued, we have not been able to discover. Nothing is said on the subject in the *Proceedings* of either the Governor and Select Committee, or the Governor in Council, for the year 1779.

There is, however, a possibility that the Badge was the *White Horse* referred to in the following correspondence with the Bombay Government. The *White Horse* appears to have been borne on the Colours of the 1st Bombay Grenadiers as early as, if not before, 1788, and to have continued in use for many years. Unfortunately, the records of the regiment, which might have afforded all necessary information, were destroyed by fire at Bombay in 1830, and nothing certain can now be ascertained regarding its origin.

FROM THE SECRETARY OF STATE FOR INDIA TO THE GOVERNMENT OF BOMBAY,

8th August, 1889, No. 49—Military.

'The Horse Guards having made inquiry as to the origin of the use of the white horse as a regimental badge by the 1st Bombay Grenadiers, I request that you will furnish such information on the subject as may be procurable.

'The earliest historical record of the regiment is apparently the G. O. of 13th November, 1788, quoted at page 2 of the Enclosures to the Despatch of the Government of India, No. 184, of 8th October, 1888, and in this the white horse is mentioned as if it were the badge already in use. I shall be glad to have a full copy of this G. O. which presumably showed the badges of the several regiments of the Bombay Army.

'A memorandum in reference to the Bombay Grenadiers, and the possible origin of the badge, is enclosed.'

ENCLOSURE.

'1st Bombay Native Infantry (Grenadiers).

'The Bombay Army List states that this regiment was raised 12th November, 1779.

'It appears to have been directed by Bombay General Order,[1] 12th November, 1779, that the Grenadier companies of the 1st, 2nd, 3rd, 4th, 5th, and 6th Regiments, Bombay Native Infantry, together with two companies of Grenadiers from the Marine Battalion, should be formed into one battalion. This battalion was apparently numbered the 8th of Bombay Native Infantry.

'In Bombay General Order,[2] 23rd November, 1783, it was stated that the 8th Battalion of Sepoys having been originally composed of Grenadiers, and having always distinguished themselves by the most exemplary valour and discipline, the President and Select Committee directed that, in consideration of their good services, and their solicitations for the honour, they should be again established into a Grenadier corps, to be called "The Bombay Grenadiers."

'Bombay General Order,[3] 18th September, 1788, directed that "the Grenadier Battalion having particularly distinguished themselves, are to be kept together, the 1st Battalion of Bombay Native Infantry, or Bombay Grenadiers, to be selected and formed from it." From September, 1788, it is accordingly presumed that the Grenadier Battalion became the 1st Battalion of the Bombay Native Infantry.

'Bombay General Order,[4] 21st July, 1796, directed that the 12 Battalions of

---

[1] Moor's *Bombay Army Regulations*, 1801, xxxii. 6.

[2] *Ibid.* xxxii. 6.   [3] *Ibid.* xxxii. 9.   [4] *Ibid.* xxxii. 17.

Native Infantry were to be newly regimented, and that the Grenadier Battalion (eight companies) with the two flank companies of the 10th Battalion, were to form the 1st or Grenadier Battalion of Native Infantry.

'With regard to the use of the *white horse* as a regimental badge by the battalion, the earliest mention appears to be in the General Order, 13th November, 1788 (at which date the battalion had become the 1st or Grenadier Battalion), quoted in the letter from the Adjutant-General, Bombay, 5th November, 1887, printed at page 1 of the enclosures to the Despatch of the Government of India of 8th October, 1888, No. 184. It is presumed that had there been anything on the regimental records beyond the quoted extract of the above General Order it would have been duly referred to by the Bombay authorities.

'The following is a *possible* explanation of the origin of the white horse badge:—

'As already shown, the 8th Bombay Battalion, afterwards the 1st, or Grenadier Battalion, was, at its formation in November, 1779, composed, as respects three-fourths of its men, of the Grenadier companies of the 1st, 2nd, 3rd, 4th, 5th, and 6th Battalions. Now it so happens that in the ill-fated expedition which was despatched from Bombay to Poona at the end of 1778, in the interest of Rugonath Row, there were six companies of select Grenadier Sepoys commanded by Captain Stewart, and after his death by Captain Hartley. In the retreat from Poona on 11th January, 1779, these six companies under Captain Hartley formed the rearguard and behaved with great gallantry, so much so that the Bombay authorities, *i.e.*, the Governor and the Select Committee, in their General Order of 3rd February, 1779, in which they promoted Captain Hartley and other officers for their good services, ordered that "their thanks be returned to the six companies of Grenadier Sepoys that composed Captain Hartley's division, for their gallant behaviour on the 12th ultimo, and that badges be given to them to commemorate the honour they gained on that occasion." This General Order does not appear in the volume of the *Proceedings* of the Select Committee for 1779 on record in this Office. It is however printed at p. 22 of a pamphlet, entitled "Journal of the march of the Bombay Detachment in 1778 under Colonel Goddard; and the proceedings of the Bombay Army under Colonel Egerton in their march towards Poona." (Indian Office Library, *Tracts*, vol. 389.)

'What form this badge took, if ever it was issued, is not known, but having regard to the circumstances, it seems not improbable that it may have been the white horse. In this way the badge, personal originally to the Grenadiers of the six companies, may have become the regimental badge of the 8th, and subsequently of the 1st Bombay Native Infantry.

'But apart from this conjecture, it would be interesting to know whether the intention of bestowing a badge on the six companies of Grenadiers was carried into effect at the time, and, if so, what was the nature of the badge. Perhaps the records at Bombay may throw some light on the point.

'MILITARY DEPARTMENT, INDIA OFFICE,
24th July, 1889.'

FROM THE GOVERNMENT OF BOMBAY TO THE SECRETARY OF STATE FOR INDIA,

23rd January, 1890, No. 8—Military.

'Refering to your Lordship's Despatches noted in the margin,[1] we have the honour

---

[1] Despatch No. 49, dated 8th August, 1819, para. 2 (M.-6359). Despatch No. 63, dated 17th October, 1889, para. 2 (M.-8027).

to forward copy of a correspondence[1] relating to the badge of the "White Horse," borne on the Colors of the 1st Bombay Grenadiers, and to state that no further information on the subject is forthcoming.'

ENCLOSURES.

'*Letter from the Adjutant-General, Poona, to the Secretary to Government, Military Department, Bombay, No.* 1550—9389, *dated* 11*th October*, 1889.

'With reference to Government Resolution No. 2861 of the 11th ultimo, I have the honour to forward the documents noted in the margin.'[2]

'*Letter from the Officer Commanding* 1*st Bombay Grenadiers, to the Adjutant-General, Poona, No.* 23—620, *dated Ahmednagar,* 5*th October*, 1889.

'In reply to your No. 1550—8432, dated 14th instant, and annexure herewith returned, I have the honour to forward, for your information, extracts from the "Digest of Services" of the Regiment under my Command relating to the badge of the "White Horse."

'2. This badge appears to have been borne on the Colours of the Regiment "at the siege of Mangalore (in the year 1782) and for many years subsequently," but no certain information as to its origin is to be found in the records. This is probably due to the fact of the original regimental records having been destroyed by fire in Bombay in the year 1830. The present records were compiled in the year 1860 by Lieut.-Colonel Honner who commanded the Regiment at the time.'

'WHITE HORSE.

'*Extract from the Digest of Services of the* 1*st Bombay Infantry* (*Grenadiers*).

'At this period of the Regiment's service, at the siege of Mangalore, and for many years subsequent to that event, the emblem of a "White Horse" was borne on the Colours, but no certain information can be obtained on the point.'[3]

'*Extract from letter from Lieut.-Colonel Dyson,* 1*st Battalion,* 1*st Grenadier Regiment, to Lieut.-Colonel Sir Willoughby Cotton, Aide-de-Camp to His Majesty and Commanding at Poona, dated Poona, December* 23*rd*, 1822.

'The Battalion was raised in the year 1779 and composed of eight companies of Grenadiers from the Battalions of the Bombay Army. It was sent to Malabar and gained the highest encomium for valour and discipline. When Mangalore was besieged by Tippoo's Army in 1782 (1783-4?) the Grenadier Battalion formed part of the garrison with His Majesty's 73rd and 42nd Regiments of Foot and was highly commended for its good behaviour and by General McLeod and Colonel Campbell.[4]

'At this period, as I have learned from the Native officers, a "White Horse" was on the Colours of the Battalion, and that emblem was continued for many years subsequent.'

---

[1] Letter from the Adjutant-General, No. 1550—9389, dated 11th October, 1889, with enclosures. Memorandum by Adjutant-General, No. 1550—11401, dated 10th December, 1889, with enclosures.

[2] 1. Letter 23—620, 5th October, 1889, from the Officer Commanding 1st Bombay Infantry, with accompaniment. 2. Copy of G. O. dated 13th November, 1788.

[3] Page 32. 1782. November 29th. [4] Page 128.

'BOMBAY, 13*th November*, 1788.
Thursday, 13*th November.*

'*General Orders.*

'PAROLE, DRAPER
COUNTERSIGN, BRERETON.

'The distinctions fixed upon by the Commander-in-Chief for the Natives of the Sepoy Corps are as follows:—

'As the jackets for the first Brigade of Native Infantry are to be laced with yellow, the turbans are to be bound round the edge with lace of the same sort. The bands and tassels are also to be yellow. Two stripes of yellow lace are to be fastened to and go round the front of the cumberband, and the short drawers are to be ornamented at their termination with stripes of blue and yellow in the same manner as at present with blue and white.

'The second Brigade to have white lace applied exactly in the same manner as the first has yellow. The turbans will have white bands, and the short drawers will of course remain as they are blue and white.

'The turbans and cumberbands of the whole, exclusive of the ornamental distinctions, are to remain blue.

'Fronts of black leather (filled up at the back with black feathers or with a fringe of black cotton thread) similar in shape to those now worn by the first or Grenadier Battalion and fastened to the turban in the same manner are to be worn by all the Native Infantry. The number of the Battalion either in yellow or white metal, according to the colour of the lace, in Roman characters three-quarters of an inch long are to be fastened to the centre of each front, unless the Officers Commanding Corps choose to apply the badges affixed as follows hereafter and which are to be paid for out of the off-reckoning fund usually divided among the Captains Commanding Sepoy Battalions in the Companies' service on this establishment upon the fronts fastened to their men's turbans as above directed when they will be placed above the number, that is, for that purpose to be brought lower down than if there be no badge. If badges are adopted, the 4th and 10th Battalions will require no detached number, they will be conspicuous in the centre of the stars. The badges may be painted or embroidered in the Regimental Colour of each Battalion. But when once decided and fixed upon by the Captains, it will always in future be expected they are kept up and adhered to strictly and with perfect uniformity.

'*Feathers.*

'Distinguishing plumes of feathers ordered to be worn in the hats and turbans of the officers, and plumes of cotton thread until feathers can conveniently be procured for the turbans of non-commissioned officers and privates of the Battalions of Native Infantry with the honorary badges allowed to be adopted by each different Corps.

'Battalions' feathers or plumes ordered, badge allowed:—

Battalions	Feathers or plumes	Badge
1st (or Grenadier)	White	White Horse.
7th ,,	Rings of black or yellow	Rays of Light.
2nd and 8th ,,	Red	Arrow.
3rd ,, 9th ,,	Blue	Crescent.
4th ,, 10th ,,	Yellow	Star.
5th ,, 11th ,,	Black	Battle Axe.
6th ,, 12th ,,	Red and orange in rings	Scimitar.
Marines	Black and blue in rings	Anchor.

'The Grenadiers of each Battalion to wear white plumes.

'The size and shape of the badges permitted may be seen at the Town Major's Office, and if not fixed upon and got ready as far as possible by the first of next

January, it is not intended they will be allowed in future. They are considered as honorary marks of distinction to the old Corps forming the peace establishment of this Presidency which is to be looked upon as a pattern to and a foundation for any greater establishment that may in future be necessary in case of war, and it is not intended that any new Corps shall be allowed badges until merited on service.

'(Signed) GEORGE HART,
'*Deputy Adjutant-General.*'

'*Memorandum from the Adjutant-General, No.* 1550—11401, *dated* 10*th December*, 1889.

'Submitted to Government with reference to Government Resolution No. 3598, 25th ultimo.'

'*Letter from the Officer Commanding* 1*st Regiment, Bombay Infantry* (*Grenadiers*), *to the District Staff Officer, Poona District, No.* 23—818, *dated Ahmednager,* 4*th December*, 1889.

'I have the honour to acknowledge the receipt of your No. 501-D., dated 28th November, 1889, forwarding Deputy Adjutant-General's endorsement on Government Resolution, Military Department, No. 3598, dated Bombay Castle, 25th November, 1889, and in reply I have the honour to state as follows :—

'2. The badge of the "White Horse" was granted to the 1st Bombay Grenadiers in G. O. 13th November, 1788, and was subsequently borne on the Regimental Colour, but there is no record to show when or how it was discontinued.

'3. From careful enquiries I have made from various sources and reference to other Corps, there appears no doubt whatever that the "White Horse of Hanover" (Courant) as shown in my sketch referred to, is the correct device and not the "Kentish White Horse."

'4. Regarding the motto *Nec aspera terrent* it appears to belong to the badge—*vide* copy of extract from records (attached) and Section I, Queen's Regulation, Precedence and Distinctions of Corps.'

'*Extract from Records.*

'In the year 1700 a medal was struck at Hanover to commemorate the accession of the Electorate of George Lewis, Duke of Hanover, afterwards King George the First. This medal bears on one side the head of the Elector and on the reverse "The White Horse" with the circumscription *Nec aspera terrent.* After the accession of the House of Hanover to the Imperial Crown of Great Britain and Ireland, the "White Horse" was introduced as a Royal badge in the standards of certain Regiments of Cavalry and Infantry.'

No. 127.

WEST OF INDIA AND GUZERAT, 1778-84,

AND

CARNATIC, 1780-84.

PLATE 15, *Nos.* 1 *and* 2.

Obv. Figure of Britannia seated on a military trophy, with her right hand holding out a wreath of laurel towards a Fort on which the British flag is flying.

Rev. Persian inscription:—In centre, 'Presented by the Calcutta Government in memory of good service and intrepid valour, A.D. 1784, A.H. 1199.' Around, 'Like this coin may it endure in the world, and the exertions of those lion-hearted Englishmen of great name, victorious from Hindostan to the Deccan, become exalted.' (Translations.)

Circular, 1·6 inch. Gold, silver. 1·25 inch. Silver.
Worn suspended round the neck by a cord through a ring or loop at the top of the medal.

This medal was given to native troops only, and it is the earliest Anglo-Indian example distributed to all ranks. It appears to have been awarded to the native portions of the two large detachments of the Bengal Army, denominated the 'Bombay Detachment' and the 'Carnatic Detachment,' which respectively took part in the campaigns in the west of India and Guzerat, 1778-84, and in the south of India, 1780-84.

THE BOMBAY DETACHMENT.

The authority for the grant of a medal to the 'Bombay Detachment' for its services in the campaign in Guzerat and the Northern Concan, is a minute of the Governor-General and Council of 19th January, 1784, in reference to certain recommendations which the Commander-in-Chief had submitted regarding the detachment which, originally commanded by General Goddard, but afterwards by Colonel Morgan, was then on its return to Bengal. One of the recommendations was that each Subadar should be awarded a gold medal; each Jemadar, a silver one; and that similar badges of inferior value should be given to the Non-warrant Officers and Sepoys.

This proposal was adopted, and negotiations were entered into with the firm of Young & Shepperd, of Calcutta, which resulted in that firm undertaking to make the medals at a charge, exclusive of the gold and silver, of half a rupee each. The dies were made by Mr. Shepperd at a cost of Rs. 600. The choice of a design was left to the Commander-in-Chief.

Hindoos of the Bombay Detachment who received this medal were, by Minute of Council of 15th July, 1784, exempted from payment of the duties levied by the authorities at Gya, the Hindoo Jerusalem.

THE CARNATIC DETACHMENT.

The medal for this detachment, commanded by Colonel Pearse, was authorised by a Minute of the Governor-General in

Council, dated 22nd January, 1785, in terms very similar to those used in reference to the Bombay Detachment. Subadars were granted gold, and Jemadars silver medals, and the lower ranks similar badges of inferior value. A subsequent Minute of 28th January, 1785, extended the grant to the artillery Lascars.

Swords of honour for this service were awarded to Colonel Pearse, and his second and third in command.

This medal has by some persons been denominated the 'Deccan,' probably because that word occurs in the inscription. Were there anything to connect the representation on the medal with the fortress of Ahmedabad in Guzerat, it would be conclusive that the medal was designed to commemorate the services of the Bombay Detachment, by which the capture of that fortress was effected, and not those of the Carnatic Detachment. The design, however, is emblematic, and though it may have originally been intended to refer to Ahmedabad, yet if other towns were taken in the course of the operations of the two Detachments, it would be as applicable in one case as in another.

A fact which would seem to identify the medal with the Bombay Detachment is that the date in the inscription, viz., 1784, is that of the grant of the medal to that Detachment; whereas the grant to the Carnatic Detachment did not take place until the following year.

Captain Buckle, in his *Memoirs of the Bengal Artillery* (p. 98), says he was 'informed by an old native officer that the medal was of the same pattern for both Detachments.'

On the whole, it seems reasonable to conjecture that, although the medal may have been originally prepared specially for the Bombay Detachment, yet, the design being of a general character, and the inscription not inappropriate, the Government afterwards decided that it should do service for the Carnatic Detachment likewise. The same firm was employed in both instances, and the dies of the medals probably remained in their hands. They are not at the Calcutta Mint.

Specimens of both sizes of the medal are in the British Museum. Attached to one is the following memorandum:— 'Medal given by ye Governor of Madras to ye Officers of ye troops who marched from Bengal, relieved that fortress, and gained other victories in the ye Carnatic, which are recorded in the

Persian characters on the reverse. Given to me by Sir John MacPherson, 20th Nov. 1787.' This supports the evidence of the native officer recorded by Buckle.

In connection with the manufacture of the medals, it appears that the contractors, Messrs. Young & Shepperd, thought, from the extraordinary softness of the gold and silver in India, that the medals might easily be struck with one blow of a hammer. They found, however, to their disappointment, that a dozen blows at least were required, and that the dies from which they intended to strike all the medals would be totally spoiled after striking fifty or sixty. They therefore declared it would be necessary to have the assistance of a large mint press, which they undertook to procure if the Government would allow them one rupee, instead of half a rupee per medal as was originally stipulated for striking. To this the Government agreed.

PROCEEDINGS OF THE GOVERNOR-GENERAL AND COUNCIL, GENERAL DEPARTMENT, *19th January*, 1784.

THE BOMBAY DETACHMENT.

'*The Governor General.*—As the Detachment from Surat under the Command of Colonel Morgan is on its approach to its destination to the Line of our own Provinces, the Governor-General informs the Board that he has requested the presence of the Commander-in-Chief for the purpose of forming such a deduction in the Military Establishment as shall be judged advisable on its arrival.

'The General attends accordingly and produces the last return which he has received from the Detachment, showing the strength of the different corps of which it is formed, and recommends.

. . . . . .

'The Commander-in-Chief further recommends that Government express in public Orders the high sense which they entertain of the behaviour and services of the Native Corps composing this Detachment, and that as a lasting mark of their approbation, they bestow on each of the Sepoy Battalions a pair of Honorary Standards, on each of the Subadars a Gold Medal, and on each of the Jemadars a Silver one, with such device motto or inscription as shall be judged applicable to the occasion, and Medals of the same sort to the Native Officers of the Cavalry and Golundauze Company, also similar Badges of inferior value to such of the Non-Warrant and Privates as have served with the Detachment from the commencement of the Expedition to its return to the Doab. And that in order to show to the Army the determined resolution of Government to punish in an exemplary manner the disobedience and sedition of any part of their Forces, however late may be the opportunity, it be published in orders and explained at the different Stations of the Army the cause of the Dismission of the 4th, 15th, and 17th Regiments of Sepoys.

'The Board agree to the recommendations of the Commander-in-Chief, and request that he will issue the necessary orders for carrying the same into execution as soon after the arrival of the Detachment in the Doab as it can conveniently be done.'

(*Bengal General Consultations*, January, 1784, p. 334.)

PROCEEDINGS OF THE GOVERNOR-GENERAL AND COUNCIL, GENERAL DEPARTMENT, 28*th June*, 1784.

'The Secretary acquaints the Board that the Acting Adjutant-General is attending with a message from the Commander-in-Chief.

'Captain Murray being called in submits sundry devices to the Board for their selection of one to make the impression of a distinguishing medal to be worn by the Sepoys who have returned from the late campaign in the Carnatic.[1]

'The Board desire Captain Murray to signify their approbation of the idea to the Commander-in-Chief, to whose judgment they wish to leave the choice of the device.

'Captain Murray withdraws.'

(*Bengal General Consultations*, June, 1784, p. 41.)

PROCEEDINGS OF THE GOVERNOR-GENERAL AND COUNCIL, GENERAL DEPARTMENT, 15*th July*, 1784.

'Read a letter from the Collector at Gya, as follows :—

'Mr. Thos. Law, 29th June, 1784.

'Honble. Sir and Sirs,—The gallant behaviour and persevering attachment of the Sepoys of the Company's service in General Goddard's Detachment having been rewarded by the most flattering marks of distinction, permit me to suggest a still further encouragement to those possessed of the medals, by annexing to them, the invaluable benefit of an exemption from the Gya duties.

'The majority of the Native Troops, now consisting of Hindoos, this desired object will call forth distinguished exertions on future occasions ; it were superfluous to give instances of religious zeal superseding every other tie, or to state the spur it gives to every furious onset. This is the Hindoo Jerusalem.

'To prevent the abuse of this favour permit me to request that the Commanding Officer of each Regiment may be ordered to transmit me the names of the Sepoys honoured with Medals, that I may regularly mark off those who avail themselves of this additional reward.

'The Aumil has promised not to claim a deduction on this account.

'I am, etc.,

'GYA, 29*th June*, 1784.' 'THOMAS LAW, *Collector*.

'*Agreed*, that the additional encouragement which Mr. Law recommends to be shown to the Sepoys who have returned from the Campaign on the other side of India be authorised, and that the Commander-in-Chief be requested to direct the Officers commanding the different Corps which composed the Bombay Detachment, to furnish Lists of the Hindoo Sepoys belonging to that Detachment, who have been honored with Medals, and to transmit their names to Mr. Thomas Law, Resident at Gya, in order that they may be exempted from the Duties of that place as a further reward of their good conduct.

'*Ordered* that information be given to Mr. Law of the above, and that the Board's approval of the favor recommended by him be signified to him.'

(*Bengal General Consultations*, July, 1784, p. 339.)

PROCEEDINGS OF THE GOVERNOR-GENERAL AND COUNCIL, MILITARY DEPARTMENT, 22*d January*, 1785.

THE CARNATIC DETACHMENT.

'The Governor General proposes the enclosed Draft of a Minute to be issued by

---

[1] A mistake, apparently, for 'West of India,' as the medal for the Carnatic was not granted until 22nd January, 1785.

the Board on the occasion of the return of the Detachment which served in the Carnatic during the late War.

'*January 22d*, 1785.

'The Governor General and Council direct that their thanks be expressed in General Orders to Colonel Pearse and the European Officers, and to the Native Officers and Privates of the several corps composing the Detachment lately returned from the Carnatic, for their gallant behaviour and useful services in the defence of the Company's territories in the Carnatic during the course of a long and unequal war. And as a lasting mark of their approbation, they bestow on each of the Sepoy Regiments a pair of Honorary Standards, on each of the Subadars a Gold Medal, and on each of the Jemadars a Silver one, with such device, motto and inscription, as shall be judged applicable to the occasion, and Medals of the same cost to the Native Officers of the Golundange Company; also similar Badges of inferior value to such of the Non-Warrant Officers and Privates, as have served with the Detachment from the commencement of the Expedition to its return into the Provinces.

'The Governor General and Council further direct that in acknowledgment of the services of the two great Detachments which have served in the late war in the Carnatic and in the West of India, an additional pay of one Rupee be granted to each Non-Commission Officer and Private, both European and Native, of the several corps composing those Detachments who were originally attached to the same on their march to their respective destinations and returned with them.

'*Mr. Macpherson.*—I agree to the first resolution in the Minute, and to the second proposition: but the proposition itself is not fully worded. The time when the additional Rupee pay is to commence should be specified, and a mode adapted for the accounts.

'*Mr. Stables.*—I most heartily concur in the inclosed Minute, and think it a right and just reward for distinguished services. The Europeans ought to have double the addition of pay intended to be given to the Sepoys.

'*Governor General.*—Agreed.

'*Mr Macpherson.*—Agreed.

'*Governor General.*—An additional pay of two Rupees per month be granted to each Non-Commissioned Officer and Private of the European Corps: and one Rupee per month to each Non-Warrant Officer and Private of the Native Corps composing these Detachments who were originally attached to the same on their march to their respective destinations and returned with them.

'The additional pay is to commence with this year which was the time of the Detachments passing the Soobaumeeka. The mode of payment may be settled hereafter. It is an official subject not immediately necessary for publication.

'*Mr. Macpherson.*—Agreed.

'*Mr. Stables.*—Agreed.'

(*Bengal Military Consultations*, January, 1785, p. 16.)

MILITARY DEPARTMENT, FORT WILLIAM, MINUTE OF COUNCIL, 28th January, 1785.

'*Ordered*, that Medals be given to the Artillery Lascars belonging to the Detachment lately returned from the Carnatic, in like manner as those given to the Sepoys of that Detachment.' (*Bengal Military Consultations*, January, 1785, p. 55.)

PROCEEDINGS OF THE GOVERNOR-GENERAL AND COUNCIL, GENERAL DEPARTMENT, *10th February*, 1785.

'Read letter (26th Jan. 1785) from the Commander-in-Chief.

'GENTLEMEN,

'I beg leave to present for your inspection two Medals which have been struck for the Warrant Officers and Sepoys which served in the Expedition to the West of India.

'I also beg leave to lay before you a letter which has been addressed to me by Mr. Shepperd, by whom the Dyes were cut, in which he represents that the Medals cannot be struck without a large press, the cost of which will be so considerable that he will not be able to strike off the Medals for a less sum than one Rupee each, instead of half a Rupee, as formerly agreed on, inclusive of the price of the Bullion of which they are made when he supposed the impression might be made with the stroke of a hammer, and as I see no way of having these honorary Medals provided at a less expense, I have agreed to the terms proposed, which will, I hope, meet with the approbation of the Board.

'I have, etc.,

'G. STIBBERT.

'FORT WILLIAM, *26th Jan.*, 1785.'

'TO GENERAL STIBBERT—

'SIR,

'Herewith we send you as a specimen a Gold and Silver Medal, and find it necessary to observe to you that the Dyes from which they were struck, will, in striking off 50 or 60, be totally spoiled. All this I was a stranger to when first I undertook to make them, thinking from the extraordinary softness of the Gold and Silver in this country, that they might with ease be struck up, with one blow of an hammer, but to my very great disappointment, they take a dozen at least, besides passing them through the fire as many times before the impression appears decent. As there are numbers of them to do, I find it impossible to complete them without the assistance of a large Mint Press, which we can get made here under our directions should it please you to enable us to pay the expense, by allowing one Rupee each for striking them off, independent of the Gold and Silver which may be worked up in the quantity required. I will be answerable that one pair of Dyes shall complete the whole provided they are struck up by Press—otherwise if an accident should happen in striking them with an hammer as before mentioned of breaking the Dyes, it would be attended not only with a double expense in sinking them again, but would be a great disappointment to you.

'We are, etc.,

'YOUNG & SHEPPERD.'

'*N.B.*—You was desirous to know the charge of the Dyes. We cannot in justice to ourselves charge less than 600 Rupees what could not be done in England for less than 40 Guineas.'

'The Board approve the Medals prepared for the Native Officers and Sepoys returned from the West of India, and allow the charge of one Rupee each for the engraving (? striking).'

(*Bengal General Consultations*, February, 1785, p. 73.)

PROCEEDINGS OF THE GOVERNOR-GENERAL AND COUNCIL, GENERAL DEPARTMENT, 20th June, 1785.

'Read letter (12th June, 1785) from the Commander-in-Chief.

'GENTLEMEN,

'I beg leave to lay before you an abstract Return of the Native Warrant and Non-Warrant Officers, Sepoys and other Native Troops lately employed on foreign service, who, by the orders of the Board, are entitled to honorary Medals, and who were alive last month.

'As the press for striking the Medals is in great forwardness, and will be ready in the course of a week, I have to request that you will give orders to the Treasurer and advance upon my draft to Messrs. Young & Shepperd, the persons employed, such sums of money as they may from time to time require for the purpose of making these Medals, which will not I believe be less than 20,000 Rupees, though an exact calculation cannot yet be made.

'I must also beg leave to submit to the Board the propriety of giving the Jemadars *Gold* instead of Silver Medals, as assigned to them by your Resolutions, otherwise there will be no distinction between the Medals of the latter, and those fixed for the Havildars, Naicks and Privates, as the whole must be struck *from one Die*, since making separate Dies for each rank would be attended with too much trouble and expense.

'I have, etc.

'G. STIBBERT.

'FORT WILLIAM, *12th June*, 1785.'

'*Ordered* that the Military Paymaster-General do advance to the Commander-in-Chief, the sum of 20,000 Rupees, for the purpose of preparing the honorary Medals ordered to the Troops late serving in the Carnatic: and to create a proper distinction between the Jemadars and the inferior Officers and Privates, the Medals of the former are directed to be gilt.'

(*Bengal General Consultations*, 1785, p. 505; and *Military Consultations*, 1785, p. 228.)

No. 128.

MEDAL FOR FIDELITY—INDIA, 1780-84.

This medal, although formally instituted, does not appear to have been ever issued.

In 1785 the Court of Directors, adverting to the sufferings of those who were prisoners with Tippoo Sultan, directed that compensation, in proportion to the hardships they had endured during their confinement, should be made to the officers and soldiers of both European and Native Armies. They likewise instructed the Government of Madras to bestow some proper mark of distinction upon such individuals of the Native Army as had resisted the many endeavours used to seduce them from the British Service, as a reward for their firmness, fidelity, and attachment, and as an encouragement to others to follow so laudable an example.

The Madras Government accordingly passed a resolution, and issued a General Order, to the effect that medals, with the inscription 'Fidelity,' would be given to such of the native officers and Sepoys as could be ascertained to be entitled to receive them, the medals for the officers to be of gold, and those of the non-commissioned officers and privates of silver. On account of the Court of Directors having given no instructions as to the 'mark of distinction' taking the shape of a medal, the idea of the medal must be attributed to the Madras Government.

The resolution was, however, never carried out. In 1797 we find the Commander-in-Chief at Madras, General George Harris, when proposing that a badge of distinction should be conferred on certain native officers and soldiers who had volunteered for the expedition to Manilla, regretting that the resolution as to the medals for fidelity, passed in 1785, had never been acted on. Probably there were difficulties in the way which have not been recorded.

FROM THE COURT OF DIRECTORS TO THE GOVERNMENT OF MADRAS, 21st Sept., 1785.

'15. Commiserating the sufferings of those who were Prisoners with Tippoo Sultaun, and in order to afford them some relief, we hereby direct that you take the same into your immediate consideration, and that you make such compensation as may be thought reasonable, to the Officers and Privates both of the European and Native Troops, in proportion to the hardships they endured during their rigorous confinement; and in this compensation you will give full indemnification to those whose Pay, being long in arrears, has been discharged by Bills which bare a great discount, so that in fact they did not receive their full pay. This is a hardship which in justice ought not to be imposed upon a Soldier, and it is bad policy ever to let him feel the effects of any grievance he is with justice entitled to complain of.

'16. We further direct that you consider of some proper mark of distinction to be given to such of the Sepoys as resisted the many endeavours used to seduce them from the British Service, as a reward for their firmness, fidelity, and attachment, and as an encouragement to others to follow so laudable an example.'

MADRAS MILITARY PROCEEDINGS, 11th April, 1786.

'General Letter from the Court of Directors of the 21st Sept., 1785, taken into consideration —Paras. 15-16.

'The Governor-General and Council having already anticipated the directions of the Company contained in the above paragraphs (15-16) relative to the prisoners with the Nabobs Hyder Ally and Tippoo Sultaun, there remains nothing but to give a Medal to those of the Commissioned, Non-commissioned and Privates among the Native Troops who gave proofs of their attachment to the Company.

'*Agreed*, that a Medal with the Inscription of the word *Fidelity* be given to the Natives above described as a mark of the attention and opinion of the Govt. in their favor. The Medals to the Commissioned Officers to be of gold, those to the Non-commissioned and Privates to be of silver.' (Pp. 661 and 662.)

H

MADRAS GENERAL ORDER, 11th April, 1786.

'*Agreed*, that a Medal with the inscription of the word *Fidelity* be given to the Natives above described as a mark of the attention and opinion of Govt. in their favor. The Medals of the Commissioned Officers to be of *gold*; those to the Non-commissioned Officers and Privates to be of *silver*. The Commander-in-Chief will therefore give orders to ascertain in the most impartial and exact manner the Native Officers and Sepoys entitled to the mark of distinction and favor now ordered, and lay the whole before the Board with the least possible delay.'

FROM THE GOVERNMENT OF MADRAS TO THE SECRETARY OF STATE FOR INDIA, 13th April, 1880, No. 44—Military.

'2. With reference to Your Lordship's Despatch, No. 73, dated 30th October, 1879, paras. 1 to 6,[1] we have the honor to forward the accompanying correspondence, from which it would appear that neither of the medals for "Fidelity" (1786) and "Vellore Mutiny" was ever issued. Our Mint records, which have been thoroughly searched, fail to throw any light on the subject, and, as Colonel Wilson remarks, it is not likely that the receipt of such medals would have been omitted from the regimental records. We can only conclude, therefore, that the matter fell through, or was forgotten, in both instances.'

GOVERNMENT OF MADRAS—MILITARY DEPARTMENT, 10th April, 1880. *No.* 2278.

MEDALS.

'Read the following papers :—

'No. 132. *Extract from a Military Despatch from the Right Honorable the Secretary of State for India, dated 30th October,* 1879, *No.* 73.

'Para. 1. Amongst the papers which accompanied your Military letter, No. 152, dated 30th October, 1877, were several lists, carefully prepared by Colonel W. J. Wilson, Madras Retired List, showing the services and honorary distinctions of the Madras Army.

'2. In List "A," which gives the "services of corps of the Local Army of the Madras Presidency engaged in campaigns, expeditions and sieges, for which war medals or honorary distinctions have been granted from 1767 to the present time," mention is made of a medal for "Fidelity" awarded by the Madras Government in 1786.

'3. The Court of Directors, in paras. 15 and 16 of their Despatch to Madras, dated 21st September, 1785, desired that a "proper mark of distinction" should be bestowed on those sepoys who, during the period of their captivity by Hyder Ally and Tippoo Sultaun, had resisted the many endeavours used to seduce them from the British service, "as a reward for their firmness, fidelity, and attachment, and as an encouragement to others to follow so laudable an example." The Government accordingly resolved (see *Madras Military Proceedings*, 11th April, 1786, pp. 661 and 662) that gold and silver medals, inscribed with the word "Fidelity," should be given to the Native officers and soldiers in question.

---

[1] Procs. of Govt., 10th April, 1880, Nos. 132-136. No. 10 in the Packet.

'4. Another medal, mentioned in List "A," is that conferred on the Native troops which took part in the suppression of the mutiny at Vellore in 1806. Colonel Wilson quotes the Madras General Order of 24th July, 1806, granting the medal, but adds, in a note, "It is doubtful whether the medals were ever issued."

'5. It appears, however, from the Madras Military Proceedings of 29th September, 1807, p. 8560, that the Government approved of a Persian inscription proposed for the medals by the Commander-in-Chief, and issued orders for the preparation of the medals at the Mint. The matter was reported to the Court of Directors in paras. 531 and 532 of Military letter of 21st October, 1807. It is evident, therefore, that some measures were taken by the Government for giving effect to their General Order.

'6. I should be glad were some further investigation to be made in regard to those two medals. Your Mint records would probably show whether the intention of having the latter medal made there was carried out, and likewise what was its design. In the event of the dies of either medal being forthcoming, some impressions in silver should be sent to this country.'

'No. 133. No. 887.

'Referred to His Excellency the Commander-in-Chief, with advertence to Proceedings of Government, No. 5887, dated 23rd October, 1877, for favor of report whether anything further in regard to these medals can be traced in the Adjutant-General's Department.

'2. The records of the Government Office show that Lieutenant-General Sir John Cradock, with a minute dated 26th August, 1807, furnished the Government with a design for the proposed Vellore Mutiny Medal, and that this was forwarded to the Mint Master, but nothing can be traced in the Mint records as to whether either of the medals referred to was actually issued, or what became of the dies.

'3. Colonel W. J. Wilson will also be requested to report whether he can furnish any information on the subject.

'H. N. D. PRENDERGAST, Colonel, R.E.,
Acting Secretary to Government.

'FORT ST. GEORGE,
9th February, 1880.

'To the Adjutant-General; Colonel W. J. Wilson.'

'No. 134. *From* Lieut.-Colonel W. J. WILSON, *Retired List, Ootacamund, to* Colonel H. N. D. PRENDERGAST, V.C., C.B., R.E., *Acting Secretary to Government, Military Department, Fort St. George; dated Ootacamund, 16th February*, 1880.

'I have the honor to acknowledge receipt of the Proceedings of Government regarding the medals granted in 1786 and 1806, respectively.[1]

'2. On the 17th October, 1797, General Harris, in a minute addressed to Government, recommended that honorary badges should be granted to the Native troops which had volunteered for the projected expedition to Manilla. In this minute he alluded to the order of April, 1786, regarding the medals to be conferred on the Native soldiers who had resisted the inducements held out to them by Hyder and Tippoo, and he remarked, with reference thereto, that "*perhaps it cannot be too much lamented that this interesting resolution was never carried into effect.*" It may therefore be fairly assumed that this medal was not issued.

---

[1] Military Department, 9th Feb., 1880, No. 887.

'3. When compiling the account of the 4th (P.W.O.) Regiment of Cavalry, I made inquiries regarding the medal furnished to the men of the Cavalry who accompanied the 19th Dragoons from Arcot to Vellore on the 10th July, 1806, but did not obtain any information tending to shew that it had been issued. On the other hand, the Officer Commanding the 4th stated that the men of that regiment did not receive any medal. When I joined my regiment in 1835, several of the Native officers were then wearing the badge for the Manilla Expedition of 1797, which they had received when privates; and as the number of men of all ranks who were entitled to the Vellore mutiny medal amounted to 412, it seems almost certain that, had it been issued, the fact of its having been worn would still be remembered in some of the regiments concerned. Moreover, the receipt of such medal was not likely to have been omitted from the records of the regiments.

'No. 135. *From* Colonel A. R. CLEPHANE, *Officiating Adjutant-General, to* Colonel H. N. D. PRENDERGAST, V.C., C.B., R.E., *Acting Secretary to Government, Military Department; dated Fort St. George, 23rd March, 1880, No. 226.*

'With reference to Proceedings of Madras Government of the 9th ultimo, No. 887, I have the honor, by Order of the Commander-in-Chief, to state that nothing can be traced in this department of the receipt or issue of either of these medals for "Fidelity" or the "Vellore Mutiny."

'No. 136. ORDER THEREON, 10th April, 1880, No. 2278.

'The Secretary of State for India will be informed accordingly.

'H. N. D. PRENDERGAST, Colonel, R.E.,
Acting Secretary to Government.'

No. 129.

CAMPAIGN IN MYSORE, 1790-92.

PLATE 15, *Nos.* 3 *and* 4.

Obv. A Sepoy holding the British colours in his right hand, and in his left the enemy's standard reversed. His left foot rests on a dismounted cannon. In the background, a fortified town.

Rev. Within a wreath: FOR SERVICES IN MYSORE, A.D. 1791-1792.

Outside the wreath in Persian: 'A memorial of devoted services to the English Government at the war of Mysore. Christian Era, 1791-1792, equivalent to the Mahomedan Era, 1205-1206.'

Circular, 1·7 inch. Gold, silver. 1·5 inch. Silver.
Mounting: A small loop of the same metal as the medal.
Worn suspended round the neck by a cord through a loop at the top of the medal.

This medal was given to a detachment of native troops of the Bengal Army sent to Madras in 1790, under Colonel Cockerell, to operate against Tippoo Sultan.

In a Minute, dated 1st April, 1793, the Governor-General, the Marquis Cornwallis, in order to perpetuate the memory of the services performed by the native troops employed in the late war against Tippoo Sultan, proposed that Honorary Medals should be bestowed on the 'Native Officers and Sepoys of the Infantry and Cavalry, and on the Artillery Lascars, who either marched by land, or proceeded by sea to the Carnatic and returned to Bengal,' as under:—

To the Subadars, . . . Gold Medals;
To the Jemadars and Serangs, . Silver Medals;
To the Havildars, Naicks, Tindals, Sepoys, and Lascars, Silver Medals of an inferior value;

with some suitable motto, inscription, or device. He recommended that the medals be made at the mint, and that their value should be in the same proportions as those given in 1785 to the Detachments which returned from the Carnatic and the west of India a few years previously. In the Governor-General's proposals the Council concurred, and the grant of the medal was notified in a General Order of 4th June, 1793.

Upon the mint master stating that the medals could not be so well struck and so neatly finished by his people as by a practical workman in gold and silver, the Government entrusted their manufacture to Mr. Mair, the principal silversmith in Calcutta. The gold medals were each to contain two gold mohurs and ten rupees; the large silver medals, two rupees ten annas each; and the small silver medals, one rupee eight annas. The dies were supplied by Mr. Mair, and probably remained in his possession. They are not at the Calcutta mint.

BENGAL MILITARY PROCEEDINGS, FORT WILLIAM, 1st April, 1793, No. 1, page 483.

MINUTE BY THE MARQUIS CORNWALLIS, GOVERNOR-GENERAL.

'Government have already expressed in the strongest terms their sense of the services performed by the Native Troops who were employed in the late war against Tippoo Sultaun, and the Gratuity of six months Batta bestowed upon them at Seringapatam, together with the additional donation of six months Batta which the Court of Directors have liberally ordered for all the Troops employed on that Service, will be an ample pecuniary Reward; but there is still something wanting to perpetuate the Memory of those Services throughout the Native part of the Army as well as to distinguish the Individuals who were partakers in the fatigues and dangers of the War and in the glory of its success.

'I therefore propose that as a public and lasting mark of the approbation of Govt., Honorary Medals be bestowed on the Native Officers and Sepoys of the Infantry and

Cavalry, and on the Artillery Lascars who either marched by land or proceeded by sea to the Carnatic, and returned to Bengal—

'To the Subadars, ... Gold Medals;
To the Jemadars and Serangs, ... Silver Medals; and
To the Havildars, Naicks, Tindals, Sepoys and Lascars, Silver Medals of an inferior value, with some suitable Motto, inscription or device.

These Memorials which exclusive of the first cost will entail no future expense upon the public, whilst they are worn with pride by the parties themselves, will create and keep alive a spirit of emulation amongst the Native Troops of the Bengal Establishment, on whose zeal, attachment, and military qualities, a high dependence must be placed in any Wars in which we may be hereafter engaged in any part of India.

'If this proposition be approved, I beg to recommend that Orders may be given to the Mint Master to make the necessary preparations for striking the Medals as soon as he shall be furnished with a Design. The value of the Medals should I think be nearly in the same proportions as those distributed on the Return of the Detachment from the Carnatic and the West of India in the beginning of the year 1785.'

'The Board concur entirely with the Governor-Genl. on the subject of His Lordship's Minute: and it is accordingly agreed that as a public and lasting mark of the approbation of Govt., Honorary Medals be bestowed on the Native Officers and Sepoys of the Infantry and Cavalry, and on the Artillery Lascars who either marched by land or proceeded by sea to the Carnatic and returned to Bengal—

'To the Subadars, ... Gold Medals;
To the Jemadars and Serangs, . . . Silver Medals; and
To the Havildars, Naicks, Tindals, Sepoys and Lascars, Silver Medals of an inferior value with some suitable Motto, inscription or device.

'*Agreed*, that the Commander-in-Chief be requested to issue the Orders necessary on this occasion, and that the Mint Master be directed to make the preparations that are requisite for striking the Medals as soon as he shall be furnished with a Design.'

FROM THE GOVERNMENT OF BENGAL TO THE COURT OF DIRECTORS, *14th May*, 1793—Military.

Cons. 1st April, 1793.—' 10. In a Minute laid before us by the Commander-in-Chief, his Lordship observed that Govt. had already expressed in the strongest terms, their sense of the services performed by the Native troops, who were employed in the late war against Tippoo Sultaun; and that the gratuity of six months' Batta given to them at Seringapatam, together with the additional donation which had been liberally ordered by your Hon'ble Court, would be an ample pecuniary reward; but his Lordship said that there was still something wanting to perpetuate the memory of those services, as well as to distinguish the individuals who were partakers in the fatigues and dangers of the war, and in the glory of its success; and his Lordship proposed that, as a public and lasting mark of the approbation of Govt., honorary Medals should be bestowed on the Native Officers and Sepoys of the Infantry and Cavalry, and on the Artillery Lascars, who either marched by land or proceeded by sea to the Carnatic, and returned to Bengal. To the Soubadars, Gold Medals, to the Jemidars and Serangs, Silver Medals, and to the Havildars, Naicks, Tindals, Sepoys and Lascars, Silver Medals of an inferior value, with some suitable motto, inscription or device. These Medals which, exclusive of the first cost, would entail no expense on the public, whilst they were worn with pride by the parties upon whom they were bestowed, would, his Lordship observed, create and keep alive a spirit of emulation amongst the Native Troops of the Bengal Establishment, on whose zeal, attachment, and military qualities a high dependence must be placed in any wars in which you might hereafter be engaged in any part of India.

'11. His Lordship was of opinion that the value of the Medals should be nearly in the same proportions as those distributed on the return of the Detachments from the Carnatic, and the West of India in the beginning of the year 1785.

'12. Our sentiments concurring entirely with those expressed by the Commander-in-Chief on this subject, and having requested that he would be pleased to issue generally the orders that were necessary in consequence, we directed the Mint Master to make the preparations that were requisite for striking the Medals, as soon as the design should be sent to him for that purpose.'

GENERAL ORDER BY THE GOVERNOR-GENERAL, 4th June, 1793.

'The Governor-Gen. in Council has been pleased to resolve that as a public and lasting mark of the approbation of Govt., Honorary Medals be bestowed on the Native Officers and Sepoys of the Infantry and Cavalry; and on the Artillery Lascars, who either marched by land or proceeded by sea to the Carnatic and returned to Bengal.

'To the Subadars, ... Gold Medals.
To the Jemadars and Serangs, ... Silver Medals, and
To the Havildars, Naicks, Tindals, Sepoys,
and Gun Lascars, ... Silver Medals of
an inferior value, with some suitable motto, inscription or device.'—
(See *The Code of Military Standing Regulations of the Bengal Establishment*, compiled by Captain Henry Grace, 1791-1799, Vol. ii. p. 69, para. 7.)

BENGAL MILITARY PROCEEDINGS, 5th August, 1793, *No.* 2.

'The Secretary has been desired to acquaint the Board that the Dies for the Medals, which, according to their orders of 1st April (1793), are to be given to the Native Officers and Sepoys of the Infantry and Cavalry, and to the Artillery Lascars who served in the War against Tippoo Sultaun, being nearly completed, it becomes necessary to determine what quantity of gold or silver shall be in each Medal, and by whom the Medals shall be struck, notwithstanding the Resolution of 1st April, which directs that the Mint Master should make the necessary preparations for striking the Medals as soon as he should be furnished with a design, for that officer is apprehensive that they cannot be struck and so neatly finished by the people employed in the Mint as by a practical workman in gold and silver. The Secretary is instructed to mention that Mr. Mair, the principal Silversmith in Calcutta, at whose shop the Dies have been executed, would prepare the Medals for receiving the impression, strike the Medals, and fix to them the loops by which they are to be suspended, and thus deliver the number of Medals that may be required, complete in every respect, for Six Thousand Sicca Rupees, this sum including the charge for the Dies, and the risk of the impressions remaining with him. It of course does not include the expense of the Gold and Silver of which the Medals will be made.

'As to the number of Medals which will be wanted, it has been computed that there will be about seven thousand large and small; but the number cannot be accurately determined, as some of the returns from corps have not been yet received.

'The Secretary has been desired further to say that an expense of Six thousand Rupees for mere labour is considerable, but that the Board will probably have in mind that mere cutting the Dies has employed an ingenious man above three months, and that any that may fail are to be replaced without additional charge; that if the Medals could be struck at the Mint, there would yet be some work to be done by a Silver Smith, and the Dies must be paid for as a separate charge, and that it is not easy in this country to estimate the value of ingenious labour.

'*It is agreed* by the Board on these considerations:—

'*1st*, That Mr. Mair shall be allowed Six thousand Sicca Rupees for the work to be executed by him as above mentioned; that for this sum he shall deliver the number of Medals required, each Medal to have a perfect impression, to be milled round the edge, and to have a loop fixed to the top for suspending it.

'*2d*, That there shall be in each Gold Medal two Gold Mohurs and ten rupees; in each large silver Medal, two Rupees and ten annas; and in each small silver medal, one Rupee and eight annas.

'*3d*, That the gold and silver shall be provided by Mr. Mair, the standard thereof being fixed by the Assay Master and the Medals examined by him, in order that the gold and silver may not be inferior to the standard fixed.

'*4th*, That Mr. Mair be allowed to make use of the Mint Fly Press.

'*5th*, That the Adjutant-Genl. be directed to lay before the Board as soon as possible a return of the number of Medals of each description that will be required, and that as the Medals shall be completed and assayed, they be sent to the Adjutant-General and be by him distributed to the Corps.

'*Ordered*, that the necessary orders in consequence of these resolutions be sent to Mr. Mair, the Mint and Assay Masters, and the Adjutant-General, and that notice thereof be transmitted to Lieut.-Colonel Ross, for the information of the Commander-in-Chief.'

FROM THE GOVERNMENT OF BENGAL TO THE COURT OF DIRECTORS, *27th October*, 1793—Military.

'176. The Secretary having reported to us that the Die for the Medals, which, according to our orders of the 1st April (1793) already communicated to you, are to be given to the Native Officers and Sepoys of the Infantry and Lascars, who served in the late war against Tippoo Sultaun, were nearly ready, it became necessary to determine what quantity of Gold and Silver should be in each Medal, and by whom the Medals should be struck, we had resolved on the date above mentioned, that the Mint Master should make the necessary preparations for striking the Medals as soon as he should be furnished with a Design, but that Officer informed us that they could not be struck and so neatly finished by the people employed in the Mint, as by a practical workman in gold and silver. We therefore entered into an engagement with Mr. Mair, the principal Silver Smith in Calcutta, who has undertaken to strike and deliver the number of Medals required for the sum of S^a^ R^s^ 6000; each Medal to have a perfect impression, to be milled round the edge, and to have a loop fixed at the top for suspending it.

'177. We have resolved that each Gold Medal shall contain two Gold Mohurs and ten Rupees: that each large Silver Medal shall contain two Rupees ten annas, and each small Silver Medal, one Rupee eight annas.

'178. An expense of Six thousand Rupees for mere labor is certainly considerable, but it is at the same time proper to mention that the mere cutting the Dyes employed an ingenious man above three months, and that any that may be imperfect are to be replaced without additional charge. Even had the Medals been struck at the Mint, there would yet have been some work to be done by a Silver Smith, and Dyes must have been paid for as a separate charge, and it is not easy in this country to estimate the value of ingenious labor.

'179. We have the honor of transmitting to you five of each of the Medals, and will hereafter communicate to you the exact expense that has been incurred in making the number required for the Troops for whom they are intended.

'180. Your Hon. Court will receive, a number in the Packet, a copy of an abstract Return of the number of Medals of each description required for the native Officers and Privates of the Cavalry and Infantry and Lascars belonging to the Artillery, to which is added, the probable number that will be required for some Corps from which Lists have not yet been received.'

GENERAL LETTER OF COURT OF DIRECTORS TO BENGAL,
24th March, 1795, *Para.* 157.

Published in General Order, 22d September, 1795. See Grace, page 130.

'157. Having perused Lord Cornwallis' Minute of 1st April, 1793, we most heartily concur in your Resolution for bestowing Honorary Medals on the Officers and Men of the Native Corps belonging to the Detachment which served in the late war against Tippoo Sultaun: and approve of the mode in which these medals are to be supplied, as advised in your Military Despatch of 27th Oct., 1793.'—(See paras. 176-180.)

No. 130.

CEYLON, 1795-6.

PLATE 16, *No.* 1.

Obv. Ins. FOR SERVICES ON THE ISLAND OF CEYLON, A.D. 1795/6.

Rev. Ins. in Persian :—'This Medal was presented to commemorate good services in Ceylon during the years of the Hegira 1209-10.'

Circular, 2 inches. Gold. Silver.
Dies engraved and preserved at the Calcutta Mint.
Mounted with a loop for suspension.

Several years elapsed before it was decided to confer a medal on the small force of Bengal Native Artillery which took part in the capture of Ceylon from the Dutch in 1795-6, and it was not until May, 1807, that a General Order granting the medal was issued.

The reason for the design of the medal being of so extremely simple a character is explained by a letter from the Adjutant-General of the Bengal Army, dated 16th November, 1810, stating that as it did not appear that the service in Ceylon had been distinguished by any particular or brilliant events affording subject for any special device or motto, the Commander-in-Chief considered that an inscription in English on one side, and in Persian on the *reverse*, of each medal would suffice.

This is the only instance of a war medal with a merely verbal design.

The medal was made at the Calcutta Mint, the numbers and cost, as shewn in the *Mint Account*, printed at p. 125, being as under :—

2 Gold, for native officers, . .	Rs. 165.13
121 Silver, for other ranks, . . .	492.10

A curious mistake was made in connection with the medals for Ceylon and Egypt. The Mint authorities had been directed to prepare the medals without, however, being furnished with any designs for them. They accordingly struck the number required from the *Seringapatam* dies. When the mistake was discovered the medals were recalled, and the design above described was adopted.

The troops employed in the expedition were the following:—

71st and 73rd Foot: Detachments.
72nd Foot.
Royal Artillery: Detachment.
Bengal Artillery: two Companies.
Madras Artillery: two Companies.
Do. Gun Lascars, six Companies.
Madras Pioneers: two Companies.
Madras Native Infantry: 1st, 7th, 9th, and 23rd Battalions.

Of the above, the Native portion of the Bengal Artillery alone received this medal.

The principal events in the course of the expedition were the captures of—

Trincomalee, on 26th August, 1795;
Fort Ostenburgh, on 31st August, 1795; and
Colombo, on 15th February, 1796.

GENERAL ORDER BY PRESIDENT OF COUNCIL.

15th and 31st May, 1807.

'All survivors of the Gun Lascars, and Native Commissioned and Non-Commissioned Officers attached, who accompanied the Detachments commanded by Captains Tomkyns and Balfour to the coast in 1799, and those commanded by Captains Barton and Clarke to Ceylon in 1795/6, are to be considered as entitled to Medals for those services.'

(*N.B.*—By G. O. G. G. 19th June, 1800, and 31st July, 1802, Medals are also granted to Gun Lascars for services in the Dukhun and in Egypt. See also Henley's *Military Code*, p. 194.)

This General Order should be read with those of 10th and 24th April, 1807, printed subsequently among the Seringapatam Papers in the Appendix.

A correspondence in reference to the mistake which had been made in striking the medals for Ceylon from the Seringapatam dies (*Bengal Military Proceedings*, 23rd August, 1808, No. 84, and 19th Sept., 1808, No. 15) is also printed among the

Seringapatam Papers, together with a *Report from the Government of Bengal to the Court of Directors*, 27th March, 1809 (Military), paragraphs 724 and 729, in regard to the preparation of medals for various services. Paragraph 729 draws attention to the mistake as to the dies.

BENGAL PUBLIC PROCEEDINGS.

30th Nov., 1810. *No.* 5.

Extract from the Proceedings of the Right Hon. the Governor-General in Council in the Military Department under date 17th Nov., 1810. (No. 44.)

'To

'JOHN ADAM, Esq.,

'Secretary to Govt., Military Dept.

'ADJUTANT GENL.'S OFFICE,
'FORT WILLIAM, *16th Nov.*, 1810.

'SIR,

'With reference to the Inducts for Medals transmitted to the Office of Secretary to Govt. Military Dept., on 28th Aug., 1807, the Commander of the Forces understanding that the Medals granted for services in Mysore and the Dukkun have been issued, that those for services in Egypt are now preparing at the Hon. Company's Mint at the Presidency, but that the preparation of the few authorised for services on the Island of Ceylon has been suspended in consequence of no suitable motto or device having been fixed on; I am directed to request you will submit to the Right Hon. the Governor Genl. in Council the recommendation of the Commander of the Forces that the Medals required for services in Ceylon may be ordered to be executed whilst those for services in Egypt are yet in hand, and as it does not appear that the service for which Medals have been authorised for the Native Artillery Details of this Estabt. which served on Ceylon, was distinguished by any particular or brilliant event affording subject for any special Motto or Device, altho' the Honorary Distinction which Medals are intended to confer is justly appropriate and due to those Troops for the attachment, zeal, and alacrity manifested by them in proceeding on distant service beyond the sea. The Commander of the Forces suggests that an inscription in English on one side and in Persian on the Reverse of each Medal in the following words would very well answer the purpose and be easily executed without any difficulty or delay: viz. For Services on the Island of Ceylon, A.D. 1795/6.

'Annexed is an abstract of the Medals required for this purpose.

'I have, etc.,

'GEORGE BALL,

'*Adjutant Genl.*'

'GUN LASCAR DETAIL.

'Sarangs, the same as Jemedars	2
1st and 2nd Tindals, same as Havaldars and Naicks . .	6
Private Lascars, same as Sepoys	85
Total Medals,	93

'*Ordered*, that the foregoing papers be recorded in the Public Dept. from whence the necessary instructions will be issued to the Mint Master for striking the Medals granted for services on the Island of Ceylon, bearing the inscription in English and Persian written on the accompanying papers.

'A true extract,

'J. ADAM,

'*Secretary to Govt.*'

'The following Order was passed on the 27th Instant (Nov., 1810):—

'*Ordered*, that a copy of the foregoing extract be transmitted to the Mint Master, with the original paper which accompanied it, and that he be directed to have the Medals struck with the Inscription in English and Persian contained in the paper in question.'

GENERAL ORDER BY THE COMMANDER-IN-CHIEF.

13th May, 1811.

'The Honorary Medals authorised to be granted to the Native Troops who were employed on service in Egypt under Major Genl. Baird, by the Orders of Govt. under date 31st July, 1802, and those subsequently authorised on account of the survivors of the Gun Lascars who embarked for service on Ceylon under Captains Barton and Clarke of Artillery, in the years 1795/96, being now in readiness for delivery, the Commr.-in-Chief directs that Rolls with figured Abstracts, agreeably to the annexed Form, of all the Native Commissioned, Non-Commd. Officers, Sepoys, Golundaz, and Gun Lascars, who are entitled to Honorary Medals for the services above referred to, be immediately prepared on foolscap paper, and transmitted to the Adjt.-Genl.'s Office by the Officers commanding the several Corps and Establishments to which the persons so entitled may now belong, in order that Medals may be transmitted them accordingly.

. . . . . .

'It is to be clearly understood that claims to Medals for Services in Egypt are only admissible on account of persons who embarked from Bengal for service in that country, and must therefore be confined to those who belonged to the 1st Battalion of Volunteers commanded by Major Broughton.' (See Henley's *Military Code*, p. 247.)

PROCLAMATION, VICE-PRESIDENT.

10th September, 1811.

Claims to Medals by Pensioned Soldiers.

Copy with Seringapatam Papers in Appendix.

BENGAL PUBLIC PROCEEDINGS.

17th April, 1812. *No.* 17.

Extract *Military Proceedings*, 11th April, 1812 (No. 229).

'Read a letter and enclosure from the Adjt.-Genl., dated 8th April, 1812.

'The Governor-Genl. in Council observing that ten more Silver Medals for services on Ceylon are required to satisfy all claims to that honorary distinction and concluding that the Die still remains at the Mint:

'*Resolved*, that the Mint Master be instructed to strike off ten Silver Medals for services on the Island of Ceylon at an early period and to forward them when finished to the Adjt.-Genl. for distribution.'

BENGAL PUBLIC PROCEEDINGS.
17th July, 1812. *No.* 30.

Military Proceedings, 11th July, 1812 (No. 233).

'Read a letter from the Asst. Adjt.-Genl. dated 9th July, 1812.

'*Ordered*, that the Mint Master be instructed to strike off twenty Silver Honorary Medals for services on the Island of Ceylon, and to forward them to the Asst. Adjt.-Genl. at the Presidency, for distribution, who has been desired to furnish a receipt for the same.'

BENGAL PUBLIC PROCEEDINGS.
25th March, 1814. *No.* 36.

CALCUTTA MINT.

CHARGES FOR THE BULLION AND FABRICATION OF SUNDRY MEDALS SINCE 25TH FEBRUARY, 1811.

Date	Item	Rs.		
1811. March 6. Egypt—Gold.	Bullion for 16 Gold Medals for *Egypt* . . Rs.	1242	15	0
	Workmen for forming and finishing 16 Medals at Rs. 4 each	64	0	0
	Fixing 16 loops to suspend the Medals by, @ Rs. 2	32	0	0
1811. March 6. Ceylon—Gold.	Bullion for 2 Gold Medals for *Ceylon* . . .	153	13	0
	Workmen for forming and finishing 2 Gold Medals	8	0	0
	2 loops to suspend the Medals by	4	0	0
1813. August 31. Mauritius—Gold.	Bullion for 45 Gold Medals for *French Islands* .	3451	14	8
	Forming and finishing 45 Gold Medals at Rs. 4 .	180	0	0
	45 loops at Rs. 2	90	0	0
1811. February 25. Egypt—Silver.	Bullion for 300 Silver Medals for *Egypt*	1217	10	0
	,, 400 do.	1642	0	0
	,, 60 do.	243	15	0
	760			
	Workmen to prepare and sink 1 pair of Dyes and for forming and finishing 760 Medals @ 4 annas .	190	0	0
	760 loops @ 2 annas	95	0	0
1811. March 6.	Bullion for 91 Silver Medals for *Ceylon*	342	4	0
1812. June 1.	,, 10 do. . . .	36	2	0
August 1.	,, 20 do. . . .	68	14	0
Ceylon—Silver.	121			
	Workmen to prepare and sink 1 pair of Dyes and for forming and finishing 121 Medals at 4 annas .	30	4	0
	121 loops at 2 annas	15	2	0
1813. August 31. Mauritius—Silver.	Bullion for 2156 Silver Medals for *French Islands* .	7280	0	0
	Sinking Dyes and forming 2156 Medals @ 4 annas .	539	0	0
	2156 loops @ 2 annas per loop	269	8	0

No. 131.

MANILLA, 1797.

BADGE FOR NATIVE VOLUNTEERS.

An arm-plate about five inches long, convex so as to lie on the arm, and sufficiently broad to come well round the outside of the (left) upper arm at each side. Inscription in English and Hindustani: 'Volunteer—Manilla—1797.'[1]

Silver, for Native Officers.
Brass, for Non-Commissioned Officers and Sepoys.

The idea of bestowing badges of distinction on native troops who had volunteered for foreign service appears to have originated with the Commander-in-Chief at Madras, Lieut.-General George Harris. In a Minute, dated 17th October, 1797, His Excellency, after referring to the merits of the native troops who had been employed on foreign service, and particularly of those who had recently volunteered for the projected expedition against Manilla, proposed that the troops in question should be distinguished by a badge, to be worn on the left arm; that for the native officers to be of silver, and that for the non-commissioned officers and privates of brass.

This proposal was agreed to by the Madras Government, and the Military Board were instructed to prepare the Badges, 66 of silver, and 2947 of brass, the cost being 1085 Pagodas. The issue of the Badges was announced to the Army in a General Order, dated 19th December, 1798.

We have not met with a specimen of this Badge. It is stated, however, by Lieut.-Colonel W. J. Wilson, one of the historians of the Madras Army, that when he first joined his regiment in 1835, several of the old native officers were wearing the Manilla Badge which they had received when privates.

It may be pretty safely assumed that it was similar to that given to the volunteers who served in Amboyna shortly afterwards. (See p. 131, No. 132.)

The original intention was to decorate all native soldiers volunteering for service across the sea, not only as a gratification

---

[1] The following is an extract from a letter to the author from Lieut.-Colonel W. J. Wilson, Madras Retired List, dated Ootacamund, 21st June, 1880:—

'The Badges (for Manilla) were arm-plates about five inches long, convex so as to lie on the arm, and sufficiently broad to come well round the outside of the arm (upper arm) at each side. To the best of my recollection the inscription was both in English and in Hindostanee to the following effect:—*Volunteer—Manilla*—1797.'

to themselves, but also as an incentive to their comrades, should occasion arise, to imitate their example. The intention was carried out on at least one other occasion, viz., in the case of the volunteers who served in the expeditions to the Moluccas, Amboyna, and Banda, 1795-1801.

It appears that the Gun Lascars and Native Pioneers were not called upon to volunteer, as they were already under obligations to serve abroad; and the Government consequently considered it would be 'injudicious to bestow an extra reward when no extraordinary sacrifice would have been made.' They accordingly did not receive the Badges.

MADRAS MILITARY PROCEEDINGS, 17th October, 1797.

'The Commander-in-Chief (Lieut.-General George Harris) delivers in the following Minute:—

MINUTE IN COUNCIL, 17th October, 1797.

'The Commander-in-Chief thinks it his duty to request the attention of Government to a subject which he conceives to be well worthy of their consideration, and on which he hopes to have the honour of their concurrence. He alludes to the merits of the Native Troops who are, or have been lately employed on foreign service, and of those who recently volunteered, and so cheerfully embarked, for the projected expedition against Manilla.

'The expediency of distinguishing these deserving men by some lasting mark of honor, which shall flatter their pride, and commemorate their merits and services, he need scarcely insist on. Rewards of this description when properly distributed, have ever been found to be no less effectual in cementing the attachment of those who have proved zealous and faithful, than in cherishing merit at large, and exciting a general spirit of emulation.

'The sentiments and wishes of the Hon. the Court of Directors, on a similar occasion, may be seen from the General Orders of 24th April, 1786, containing a paragraph (16) of their General Letter under date 21st September, 1785, and a subsequent Resolution of Govt. by which it was agreed that Gold and Silver Medals with the inscription of the word "Fidelity" should be given to the Native Troops, who, during the Mysore War that commenced in 1780, had resisted the many endeavours used to seduce them from the British Service; and perhaps it cannot be too much lamented that this interesting resolution was never carried into effect.

'In recommending a measure then which professedly offers such valuable consequences, the Commander-in-Chief would feel himself justified in laying no great stress on the article of expense, as it has been well observed, however, of honorary rewards, that the less they cost the public, the more do they still contribute to its advantage, he is permitted to keep economy in view without detriment to his object.

'Under these several considerations, the Commander-in-Chief proposes that the Troops alluded to shall be distinguished by a Badge to be worn on the left arm, those for the Native Commissioned Officers to be of Silver, and those for the Non-Commissioned and Privates of Brass, agreeable to patterns now submitted to the Board, or of such form as may be determined on. If Govt. be induced to consent to the measure, and fix on the patterns, the Military Board may be entrusted to ascertain how they may be most conveniently made up, and report the expense of the whole to Govt.

'GEORGE HARRIS.'

MINUTE THEREON.

'The Board entirely concur in the suggestion of the Commander-in-Chief for distinguishing by a Badge the whole of the Native Troops who are now, or who have been, employed on foreign service:

'*Resolved* therefore, to desire the Military Board to ascertain how the Badges can be most conveniently made, and report the expense of the whole.' (Page 6194.)

TO THE MILITARY BOARD.

'GENTLEMEN,

I am directed to inform you that being fully sensible of the merits of the Native Troops, who are or have been employed on foreign service, as well as of those who recently volunteered and so cheerfully embarked for the projected expedition against Manilla, the Right Hon. the President in Council has adopted a suggestion of the Commander-in-Chief for distinguishing the whole by a Badge to be worn on the left arm; those for the Native Commissioned Officers to be of silver, those for the Non-Commissioned and Privates of brass, according to a plate which is herewith enclosed. His Lordship in Council therefore desires that you will ascertain how the Badges may be most conveniently made, and report the expense of the whole for his information.

. . . .

'I have, etc.,

'J. WEBBE,
Secretary to Govt.

'FORT ST. GEORGE,
17th October, 1797.'

(Page 6241.)

MADRAS MILITARY PROCEEDINGS, *28th November*, 1797.

Letter from the Military Board, dated Fort St. George, 25th November, 1797.

'Having made the necessary enquiries respecting the most convenient mode of having the Badges made for the Native Volunteers of the late projected Expedition, we find that the whole can be executed in a proper manner for Pagodas 1085 : 18 : 40, agreeably to the accompanying Statement, which your Lordship will observe, does not extend to the Gun Lascars and Native Pioneers, from their not having been called upon to volunteer, and strictly speaking are not therefore comprehended in Mr. Secretary Webbe's letter of 17th ultimo.' (Page 7211.)

'Abstract Return of the Native Officers and Soldiers who volunteered for the projected Expedition against Manilla. (Page 7216):—

	Commissioned Officers.	Non-Commissioned Officers, Rank and File.	Farriers or Native Doctors.	Drums and Fifes.	Puckallies.
Detachments of Native Cavalry . . .	6	150	1	2	2
2nd Battalion, 5th Regt. (7 Companies) .	15	682	1	14	7
Major Oram's Corps (6 do.) .	13	656	...	10	6
33 Battalions Native Infantry . . .	16	686	...	9	5
34 do. do. . . .	16	695	1	10	10
TOTAL .	66	2869	3	45	30

'Statement of the cost of making Badges to distinguish the Native Volunteers for the projected Expedition against Manilla :—

To be made	Corps.	Officers.	Privates, etc.	Rate.	P. F. C.	P. F. C.
By Mr. Gordon, Jeweller	Cavalry	66	...	1 33 0	115 22 0	
		...	155	0 22 0	77 22 0	
						193 0 0
At Pondicherry	33 and 34 Battalions	...	1416	0 14 5	452 28 40	452 28 40
Under the superintendence of Captain Hill	2 Battalions 5 Regiments and Major Oram's Corps	...	1376	0 14 5	439 34 0	439 34 0
		66	2947		Pagodas	1085 18 40

'FRED. PIERCE,
Secretary, Military Board.'

MADRAS MILITARY PROCEEDINGS, 7th December, 1797.

Letter to the Military Board, dated Fort St. George, 6th December, 1797.

'We are happy to observe that the Badges intended for the Native Volunteers can be completed at so reasonable a rate; and desire that orders may be issued for furnishing them according to the statement you have laid before us. We shall accordingly instruct the Military Auditor-Genl. to comply with the application of your Secretary to the amount of Pagodas 1085 : 18 : 40, on this account.

'We certainly concur with you that there is a great difference between the Volunteers of the different Native Corps and the Gun Lascars and the Native Pioneers; and therefore think it might be injudicious to bestow an extra reward when no extraordinary sacrifice would have been made.' (Page 7381.)

MADRAS MILITARY PROCEEDINGS, 18th December, 1798.

Letter from the Military Board, dated Fort St. George, 12th December, 1798.

'5. We do ourselves the honor to report that the number of Silver and Brass honorary Badges, which were ordered by Govt. under date 6 Decr., 1797, to be made up for the Native Cavalry and Infantry, who volunteered for the expedition against Manilla, are completed, and in readiness for disposal in such manner as your Lordship may be pleased to direct.' (Page 8152.)

Resolution thereon.

'*Resolved* that the Volunteers be informed in General Orders that a distribution of the Badges has been ordered to take place; and the Commander-in-Chief is requested to forward the Badges to the different Corps for delivery to the Commissioned, Non-Commissioned and Private Volunteers.

'*Resolved* at the same time, that the Officers commanding Corps be desired to explain to the Volunteers, that merit, however obscure, can never be indifferent to a just and even Government, and that the successors of those who have the present pleasure of bestowing these Badges of distinction, will feel an equal satisfaction in recognising in the descendants of the Volunteers, these testimonials of fidelity.' (Page 8156.)

GENERAL ORDER BY THE GOVERNMENT, Fort St. George, 19th December, 1798.

'The Right Honorable the Governor in Council, impressed with a just sense of the zeal and order manifested by the Native Troops who volunteered for the projected expedition against Manilla, has caused Badges to be prepared in commemoration of their spirit and attachment to the Service.

'His Lordship in Council has particular pleasure at this period in ordering the distribution of these honorable pledges; and they will accordingly be forwarded by the Military Board to the Officers commanding Corps, for delivery to the Commissioned, Non-Commissioned, and Private "Volunteers."

'The Officers commanding Corps are desired to explain to the Volunteers that merit, however obscure, can never be indifferent to a just and wise Government, and that the successors of those who have the present pleasure of bestowing these badges of distinction, will feel an equal satisfaction in recognising in the descendants of the Volunteers, these testimonials of fidelity and worth.

'By Order of the Right Hon. the President in Council.

'J. WEBBE,
Secretary to Govt.'

MADRAS MILITARY PROCEEDINGS, 20th December, 1798.

Letter to the Military Board, dated Fort St. George, 19th December, 1798.

'We have ordered a distribution in General Orders of the Badges provided for the Volunteers who turned out for the Manilla Expedition.' (Page 8358.)

FROM THE SECRETARY OF STATE FOR INDIA TO THE GOVERNMENT OF MADRAS, 15th July, 1880—Military, No. 45.

(Reply to No. 44 of 13th April, 1880, p. 2.)

'5. In the letter of Lieutenant-Colonel W. J. Wilson, regarding the medals for fidelity (1786) and the Vellore mutiny, forwarded by you, mention is made of the grant of honorary badges to the troops who volunteered in 1797 for an expedition to Manilla.

'From the Military Proceedings of the Madras Government of 17th October, 1797, pages 6194 and 6241, it appears that the Government resolved to give badges "to the whole of the native troops" (in silver to the Commissioned Officers and in brass to the Non-commissioned Officers and Sepoys) "who are or have been employed on foreign service, as well as of those who recently volunteered and so cheerfully embarked for the projected expedition against Manilla."

'The further Proceedings on the subject, noted in the margin,[1] show, however, that this intention was carried into effect in respect only of the troops who volunteered for the Manilla expedition.[2]

---

[1] 28th November, 1797, pp. 7211-7216. 7th December, 1797, p. 7381. 18th December, 1798, pp. 8152-8156. 20th December, 1798, p. 8358.

[2] This is not quite correct, because a similar Badge apparently was conferred on the Native Volunteers who took part in the expedition to the Moluccas, 1795-1801.

'In the Proceedings of 18th December, 1798, it is stated that the grant of the badges was to be announced in a General Order. There being no Madras General Orders in this Office of an earlier date than 1800, I shall be glad if you will forward a copy of the General Order which, it is presumed, was issued in due course.

'Should any of these badges, which appear to have been obtained originally through the agency of the Military Board, be now procurable, I request you will furnish me with some specimens.'

FROM THE GOVERNMENT OF MADRAS TO THE SECRETARY OF STATE FOR INDIA, 1st October, 1880—Military, No. 121.

'4. With reference to para. 5 of your Lordship's Despatch No. 45, dated 15th July, 1880, we beg to forward a copy of General Order by this Govt., dated 19th December, 1798,[1] and to report that no specimens of the Badges granted to the Troops who volunteered for an expedition to Manilla, in 1797, can now be traced.'

No. 132.

MOLUCCAS, AMBOYNA, BANDA 1795-1801.

BADGE FOR NATIVE VOLUNTEERS.

The 2nd Battalion 1st Madras N.I., and a battalion composed of volunteers from other native infantry regiments, had been on foreign service since 1795, including the expeditions to the Moluccas, Amboyna, and Banda. On their return to Madras in 1801, a General Order was issued by the General commanding, thanking them, and announcing that certain indulgences would be extended to them in consideration of their good service; also, that honorary Badges would be presented to them.[2]

An illustration of the Badge for Amboyna, on a reduced scale, is subjoined. The actual size of the Badge is 2.7 by 2.3 inches. It was exhibited by Major-General J. B. Knocker, late Madras Army, in the Loan Collection of Relics of the East India Company at the Empire of India Exhibition, held in London in 1895. (See *Catalogue*, No. 362.)

From the Proceedings of the Madras Government for February, 1801, it appears that these Badges were prepared under the same authority as those given to the troops who

---

[1] Proceedings of Government, 23rd September, 1880. Nos. 453, 454—R.

[2] See Wilson's *History of the Madras Army*, vol. ii. p. 259, and vol. iii. p. 95.

volunteered for the Manilla Expedition in 1797, viz.:—a Minute of the Government, dated 17th October, 1797, concurring in the suggestion of the Commander-in-Chief for distinguishing by a Badge the whole of the native troops who were then, or who had been, employed on foreign service.

It is presumed, therefore, that the Badge given on the present occasion was of the same description as that bestowed on the volunteers for Manilla, viz.:—an arm-plate, with an inscription

in English and Hindustani to the effect that the wearer had been a volunteer in the Expedition to the Moluccas; the Badges of the officers being of silver, and those of the non-commissioned officers and Sepoys of brass.

It appears that in 1800 the officer in command at the Moluccas recommended that the men should have medals presented to them; but at the time he made the recommendation he was probably unaware that action had already been taken, and that Badges were in course of preparation.

MADRAS MILITARY PROCEEDINGS, February, 1801.

Letter from the Military Board to the Governor in Council, 17th February, 1801.

'Having in consequence of the authority contained in a letter from Mr. Secretary Webbe, under date 17th October, 1797,[1] taken measures for providing Honorary

---

[1] See page 128. Badge for Manilla Volunteers.

Badges for the Native Volunteers expected from Molucca and Amboyna, we beg leave to request that authority may be given to the Military Paymaster-General for making an advance to our Secretary of 200 Pagodas on that account.' (Page 960.)

GENERAL ORDER BY THE COMMANDER-IN-CHIEF, MADRAS, 29th May, 1801.

'The General derives particular pleasure also in announcing to these corps the resolution of the Governor in Council to testify his sense of their faithful attachment to the British Govt. during a period of more than five years on foreign service, by bestowing on them individually a Badge to be worn as an honorary mark of distinction, and which the General hopes may be in readiness for delivery previous to the departure of the corps from the Presidency.'

MADRAS MILITARY PROCEEDINGS, 28th April, 1801.

'Read the following letter from the officer commanding the Molucca Islands:—

'To JOSIAH WEBBE, Esq.,
Chief Secretary to Govt.,
Fort St. George.

'FORT VICTORIA, AMBOYNA,
31*st Decr.*, 1800.

'1. The men of the Volunteer Battalion, and 2nd Battalion, 1st Native Regiment, who have volunteered to continue to serve at Amboyna, having complied so readily with my request, notwithstanding their unprecedented long absence from their families, and the many hardships the situation unavoidably exposes them to, induces me to wish that some gracious mark of Government's approbation may be conferred on them, which will not only prove gratifying to them in the present instance, but at the same time inspire others on similar occasions with a spirit of emulation that may prove beneficial to the service. With this object in view, I take the liberty of sending by this conveyance musters of a Medal for the inspection of the Right Honourable the Governor in Council, requesting that each of the Sepoys who have so handsomely come forward to continue to serve at the Moluccas, may have one presented him by Government as a mark of the sense that is entertained of their military spirit and their distinguished fidelity to their Honourable Masters. Should this request meet the approbation of the Right Honorable the Governor in Council, I beg that the Medals may be struck at Fort St. George, for which purpose the Brigade-Major will transmit a list of the names of the Volunteers to the Adjutant-General, as from the want of handicraftsmen it would not be practicable to have them done here. Should the Right Honorable the Governor in Council think proper to express his approbation of the conduct of the men in this particular instance in any other manner he may think more suitable, it will afford me particular pleasure and satisfaction in publishing the sentiments of Govt. to those meritorious soldiers.

. . . . .

'D. BURR, *Colonel,*
Commanding the Moluccas.'

'Ordered to lie on the table for future consideration.' (Page 2665.)

No. 133.

SERINGAPATAM, 1799.

There are two Seringapatam Medals: one (No. 1) made in England at the Soho Mint, Birmingham, and the other (No. 2) at the Calcutta Mint, the latter being copied from the former.

MEDAL, No. 1.

PLATE 16, *No.* 2.

Obv. Representation of the storming of the breach at Seringapatam, from a drawing made on the spot, with the meridian sun denoting the time of the storm. In the *exergue*, in Persian:—'The Fort of Seringapatam, the gift of God, the 4th May, 1799.'

On the ground to the left, the initial K.

Rev. The British Lion subduing the Tiger, the emblem of Tippoo Sultan's Government. On a banner, the Union badge, and the following words in Arabic:—'Assud otta-ul Ghaulib'; signifying: 'The Lion of God is the conqueror,' or 'The conquering Lion of God.'

On the ground below the tiger the initials, C. H. K. In the *exergue*:—IV. MAY. MDCCXCIX.

Circular, 1·9 inch. Gold. Silver-gilt. Silver. Copper bronzed. Pure grain tin.

Artist, C. H. Küchler. Struck at the Soho Mint, Birmingham.

Dies in possession of Messrs. Taylor, Medallists, 70 Red Lion Street, London.

Ribbons, Crimson with blue borders. Yellow watered.

Worn by general officers round the neck; by others, on the left breast.

MEDAL, No. 2.

Obv. Same as No. 1.

Rev. Same as No. 1—except that the initials on the ground below the tiger are rendered 'C. Ж. H.'

Circular, 1·8 inch. Gold. Silver.

Dies engraved and preserved at the Calcutta Mint.

Mounted with a loop for suspension.

As already observed, this medal is copied from that made at the Soho Mint. It is less in diameter by one-tenth of an inch, and is in some respects inferior in execution. On the *obverse*, the ramparts and buildings are indistinct, although the troops in the foreground and certain other details are well worked out. On the *reverse*, the bodies of the lion and tiger are imperfect, as likewise is the ground. Native workmanship is revealed by the mistake in the initials of the artist, which are rendered 'C. Ж. H.,' instead of 'C. H. K.'

SERINGAPATAM MEDAL, No. 1.

The Court of Directors of the East India Company on 24th September, 1799, resolved that the thanks of the Court be given to the Earl of Mornington, Governor-General; Lord Clive, Governor of Madras; Jonathan Duncan, Esq., Governor of Bombay; Lieutenant-General George Harris, Commander-in-Chief at Seringapatam; the Officers of the King's and Company's Armies engaged at Seringapatam on 4th May, 1799; and Lieutenant-General Stuart, Commanding the Bombay Army, for their services in, and in connection with, the campaign which resulted in the capture of Seringapatam on 4th May, 1799. On 13th November, 1799, the General Court of the East India Company passed identical resolutions.

These resolutions make no mention of a medal. In February, 1801, orders were, however, given for the preparation of 30 gold medals, 185 silver gilt, 850 silver, 5000 copper bronzed, and 45,000 pure tin. The cost amounted to £3915, 13s. 11d.

This medal, like Mr. Davison's for the Battle of the Nile, was designed by Mr. C. H. Küchler, and made by Mr. Matthew Boulton at the Soho Mint, Birmingham. The artist carried out the same idea on both medals—viz. a representation of the action and an indication, by the position of the sun, of the time of day at which it took place. The use of different metals for the various ranks was an adaptation of Mr. Davison's idea in the case of the Nile Medal.[1] The medals were made in 1801-2, but, for some reason which is not apparent, none were sent to India for distribution until 1808.

The Royal sanction for wearing this medal was accorded, in respect of the Company's officers, in 1815. There does not appear to have been any similar sanction in regard to the Royal Army until 1851, when, in the Horse Guards General Order announcing the grant of the 'India, 1799-1826' Medal, it was stated that the officers and soldiers of the Crown who had received the Seringapatam Medal, had Her Majesty's permission to wear the same.

There is some uncertainty as to how, and with what ribbon, these medals were generally worn. There is no doubt that they

[1] The Nile Medal was executed before the capture of Seringapatam.

were issued unmounted, and, as no directions had been given by the authorities, details as to ribbon and mountings devolved on the recipients, who exercised their own discretion and taste. It is, however, probable that the European officers wore them as the gold medals for the Peninsula and other campaigns were worn—*i.e.* round the neck, or at the button-hole, according to rank. Some added a clasp bearing the word 'Seringapatam.'

Three patterns of ribbon, at least, appear to have been used, viz., red with blue borders, yellow watered, and plain red. That the first was used under some sort of authority is gathered from a discussion which took place between the Madras Government and Commander-in-Chief in 1831, on the occasion of the distribution of the medals awarded to the native troops for the first Burmese War. The Commander-in-Chief had proposed that a piece of red ribbon with blue borders should be issued with each medal. The Government assented to the issue of ribbon, but objected to the pattern on the ground of its resemblance to the Waterloo ribbon. To this the Commander-in-Chief replied that the ribbon he had proposed was common to all medals granted by His Majesty in modern times, and was considered to be the medal ribbon of England. He added:—'The medals of Seringapatam and Java (the gold medal) are both suspended from it, and both are so worn with the sanction of His Majesty.'

This is authoritative evidence of the medal being worn with the only military medal ribbon then in use.

Lord Harris, who commanded at Seringapatam, wore his medal (gold) suspended round his neck by the red, blue-bordered ribbon, as the gold war medal was worn by general officers. A bust of his lordship was at the Royal Military Exhibition at Chelsea in 1890 (*Catalogue*, No. 899). This showed the medal worn round the neck, with a clasp inscribed 'Seringapatam.' The ribbon is crosswise, as in the 'Empress' medal. His son, the second Lord Harris, who was present at Seringapatam as a lieutenant, used the same ribbon, the medal being worn on the breast.

The medal (gold) of Sir David Baird, Bart., who was second in command under Lord Harris, has the same ribbon attached to it.

On the other hand, the Duke of Wellington's medal[1] (silver

[1] The mounting of the Duke's medal is similar to the mounting of the Sutlej, Punjab, Long Service, and several other medals; it is of comparatively modern date, and probably superseded an earlier mounting.

gilt) has the yellow ribbon; and Carter, in his *Medals of the British Army*, Part III. p. 6, quotes General Sir James L. Caldwell, of the Madras Engineers, who received the Seringapatam medal, and Mr. Albert Woods, Lancaster Herald, to the effect that no ribbon accompanied the medal: but the recipients were given to understand that the ribbon was to be of a deep yellow colour, about an inch wide. This colour was adopted in reference to the tiger, Tippoo Sultan's favourite emblem, the shading on the ribbon being intended to represent the stripes in the tiger's fur.

MINUTES OF THE COMMITTEE OF CORRESPONDENCE OF THE COURT OF DIRECTORS OF THE EAST INDIA COMPANY,
4th February, 1801.

'*Ordered*, that 30 gold medals at 8½ guineas each
185 silver gilt at 17s. 1d. each
850 silver at 14s. 1d. each
5,000 copper bronzed at 2s. 6d. each
and 45,000 of pure tin at 1s. 0d. each
in commemoration of the capture of Seringapatam, be made and distributed agreeably to a List now approved by the Committee.'

AT A COURT OF DIRECTORS, 5th August, 1801.

'*Ordered*, that a Warrant be made out to Mr. Matthew Boulton for £987, 3s. 1d. in payment for the Gold and Silver Medals which were struck to commemorate the capture of the Capital and Country of Mysore.'

25th August, 1801.

'*Ordered*, that a Warrant be made out to Mr. Matthew Boulton for £626, 2s. 6d. in payment for Copper bronzed Medals, which were struck to commemorate the capture of the Capital and Country of Mysore.'

10th March, 1802.

'*Ordered*, that a Warrant be made out to Mr. Matthew Boulton for £2302, 8s. 4½d. for Medals for the Troops employed in the late Mysore Campaign against Tippoo Sultaun.'

MINUTES OF THE COMMITTEE OF CORRESPONDENCE OF THE COURT OF DIRECTORS OF THE EAST INDIA COMPANY,
8th January, 1808.

'A list of the Gold Medals struck in commemoration of the success of the British Arms in Mysore, which are now remaining at the India House, was laid before the Committee.

'The Chairman and Deputy-Chairman undertook to present those intended for His Majesty and Lord Melville.

'Letters were ordered to be written to the Field Officers who have not yet received their Medals, transmitting the same to them.

'And the remaining Medals were ordered to be sent to India as advised in the Paragraphs for Bengal, Madras, and Bombay, already approved.'

FROM THE COURT OF DIRECTORS TO THE GOVT. OF FORT ST. GEORGE, 26th Feb., 1808—Military.

'2. Some time ago we caused a Medal to be executed by one of the most eminent artists in this country, in commemoration of the brilliant success of the British Arms in Mysore in 1799, for distribution amongst the Officers and Soldiers (European and Native) employed on that glorious occasion. On one side of it is represented the storming the breach of Seringapatam, from an actual drawing on the spot, with the meridian sun, denoting the time of the storm, with the following inscription in Persian underneath. "The Fort of Seringapatam, the gift of God, the 4th May 1799." On the reverse side is the British Lion subduing the Tiger, the emblem of the late Tippoo Sultaun's Govt., with the period when it was effected, and the following words in Arabic on the banner, "Assud otta-ul Ghaulib," signifying the Lion of God is the Conqueror, or the Conquering Lion of God.

'3. Of these Medals Gold ones have been struck for His Majesty, the Right Honorable Lord Melville, the Governor-General in India at the time, Marquis Cornwallis, the Nizam and his two Ministers, the Peishwah and his Minister, the Nabobs of Arcot and Oude, and the Rajahs of Tanjore, Travancore, Mysore, Coorg and Berar. Dowlut Row Scindia, the Commander-in-Chief, General Officers on the Staff employed in the Service, and for the Oriental Museum.

'Silver Gilt for the Members of Council at the three Presidencies, the Residents of Hydrabad and Poonah, the Field Officers, and the General Staff on the service.

'Silver, for the Captains and Subalterns on the service.

'Copper bronzed, for the Non-Commissioned, and

'Pure Grain Tin, for the Privates.

'4. We have estimated the Army employed before Seringapatam at 51,000, exclusive of General Officers, but including all others, and an equal number of Medals have been struck, and these are now forwarded to your Presidency, Four Gold Medals, to be presented to the Nabob of Arcot, the Rajahs of Tanjore, Travancore and Coorg.

'5. The Medals for the late Governor of Madras, for Generals Stuart and Bridges, and the late Generals Brathwaite and Hartley, have been presented here, and as all the remaining General Officers employed on the Expedition are in this Country, they will receive the Medals here.

'6. One hundred Silver Gilt Medals, for the Members of Council in May, 1799, for the Residents at Hyderabad and Poonah at the same period, and for the Field Officers and General Staff of the Army employed on the Expedition, have been forwarded to your Presidency for distribution, the calculation is founded on the Returns sent in by the Adjutant-General in 1800, from which the number of the Staff entitled to be considered as Field Officers had been computed at forty-two, but you will determine on the accuracy of this calculation. These were forwarded by the *Albion* in September, 1805.

'7. The Medals for Officers of the foregoing description belonging to the other Presidencies are to be forwarded thither to them.

'8. Eight hundred Silver Medals for Captains and Subalterns, including such of the General Staff as are to be considered of those ranks, were also forwarded by the *Albion*, and are to be considered under similar directions to the foregoing.

'9. Five thousand bronzed Medals are now sent to be distributed to the Native Commissioned and Non-Commissioned Officers as are in the margin, to Sergeants, Drummers or Fifers, and Trumpeters of European Corps, and to Conductors and others of the General Staff, considered as Non-Commissioned Officers. The number of these, according to the Returns above mentioned, appears to be 4331.

Subadars.
Jemadars.
Syrangs.
1st Tindals.
Havildars.
Trumpeters.
Drummers and Fifers.
Head Guides.

'10. Forty-five thousand Tin Medals are likewise now sent, for Corporals, Gunners and Private Europeans, and for Naicks, Farriers, Native Doctors, Golundauze, Private Sepoys, Second Tindals, Lascars, Puckallies and Guides of the Native Troops, the number of these from the Returns was about 42,450.

'11. In regard to the Medals of the two last descriptions for the Troops belonging to the other Presidencies, we must call your attention to what is said above respecting the Silver Medals.

'12. As many of the Troops serving under your Presidency employed in the siege of Seringapatam, must have since deceased, you will endeavour to learn the situation of their families or heirs, and forward the Medals to them.

'13. A List of Officers who have received Medals in this Country is likewise now forwarded.'

The above was published in Madras G.G.O. 6th July, 1808, and republished in G.O.C.C. Madras, 18th July, 1808 (at p. 10 of Vol. of G.O. for that period).

FROM THE COURT OF DIRECTORS TO THE GOVERNMENT OF BENGAL, 26th February, 1808—Military.

'2. We forward in the Packet one of the Gold Medals struck in commemoration of the brilliant success of the British Arms in Mysore in 1799, which is to be presented to Governor Duncan. We also enclose in the Packet a copy of our Despatch to Madras (26th February, 1808) on the subject of the Medals struck on that occasion.'

GENERAL ORDER BY THE COMMANDER-IN-CHIEF, MADRAS, 5th January, 1811,

Prescribing the mode in which claims to the Seringapatam Medal are to be prepared.

'EAST INDIA HOUSE,
16th August, 1815.

'MY LORD,

'Several years have elapsed since the Court of Directors, with the approbation and concurrence of His Majesty's Ministers, caused a great number of Medals, in commemoration of the storming of Seringapatam, and of the other splendid successes of the British Army in Mysore in 1799, to be executed by an eminent artist and distributed to the Officers and Soldiers both of His Majesty's and of the Company's Troops who served in that brilliant and decisive campaign.

'The European Officers of the Company's Service have represented to us that, highly as they have been gratified with the receipt of those honorable testimonials, they experienced considerable mortification in not feeling themselves at liberty to wear them on great public occasions, such as being presented at Court, and at the Military Levees of His Royal Highness the Commander-in-Chief.

'This sentiment necessarily strikes them with peculiar force at the present period, when all the Officers of Europe, who have distinguished themselves in the service of their several Sovereigns, appear upon all public occasions, decorated with the honorable badges of their services and glory.

'We therefore intreat your Lordship to transmit these circumstances to His Royal Highness the Prince Regent, and to solicit his gracious permission, that the Medals granted by the East India Company on the occasion of the capture of Seringapatam by storm on the 4th May, 1799, and the other splendid successes of the British Arms in Mysore in that year, may be worn by the Officers who have received them, in such manner and at such times as to His Royal Highness may appear proper.

'We have, etc.,

'CHARLES GRANT.
THOS. REID.

'The Right Honourable
The EARL OF BUCKINGHAMSHIRE,
President of the Board of Commissioners
for the Affairs of India.'

'WHITEHALL,
29th August, 1815.

'GENTLEMEN,

'Your application on behalf of the Officers of the Company's Army, to whom Medals have been granted with the concurrence and approbation of His Majesty's Government, in consideration of their services, having been laid before his Royal Highness the Prince Regent, I have now the satisfaction of informing you, that His Royal Highness has been pleased to grant his gracious permission, that such Officers may wear their Medals in any part of His Majesty's dominions.

'I have, etc.,

'BUCKINGHAMSHIRE.

'To the Chairman and Deputy Chairman
of the East India Company.'

FROM THE COURT OF DIRECTORS TO THE GOVERNMENT OF BENGAL, 20th November, 1816—Military.

Paragraph 5 requests the return of Seringapatam Medals of Officers who have gone to England.

The following troops were present at the capture of Seringapatam :—

European—

Madras Engineers.
Bengal Artillery—Detachment.
Madras ,, 1st and 2nd Battalions.
Bombay ,, Detachment.
H.M.'s 12th, 33rd, 73rd, 74th, 75th, and 77th Foot.
Scotch Brigade.
Regiment de Meuron.
Bombay European Regiment.

Native—

Bengal[1]	10th N. I.—1st and 2nd Battalions.	
	1st, 2nd and 3rd Battalions of Volunteers.	
Madras	1st N. I. 1st Batt.	2nd N. I. 2nd Batt.
	3rd N. I. 2nd Batt.	5th N. I. 2nd Batt.
	6th N. I. 1st Batt.	7th N. I. 2nd Batt.
	8th N. I. 1st Batt.	9th N. I. 2nd Batt.
	11th N. I. 1st and 2nd Batts.	12th N. I. 1st and 2nd Batts.
	Pioneer Corps.	
Bombay	2nd N. I. 1st and 2nd Batts.	3rd N. I. 1st and 2nd Batts.
	4th N. I. 1st Batt.	5th N. I. 1st Batt.
	Pioneer Corps.	

SERINGAPATAM MEDAL. No. 2.

On the return to Bengal of the native troops belonging to that Presidency who had been in service in Southern India, and were present at Seringapatam—viz. the 10th Native Infantry, three battalions of Volunteers, and detachments of Artillery Lascars—the Commander-in-Chief suggested that Government should mark their approbation of the distinguished services of those corps by the bestowal of a medal as on former occasions. The Governor-General concurred, and General Orders were published granting medals to the native ranks of the troops in question.

The official records are for several years silent regarding this medal, and the next mention of it appears to be in a General Order of the Commander-in-Chief, dated 10th April, 1807, calling for lists of those entitled to receive it.

Nothing is said in the General Orders conferring the medal as to the metal of which it was to be made. Precedent appears, however, to have been followed; and the medals of the native officers were made of gold, and those for the other ranks of silver. In this respect therefore the Bengal native soldiers were far more highly favoured than any of the other troops, European or Native, who served in the campaign; inasmuch as whilst the other native troops received bronze and tin medals for officers and men respectively, those of Bengal obtained gold and silver, the officers, as regarded their decorations, being thus placed on an equality with British general officers, and the men with British captains and subalterns. The Bengal Government, in adhering to precedent, can scarcely have been aware of what had been done in England.

[1] The natives of the Bengal portion of the force did not receive this medal, but the one in gold and silver, granted by the Bengal Government. See Medal No. 2.

The manufacture of the medals was entrusted to the Calcutta Mint, and in May, 1808, the Mint Master delivered specimens, and expressed the hope that they would meet with the approbation of Government. The cost per medal was :—

Gold . . .	Rs. 72.9
Silver . . .	3.5

and the numbers were—gold, 83, and silver, 2786. (See Abstract in *Bengal Military Proceedings*, 23rd August, 1808, No. 84.)

From a report by the officer commanding the 1st Battalion of the 10th N. I., we learn that the medals of the officers and men of that corps were presented to them on parade, in front of the colours, at Rewarrie, on 3d March, 1809.

BENGAL MILITARY PROCEEDINGS, 19th June, 1800.

No. 1. *Minute by the Commander-in-Chief, dated 12th June,* 1800.

'I had the honor to report the arrival of the 10th Regt. N. I. at Cawnpore through the usual official channel some days ago, and I now feel myself called upon, in consequence of the repeated favorable reports of the exemplary good conduct of this Corps in every situation it has been employed during the long period of more than three years and a half that it has been detached from this Presidency on active and important service, to submit for your Lordship's consideration the propriety of Government's making some public declaration of the sense it entertains of its fidelity and discipline, which cannot but be highly gratifying to the officers respectively under whose command and attention it has so deservedly acquired the good reputation it bears, as well as to every individual now serving with it, and be a strong incitement for the army at large to avail themselves of every future opportunity to merit an equally honorable mark of the approbation of your Lordship in Council.

'Upon some former occasions, and no one appears to me to have deserved it better than the present, this has been done, and an honorary Badge or Medal, which is very gratifying to the Native Troops, given with it. What expense this would occasion I cannot say, but if it is not very great, I am sure it would be more than compensated by the effect it would have on the minds of the soldiers.

'ALURED CLARKE.'

No. 2. *Resolutions on the foregoing.*

'The Governor-Genl. in Council directs that the following be published in General Orders to the Army.

'FORT WILLIAM, *June 19th,* 1800.

'The 10th Regt. of Native Infantry having arrived at Cawnpore, after an absence from this Presidency of more than three years and a half, the Most Noble the Governor-Genl. in Council has great satisfaction in expressing his entire approbation of the exemplary conduct of this distinguished Regiment in the several arduous and important services on which it has been employed in the Peninsula of India during its long absence from these Provinces.

'His Lordship in Council is happy to bear this public testimony to the merits of the European Officers under whose command this Corps has attained so high a state of discipline, regularity and order, and he entertains a just sense of the fidelity and attachment to the Service manifested by the Native Officers and Private Soldiers of the Regt. throughout the whole period of their laborious duties at Hydrabad, in Mysoor, and during their long march from the Deccan to the Province of Oude.

'The conduct of the Artillery and Lascars, who have been attached to the Regt. during the time of its absence from these Provinces, is equally entitled to commendation.

'To perpetuate the memory of the services of the 10th Regt., to distinguish the individuals who have served in the Corps, and to recommend their laudable example to the emulation of the whole Native Service, the Most Noble the Governor-Genl. in Council is pleased to order that honorary Medals be conferred on the Native Commissioned and Non-commissioned Officers and Sepoys of the 10th Regt., and also on the Lascars belonging to the Artillery, attached to that Regt., during the time of its absence from these Provinces.'

BENGAL MILITARY PROCEEDINGS, 7th August, 1800. *No.* 1.

Minute by the Commander-in-Chief, dated 23rd July, 1800.

'I have the honor to report the arrival of the three Battalions of Bengal Volunteers under the command of Lieut.-Colonel Gardiner at Midnapore, on 16th instant.

'These Corps having been made the foundation of the 18th and 19th Regiments of Native Infantry, I have directed such part of them as is allotted for the former to proceed without loss of time to Berhampore, and that for the latter to Barrackpore, as the most convenient places for affording them immediate shelter, and completing their formation.

'The alacrity and spirit with which every individual composing the Volunteer Battalions offered his service and embarked for the coast, at a period when the speedy augmentation of the Army there was of the utmost importance, are well known to Govt.; and I have great satisfaction in remarking to your Lordship in Council that every account I have received of their conduct since has been equally honorable to themselves and beneficial to the State, even to the very moment of their departure from the Northern Circars, where their meritorious services were honorably noticed by the Govt. of Fort St. George.

'Under these circumstances I have no doubt of your Lordship's ready disposition to gratify the feelings of this valuable Corps, by expressing the favourable sentiments entertained by this Govt. of its zeal and fidelity, and by granting a similar indulgence of Honorary Medals to that lately bestowed on the Native Troops from Hyderabad, which I am fully of opinion they merit.

'ALURED CLARKE.'

The following General Orders were issued by the Governor-General in Council on the 6th instant (August, 1800):—

GENERAL ORDER.

'The Most Noble the Governor-General in Council having received from H.E. the Commander-in-Chief the notification of the arrival within these Provinces of the three Battalions of Bengal Volunteers, under the command of Lieut.-Colonel Gardiner, feels a peculiar satisfaction in publishing to the Army His Lordship's most cordial approbation of the distinguished services rendered to the British Empire in India by the European and Native Officers and Privates of those gallant and meritorious Corps, during the late arduous crisis of public affairs. His Lordship remarked with the warmest sentiments of gratitude the alacrity and zeal manifested by the

Native Officers and Privates in their voluntary embarkation for the coast of Coromandel at the eve of the late glorious war: after the commencement of the war, the exemplary discipline, valour and steadiness of the Bengal Volunteers were eminently conspicuous on various important occasions: and the official reports which His Lordship repeatedly received from the field during his residence at Fort St. George, justify in attributing to the Bengal Volunteers, a considerable portion of the glory and honor acquired by the British Arms during the brilliant and memorable campaign in Mysore.

'After the reduction of Seringapatam, the Most Noble the Governor-General in Council was happy to observe the laudable and unabated exertions of the Bengal Volunteers in accompanying the rapid movements of the army upon the Northern frontiers of the dominions of the Rajah of Mysoor.

'When the service in Mysoor had been brought to a conclusion, the conduct of the Bengal Volunteer Battalions in the Northern Circars was such as to receive the most honorable testimony of approbation from the Right Hon. the Governor in Council at Fort St. George.

'In addition to these circumstances which have fallen under the immediate observation of the Governor-General in Council, the favorable reports which His Lordship has received from H.E. the Commander-in-Chief, of the uniform fidelity, attachment, dutiful subordination, and determined courage manifested by these valuable Corps on every emergency, require that His Lordship in Council should confer a mark of Honorary distinction on the Bengal Volunteers, for the purpose of commemorating their services and of recommending their example to the imitation of their fellow-soldiers.

'The Most Noble the Governor-General in Council is therefore pleased to order that honorary Medals be conferred on all the Native Commissioned, and Non-commissioned Officers and Sepoys of the three Battalions of Bengal Volunteers recently returned from the Coast of Coromandel.'

GENERAL ORDER BY THE PROVINCIAL COMMANDER-IN-CHIEF, 10th April, 1807.

'Regulations for the preparation of Rolls, etc. for Honorary Medals granted to Native Troops.

'With reference to G. O. by the Govr.-Genl. in Council dated 19th June, 1800, granting Honorary Medals to the Native Commissioned, Non-commissioned Officers and Privates of the 10th Regt. N.I., as also to the Gun Lascars who were attached to that Regt. during its absence from these Provinces: With reference also to G. O. by the Govr.-General in Council dated 6th Aug., 1800, granting Honorary Medals to all the Native Commissioned, Non-commissioned Officers and Sepoys who composed the three Battalions of Bengal Volunteers which were engaged in the last war in Mysore: and with reference to G. O. by the Govr.-Gen. in Council dated 31st July, 1802, granting Honorary Medals to all the Native Commissioned Officers, Troopers, Sepoys, Golundaz and Gun Lascars, who were employed on service in Egypt under Major-Genl. Baird; the Provincial Commr.-in-Chief directs that Rolls with figured abstracts of all the Native Commissioned, Non-commissioned Officers, Troopers and Sepoys, Golundaz and Gun Lascars, who are entitled to Honorary Medals for the occasions above referred to, be immediately prepared on foolscap paper and transmitted to the Adjt.-Genl.'s Office, by the Officers commanding the several Corps and Establishments to which the persons so entitled may now belong.

'The Rolls from the 10th, 18th and 19th Regts. N.I. to be prepared by Companies, and to be countersigned and transmitted by Commanding Officers of Battalions, with the signature also of the Colonel Commandant, when present with the Corps.

'One Roll and Abstract only is to be prepared by every other Corps, in which is to be comprised all those now belonging to such Corps who may be entitled to Honorary Medals for any of the occasions above referred to, under the distinct heads of "10th Regt. in the Dukhun"—"Bengal Volunteers in Mysore"—"Bengal Volunteers in Egypt."

'*N.B.*—By Minutes of Council [19th January, 1784], 22nd Jan., 1785, and by G. O. 4th June, 1793, Honorary Medals were granted to Native Troops for Service in Guzerat and the Carnatic and Mysore.'

GENERAL ORDER BY THE PROVINCIAL COMMANDER-IN-CHIEF, 24th April, 1807.

'All Volunteers who embarked for service on account of which Medals are granted, are entitled to them, whether they reached their destination or not.

'All Volunteers who embarked from Bengal for service in Egypt, or who proceeded from Bengal on other foreign services referred to in G. O. of 10th April, 1807, and who have returned to this Presidency and are now alive, are to be considered as entitled to Medals, and to be included in the Rolls accordingly, whether they reached the place of their original destination or not.'

PROCLAMATION, VICE-PRESIDENT, 10th Sept., 1811.

'Directions for the issue of Medals and Gratuities to Native Invalids on the Pension Estabt.

'In the case of claims preferred to Honorary Medals, that it be stated by the Collector from what service the claim arises; whether for those in the Dukhun and Mysoor, in Egypt under Genl. Baird, or on the Island of Ceylon, in order that the Officers of the Invalid Depts. may direct their inquiries accordingly.' (See Henley's *Military Code*, pp. 246, 247, and 698.)

Further papers relative to the grant of this medal will be found in the Appendix.

No. 134.

EGYPT, 1801.

PLATE 16, *No.* 3.

Obv. A Sepoy holding the Union flag in his right hand; in the background a camp. In the *exergue*, in Persian:—'This medal has been presented in commemoration of the defeat of the French Army in Egypt by the victorious and brave English Army.'

Rev. A British ship sailing towards the coast of Egypt. In the background, an obelisk and four pyramids. In the *exergue*, MDCCCI.

Circular, 1·9 inch. Gold. Silver.
Mounted with a loop for suspension.
Dies engraved and preserved at the Calcutta Mint.

The grant of this medal was announced in the General Order issued by the Governor-General on the return to India of the Egypt Expeditionary Force under General Baird in 1802.

The General Order does not specify the metals of which the medals were to be made, but it appears from the Calcutta Mint Accounts for 1811 that they were of gold and silver for native officers and soldiers respectively, the cost being as under:—

16 gold medals with loops, . .	Rs.	1338	15	0
760 silver medals with loops, .		3388	9	0

The same mistake occurred in the case of the Egypt medal as in that of the medal for Ceylon, namely, that impressions from the Seringapatam die were in the first instance struck for distribution. The discovery of the error led to the submission by the Adjutant-General in August, 1810, of specific designs for the Egypt medal.

In Williams' *History of the Bengal Native Infantry* it is stated (p. 277) that the Hindoo Sepoys, who had volunteered for Egypt, were exempted from the duties levied on the performance of their religious ceremonies at Gya. This was an indulgence similar to that accorded to the troops who received the medal for the campaign in the West of India, 1778-84.

The medals referred to above were for the Bengal portion of the Egypt army.

In 1803 the Government of Bombay reported to the Court of Directors that they had given orders for the bestowal of medals on the Bombay portion of the force, a proceeding of which the Court duly expressed approval.

No active measures seem to have been taken in respect to the preparation of the medal until 1812, when the Bombay Government applied for a specimen of the medal struck at the Calcutta Mint to enable them to prepare similar ones. Bombay appears, however, to have been unequal to the occasion, inasmuch as the specimen was returned to Calcutta with a request that 1439 similar medals, each with a ring attached 'for the purpose of suspending it on the soldier by whom it is worn,' might be struck at the Calcutta Mint, and forwarded to Bombay upon the first opportunity. The Calcutta Mint Accounts for 1814 show that all these medals were made of silver. The Bombay native officers and soldiers must therefore have fared alike. The total cost of the medals was Rs. 5519.8.

The total numbers of medals struck were therefore—

Bengal—Commissioned Officers, .	16 gold.
Other Ranks, ...	760 silver.
Bombay—All Ranks, ...	1439 silver.

GENERAL ORDERS BY HIS EXCELLENCY THE MOST NOBLE THE GOVERNOR-GENERAL IN COUNCIL, Fort William, 31st July, 1802.

'Under a grateful impression of the important aid derived to the common cause of our country by the able and successful conduct of the Expedition from India to Egypt, the Governor-General in Council notifies his public thanks to Major-General Baird, and to all the Officers and Troops employed under his command in Egypt. His Excellency in Council is further pleased to order that honorary medals be conferred on all the native Commissioned and Non-Commissioned Officers, Troopers and Sepoys, Golundauze and Gun Lascars, who have been employed on Service in Egypt.'

(*Bengal Military Consultations*, 7th August, 1802.)

FROM THE GOVERNMENT OF BENGAL TO THE COURT OF DIRECTORS, 30th Sept., 1802—Military.

'145. Under a grateful impression of the important aid derived to the common cause of our Country by the able and successful conduct of the expedition from India to Egypt, the Governor-General in Council notified his public thanks to Major-General Baird and to all the Officers and Troops employed under his command in Egypt. His Excellency in Council was further pleased to order that honorary Medals be conferred on all the Native Commissioned and Non-Commissioned Officers, the Troopers, the Sepoys, the Golundauze, and the Gun Lascars, who have been employed on service in Egypt.'

FROM THE COURT OF DIRECTORS TO THE GOVERNMENT OF BENGAL, 14th Sept., 1803—Military.

'54. In the General Orders issued by you on 31st July, 1802, you have fully expressed the sense which we ourselves entertain of the services rendered by Major-General Baird, and the Officers and Soldiers under him, and we entirely approve of your having notified to Major-General Baird, and to all Officers and Troops employed under his command in Egypt, your public thanks for the services rendered to the Nation by their exemplary conduct.'

'55. Considering also your representation of the cheerful alacrity displayed by our Native Troops in surmounting the difficulties to which they were unavoidably exposed from the nature of the country, and in embarking on a service of which the object was unknown to them until they had reached the point of their destination, we have further to signify our approbation of your having directed that honorary Medals be conferred on all the Native Commissioned and Non-Commissioned Officers, Troopers and Sepoys, Golundauze and Gun Lascars, who have been employed on this service.'

FROM THE GOVERNMENT OF BOMBAY TO THE COURT OF DIRECTORS, 5th Feb., 1803—Military.

'75. H.E. the Most Noble the Governor-General in Council having been pleased to order that Honorary Medals should be conferred on all the Native Commissioned Officers, Sepoys and Gun Lascars, who were employed on service in Egypt; it appeared to us equally necessary and incumbent that a similar mark of attention and approbation should be bestowed on the Native Corps under this Presidency, who were on the same foreign service: and orders were accordingly issued to carry this intention into effect, under the date specified in the margin.'—(*Bombay Military Consultations*, 8th Oct., 1802.)

FROM THE COURT OF DIRECTORS TO THE GOVERNMENT OF BOMBAY, 30th January, 1805—Military.

Letter dated 5th Feb., 1803. 75. Honorary Medals granted to Troops in Egypt.

'47. We approve of your Resolution on this subject.'

FROM THE GOVERNMENT OF BOMBAY TO THE COURT OF DIRECTORS, 23d July, 1806—Military.

Reply to p. 47 of Court's letter, dated 30th Jan., 1805.
Honorary Medals given to Troops in Egypt, approved.

'34. The Commanding Officer of the Forces has been called on to report what ultimate proceedings have been held in the execution of the orders issued on this subject.'

Copies of the following documents will be found among the Seringapatam papers in the Appendix—*General Order by Provisional Commander-in-Chief*, 10th April, 1807, directing the preparation of Rolls of the native officers and soldiers entitled to the medal; another General Order of 24th April, 1807, providing that all the troops who volunteered for service in Egypt are to be considered entitled to medals, whether they reached their destination or not; an abstract of the medals required, from *Bengal Military Proceedings*, 23rd August, 1808, No. 84; a correspondence from the same source, 19th September, 1808, No. 15, in which it is brought to notice that the medals, which had been prepared for issue to the troops who had served in Ceylon and Egypt, had been struck from the Seringapatam dies, whereupon the Government directed that fresh medals with appropriate devices should be prepared for the troops in question; and a report as to the preparation of Seringapatam, Ceylon, and Egypt medals, *From the Government of Bengal to the Court of Directors*, 27th March, 1809—Military, paras. 724-7 and 729.

BENGAL PUBLIC PROCEEDINGS, 14th Sept., 1810. *No.* 46.

Extract from the Proceedings of the Right Hon. the Governor-General in Council in the Military Department, under date 8th Sept., 1810. (No. 45.)

No. 913.

'To JOHN ADAM, Esq.,

'Secretary to Govt., Military Dept.

'SIR,

'With reference to General Orders by Govt. under date 31st July, 1802, authorising Medals to be granted to the Native Troops employed under Major-Genl. Baird in Egypt; I have the honor to forward to you to be submitted for the approbation of the Right Hon. the Governor-Genl. in Council, the enclosed drawings exhibiting an inscription and devices which it is humbly conceived might be suitably adopted as those of the Medal above referred to.

'I beg leave to observe to you for the notice of the Right Hon. the Governor Genl. in Council, that under the General Orders by Govt. above mentioned, 16 Gold and 700 Silver Medals will be required to answer the claims to this honorary distinction.

'I have, etc.,

'GEORGE BALL,
Adjt.-Genl.

'ADJUTANT-GENL.'S OFFICE,
30*th Aug.*, 1810.'

'*Ordered*, that a copy of the foregoing letter with the drawings of the Medals therein referred to be sent to the Public Dept., whence the Mint Master is to be instructed to strike 16 Gold and 700 Silver Medals, to answer the claims of the Native Troops employed under Major-Genl. Baird in Egypt.

'*Ordered also*, that the Mint Master be directed at the same time to deliver the Medals when finished to the Adjt.-Genl., taking his receipt for the number supplied.

'True Extract.

'J. ADAM,
Sec. to Govt.'

'*Ordered*, that a copy of the foregoing extract, with the drawings of Medals referred to therein, be transmitted to the Acting Mint Master with directions to him to carry the Resolutions of Govt. into effect.'

GENERAL ORDER BY THE COMMANDER-IN-CHIEF, 13*th May*, 1811.

This General Order directs the preparation of Rolls of troops entitled to medals for Egypt and Ceylon. A copy will be found among the Ceylon papers in the Appendix.

BENGAL PUBLIC PROCEEDINGS, 21*st June*, 1811. *No.* 3.

Extract from the Proceedings of His Excellency the Vice-President in Council in the Military Department, under date 11th June, 1811. (No. 19.)

'To
C. W. GARDINER, Esq.,
Acting Secretary to Govt.,
Military Dept.

'SIR,

'With reference to my letter under date 30th Aug., 1810, on the subject of Honorary Medals granted to the Native Troops for service in Egypt, it being then stated that the number of Medals required to answer claims to this Honorary distinction was 16 of Gold and 700 of Silver, whereas the actual number now appears to be 760 of the latter description according to the Rolls of Claimants recorded in this Office; I am directed by the Commander-in-Chief to request you will submit His Excellency's recommendation that instructions may be given to the Assay Master to furnish a further supply of 60 Silver Medals to complete the number required for the services above mentioned.

'I am, etc.,

'GEORGE BALL,
Adjt.-Genl.

'ADJUTANT-GENL.'S OFFICE,
FORT WILLIAM, 10*th June*, 1811.'

'*Resolved*, that a copy of the foregoing letter be transmitted to the Public Dept. whence the Mint Master is to be instructed to strike off a further supply of Sixty honorary Silver Medals to complete the number required to answer the claims of the Native Troops employed under Major-Genl. Baird in Egypt.

'*Ordered*, that the Mint Master be directed at the same time to deliver the Silver Medals when finished to the Adjutant-Genl., taking his receipt for the number supplied.

'*Ordered*, that an extract from the proceedings be recorded in the Public Dept. for the purpose above specified.

'True Extract.

'C. W. GARDINER,
Acting Secretary to Govt.
Military Dept.'

'*Ordered*, that a copy of the foregoing extract be transmitted to the Mint Master, and that he be directed to carry into execution the Orders of Govt. therein communicated.'

PROCLAMATION BY VICE-PRESIDENT, 10*th September*, 1811.

A copy of this Proclamation, referring to the claims of pensioned native soldiers to the medal for Egypt, is included among the Seringapatam papers in the Appendix.

BENGAL PUBLIC PROCEEDINGS, 8*th May*, 1812. *No.* 11.

Military Proceedings, 2nd May, 1812 (No. 20).

'Read letter from the Secretary to the Govt. at Bombay dated 10th April, 1812.

'*Resolved*, that the Mint Master be instructed to furnish the Military Dept. with one Silver Medal for services in Egypt, for the purpose of being transmitted to Bombay to enable the Govt. to prepare similar Medals for distribution to the Troops belonging to that Establishment who are entitled to that honorary mark of distinction.

BENGAL PUBLIC PROCEEDINGS, 30*th July*, 1813. *No.* 47.

Military Proceedings, 24th July, 1813 (No. 387).

'To

C. W. GARDINER, Esq.,
Secretary, Military Dept., Fort William.

'BOMBAY CASTLE,
26*th June*, 1813.

'SIR,

'I am directed to desire you will submit to the Right Hon. the Governor-Genl. in Council, the request of the Right Hon. the Governor in Council (Bombay) that he will have the goodness to cause to be struck at Bengal and forwarded to Bombay by the first opportunity 1439 Medals for distribution to the Native Troops from this Presidency who served in Egypt, of the pattern transmitted with Mr. Secretary Adam's letter of 30th May, 1812, which is herewith returned, and to desire that a ring may be attached to each, for the purpose of suspending it on the soldier by whom it is worn.

'I have, etc.,

'J. FARISH,
Secretary to Govt.'

'*Ordered*, that a copy of the foregoing letter, together with the Medal which accompanied it, be transmitted to the Public Dept. whence the Mint Master will be instructed to strike off the number of Medals, with a ring attached to each of the descriptions therein required by the Govt. of Bombay, and to forward them when finished to the Military Dept. ready packed for transmission to that Presidency.'

BENGAL PUBLIC PROCEEDINGS, 25th March, 1814. *No.* 36.

This is the Calcutta Mint Account for preparation of medals. A copy is given with the Ceylon papers in the Appendix.

BENGAL PUBLIC PROCEEDINGS, 27th May, 1814. *Nos.* 7 *and* 8.

Military Proceedings, 14th May, 1814 (No. 200).

'To

C. W. GARDINER, Esq.,
Secretary to Govt., Military Dept.

'SIR,

'I beg leave to forward an account[1] of the charges for the Bullion and fabrication of Medals struck in the Calcutta Mint for the Bombay Presidency conformably to the orders of Govt. under date 24th July, 1813, and have to request your procuring from H.E. the Governor-Genl. in Council an order in favor of the Mint for Sa. Rs. 5629.7,—the amount thereof.

(Recommends remuneration to Foreman.)

'The Muster Medal is herewith returned.

'I have, etc.,

'MALCOLM M'LEOD,
Acting Mint Master.

'CALCUTTA MINT,
11*th May*, 1814.'

No. 135.

ASSAYE, 1803.

ELEPHANT BADGE.

Silver. Copper.

The Government of Madras in 1811 resolved to confer Honorary Badges on the native troops who were present at the battle of Assaye on 23rd September, 1803. The Badge was to

---

[1] EXTRACT OF ACCOUNT.

1814.		Rs.	a.	p.
Feb. 1.	Bullion for 1439 Silver Medals for Egypt for the Native Troops that proceeded from Bombay	4979	14	0
	For 1 pair of Dyes and for forming and finishing 1439 Medals @ 4 annas	359	12	0
	1439 Loops @ 2 annas	179	14	0

be the figure of an elephant in silver for the officers, and copper for the men, and it was to be similar to that worn by the British regiments which were present at the battle. It was to be worn in the turbands, and it may therefore be inferred that the British soldiers wore their Badges on their head-dresses. As the Badge was intended only for those who were actually present at the battle, it was in the nature of a personal decoration and not of a regimental 'appointment.'

The Badges were made at the Madras Mint—179 of silver, and 7269 of copper, at a cost of 1021 Pagodas. (Pagoda = Rs. 3½.) They were ready for distribution in 1813, and their issue to the troops was directed in a Minute of the Government, dated 1st June, 1813.

MADRAS MILITARY CONSULTATIONS, 22nd October, 1811.

'From the ADJUTANT-GENERAL of the Army,
To the CHIEF SECRETARY to Govt.,
Fort St. George.

'It having been directed by the Right Honorable the Governor-General in Council, that the Corps which served in the Army under Major-General Wellesley at the Battle of Assaye, on 23rd Sept., 1803, shall be presented with Honorary Colours,[1] with a device properly suited to commemorate that splendid and signal victory, which are now nearly ready for delivery, and the Corps of this Establishment having also adopted with the Commander-in-Chief's permission, the figure of an Elephant, as an Honorary device, similar to that worn by His Majesty's regiments which were present on the same occasion, it appears to the Commander-in-Chief to be proper that the Native Commissioned, Non-Commissioned, Rank and File of the Corps of Native Cavalry, Infantry and Pioneers which served in that Army, should wear a similar device in their Turbands, and that it should be presented to them by the Government; I am accordingly directed to request the sanction of the Honorable the Governor in Council, to the adoption of the measure, and to propose, as the cheapest mode of preparing the Honorary Badges, that authority may be given for making them up in the Clothing Dept., and allowing the Agent to charge the expense to Government.

'Mr. Ogilvie, the Mint Master, has, on this as well as many other occasions, kindly given his aid to the Department of the Agent for Army Clothing, by employing the facilities which the Mint Establishment affords, in cutting and preparing dies of different descriptions, which has not only been a considerable saving of expense to the Dept., but forwarded the progress of the issue of clothing most materially.

'The number of Elephants required will be 179 Silver, and 7269 Copper.

'Copper can be furnished on an indent from the Public Stores, and the Silver, with the sanction of the Honorable the Governor in Council, from the Mint, the value of which being debited to the Agent for Army Clothing, the whole expense will appear in his Bills, and will not materially exceed the value of the metals.

'FORT ST. GEORGE,
14th Oct., 1811.'

'The Board are happy to concur in the suggestion of the Officer Commanding the Army, for presenting Honorary Badges to the Native Troops who served under the

---

[1] *Vide* General Order by the Governor-General, 14th October, 1803.

command of Major-General Wellesley at the Battle of Assaye. They also approve the mode in which it is proposed that the Badges shall be prepared.

'*Ordered*, accordingly, that the Officer Commanding the Army be requested to give the necessary directions to the Agent for Army Clothing; and that the Board of Trade and the Mint Master be severally authorised to supply the copper and the silver which may be required by the Agent for the stated purpose.

'*Ordered* also, that the Officer Commanding the Army be requested to report to the Board when the Badges may be ready for distribution, that a General Order on the occasion may be issued by the Governor in Council.'

MADRAS MILITARY CONSULTATIONS, 1st June, 1813. *No.* 15.

'From the ADJUTANT-GENERAL of the Army,
To the CHIEF SECRETARY to Government,
Fort St. George.

'With reference to the Minutes of Council of 22nd Oct., 1811, I have the honor to report that the Honorary Badges, authorised to be made up for the Corps which served under Major-General Wellesley at the Battle of Assaye, have been received from the Mint, and are now ready for delivery, when Orders may be issued to that effect.

'FORT ST. GEORGE,
26th May, 1813.'

MINUTE THEREON (No. 16).

'It was the intention of the Governor in Council, as recorded in the Proceedings of this Dept. under date 22nd Oct., 1811, that a General Order by the Government should have been published on the occasion of distributing Honorary Badges to the Native troops who served at the Battle of Assaye, but as Honorary Colours have already been presented to those Corps by the late Commander-in-Chief, and as the European Officers have been permitted to wear Badges of Distinction under the same authority, it appears to be unnecessary that a General Order by the Govt. should now be issued.

'*Resolved*, therefore, that the Commander-in-Chief be authorised and requested to issue such directions as he may deem proper for distributing to the Native troops who served at the Battle of Assaye, the Badges which have been prepared for them in commemoration of that victory.'

MADRAS MILITARY CONSULTATIONS, 9th July, 1813. *No.* 21.

'From the ADJUTANT-GENERAL of the Army,
To the CHIEF SECRETARY to Govt.,
Fort St. George.

'I have the honor, by desire of His Excellency the Commander-in-Chief, to enclose a Bill for the amount of charges for articles and workmanship used in preparing silver and brass Honorary Badges for the troops who served under Major-General Wellesley at the Battle of Assaye; provided under the authority of the Minutes of the Honorable the Governor in Council, dated 22nd October, 1811, and request you will obtain authority for its being discharged.

'FORT ST. GEORGE,
5th July, 1813.'

ORDER THEREON (No. 22).

'*Ordered*, that authority be given for the payment of the bill submitted with the foregoing letter, amounting to Pagodas 1021.'

FROM THE GOVERNMENT OF MADRAS TO THE COURT OF DIRECTORS, 31*st December*, 1813—Military.

'57. At our Consultation of 1st June, we were informed by a Report from the Adjutant-General of the Army, that the honorary badges prepared under our directions of 22nd October, 1811, in commemoration of the Battle of Assaye, were in readiness to be issued to the troops. It was our intention to have published a General Order on the occasion of distributing these badges, but as Honorary Colours had already been presented to the Corps engaged in that Battle by the late Commander-in-Chief, and as the European Officers had been permitted to wear badges of distinction under the same authority, we deemed it sufficient to request the present Commander-in-Chief to give the necessary directions for the distribution.

'58. We have since authorised the payment of the bill for the preparation of these badges, amounting to Pagodas 1021.'

No. 136.

VELLORE MUTINY, 1806.

In order to reward the native cavalry who took part in the suppression of the mutiny at Vellore in July, 1806, the Government resolved to present them with medals, gold for the officers, and silver for the non-commissioned officers and men. A description of the projected medal will be found in Sir John Cradock's Minute in the Madras Military Proceedings for 29th September, 1807.

Notwithstanding the very clear orders passed in regard to the preparation of the medal, and likewise the fact that the grant had been approved by the Court of Directors, no further steps appear ever to have been taken, and nothing in reference to its manufacture or distribution can be traced in the Mint or other records at Madras. (See correspondence with the Madras Government, with papers regarding the Medal for Fidelity, No. 128, p. 112.)

A gold medal was, however, presented to Sepoy Mustapha Beg, 1st Battalion 1st Madras N.I., who gave information to the authorities of the projected mutiny. (See No. 143.)

The report of a Commission appointed to investigate the circumstances connected with the mutiny at Vellore was printed as a Parliamentary paper in May, 1861. The conclusions arrived at by the Commission were that certain innovations in the dress and appearance of the Sepoys were the leading cause of the mutiny; a secondary cause being the residence of the family of the late Tippoo Sultan at Vellore.

GENERAL ORDER BY THE GOVERNMENT OF MADRAS, 24th July, 1806.

'It has been in every instance the earnest desire of this Govt. to distinguish such of the Native Troops as may have particularly signalised themselves in the performance of their duty: and the Right Hon. the Governor in Council considers the application of this principle to be forcibly called for in the case of the Detachment of Native Cavalry which proceeded to Vellore under the command of Colonel Gillespie.

'In adverting to the circumstances with which the insurrection at Vellore was attended, His Lordship in Council considers the alacrity and ardour manifested by the Native Cavalry in the re-establishment of order, to have been in the highest degree meritorious; and His Lordship has accordingly resolved to confer on the Native Officers and Troopers of the Cavalry who shared in the honor of that Service, a reward proportioned to their merit.

'His Lordship in Council has been pleased to resolve that a Gold Medal with a suitable inscription shall be presented to each of the Native Commissioned Officers, and that a Silver Medal shall be presented to each Non-commissioned Officer and Private Trooper who accompanied the party of Troops which proceeded from Arcot on the morning of the 10th Instant: and it has been at the same time resolved to make a similar provision for the families of those Officers and Troopers in the event of their death as was conferred by the G. O. of 3rd Sep., 1804, on the families of the Native Officers and Soldiers who lost their lives during the late Mahratta Campaign.

'The Commander-in-Chief is requested to give every practicable degree of publicity to the intention which has been stated in this Order.' (Page 152.)

MADRAS MILITARY PROCEEDINGS, 29th Sept., 1807.

'The following Minute of the late Commander-in-Chief having returned from circulation, is ordered to be recorded.

'MINUTE BY THE COMMANDER-IN-CHIEF.

'I have the honor to submit to the Board agreeably to the Resolution on that subject, the inscription proposed to be stamped on the Medals for the Native Officers and soldiers who distinguished themselves by their fidelity, on the suppression of the insurrection at Vellore, with a translation, that the Board may determine on its propriety or suggest such amendment as may seem to be required.

'The Persian inscription is written on the proposed size of the Medals, leaving a blank in which the name of the person to whom it is given should be engraved, the Medals for the Commissioned Officers to be of Gold; those for the Non-commissioned and Privates of Silver.

'It may be proper to make a distinction in size between the Medals of Subadars and Jemadars, and those of Havildars and rank and file. Should this be deemed expedient, the small number required for those ranks may be made a size larger than the patterns now submitted.

'The Adjutant-Genl. has communicated with different workmen at the Presidency to prepare the Medals, but finds they do not possess the requisite machinery to prepare them properly. I therefore suggest that when the Device and size shall be determined, the Officers of the Honorable Company's Mint shall be instructed to prepare the Dies and to strike off the number of Medals required of each sort, a statement of which will be furnished by the Adjutant-Genl. for their guidance.

'This will be the most efficient and least expensive mode of procuring the Medals required.

'J. F. CRADOCK, *Lieut.-Genl.*

'*26th August*, 1807.'

'TRANSLATION OF THE PERSIAN INSCRIPTION.

'Distinguished by courage and fidelity (*name of recipient*) has received this mark of honor in consequence of his devotion to the Sirkar of the English Company Bahadur.'

'RESOLUTION.

'The Board approve the proposed inscription for the Medals which it has been determined to present to the Native Officers and Soldiers who distinguished themselves in the suppression of the Mutiny at Vellore: as also the further suggestions of Sir John Cradock on that subject. Ordered accordingly, that a copy of the foregoing Minute be furnished to the Mint Master for his information and guidance.' (Page 8560.)

FROM THE GOVERNMENT OF MADRAS TO THE COURT OF DIRECTORS, *21st October*, 1807—Military.

'531. Your Hon. Court have been apprised of the determination which we published in General Orders, of presenting Medals to the Native Officers and Soldiers who distinguished themselves by their fidelity in the suppression of the Mutiny at Vellore.

'532. We have now the honor to refer you to a Minute by Sir John Cradock, recorded on our proceedings of 29th ultimo, for a particular description of the intended Medals. We have resolved, conformably to the suggestion therein stated, that the Medals shall be prepared at the Mint, and that they shall vary in size according to the rank of the persons to whom they may be presented.'

FROM THE COURT OF DIRECTORS TO THE GOVERNMENT OF MADRAS, *25th April*, 1810—Military.

'LETTER, DATED 21ST OCT., 1807.	
'530. Native Troops rewarded for good conduct at Vellore permitted to retire when become prematurely unfit for Service on same pensions as if they had completed the required term. '531-2. Medals to Native Troops who distinguished themselves by fidelity at Vellore.	'211. We approve these resolutions.'

No. 137.

RODRIGUES, BOURBON, AND MAURITIUS, 1809-10.

PLATE 17, *No.* 1.

Obv. A Sepoy standing, having the British Colours in his right hand, and in his left, a musket with fixed bayonet. His left foot rests on a fallen eagle standard; beside him is a cannon; in the background, sea and ships.

Rev. Within a wreath, in Persian:—'This Medal was conferred in commemoration of the bravery and devotion exhibited by the Sepoys of the English Company in the capture of the Islands of Rodrigues, Bourbon, and Mauritius, in the year of the Hegira 1226.'

In the circumference, in English:—RODRIGUES VI JULY MDCCCIX. BOURBON VIII JULY & ISLE OF FRANCE III DEC MDCCCX.

Circular, 1·9 inch. Gold. Silver.
Mounted with a loop for suspension.
Dies engraved and preserved at the Calcutta Mint.

At the conclusion of the expedition from India to the French Islands of Rodrigues, Bourbon, and Mauritius in 1809-10, the Government of Bengal, acting on precedents, determined to bestow medals on the native troops belonging to that Presidency which had taken part in the expedition; and they suggested to the Governments of Madras and Bombay that the troops of those Presidencies which had also taken part in the expedition should be similarly rewarded. It does not appear, however, that those Governments acted on the suggestion. Only Bengal troops therefore received the medal. The native officers had gold, and other ranks silver medals.

From the Calcutta Mint Accounts of 1813 it appears that the numbers and cost of the medals struck were as follows:—

45 gold, with loops for suspension	Rs.	3721	14	8
2156 silver do. do.	„	8088	8	0

(See *Bengal Public Proceedings*, 25th March, 1814, No. 36. Copy with Ceylon papers in the Appendix.)

The Governor-General, Lord Minto, in a Despatch to the Court of Directors, dated 25th April, 1812, announced his intention of erecting at his own expense a monument to the memory of the officers and men who fell in this expedition. A copy of the Despatch may be read with the Java papers in the Appendix.

GENERAL ORDER BY HIS EXCELLENCY THE VICE-PRESIDENT IN COUNCIL, Fort William, 10th September, 1811.

'On the occasion of the approaching return from the late French Islands of the Volunteers from Bengal, Fort St. George and Bombay, to the Presidencies to which they respectively belong, His Excellency the Vice-President in Council considers it to be no less an act of justice than of indispensable public duty, to record the high sense he entertains of the services performed by the Native Soldiery who were employed in concert with His Majesty's and the Honorable Company's European Troops, in the reduction of the Islands of Rodriguez, Bourbon, and Mauritius.

'His Excellency in Council is pleased to signify his approbation of the distinguished merits of the Volunteers from the three Presidencies, by conferring honorary Medals on all the Native Commissioned and Non-Commissioned Officers, Troopers and

Sepoys, Gaulundauze, and Gun Lascars, employed on that service from this Presidency, and by suggesting for the consideration of the Governments of Fort St. George and Bombay, that corresponding Medals shall be conferred on the Native Troops from those Establishments, as a public mark and honorable testimony of their individual exertions and praiseworthy conduct.

'His Excellency the Commander-in-Chief is requested to cause the subject of this Order to be explained to the Volunteers on their return to Bengal.'

FROM THE GOVERNMENT OF INDIA TO THE COURT OF DIRECTORS, 17th September, 1811—Military.

'11. On the occasion of the approaching return from the late French Islands of the Volunteers from Bengal, Fort St. George, and Bombay, to the Presidencies to which they respectively belong, as directed by His Majesty's Ministers, we considered it to be no less an act of justice, than of indispensable duty, to record in General Orders the high sense we entertained of the services performed by the Native Soldiery who were employed in concert with His Majesty's and the Honorable Company's European Troops in the reduction of the Islands of Rodrigues, Bourbon, and Mauritius.

'12. We have determined with reference to the precedents which appear upon the records of Govt., to signify our approbation of the distinguished merits of the Volunteers from the three Presidencies, by conferring Honorary Medals on all the Native Commissioned and Non-Commissioned Officers, Troopers and Sepoys, Golundauze, and Gun Lascars from this Presidency, and by suggesting to the consideration of the Governments of Fort St. George and Bombay, that corresponding Medals shall be conferred on the Native Troops from those Establishments as a public mark and honorable testimony of their individual exertions and laudable conduct.'

FROM THE COURT OF DIRECTORS TO THE GOVERNMENT OF BENGAL, 3rd September, 1813—Military.

Reply to Separate Letter dated 17th September, 1811.

'P. 11 & 12. G. O. expressive of the high sense entertained of the services of the Volunteers from the three Presidencies in concert with H.M. and the Company's European Troops, in the reduction of the Islands Rodriguez, Bourbon, and Mauritius. Honorary Medals granted to the Native Commissioned and Non-Commissioned Officers.'

'167. Your sentiments and orders on this subject are entirely approved.'

BENGAL PUBLIC PROCEEDINGS, 14th May, 1813. *No.* 12.

Military Proceedings of 8th May, 1813.

'To C. W. Gardiner, Esq.,
Secretary to Govt. Military Dept.

'Adjt.-Genl.'s Office,
Fort William, *6th May*, 1813.

'Sir,

'The Mint Master having reported that the Honorary Medals for the Troops employed in the expedition against the French Islands are ready for delivery, I have the honor to beg you will express to the Governor-Genl. in Council my request that the Medals may be permitted to remain in the Mint, which I understand can be done without inconvenience, or any other place of security, until the orders of H.E. the Commander-in-Chief shall be obtained respecting them, and the necessary information received by which the distribution of them will be regulated; for though I have a small guard at the Office, I feel unwilling to expose such articles to risk by keeping them here.

'I have, etc.,

'C. STUART,
Acting Adjt.-Genl.'

'The Governor-Genl. in Council is pleased to comply with the request of the Asst. Adjt.-Genl.'

No. 138.

JAVA, 1811.

PLATE 17, *No.* 2.

Obv. Representation of the storming of the Lines of Cornelis. Above, the word CORNELIS.

Rev. In Persian:—'This Medal was conferred in commemoration of the bravery and courage exhibited by the Sepoys of the English Company in the capture of Java, 1228, Hegira.'

In the circumference, in English:—

JAVA CONQUERED XXVI AUGUST MDCCCXI.

Circular, 1·9 inch. Gold. Silver.
Mounted with a loop for suspension.
Dies engraved and preserved at the Calcutta Mint.

The expedition to Java was composed of British and Indian troops, commanded by Lieutenant-General Sir Samuel Auchmuty, and accompanied by Lord Minto, the Governor-General of India. The grant of the medal was made in a General Order by the Governor-General, dated 11th February, 1812, on his return to India.

As on previous occasions, the medals were given to native troops only, in gold to the officers, and silver to the men. They were made at Calcutta Mint, the numbers and cost being as under:—

133 Gold Medals with Loops, Bullion and manufacture, . . .	Rs. 10,596	15	6
6519 Silver Medals with Loops, Bullion and manufacture, . . .	„ 24,896	8	0

(See Mint Account, 1814, *Bengal Public Proceedings*, 16th September, 1814, No. 16. Copy with Seringapatam papers in the Appendix).

In a Despatch to the Court of Directors, dated 25th April, 1812, the Governor-General intimated his intention of erecting, at his own expense, a monument to the memory of the officers and men who fell in this expedition.

The Military Gold Medal (No. 155) was awarded by the king to the general and other officers of the Royal and Company's armies who were eligible for it. The Naval Gold Medal (No. 150) does not appear to have been awarded. The Silver Naval and Military War Medals, instituted in 1847 (Nos. 175 and 174), were given to the survivors of both services. The last-named medal was also given to the European officers and soldiers of the Company's service. There were thus four descriptions of medals for Java.

FROM THE GOVERNMENT OF BENGAL TO THE COURT OF DIRECTORS, *12th Nov.*, 1811—Military.

'196. On the Proceedings of the annexed date are recorded the official details of the operations of the British Troops under the command of H.E. Lieut.-General Sir Samuel Auchmuty on the Island of Java, and a copy of the General Orders which were issued at Fort William on the occasion, and we have heartfelt satisfaction in congratulating your Honble. Court and our country at large, on the brilliant and successful achievements of His Majesty's and the Hon. Company's Troops, which may be considered to have placed under the Dominion of the Crown of Great Britain, the last and most important of the enemy's possessions to the eastward of the Cape of Good Hope.' (*Cons.* 15th Oct., No. 111. *Cons.* 22nd Oct., No. 103.)

GENERAL ORDER BY THE GOVERNOR-GENERAL, *Fort William*, *11th Feb.*, 1812.

'The Governor-General in Council would scarcely think himself justified in reciting in his own name, however grateful it would be to himself, the merited notice which His Excellency Sir Samuel Auchmuty, the Commander-in-Chief of the Expedition, has taken of individual Officers and Corps who have justly obtained his commendation, but in recording in full concurrence with His Excellency His Lordship's cordial and lively sense of the glory which has been won by the whole Army in this signal service, the Governor-General in Council cannot omit from the seat of his more immediate authority, congratulating the Army of Bengal on the distinguished honor which has fallen on the Native Troops of this Presidency serving in Java.

'Opposed as they have rarely been to a European enemy, they attracted the unanimous applause of the whole Army, and by steady as well as ardent valor displayed in the most trying scenes of war, proved themselves fit comrades of our brave and illustrious countrymen, whose triumph and glory they shared. But verbal applause alone to this Army, would be a feeble and imperfect acknowledgment of services so important and merits so transcendent.

'The Governor-General before his departure from Java had announced his resolution to propose the commemoration of this conquest, and of the noble efforts of valor and discipline to which the country owes so great a benefit, by Medals to be distributed to the Troops, and His Lordship had the gratification of finding on his return to Bengal, that his wishes had been anticipated, and that the measure was already in progress by the orders of His Excellency the Vice-President in Council.'—(*Bengal Military Proceedings*, 18th Feb., 1812, No. 117.)

FROM THE GOVERNMENT OF BENGAL TO THE COURT OF DIRECTORS, 25th April, 1812—Military.

'7. The success of the late measures for the reduction of the French power in Java, and the splendid achievements of the Army employed on that enterprise, were in substance communicated to the Public, by Order of His Excellency Lieut.-General Hewett, the late Vice-President in Council, at two several periods when the official relations had not yet been received, and the sense entertained by His Excellency in Council of events so favorable to the public interest, so grateful to this Govt., and so glorious to the Troops, was published under the same circumstances to the Army of this Presidency. (*Cons.* 18th Feb., 1812. No. 117.)

. . . . . .

'13. Opposed as they have rarely been to an European enemy, they (the Native Troops) attracted the unanimous applause of the whole Army, and by steady as well as ardent valor, displayed in the most trying scenes of War, proved themselves fit comrades of our brave and illustrious countrymen, whose triumph and glory they shared. But verbal applause alone to this Army would be a feeble and imperfect acknowledgment of services so important and merits so transcendent.

'14. The Governor-General before his departure from Java had announced his resolution to propose the commemoration of this conquest, and of the noble efforts of valor and discipline to which the country owes so great a benefit, by Medals to be distributed to the Troops. And His Lordship had the gratification of finding on his return to Bengal that his wishes had been anticipated, and that the measure was already in progress by the order of H.E. the Vice-President in Council.

'15. To this authentic and public approbation the Governor-Genl. has indulged the earnest desire of adding a testimony of his private sentiments, by resolving to erect at his own expense a monument to the memory of those brave men, who, in the short but arduous war in Java, purchased the triumph of their country, and perfected their own title to immortal fame, by illustrious death in the very bosom of victory.

'16. As just objects of similar honors merited in the strenuous discharge of duties closely connected with the same system of national services, His Lordship proposes to consecrate this memorial to the manes also of those gallant and lamented officers and men who, animated with the same spirit, fell gloriously in the conquests of the Isles of Bourbon and Mauritius.'

FROM THE COURT OF DIRECTORS TO THE GOVERNMENT OF BENGAL, 16th February, 1814—Military.

'12. The glorious achievements of Lieut.-General Sir Samuel Auchmuty, and the officers and soldiers under his command, as well Native as European, adverted to in these paragraphs [of Letters, 12th Nov., 1811], and in paragraphs 13 to 18 of your Military Letter of 13th January, and paras. 7 to 17 of that of 25th April, 1812, are entitled to our highest applause and admiration.

'13. We cannot convey these our sentiments in terms more appropriate than those used by you in your General Orders of 11th Feb., 1812. We therefore desire that you will notify to the Army our cordial participation in the sentiments expressed by you upon that occasion, and our entire approbation of the distinctions proposed to be conferred on the Troops engaged in these splendid and successful achievements.'

A copy of the *Calcutta Mint Accounts*, 1814, relating to this medal (*Bengal Public Proceedings*, 16th September, 1814, No. 16) will be found in the Appendix among the Seringapatam papers.

No. 139.

NEPAL, 1814-16.

PLATE 17, *No.* 3.

Obv. Hills crowned with stockades; in left foreground, a cannon; on the right, colours and bayonets of an attacking force.

Rev. In Persian:—'This Medal was conferred by the Nawab Governor-General Bahadoor in testimony of the energy, good service, skill and intrepidity, which were displayed during the campaigns in the Hills in the years of the Hegira 1229 and 1230.'

Circular, 2 inches. Silver.
Dies engraved and preserved at the Calcutta Mint.
Mounted with a loop for suspension.

This medal was awarded to native troops who were employed in the operations in Nepal in 1814-16. Its grant was announced in a General Order by the Governor-General, dated 20th March, 1816. The terms of this grant were, however, different from those employed on previous occasions. Silver medals were to be presented to every native officer who actually served within the Hills, and to as many of the non-commissioned officers and privates as might be recommended by the commanders of their respective battalions for distinguished zeal or gallantry in the course of that duty. The medal was to be of the same metal for all ranks, and the previous custom of giving *gold* medals to officers was therefore departed from. Why this was so does not appear, but it is possible it may have been thought that there had been too much expenditure on medals on former occasions, and that they had been given too plentifully. It will be remembered that in the cases of the Mysore (Seringapatam) and Egypt medals it was ruled that all who had started on the expeditions, albeit they never reached their destinations, were entitled to medals. It is true that the men in question were mostly *volunteers*, and that the mere fact of volunteering was held, as in the cases of volunteering for Manilla and the Moluccas, to be a highly meritorious action deserving of honorary reward. But, for whatever reason, it was distinctly laid down in regard to the Nepal campaign that actual service within the Hills was essential, coupled with the proviso that in the case of non-commissioned officers and men, only such as were specially recommended were to be eligible.

The 'India, 1799-1826,' Medal, with clasp for 'Nepal,' was granted in 1850 to the then surviving European officers and soldiers of the Royal and Company's armies who were engaged in the war, and afterwards to such of the native soldiers as did not receive this medal.

The Court of Directors had resolved in 1853 that such of the native soldiers as were not originally recommended for the medal of 1816, in accordance with the terms of the General Order, should then be granted it. On the representation, however, of the Commander-in-Chief in India, that as the medal of 1816 had been bestowed only on such native soldiers as were at the time specially recommended on account of their 'distinguished zeal and gallantry,' it would not be proper to admit parties who were not so recommended, but that the 'India' medal would be a more suitable distinction, the Court modified their decision, and adopted the Commander-in-Chief's suggestion.

Two descriptions of medals were therefore given for this campaign.

On the conclusion of the Nepal war the Court of Directors, being desirous of conferring every mark of distinction on the army in India, resolved to institute gold medals and crosses, and adopted a code of regulations similar to those applicable to the King's Service, which had been promulgated in 1813. The Court resolved, also, that those officers who had been specially mentioned as having distinguished themselves in Nepal should enjoy the privilege of bearing such badges. In consequence, however, of the enlargement of the Order of the Bath, and the means thereby afforded for providing decorations for officers of superior rank, the above project was abandoned. (See No. 156.)

GENERAL ORDER BY THE GOVERNOR-GENERAL,
Fort William, 20th March, 1816.

'11. The nature of the country, and the climate, were so novel to the Native Troops, that a greater degree of merit must be attached to intrepidity under such circumstances, at the same time that a testimonial of exemplary behaviour in such a service must have more than ordinary value to those on whom it may be bestowed. Govt. has therefore determined that Silver Medals shall be presented to every Native Officer who actually served within the hills, and to as many of the Non-commissioned Officers and Privates as shall be recommended by the Commanders of their respective Battalions for distinguished zeal or gallantry in the course of that duty.'

No. 140.

SUBADAR ABDUL CAWDER, 1795.

GOLD MEDAL AND CHAIN.

The medal bore on one side the inscription, 'For conduct and courage on all occasions,' and on the other, 'By Government, 7th June, 1795.'

This medal and chain were presented by the Government of Madras to Subadar Abdul Cawder, of the 5th Battalion Madras Native Infantry, in recognition of his conduct in an affair at Manapar, near Trichinopoly, on 7th June, 1795, in which a small British force under Lieutenant Oliphant resisted a large number of the enemy.—(Wilson's *History of the Madras Army*, ii. 249.)

No. 141.

JEMADAR BOODH SING, 1795.

GOLD MEDAL.

The medal bore on one side the inscription, 'Courage and Fidelity,' and on the other, 'By Government, 7th October, 1795.'

The medal was presented by the Government of Madras to Jemadar Boodh Sing, 13th Battalion Madras Native Infantry, as a reward for the good service rendered by him in the surprise and capture of the Polygar of Pylney in his Fort at Paulsamoodrum, in the district of Madura, on 7th October, 1795.—(Wilson's *History of the Madras Army*, ii. 249.)

No. 142.

HAVILDAR SUBAUNNAC WAUGNAC, 1798.

SILVER CHAIN AND BADGE.

GENERAL ORDER BY THE COMMANDER-IN-CHIEF,
Bombay, 21st January, 1798.

'The firmness and bravery evinced by the Detachment of the Marine Battalion on duty in the *Viper* during her last trip up the Gulph of Persia, in defending the vessel when attacked under circumstances of peculiar difficulty, are considered by Government as highly meritorious, and the Commander-in-Chief receives particular satisfaction in conveying these sentiments to the Detachment. The Board, ever happy to have it in their power to encourage fidelity and bravery, by a due notice thereof, have been pleased to direct that the notification of the high sense they entertain of such meritorious conduct, be accompanied by a Gratuity of one month's full pay to the aforesaid Marine Detachment, and by a Present of a Silver Chain and Badge, of the value of one hundred Rupees, to Subaunnac Waugnac, Hauvildaur,[1] who commanded the Party. The Badge to be engraved with the figure of a ship with a Viper Head, and inscribed with the words, "The Reward of Fidelity and Valour."

'The Commanding Officer of the Marine Battalion is directed to cause these Orders to be fully and clearly explained to the Corps, and to send to the Adjutant-General's Office a List of the Non-commissioned Officers and Men composing the Detachment.'—(*I.O. Records.* G.O.'s by Commander-in-Chief, Bombay: vol. in MS.)

---

[1] In Low's *History of the Indian Navy*, vol. i. p. 376, this General Order is quoted, but the name of the Havildar is given as Sheikh Gunny.

No. 143.

SEPOY MUSTAPHA BEG, 1806.

GOLD MEDAL.

The story of this medal, to which allusion has already been made under No. 136, Vellore Mutiny, is told in the following General Order:—

GENERAL ORDER BY THE GOVERNMENT OF MADRAS, 7th August, 1806.

'The Right Honorable the Governor in Council has derived great satisfaction from the information that the Sepoy named Mustapha Beg, of the 1st Battalion, 1st Native Infantry, who gave the only intimation which was received of the projected mutiny at Vellore previously to the occurrence of that unhappy event, has returned in safety to that garrison.

'His Lordship in Council regrets the circumstances which precluded a more early attention to the intelligence which was conveyed by that faithful Sepoy of the treacherous intention of the Native Troops of the garrison of Vellore; but His Lordship has the highest satisfaction in conferring on Mustapha Beg a reward proportioned to the honorable proof which he manifested of his fidelity and attachment to the British Service.

'His Lordship in Council has accordingly resolved that the sum of two thousand Pagodas shall be immediately presented to Mustapha Beg, and that he shall receive for the remainder of his life a pension equal to that of a Subadar of Infantry. His Lordship has further resolved, that Mustapha Beg shall be presented with a Gold Medal in the name of the Governor in Council, as a Badge of honor and distinction.'

No. 144.

SEPOYS OF THE BOMBAY MARINE BATTALION, 1811.

SILVER BADGES.

A detachment of the Bombay Marine Battalion was serving on board the East India Company's cruiser *Aurora*, at the time of her capture by two French frigates on 21st September, 1810. The men resisted all attempts to induce them to enter the French service, and as a reward they received from the Bombay Government promotion and extra pay, and were presented with silver badges bearing suitable inscriptions.[1]

GENERAL ORDER BY THE HONOURABLE THE GOVERNOR IN COUNCIL, Bombay Castle, 3rd April, 1811.

'The Hon'ble the Governor in Council having received official intimation from the commander of the *Aurora* cruizer, that the late Government of the Isle of France

[1] Low's *History of the Indian Navy*, i. p. 379.

and its officers, had endeavoured to prevail upon a Detachment of the Marine Battalion, embarked on board of the vessel, to enter the French service after her capture by the French Frigates *Astrea* and *Iphigenia* on the 21st September last, and that various ineffectual means, as well of a persuasive as of a coercive nature, had been resorted to, to induce the Sepoys to swerve from their allegiance to the Hon'ble Company, deemed it proper to cause the circumstances of this transaction to be thoroughly investigated.

'The Board of Officers appointed for that purpose having closed their proceedings, the Governor in Council has sincere satisfaction in announcing that the result of the enquiry has afforded another distinguished proof of the fidelity and attachment of the native army of this Establishment under circumstances of a very trying nature.

'It appears that in addition to repeated offers of encouragement, and failing in that, to the infliction of severe and even cruel treatment, to induce and to compel the Detachment generally to betray their duty to the Hon'ble Company, Sheikh Boodh in particular on refusing to enter the French Service was thrice severely wounded in the arm, and once on the head, the effects of which have (it is apprehended) entirely incapacitated this faithful native soldier from the performance of further duty.

'The conduct of this Detachment, though not unpreceded by various examples of similar attachment in the Native Troops of this Establishment, being accordingly considered as highly worthy of a marked testimonial of public approbation, the Governor in Council is for this purpose pleased to direct that a Silver Badge with a suitable inscription, be presented to each man of the Party as enumerated in the following List; that Launce Havildaur Dhondnac Pudnac be promoted to the rank of Havildaur; Moosahib Cawn, Launce Naique, to that of Naique; and that each of the Privates receive the pay of Naique until respectively promoted to that rank by vacancies in the corps to which they may severally belong.

'List of Detachment embarked on board the Hon'ble Company's cruizer *Aurora.*'

[Here follow the names of Naique Dhondnac Pudnac,—Launce Havildaur, Sepoy Moosahib Khan,—Launce Naique, and fourteen other Sepoys of the Marine Battalion.]

(*Bombay Proceedings*, 6th April, 1811—Military, page 1541.)

FROM THE GOVERNMENT OF BOMBAY TO THE COURT OF DIRECTORS, *29th October*, 1811—Military.[1]

'255. We have much pleasure in noticing to your Hon'ble Court the very honorable and faithful conduct of the Detachment of the Marine Battalion serving as Marines on board the Hon'ble Company's Cruizer *Aurora*, on the capture of that vessel by the *Iphigenia* and *Astrea*, French frigates on the 21st Sept. last, in having resisted the means resorted to by the enemy, both of a persuasive and of a coercive nature, to induce them to swerve from their allegiance to the Hon'ble Company, and which obtained for them from the late Government a distinguished and merited mark of their approbation as expressed in their Resolution of the 3rd April last.'

FROM THE COURT OF DIRECTORS TO THE GOVERNMENT OF BOMBAY, *6th June*, 1814—Military.

In reply to Para. 255 of Despatch from Bombay, dated 29th October, 1811.

'151. The conduct of the Native Marines in refusing to enter into the French

[1] *Cons.* 1811—22nd March, Fol. 1147. 6th April, Fol. 1526.

service under the circumstances described is highly creditable to their fidelity, and well deserving of the rewards which you have bestowed upon them.

'152. We desire that you will cause these our sentiments of approbation to be officially communicated to them, as well as our sanction of the rewards conferred on them.'

No. 145.

JEMADAR IYALOO, 1813.

GOLD MEDAL.

Jemadar Iyaloo, of the 14th Madras N.I., had revealed the existence of a conspiracy to murder the officers quartered at Quilon, the design of the conspiracy being to confer the sovereignty of Travancore upon the Pychy Rajah. The conspirators were seized and executed. Jemadar Iyaloo was promoted to Subadar, and was presented by the Madras Government in 1813 with a gold medal and a donation of Rs. 1000.—(Wilson's *History of the Madras Army*, vol. iii. p. 357.)

No. 146.

GOLD MEDALS OF THE PERSIAN ORDER OF THE SUN, 1813.

Certain detachments of the Body Guard of the Governor of Madras, and of the 1st Regiment Madras Native Cavalry, appear to have served in Persia as escort to the British Ambassador in that country. The Prince Royal of Persia having conferred gold medals of the Order of the Sun on some of the native officers, the Court of Directors, as a special mark of favour, gave them permission to wear the same.

GENERAL ORDER BY THE GOVERNMENT OF MADRAS,
Fort St. George, 15th June, 1813.

'His Excellency the Governor in Council is pleased to direct that the following extract of a letter, dated 21st October, 1812, from the Honorable the Court of Directors to the Right Honorable the Governor-General in Council, shall be published in General Orders:—

'Para. 17. "Sir Harford Jones having stated to us that His Royal Highness the Prince Royal had been pleased to confer on the Subidar of the Horse Artillery left by General Malcolm, and on Syed Hoossein and Hoosseinee Beg, the Jemidars of Sir Harford's escort, Gold Medals of the Order of the Sun, we direct, as a special mark of our favour, that our permission to wear these honorable testimonies of their good behaviour be publicly announced to these persons."'

No. 147.

SUBADAR MUCKRUND SING, 1814.

GOLD MEDAL.

This medal was presented by the Government of India, in 1814, to Subadar Muckrund Sing, of the 1st Battalion 2nd Bengal N.I., as a reward for his valuable services in bringing over to the British several battalions of the enemy during the siege of Agra by Lord Lake in October, 1803. The Subadar preferred a medal to a gold necklace because, as he said, the medal would 'for ever remain a monument of pride to his family.' He received likewise a grant of land and a special pension.

The medal was ordered to be of a larger size than usual, with a suitable inscription in English and Persian. It probably also bore the arms of the East India Company. From the Calcutta Mint Accounts it appears that its cost was Rs. 159. (See *Bengal Public Proceedings*, 16th September, 1814, No. 16. With Seringapatam Papers.)

BENGAL MILITARY PROCEEDINGS, *26th February*, 1814. *Nos.* 15 *and* 16.

'To
C. W. GARDINER, Esq.,
Secretary to Govt., Military Dept.

'SIR,

With reference to my letter No. 153 of 31st Aug. last, and the reply to the communication as contained in your letter, No. 188 of 11th Sept., 1813, respecting the compensation and honorary distinction which, in the opinion of the Commander-in-Chief, it would be proper to offer to Subedar Muckrund Sing, 1st Battn. 2nd Regt. N.I., I am directed by H.E. to transmit to you for the information of the Govr.-Genl. in Council the accompanying copy of a letter, under date 8th Oct. last, from Major Muller, commanding 1st Batt. 2nd Regt., with the Persian one, to my address from Muckrund Sing, in reply to a communication made from this Office by order of the Commander-in-Chief, in order to ascertain what distinction would be most gratifying to the Subedar.

'As the Subedar has, for the reason stated in Major Muller's letter, given the preference to a Gold Medal, the Commander-in-Chief begs leave to suggest that the necessary instructions may be given for the preparation of one; and adverting to the grounds on which the distinction has been granted, H.E. hopes the Governor-General in Council will concur with him in opinion that the Medal should be distinguished from those usually bestowed on soldiers who have been on foreign service, not only in the difference of the device, but also in its size and consequently in its intrinsic value.

'The Commander-in-Chief is not aware that it is of consequence to adopt any particular device for the occasion, but if it can be done without the trouble of preparing a die for the express purpose, the Arms or Crest of the Hon. Company on one side, and on the other a few words in Persian commemorative of the service or merits of the individual, appear to be well adapted to an Honorary Medal granted under such circumstances.

'With respect to the quantity of land to be assigned to the Subedar as a Jaghire, the Commander-in-Chief is of opinion that the grant of 150 Beegahs, at or as near to Soorajpore in the Dooab as it can be procured, would be an ample allowance, in addition to which H.E. wishes to submit for the consideration of His Lordship in Council the propriety of permitting the Subedar to retire on a pension of Fifty Rupees, should it be his desire to quit the Service, and retire to his Jaghire, or should it not be his wish to do so immediately on having it intimated to him that a Pension of such amount will be granted to him instead of the usual invalid pay of his rank, whenever in regular course of time he may be deemed unfit for further service.—I have, etc.,

'G. H. FAGAN,
Adj.-Genl.

'ADJUTANT-GENL'S. OFFICE,
FORT WILLIAM, 29*th Dec.*, 1813.'

'To LT.-COL. FAGAN, Adjutant-Genl.

'SIR,

I have been duly favored on 4th inst. with your official letter of 21st ult. enclosing the Persian letter for Subadar Muckrund Sing of the 1st Batt. 2nd Regt. I have now the pleasure to transmit the Subadar's reply, and further to state to you for the information of H.E. the Commander-in-Chief, that as H.E. has been so condescending to leave to the Subadar the choice of an honorary mark of approbation of his conduct (over and above the grant of land promised near to Siradgepore in the Dooab), that he humbly begs to prefer a Medal rather than a Gold Necklace, and I must beg permission to add in his own words, "The former will for ever remain a monument of pride to my family, whereas the latter can at least only be considered as a gift, the value of which will sink to its mere intrinsic worth after my demise."—I have, etc.

'F. MULLER, *Major*,
Commg. 1st Battn. 2nd Regt.

'ADJIE GHIER,
8*th Oct.* 1813.'

'*Ordered* that the following letter be written to the Adjutant-General in reply :—

No. 168.

To LT.-COL. G. H. FAGAN, Adjt.-Genl.

'SIR,

I am directed by H.E. the Rt. Hon. the Govr.-Genl. in Council to acknowledge the receipt of your letter under date 29th Dec. last, with the enclosure, and in reply to acquaint you that the Acting Mint Master has been desired to prepare a Gold Medal of a size larger than what has usually been bestowed on soldiers who have been on foreign service, with a suitable inscription in English and Persian, to be presented to Muckrund Sing, Subadar 1st Batt. 2nd Regt. N.I., for valuable service rendered by him to the Hon. Company at the siege of Agra in Oct., 1803.

[The remainder of the letter refers to the grant of land and pension which the Government decided to make to the Subadar as proposed by the Commander-in-Chief.]

'C. W. GARDINER,
Secretary to Govt. Military Dept.

'COUNCIL CHAMBER,
26*th Feb.*, 1814.'

'*Ordered* that the requisite instructions be transmitted to the Acting Mint Master, and that an extract from the Proceedings be recorded in the Revenue Dept., whence the necessary orders will be issued for the quantity of land above specified being granted to Muckrund Sing, Subadar.'

FROM THE GOVERNMENT OF BENGAL TO THE COURT OF DIRECTORS, 23*rd June*, 1814—Military.

'381. On the Proceedings noted in the margin,[1] is recorded a correspondence which has taken place relative to a claim preferred by Subedar Muckrund Sing, of the 1st Battalion, 2nd Regiment Native Infantry, for a reward for his services in bringing over to the British Standard several of the Enemy's Battalions, in the month of October, 1803, while the Army commanded by Lord Lake was before the Fort of Agra.

'382. The facts stated by Muckrund Sing having been most satisfactorily substantiated by Major-General Blair, who commanded the 1st Battalion of the 2nd Regt. Native Infantry at the siege of Agra, and other Officers who were then present with the Battalion, we have presented him with a Gold Medal, of a size larger than what has usually been bestowed on Soldiers who have been on Foreign Service, for the valuable services rendered by him to the Honorable Company at the Siege of Agra in 1803.

'383. As a further mark of the sense which we entertained of his conduct, we have resolved to grant him One hundred and fifty Begahs of Land as a Jagheer, with the promise of a pension of 50 Sonant Rupees per mensem, in lieu of the usual Invalid pay of his rank, whenever he may be desirous to quit the Service and retire to his Jagheer.'

BENGAL MILITARY PROCEEDINGS, 10*th Sept.*, 1814. *No.* 78.

TO THE MINT.

	Rs.		
'April 14, 1814.—To Bullion for one Gold Medal for Moohammed Sing—agreeable to orders of Govt. 26th Feb. 1814—weighing Sicca weight 10.4 @ Rs. 1554, per Sicca weight, etc., . .	157	2	8
Loop for—do.—mounting, etc., ...	8	2	6
	Rs. 165	5	2

'CALCUTTA MINT,
10 *Sep.*, 1814.'

'FORT WILLIAM, 14*th April*, 1814.

'Received from Malcolm M'Leod, Esq., Acting Mint Master, a Gold Medal weighing Sicca weight Ten and four annas, as ordered to be prepared in the Proceedings of H.E. the Right Hon. the Govr.-Genl. in Council in the Military Dept., under date 26th Feb., 1814.

'C. W. GARDINER,
Secretary to Govt. Military Dept.

---

1 *Cons.* 11th Sept., 1813, Nos. 17 to 20. *Cons.* 26th Feb., 1814, Nos. 15 to 17. *Cons.* 16th April, Nos. 40 to 42.

No. 148.

SUBADAR HOOLAS PUNDIT, 1817.

GOLD MEDAL.

Subadar Hoolas Pundit, 14th Bengal N.I., served under Sir David Ochterlony at the siege of Cuddalore in 1783, and twenty years later under the same officer in the memorable defence of Delhi against Holkar in 1804, where Sir David entrusted him with the separate defence of one of the city gates.

FROM THE GOVERNMENT OF BENGAL TO THE COURT OF DIRECTORS, 11th April, 1817—Military.

'168. On the Consultations of 11th April your Honble. Court will find recorded a Petition from Hoolas Pundit, Subadar 14th Native Infantry, stating his long and special services, and praying for some mark of the approbation of Govt. which should yield a comfortable provision for his old age and infirmities.

'169. The Resolutions which we recorded on this case we are well assured will meet with the cordial approval of your Honorable Court. They are conceived as we hope in the spirit of your gratifying injunctions to us contained in your General Letter (Novr. 14th) and we are of opinion that the case of this deserving veteran officer was exactly such as your Hon. Court contemplated when you assured us of your strong desire to distinguish by striking marks of your favor such of the Native Officers as should have deserved well of the British Govt.

'170. Foremost among the Testimonials to the merits of Subadar Hoolas Pundit, stands that afforded him by Major-Genl. Sir D. Ochterlony, under whom it was the Subadar's good fortune to serve in the trenches at the celebrated siege of Cuddalore in 1783, and more than 20 years afterwards, in the memorable defence of Delhi against Holkar in 1804, when Sir David distinguished him by entrusting him with the separate defence of one of the City gates. Your Honorable Court will derive no common gratification from the perusal of these interesting documents, and we trust that you will think we have done what was politic and right in determining to notice the particular services of Subadar Hoolas Pundit in General Orders, and to request that the Commander-in-Chief shall publicly confer on him a Gold Medal on which they are engraven.'

FROM THE COURT OF DIRECTORS TO THE GOVERNMENT OF BENGAL, 30th March, 1819—Military.

Reply to Military Letter, dated 11th April, 1817, paras. 168 and 170,

Submitting the petition of Hoolas Pundit, Subadar 14th N.I., and the Resolutions passed on his case, which the Govt. are assured will meet with the cordial approval of Court, when his particular services are considered: and stating that those services have been published in G. O., and that the Commander-in Chief has been requested to present him with a Gold Medal, on which they are engraven.

'58. Your Resolutions in favour of the distinguished Native Officer mentioned in these Paragraphs, Subadar Hoolas Pundit, have our entire approbation.'

No. 149.

SUBADAR BUGWUNT SING, 1818.

GOLD MEDAL.

This medal was presented by the Government of India in 1818 to Subadar Bugwunt Sing, 6th Bengal Light Cavalry, as a reward for his distinguished fidelity and gallantry. He likewise received a grant of land and a special pension.

FROM THE GOVERNMENT OF BENGAL TO THE COURT OF DIRECTORS, 26th Dec., 1818—Military.

'Para. 388. [Grant to Subadar Bugwunt Sing, 6th Bengal Light Cavalry, on the same principle as was observed in the case of Subadar Hoolas Pundit, of a Pension of Rs. 100—of 300 Begahs of land.]

'As a personal mark of the approbation with which the Govt. viewed the distinguished fidelity and gallantry which the Subadar had displayed in its service, we at the same time caused a Golden Medal to be presented to him, having an appropriate inscription on it commemorative of the merits of this faithful veteran.'

No. 150.

NAVY GOLD MEDALS, 1794.

GOLD MEDAL—LARGE.

PLATE 19.

Obv. An antique galley, on the prow of which is Victory placing a wreath on the head of Britannia, who stands on the galley with her right foot on a helmet, and holding a spear in her left hand. Behind her, the Union shield.

Rev. Within a wreath of oak and laurel, the name of the recipient, together with the event for which the Medal was conferred.

Circular, 2 inches. Gold.

Mounting. Plain gold ring.
Ribbon. 1¾ inch. White, with blue borders.
Worn round the neck.

Dies at the Admiralty. The name 'R. Wood' stamped on both.

GOLD MEDAL—SMALL.

NAVY, 1794.

PLATE 19.

Obv. Same as the large Medal.

Rev. The name of the recipient, and the event for which the Medal was conferred.

Circular, 1.3 inch. Gold.

Mounting. Plain gold ring and bar.
Ribbon. White, with blue borders.
Worn at a button-hole on the left breast.

The following are the actions for which the medal was awarded. (See Admiralty Notice of 1st June, 1847, published in the *London Gazette* of 1st and 4th June, 1847; and see No. 175):—

1 June, 1794. Lord Howe's victory.
14 February, 1797. Lord St. Vincent's action, off Cape St. Vincent.
11 October, 1797. Lord Duncan's battle, off Camperdown.
1 August, 1798. Battle of the Nile.
25 October, 1799. Recapture of the *Hermione* by H.M.S. *Surprise*.
21 October, 1805. Battle of Trafalgar.
4 November, 1805. Sir Richard Strachan's action.
6 February, 1806. Sir John Duckworth's action, off St. Domingo.
1 January, 1807. Capture of the island of Curaçoa.
10 November, 1808. Capture of the *Thetis* by H.M.S. *Amethyst*.
6 July, 1808. Capture of the *Badere Zaffer* by H.M.S. *Seahorse*.
6 July, 1809. Capture of the *Furieuse* by H.M.S. *Bonne Citoyenne*.
13 March, 1811. Sir William Hoste's action, off Sissa.
9 August, 1811. Capture of the island of Banda Neira.
22 February, 1812. Capture of the *Rivoli* by H.M.S. *Victorious*.
1 June, 1813. Capture of the *Chesapeake* by H.M.S. *Shannon*.
27 March, 1814. Capture of *L'Etoile* by H.M.S. *Hebrus*.
15 January, 1815. Action between the *President* and H.M.S. *Endymion*.

The Naval Gold Medals were instituted on the occasion of Lord Howe's victory over the French fleet on 1st June, 1794. The larger medal was given to admirals, the smaller to captains.

Since the commencement of the eighteenth century the practice of giving medals for sea service had fallen very much into desuetude. On the other hand, a much more important mode of reward had been introduced, namely, that of bestowing peerages, baronetcies, and knighthoods on the victorious commanders and their principal officers. That a peerage was looked forward to by an admiral in command of a fleet is clear from Nelson's traditional exclamation before the battle of the Nile: 'A peerage, or Westminster Abbey!' And when an admiral was created a peer, or was elevated in the peerage, his subordinate flag-officers often received baronetcies. The revived Order of the Bath was also utilised as a reward for important warlike achievements, and was highly esteemed.

But although from the time of Queen Elizabeth medals had been bestowed for sea services, and although statutory provision had been made on the subject in later years, the victory of the glorious First of June was the occasion which led to the institution of a 'regulation' medal for naval officers.

On the return of the British fleet to Spithead, the King went down to Portsmouth, and on board the *Queen Charlotte* presented to Lord Howe a diamond-hilted sword as a mark of His Majesty's approbation of his conduct. The King also presented gold chains, to which medals were afterwards to be attached, to Lord Howe, to Admiral Sir Alexander Hood, Rear-Admiral Alan Gardner, and the Captain of the Fleet, Sir Roger Curtis. Rear-Admirals George Bowyer and Thomas Pasley, who had each lost a leg and were unable to attend, also received gold chains.[1]

In the Painted Hall at Greenwich Hospital there is a picture by Briggs of George III. presenting the sword to Lord Howe on board the *Queen Charlotte*. The gold chains are not, however, introduced into the picture. The statue of Lord Howe in St. Paul's Cathedral shows a chain of oval links of about an inch in length. The chain appears to be about a yard long.

The medals for the First of June were given to the several admirals and to the fourteen captains honourably mentioned in Lord Howe's Despatch of 21st June, 1794. They were not distributed until November, 1796, when they were transmitted to the recipients with the following letter from the First Lord of the Admiralty, Earl Spencer.[2]

'ADMIRALTY, *9th November*, 1796.

'SIR,

The King having been pleased to order a certain number of Gold Medals to be struck, in commemoration of the Victory obtained by His Majesty's Fleet under the command of Earl Howe over that of the Enemy, in the Actions of 22nd May and 1st June, 1794, I am commanded by His Majesty to present to you one of the Medals above mentioned, and signify His Majesty's pleasure that you should wear it when in your uniform, in the manner described by the direction, which (together with the Medal and Ribband belonging to it) I have the honor to transmit to you.

'I am also commanded by His Majesty to acquaint you, that had it been possible for all the Officers on whom His Majesty is pleased to confer this mark of approbation to attend personally in London, His Majesty would have presented the Medal to each of them in person; but that being from various causes at this time impossible, His Majesty, in order to obviate all further delay, has therefore been pleased to direct them to be forwarded in this manner.

'Allow me to express the great satisfaction I feel in being made the channel of communicating to you so distinguished a mark of His Majesty's approbation.

'I have, etc.,

'SPENCER.

'*Direction.*

'The Admirals to wear the Medal suspended by a ribband round their necks. The Captains to wear the Medal suspended to a ribband, but fastened through the third or fourth button-hole on the left side. The color of the ribband, blue and white.'

---

[1] *Annual Register*, June, 1794.

[2] *Ibid.* 30th November, 1796.

In the case of the admirals, the ribbon would not, of course, have been in supersession of the gold chains already presented to them; and they probably exercised their own discretion as to the occasions on which they wore chain or ribbon.

The grant of the medal for the battle of the Nile was announced in a letter from Earl Spencer to Lord Nelson, dated 7th October, 1798. A further letter, dated 9th January, 1799, forwarded Lord Nelson's medal to him:—

From EARL SPENCER *to* LORD NELSON.[1]

'MY DEAR LORD, 'ADMIRALTY, *7th October*, 1798.

I have the greatest satisfaction in obeying His Majesty's commands by acquainting you that His Majesty has been graciously pleased to testify His Royal approbation of your conduct in the signal and brilliant victory you obtained over the French Fleet on 1st August, by conferring on you the dignity of a Baron of Great Britain by the name, style and title of Baron Nelson of the Nile, and of Burnham Thorpe, in the County of Norfolk. In congratulating your Lordship on this high distinction, I have particular pleasure in remarking that it is the highest honour that has ever been conferred on an Officer of your standing in the Service, and who was not a Commander-in-Chief; and the addition to the Title is meant more especially to mark the occasion on which it was granted, which, however, without any such precaution, is certainly of a nature never to be forgotten. His Majesty has also been pleased to signify his intention of accompanying this grant of Honour by a suitable provision, which cannot, however, be completed till Parliament shall have met; and I am likewise commanded to take the necessary steps for presenting your Lordship and the Captains who served under your orders on that occasion with Gold Medals, similar to those which have been given in the other great actions fought this War. The First Lieutenants of the ships engaged will also be distinguished by promotion, the necessary directions for which will be sent to Lord St. Vincent; and the Senior Marine Officer of the Squadron will be recommended to H.R.H. the Commander-in-Chief, that he may have a step in Brevet rank conferred upon him.

'I have, etc., SPENCER.'

From EARL SPENCER *to* LORD NELSON.[2]

'MY LORD, 'ADMIRALTY, *9th January*, 1799.

'The King having been pleased to order a certain number of Gold Medals to be struck, in commemoration of the Victory obtained by His Majesty's Fleet under your Lordship's command, over that of the French, on the 1st and 2nd of August last, off the coast of Egypt, I am commanded by His Majesty to present to your Lordship one of the Medals above mentioned, and to signify His Majesty's pleasure that you should wear it when in your uniform, in the manner described by the directions which (together with the Medal and Riband belonging to it) I have the honour to transmit to your Lordship.

'I am also commanded to communicate to you the King's pleasure that your Lordship shall be presented to His Majesty the first time you appear at St. James's, with this Decoration.

'Allow me to express the great satisfaction I feel in being made the channel of communicating to you so distinguished a mark of His Majesty's approbation.

'I have, etc.,

'SPENCER.'

---

[1] Nicolas's *Life of Nelson*, iii. p. 75.

[2] *Ibid.* iii. p. 473.

'*Directions for wearing the Medal.*

'In the same manner as the Medal which Lord Nelson received on the occasion of the Victory obtained by His Majesty's Fleet under Lord St. Vincent's command is worn; hanging it a little higher or lower than that, as may be most convenient, so that both the Medals may be distinctly seen.

'A spare parcel of Riband is sent herewith, and more may be had (if wanted) at Potter's, Haberdasher, Charing Cross.'

It will be observed that the battle of Copenhagen, fought on 2nd April, 1801, is not included in the list of actions for which the medal was awarded, and there was much heart-burning on the part of Lord Nelson and his officers at the refusal of the Government to allow a medal for that event. The correspondence on the subject will be found in the Appendix. It is not clear why the Government so strongly objected to grant the medal, inasmuch as the thanks of Parliament had been awarded to the fleet, Lord Nelson had been created a Viscount, Rear-Admiral Graves had been made a Knight of the Bath, and several officers had been promoted. (*London Gazette*, 19th May, 1801.) That Nelson felt the matter keenly is evident from the energetic representations which he made to the First Lord of the Admiralty, Earl St. Vincent, and the Prime Minister, Mr. Addington. He was much annoyed also on account of the City having refrained from voting thanks to the fleet for the victory, and he wrote a strong letter to the Lord Mayor on the subject, which letter, however, he subsequently withdrew by the advice of Mr. Addington.

Nelson set an extremely high value on medals. In a letter to Lord St. Vincent, written on 23rd September, 1801, he says: 'I feel myself, my dear Lord, as anxious to get a medal as a step in the Peerage, as if I had never got either, for if it be a sin to court glory, I am the most offending soul alive.' [1]

To Captain Foley, his flag-captain at Copenhagen, Nelson declared he would never wear his other medals until that for Copenhagen was granted.[2]

On a change of administration in 1804, Lord Nelson recurred to the subject in a letter to the First Lord of the Admiralty, Lord Melville. But his plea was again rejected; Lord Melville, whilst alleging ignorance of the reasons which had existed against the grant of the medal, stating that a compliance with the request at that period might hurt the feelings of the Danes, and tend to injure our alliance with them: an excuse which can

[1] Nicolas's *Life of Nelson*, vii. p. 230.

[2] *Ibid.* iv. p. 527.

scarcely have carried conviction to the minds of Nelson and his comrades.

On the extension of the Order of the Bath in 1815, the surviving captains who had been in command of ships at Copenhagen, and who had not subsequently had the opportunity of gaining distinction, presented a memorial to the Lord High Admiral, the Duke of Clarence, praying His Royal Highness to obtain for them the medals they conceived themselves entitled to, and also the honour of Knight Commander of the Bath. The reply of His Royal Highness was to the effect that he had referred the matter to the Duke of Wellington, who stated that although the Government were most fully sensible of the eminent services of the officers in question, they regretted that they could not, at that late period, advise the King to grant medals. The claim of the officers to the honour of K.C.B. does not appear to have been put forward by the Duke of Clarence.

On the accession of William IV., the same officers renewed their application. They were, however, informed that sensible as His Majesty was of their distinguished merit, there were general considerations connected with the subject which prevented his complying with their request.[1]

The gold medal was, consequently, never granted for Copenhagen.

Lord Nelson's friend, Lord Collingwood, also had a grievance in reference to the gold medal. He commanded the *Barfleur*, of 98 guns, on 1st June, but he was not included amongst those on whom the medal was originally conferred, and the omission mortified him highly. He subsequently, however, received it, although not until after the battle of St. Vincent, for which he had been duly recommended for a medal, but in respect of which he had told Lord St. Vincent that he could not consent to receive it while that for the 1st of June was still withheld.

A full list of the officers on whom the Naval Gold Medals were conferred is given at pp. i.-vii., History of War Medals, in vol. iv. of Sir H. Nicolas's *History of the Orders of Knighthood.*

The total numbers appear to have been :—

Large medals, . . .	22
Small medals, . . .	117

The 1st June, 1794, was the only occasion on which gold chains were also given.

---

[1] Nicolas's *Life of Nelson*, iv. p. 528.

No. 151.

BATTLE OF THE NILE, 1798.

DAVISON'S MEDAL.

PLATE 18, *No.* 1.

Obv. Hope standing on a rock in the sea, having in her right hand an olive branch. On her left side she supports an oval shield on which is the bust of Lord Nelson, surrounded by the words, EUROPE'S HOPE AND BRITAIN'S GLORY. Behind her is an anchor.

Leg. REAR-ADMIRAL LORD NELSON OF THE NILE. At the base of the rock, the initials C. H. K.

Rev. The French fleet at anchor in Aboukir Bay, the British fleet advancing to the attack, the setting sun denoting the time of day.

Leg. ALMIGHTY GOD HAS BLESSED HIS MAJESTY'S ARMS.

Exergue. VICTORY OF THE NILE AUGUST 1. 1798. Also, in small letters, 'M. B. Soho,' and 'C. H. Küchler, fec:'

Round the rim. A tribute of regard from Alexr. Davison, Esq., St. James's Square.

Circular, 1·85 inch. Gold. Silver. Copper gilt. Copper bronzed.

Artist. C. H. Küchler.
Struck at the Soho Mint, Birmingham.

Mr. Alexander Davison had been appointed by Lord Nelson agent for the prizes taken at the Battle of the Nile, and by way of expressing his gratitude for the appointment he caused this medal to be struck at an expense of nearly £2000,[1] and presented to all the British officers and men engaged in the battle. The medal was of gold for the admiral and captains; of silver for lieutenants and officers ranking with them; of copper gilt for warrant and inferior officers; and of copper bronzed for the men. It was designed and executed by C. H. Küchler, and struck at the Soho Mint by Matthew Boulton.

The topography of the *reverse* of the medal is inaccurate, since the land shown on the right should really be on the left, the promontory at the end of which stands the town of Aboukir forming the western side of the Bay of Aboukir, in which the battle took place, and not the eastern. The sun is also wrongly placed. This mistake has probably arisen from the engraver

[1] Clarke and M'Arthur's *Life of Nelson*, 1809, vol. ii. p. 110.

having neglected to transpose the position of the objects when sinking the die.

There is reason to believe that Lord Nelson wore this medal as one of his decorations,[1] and a specimen is hung round the neck of his funeral effigy in Westminster Abbey, the ribbon being the naval ribbon of England (white with blue borders), with which, therefore, he probably used to wear it.[2] His own impression, which belongs to the present holder of the title, was shown at the Guelph Exhibition in London in 1891; No. 1217 in the *Catalogue*.

Many Nelson relics, including presentation plate, medals, and orders, were in 1895 the property of Lord Bridport, and were advertised for sale by public auction held on 13th July in that year. The medals and orders, however, were purchased by the Government previous to the sale.

Two gold specimens of Davison's Nile Medal were included in the auction, and were not among those secured for the nation. They realised 145 guineas each, and were purchased respectively by Glendinning and Spink.[3]

---

[1] NOTE BY EARL NELSON.

'TRAFALGAR, SALISBURY, *May* 4, 1890.

'The Nile medal was given by Mr. A. Davison out of the profits made by him by the sale of the prizes taken at the battle of the Nile. Therefore, as it had nothing to do with the Government, there was no authorised ribbon to wear with it, nor was it authorised to be worn at all. Nevertheless, I believe my great-uncle always wore it, and I have his medal in a red Russian leather case with a gold ring through the top of it by which it was hung round the neck. NELSON.'

[2] It is singular that neither of the Navy gold medals (St. Vincent and Nile) which Lord Nelson possessed are represented on the effigy, although the stars of four orders of knighthood are. But see Nelson's declaration to Captain Foley, quoted at p. 176.

[3] 'THE NELSON RELICS.

'The old English silver and silver-gilt presentation plate, enamelled gold boxes, gold sword-hilts, medals, orders, and other highly interesting objects, formerly in the possession of Admiral Viscount Nelson, and other old English and foreign silver plate, the property of Viscount Bridport, came under the hammer at Christie's yesterday. As late as Thursday Messrs. Christie received from Messrs. Capel-Cure and Ball, of 32, Fenchurch Street, E.C., a communication requesting them to withdraw the eleven medals and orders, with their original ribands, which were worn by Lord Nelson at the time he was killed at Trafalgar, and to "inform the public who attend the sale that the nation has purchased them." The price paid by the Government for this most interesting series is understood to be £2500. The medals and orders were the service gold medal of St. Vincent, the service gold medal of the victory of the Nile, the jewel of the Order of the Bath, the jewel of the Sardinian Order of San Joachim, the grand cross of the Order of San Joachim, the jewel of the Neapolitan Order of San Ferdinando, the grand cross of the same order, the gold

In the subjoined letter to Lord Nelson Mr. Davison expressed his intention of presenting the medal:—

To Lord Nelson.

'St. James's Square, *18th March*, 1799.

'My dear Lord,

The very kind and truly flattering manner in which your Lordship, and the officers under your command, have conferred upon me the sole Agency for the sale of the French Ships of war, taken by you at the ever-memorable Battle of the Nile, commands my warmest acknowledgments. But being anxious to express these sentiments in the strongest possible degree, it occurred to me that a Medal, to commemorate this unparalleled achievement, would convey in the most durable manner the respect which I entertain for this mark of your confidence, and the admiration which I am impressed with upon this truly glorious event.

'I have therefore thus gratified my inclination, and I hope and trust that your Lordship, and all the officers and men who were then under your command, will do me the honor to receive it as a tribute of my respect and admiration.

'I have the honor to be, my dear Lord, Your Lordship's most faithful and obliged friend and humble servant,

'ALEXANDER DAVISON.

'*P.S.*—The Medals I have had struck for your Lordship and the Captains of your Fleet are of gold, those for the Lieutenants and officers who rank with them are of silver, those for the warrant and inferior officers are of copper gilt, and those for the men are of copper bronzed.'

---

star of the Turkish Order of the Crescent, two badges of the same order, and the gold medal for the victory of Trafalgar.

'As regards the articles which were sold, the highest amount was paid for a brilliant necklace, consisting of the stones removed from the Sword of Honour presented to Lord Nelson by the King of Naples—£1250 (Haws); the gold sword-hilt itself chased and spirally fluted, and thickly studded with paste diamonds, realised £170 (Hood); an aigrette of rose diamonds, presented to Lord Nelson by the Sultan of Turkey after the battle of the Nile—£710 (Haws); Lord Nelson's inkstand, oval shaped, silver-gilt, with open gallery of interleaved circles and beaded border, etc., inscribed "William and Emma Hamilton to Nelson, Duke of Bronté, their dear friend," started at £100, and was knocked down to Lady Llangattock for £520; its weight is only 17 ozs. An oval gold box, presented to Lord Nelson with the freedom of the City of London, the corners chased with wreaths of oak and laurel foliage, the lid inlaid with a large oval enamel painted with a naval engagement, and with eleven smaller enamels round the sides. For this beautiful article the bidding started at £450 and reached £1050 (Murray). The gold sword-hilt, presented by the Captains of the Fleet, formed as a terminal figure of a crocodile, enamelled with an allegorical group of Britannia and Africa, and the arms of Lord Nelson, sold for £1080 (Murray). The inscription runs thus:—"The captains of the squadron under the orders of Rear-Admiral Sir Horatio Nelson, K.B., desirous of testifying the high sense they entertain of his prompt decision and intrepid conduct in the attack of the French Fleet in Bequir Road of the Nile, the 1st of August, 1798, request his acceptance of a sword, and as a further proof of their esteem and regard hope that he will permit his portrait to be taken and hung up in the Egyptian Club now established in commemoration of that glorious day. Dated on board his Majesty's ship *Orion*, on this 3rd of August, 1798," etc.' (*The Times*, 13th July, 1895.)

An extract from a further letter from Mr. Davison to Lord Nelson respecting the medal is interesting, as indicating the regard the King entertained for the Admiral:—

'ST. JAMES'S SQUARE, *6th April*, 1799.

'I waited upon the King early last Sunday morning, at the Queen's House, and presented him with a gold and a silver medal. He received them most graciously and with much joy and pleasure, and paid me many compliments upon the occasion. I was *alone* with the King a full hour, when much of the conversation was about you. It is impossible to express how warmly he spoke of you, and asked me a thousand questions about you. I promised His Majesty a copper-gilt and a bronze medal as soon as I received them, which I shall have also the honor of presenting.'

The following letters of Lord Nelson show that he highly appreciated the gift of the medal:—

To A. DAVISON, Esq.[1]

'PALERMO, *21st April*, 1799.

'I well know, my dear Davison, the value to be put on your friendship, and I rejoice in having such a friend. I am fancied rich: you may now know the contrary. A mind like mine is not formed to take the road of wealth. I wish you had sent me your Medal; I long to wear it.

'NELSON.'

To A. DAVISON, Esq.[2]

'PALERMO, *15th August*, 1799.

'MY DEAR FRIEND,

Yesterday brought me your letters of the beginning of April, together with your elegant Medals, which cannot fail to be as highly grateful to all the brethren of the Nile as they are to your old friend. The spare gold Medal which you was so good as to send me I presented to the man that all Europe is obliged to for his encouragement of the Arts, as well as many other acts of a public benefit. You will know this person can only be Sir William Hamilton. I have also sent all the boxes as directed. In your postscript I see you intend gold Medals for all the Captains. I have presented the other gold one to Captain Hardy in your name, as I am confident it was not your intention to exclude Captain Hardy, who was a Captain in the Battle of the Nile. I assure you, my dear friend, it hurt me to part with your kind and invaluable present, but I considered you before myself. A silver, or even a copper, one I shall esteem as equally valuable.

. . . . . .

'*August* 24.—Poor dear Miller is dead; so will be your Nelson, but I trust till death that your friend longs to wear your present: therefore I have kept Miller's, and hope you will send another to his family. If that cannot be, they shall have this, which I have unjustly kept.

'NELSON.'

---

[1] Nicolas's *Life of Nelson*, vol. vii. Addenda, p. 180.

[2] *Ibid.* vol. vii. Addenda, p. 189.

From the following letter it appears that Lord Nelson presented a specimen of the medal to the King of the Two Sicilies:—

'TO HIS SACRED MAJESTY THE KING OF THE TWO SICILIES.[1]

'PALERMO, *2nd June*, 1800.

'SIRE,

The Almighty, who granted to my legitimate Sovereign's arms the Battle of the Nile, impressed your Majesty with a favorable opinion of me, which has led your Royal heart to grant me the most distinguished honors, and a fortune which I never had an idea of expecting. I presume, therefore, to request that your Majesty will permit me to lay on your table a gold Medal, highly flattering to your Majesty's devoted and faithful

'BRONTE NELSON OF THE NILE.'

It is stated in a footnote to Clarke and M'Arthur's *Life of Nelson*, 1809, vol. ii. p. 110, that 'many of these medals were afterwards found by the Russian sailors scattered over the Island of Tenedos in 1807, after the explosion that took place on board the *Ajax*, when that ship was burnt in the roads of Tenedos.'

Mr. Alexander Davison married in February, 1788, Harriet, daughter of Robert Gosling, Esq., Banker, Fleet Street, by whom he had three sons:—Colonel Hugh Percy Davison; Lieutenant-Colonel Sir William Davison, K.H.; and Alexander (died young), and three daughters. He died at Brighton in his eightieth year in December, 1829.[2]

No. 152.

BATTLE OF TRAFALGAR, 1805.

BOULTON'S MEDAL.

PLATE 18, *No.* 2.

Obv. Bust of Lord Nelson in uniform, *l.*

Leg. HORATIO . VISCOUNT NELSON . K.B. DUKE OF BRONTE &c.

Rev. Representation of the battle of Trafalgar.

Leg. On a scroll, ENGLAND EXPECTS EVERY MAN WILL DO HIS DUTY
Exergue, TRAFALGAR OCT^{R}. 21 . 1805.
Round the rim. From M. Boulton. To the Heroes of Trafalgar.

---

[1] Nicolas's *Life of Nelson*, vol. iv. p. 244. [2] *Ibid.* vol. v. p. 42.

Circular, 1·9 inch. Various metals.
Artist. C. H. Küchler.
Struck at the Soho Mint, Birmingham.
Dies in possession of Messrs. Taylor, Medallists, 70 Red Lion Street, London.

Mounting
Ribbon } Various.
How worn

Instigated by the example of Mr. Davison on the occasion of the victory of the Nile, Mr. Matthew Boulton of the Soho Mint, by whom the Davison Medal was struck, determined to present a medal to the officers and crews of the English ships which took part in the battle of Trafalgar. The artist Küchler was again employed.

No. 153.

MAIDA, 1806.

PLATE 22.

Obv. Head of George III., laureated *l.*

Leg. GEORGIVS TERTIVS REX.

Rev. Britannia casting a spear with her right hand: on her left arm the Union shield. Above, Victory flying holding out a wreath. In front of Britannia, MAIDA . IVL . IV . MDCCCVI. Behind her, the triquetra or trinacria, the symbol of the Island of Sicily. Crossed spears in *exergue.* In circumference, PIDGEON . F.

Circular, 1.5 inch. Gold.
Artist. G. F. Pidgeon.
Mounting. Plain gold bar.
Ribbon. Crimson, with blue borders.
Worn on left breast from button of coat.

This medal was given to the thirteen superior officers who took part in the battle of Maida on 4th July, 1806. It was the first medal given by the Crown for a land battle, and it was the forerunner of the many gold medals and crosses distributed during the next few years. The grant of it was doubtless suggested by the practice of bestowing gold medals on superior officers of the sister service, which had been introduced in 1794 to commemorate the victory of the glorious First of June.

The grant of the medal was announced in the following General Order by H.R.H. the Duke of York, Commander-in-Chief, printed in the *London Gazette* of 23rd February, 1808, p. 265. Instructions are given as to the ribbon to be used; and it will be noticed that the mode of wearing the medal is similar to that prescribed for Captains in the case of the Naval Gold Medal.

'HORSE GUARDS, *February* 22, 1808.

'His Majesty having been graciously pleased to command that, in commemoration of the brilliant and decisive victory obtained by a Division of his Army under the command of Major-General Sir John Stuart, 4th July, 1806, on the Plains of Maida, the undermentioned officers of the Army, engaged on that day, should enjoy the privilege of bearing a Medal; and His Majesty having approved of the Medal which has been struck upon this occasion, is pleased to command that it should be worn suspended by a Ribband of the color of the Sash, with a blue edge, from a button of the coat on the left side.

'Major-General Sir John Stuart, K.B.

'*Commanders of Brigades.*

Brigadier-General Hon. George Lowrey Cole, 1st Brigade.
Brigadier-General W. Palmer Acland, 2nd Brigade.
Colonel John Oswald, 3rd Brigade.

'*Commanders of Corps, having the rank of Lieutenant-Colonel.*

Lieut.-Colonel James Kempt, commanding Battalion Light Infantry.
Lieut.-Colonel Hon. K. W. O'Callaghan, Battalion Grenadiers.
Lieut.-Colonel Robert Ross, 20th Regiment.
Lieut.-Colonel Haviland Smith, 27th do.
Lieut.-Colonel George Johnson, 58th do. since dead.
Lieut.-Colonel Patrick Macleod, 78th do. since dead.
Lieut.-Colonel Louis de Watteville, Watteville's Corps.
Lieut.-Colonel John Lemaine, Royal Artillery.
Lieut.-Colonel Henry Edward Bunbury, Deputy Quarter-Master-General.

'FREDERICK,
Commander-in-Chief.'

No. 154.

CAPTAIN JAMES WOOLDRIDGE, R.N., 1809.

GOLD MEDAL AND CHAIN.

PLATE 18, *No.* 3.

Obv. A British ship in flames approaching the French ships, and in the act of breaking a boom.

Below, chased on a scroll, XI. APRIL . MDCCCIX.

Rev. Within a wreath of oak and laurel, held together at the base by a scallop shell, the inscription:—CAPTAIN JAMES WOOLDRIDGE LED THE BRITISH FIRE SHIPS

WHEN FOUR FRENCH SAIL OF THE LINE WERE BURNT UNDER THEIR OWN BATTERIES IN AIX ROADS.

Circular, 1·7 inch. Gold.
Dies at the Admiralty.

The Medal is encircled by a cable, ⅛ inch thick, and has a gold chain attached to it.

The medal was made by Mr. R. W. Silvester, Seal and Copper-plate Engraver, at the cost of £105.

The dies are at the Admiralty in the box in which they were originally supplied.

In the grant of this medal and chain, we have a recurrence to the practice of specially rewarding captains of fireships. It is believed to be the last case of the kind.

From Captain Wooldridge's letter to the Admiralty, dated 15th February, 1812, we learn that in a letter addressed to him by the Earl of Mulgrave, First Lord of the Admiralty, of 25th May, 1809, it was stated that the King had been pleased to direct that he should receive a gold chain and medal 'according to the provision of the ancient fighting instructions regarding fireships.'[1]

The announcement of the grant of the medal and chain followed pretty promptly the service for which they were awarded; and it was not until after waiting nearly three years without hearing anything further about them, that Captain Wooldridge ventured to make inquiries of the Admiralty. He was then informed that although every effort had been made to get the medal executed, it was not ready, but that it was hoped it soon would be. The medal and chain were ready on 24th November, 1812, and Captain Wooldridge was invited to attend at the Admiralty to receive them. His health did not, however, permit of his so doing, and they were consequently delivered to his brother on his behalf.

Captain Wooldridge commanded the British fireships in Aix Roads on 11th April, 1809, when four French sail of the line were burnt. His ship was the *Mediator*, and in the course of the action he sustained very severe injuries, on account of which he was granted a special pension of £200 a year.

The following is a quotation from the Order in Council, 18th December, 1811, granting the pension:—

'While serving as a Commander in the command of His Majesty's Ship *Mediator*, which had been previously fitted as a Fireship, he had the honor on the 12th April,

[1] See section in Introduction on rewards for services in fireships.

1809, to lead the attack against the Enemy's Fleet in Basque Roads, and to break the Boom which was fixed for their defence. That when in the act of grappling with the French Admiral's ship, the *Mediator* having been then several minutes on fire, he was, with his two Lieutenants the only persons then on board, blown up by an unexpected explosion of Congreve's rockets, and forced overboard through the port. That in consequence of his sufferings on that occasion he has become blind of his left eye, and that the sight of the other is much impaired. That he has entirely lost the hearing of the left ear, and further has suffered the loss of seven teeth.'

Captain Wooldridge died on 31st August, 1814, and his widow presented a Memorial to the Prince Regent which resulted in her being, by an Order in Council, dated 13th February, 1815, granted a pension of £120 a year, with pensions of £25 each to her three children.

In Mrs. Wooldridge's Memorial occurs the following passage:—

'That your Royal Highness was most graciously pleased to grant to the late husband of your Memorialist, for his services in His Majesty's Royal Navy, but particularly when in command of His Majesty's Ship *Mediator*, on the 12th of April, 1809, a pension of £200, in addition to a Chain and Medal granted by His Majesty to remain as a token of Honor to him and his posterity.'[1]

The following letters are taken from the *Admiralty Records*:—

CAPTAINS' LETTERS—W.

'PENZANCE, CORNWALL, *Feb. 15th*, 1812.

'SIR,

On the 25th May, 1809, Lord Mulgrave did me the honour to inform me by letter that His Majesty had been most graciously pleased to direct that I should receive a Gold Chain and Medal, "according to the provision of the ancient fighting instructions regarding Fireships, to remain as a token of Honor to me and my posterity," in consequence of my conduct when commanding His Majesty's late Fireship *Mediator* at the attack of the Enemies' ships in the Road D'Aix on the night of the 11th of April preceding.

'I beg to inform you for the information of my Lords Commissioners of the Admiralty, that this honorable badge has not yet reached me, and as three years have nearly elapsed, during which time many officers, I believe both Navy and Army, particularly the latter, have received distinctions of a similar nature, and being anxious to obtain so distinguished a mark of His Majesty's approbation, I have to solicit their Lordships to give such directions as to them may seem most proper.

'I am, Sir,
Your most Obedt. Servt.,

'J. WOOLDRIDGE,
Captain, Royal Navy.

'J. W. CROKER, Esq.'

---

[1] How long the medal and chain remained in the Wooldridge family we do not know, but they formed part of the collection of Captain John Hamilton, which at his decease was purchased by Mr. James Sanders, by whom it was resold at Sotheby's in May, 1882, when this medal and chain fetched £95. They now belong to Colonel Murray of Polmaise, who kindly afforded facilities for the production of the illustration on Plate 18.

SECRETARY'S COMMON LETTERS TO CAPTAINS, R.N.

(No. 15.)

'18*th Feb.*, 1812.

'SIR,

Having laid before my Lords Commissioners of the Admiralty your letter of the 15th inst. requesting that measures may be taken for your obtaining the Medal, which, under a communication made to you on the 21st May, 1809, you have expected to be furnished to you for your conduct on the *Mediator* in Basque Roads; I am commanded by their Lordships to acquaint you that every effort has been made, but without effect, to have that Medal executed; but that My Lords hope shortly to be able to have it accomplished.

'I am, etc.,

'J. B.

[John Barrow, Secretary of the Admiralty.]

'CAPTN. J. WOOLDRIDGE,
Penzance, Cornwall.'

ADMIRALTY MINUTE.

Nov. 24, 1812.

'Acquaint Capt. James Wooldridge that the Gold Medal and Chain for his services in the *Mediator* are ready for delivery, and that, if convenient to him to attend, he may receive them at the Board; if not, that they shall be transmitted to him.'

CAPTAINS' LETTERS—W.

'PENZANCE, CORNWALL, *Novr.* 27*th*, 1812.

'SIR,

I have been honored by yours of the 24th inst., acquainting me that the Gold Medal and Chain ordered for me is now ready for delivery.

'I feel much indebted to their Lordships for their indulgence in considering my convenience, and as my state of health continues such as at present to prevent my undertaking so long a journey, I have requested my brother, Capt. W. Wooldridge, who is at present in town, to wait on you and receive it for me.

'I am, Sir,
Your very Obdt. Servt.,
'J. WOOLDRIDGE.

'JAS. WILSON CROKER, Esq., Admiralty.'

LORDS' LETTERS—WAGES AND ACCOUNTS. No. 21.

'20*th April*, 1813.

'GENTN.

Mr. R, W. Silvester, Seal and Copper Plate Engraver, having laid before Us an Account of Work performed and Articles supplied for this Office, amounting to the Sum of Two hundred and Fifty-Five Pounds One Shilling, we transmit to you herewith the said Account and do hereby desire and direct you to cause the same to be paid.

'We are, etc.,

'WM. DOMETT.
'J. S. YORKE.
'G. WARRENDER.

'NAVY BOARD.'

'J. W. CROKER, Esq.,

'To R. W. SILVESTER (Seal and Copper Plate Engraver).

		£	s.	d.
18th Novr., 1812.	A Pair of Dies, a Gold Medal, Case, etc., complete, Captn. Wooldridge, Naval Action 1809, ...	105	0	0
	A Case for Dies with Lock, etc., complete,	1	1	0
2nd Jany., 1813.	Modelling a Bust of His Majesty, . .	14	14	0
	A Medal Die Do. 2 Dies for Reverses, First and Second Mathematical Prizes, Royal Naval College, 2 Gold and 15 Silver Medals and Cases Do., . .	132	14	6
	A Case for Dies with Lock, etc., complete,	1	11	6
		£255	1	0

The following is an extract from the *Naval Chronicle*, 1814, vol. xxxii. (p. 352).

'DEATHS.

'On the 31st Augt. suddenly in the prime of life at Penzance, Capt: James Wooldridge of the Royal Navy. This gallant Officer commanded the *Mediator* frigate under Lord Cochrane at Basque Roads, and had the honour of breaking the enemy's boom, for which he was presented with a gold chain and medal by order of the Lords of the Admiralty, but the wounds he received disabled him from serving his country again, he being obliged afterwards to resign the command of the *Rainbow* which had been assigned to him in testimony of his gallantry.'

No. 155.

ARMY GOLD MEDALS AND CROSS, 1808-14.

GOLD MEDALS—LARGE AND SMALL.

PLATE 20.

Obv. Britannia, *l.*, seated on a globe, holding in her right hand a laurel wreath, and in her left a palm branch. Beside her, right, a lion; left, the Union shield.

Rev. A wreath of laurel, encircling the name of the battle for which the Medal was granted.

Circular, 2·1 inches for General Officers.
1·3 inch for other Officers.

Mounting. Large Medal, a gold ring.
Small Medal, a gold bar.

Clasps. 2 by ·6 inches. Within a border of laurel, the name of a battle.

Ribbon. 1⅝ inch. Crimson, with blue borders.

Large Medal. Worn round the neck.
Small Medal. Worn at the button-hole.

GOLD CROSS.

PLATE 21.

A Maltese Cross, 1½ inch in diameter, with ornamental border ; in the centre, a lion, *r.* ; on each limb of the Cross the name of a battle. The back of the Cross is the same as the front.

Clasps. 2 by ·6 inches. Within a border of laurel, the name of a battle.
Ribbon. 1¾ inch. Crimson, with blue borders.

Worn by General Officers round the neck, the ribbon passing through a gold ring of laurel attached to the Cross or the top Clasp. By other Officers, at the button-hole.

The precedent set in the grant of a medal for Maida was followed a few years later in order to reward the officers engaged in the Peninsular War.

On 9th September, 1810, a General Order was issued by the Horse Guards, announcing that the King had commanded that in commemoration of the brilliant victories obtained over the French in the battles of Roleia, Vimiera, Corunna, and Talavera, and in several cavalry encounters, the 107 general and field-officers specified, who were present on those occasions, should enjoy the privilege of bearing a medal. The General Orders likewise provided that the medals which would have been conferred upon the officers who had fallen at, or died since, the actions in question, should be delivered to their respective families.

Inconvenience having arisen in consequence of the issue of a separate medal for each action, it was decided that in future one medal only should be issued to an officer, and that for the second and third events a gold clasp should be attached to the ribbon ; also, that for a fourth event a gold cross, having the names of the four events inscribed on it, should be substituted for the medal, such cross to be in its turn supplemented by clasps in the event of the bearer earning further distinctions. (See *Horse Guards' General Order*, 7th October, 1813.)

A good many questions arose in connection with the grant of the MEDAL and CROSS, most of which appear to have been determined in consultation with the Duke of Wellington. It was originally intended that the medals for the Army should be awarded on the same principle as was observed in reference to the Navy ; that is to say, that only general officers and officers commanding regiments should be eligible to receive them. But, inasmuch as there were in the Army many important officers for whom there were, and could be, no equivalents in the Navy, these, had the analogy been strictly followed, would have been debarred from the distinction. This would have been unfair, and the principle had therefore to be modified so as to include all officers of the proper ranks who were considered to deserve the distinction.

On the termination of the Peninsular War the issue of the MEDAL and CROSS ceased, the recent enlargement of the Order of the Bath affording the means of rewarding those who, under the old system, would have received gold medals, crosses, or clasps. This is explained in a letter from the Military Secretary at the Horse Guards to the Commander-in-Chief at Madras, dated 15th October, 1818, on the occasion of the submission by His Excellency, under the idea that the old system still prevailed, of the names of officers who had been particularly engaged in the battle of Mahidpore.

A full list of the officers on whom the gold medals and crosses were conferred is given at pp. xi.–xxxvii., History of War Medals, in vol. iv. of Sir H. Nicolas's *History of the Orders of Knighthood.*

With reference to the mode of wearing these medals, it will be seen from the Duke of Wellington's correspondence that he was in favour of the large medal being worn, like the small one, at the button-hole instead of round the neck.

We have been unable to ascertain by whom the medals and cross were designed. They were, however, probably made by Messrs. Rundell and Bridge, of London, the firm which executed the collar given to the Duke of Wellington by George IV. (See No. 158.)

It is curious that the illustration of the large medal given at p. 23 of Nicolas's *History of War Medals*, does not agree with the pattern issued, as shown in Plate 20. The subject is the same, but certain details are different—*e.g.* Britannia wears a helmet of another shape, the lion's head is above her knee, and the shield is placed obliquely. Whether any medals of this design were ever executed and distributed is uncertain, but it is difficult to understand how Nicolas could have given the illustration unless a medal had existed from which it was copied.

The following are the services for which the gold medal and cross were awarded :—

BATTLE, ETC.	DATE.	H. G. G. O.	'LONDON GAZETTE.'
Roleia	17 Aug., 1808	9 Sept., 1810 7 Oct., 1813 1 June, 1814	11 Sept., 1810 9 Oct., 1813 13 Sept., 1814
Vimiera	21 Aug., 1808	9 Sept., 1810 7 Oct., 1813 1 June, 1814	11 Sept., 1810 9 Oct., 1813 13 Sept., 1814
Sahagan, Benevente	Dec., 1808, and Jan., 1809	......	11 Sept., 1810
Corunna	16 Jan., 1809	9 Sept., 1810 7 Oct., 1813 1 June, 1814	11 Sept., 1810 9 Oct., 1813 13 Sept., 1814
Martinique	Feb., 1809	......	......
Talavera	27 and 28 July, 1809	9 Sept., 1810 7 Oct., 1813 1 June, 1814	11 Sept., 1810 9 Oct., 1813 13 Sept., 1814
Guadaloupe	Jan. and Feb., 1810	......	......
Busaco	27 Sept., 1810	7 Oct., 1813 1 June, 1814	9 Oct., 1813 13 Sept., 1814
Barossa	5 Mar., 1811	7 Oct., 1813 1 June, 1814	9 Oct., 1813 13 Sept., 1814
Fuentes d'Onor	5 May, 1811	7 Oct., 1813 1 June, 1814	9 Oct., 1813 13 Sept., 1814
Albuhera	16 May, 1811	7 Oct., 1813 1 June, 1814	9 Oct., 1813 13 Sept., 1814
Java	Aug. and Sept., 1811	25 May, 1814	27 Aug., 1814
Ciudad Rodrigo	Jan., 1812	7 Oct., 1813 1 June, 1814	9 Oct., 1813 13 Sept., 1814
Badajoz	17 Mar. and 16 Apr., 1812	7 Oct., 1813 1 June, 1814	9 Oct., 1813 13 Sept., 1814
Salamanca	22 July, 1812	7 Oct., 1813 1 June, 1814	9 Oct., 1813 13 Sept., 1814
Fort Detroit, America	Aug., 1812	......	......
Vittoria	21 June, 1813	28 Mar., 1814	19 Apr., and 13 Sept., 1814
Pyrenees	28 July to 2 Aug., 1813	1 June, 1814	13 Sept., 1814
St. Sebastian	Aug. and Sept., 1813	1 June, 1814	13 Sept., 1814
Chateauguay, America	26 Oct., 1813	......	......
Nivelle	10 Nov., 1813	1 June, 1814	13 Sept., 1814
Chrystler's Farm, America	11 Nov., 1813	......	......
Nive	9 to 13 Dec., 1813	......	......
Orthes	27 Feb., 1814	......	......
Toulouse	10 Apr., 1814	......	......

ORIGINAL GRANT.

'HORSE GUARDS, *September* 9, 1810.

'His Majesty having been graciously pleased to command that, in commemoration of the brilliant victories obtained by Divisions of His Army over the Enemy in the Battles of Roleia, Vimiera, also in the several instances where the Cavalry had an opportunity of distinguishing themselves against the Enemy in Spain, and in the Battles of Corunna and Talavera de la Reyna, the undermentioned Officers of the Army, present on those occasions, should enjoy the privilege of bearing a Medal; and His Majesty having approved of the Medal which has been struck, is pleased to command that it should be worn by the General Officers, suspended by a Ribbon of the colour of the Sash, with a blue edge, round the neck; and by the Commanding

Officers of Corps, (not being of rank inferior to Lieutenant-Colonel), and the Chiefs of Military Departments, attached by a Ribbon of the same colour to the button-hole of their Uniform.

'His Majesty has also been pleased to command that the Medals, which would have been conferred upon the Officers who have fallen at or died since the above-named Actions, shall, as a token of respect for their memories, be deposited with their respective families.

. . . .

[Here follow the names of 107 Officers, viz. : 6 Lieut.-Generals, 14 Major-Generals, 16 Brigadier-Generals, 12 Colonels, and 59 Lieutenant-Colonels.]

'By His Majesty's Command,

'DAVID DUNDAS,
Commander-in-Chief.

'H. TORRENS,
Lieut.-Col. and Mil. Sec.'

(*London Gazette*, 11th September, 1810, p. 1365.)

'HORSE GUARDS, *October* 7, 1813.

'Whereas considerable inconvenience having been found to attend the increased number of Medals that have been issued in commemoration of the brilliant and distinguished events in which the success of His Majesty's Arms has received the royal approbation, the Prince Regent has been pleased to command, in the name and on the behalf of His Majesty, that the following regulations shall be adopted in the grant and circulation of such marks of distinction, viz. :—

'1st. That one Medal only shall be borne by each Officer recommended for such distinction.

'2nd. That for the second and third events, which may be subsequently commemorated in like manner, each individual recommended to bear the distinction shall carry a gold clasp attached to the Ribbon to which the Medal is suspended, and inscribed with the name of the Battle or siege to which it relates.

'3rd. That upon a claim being admitted to a fourth mark of distinction, a cross shall be borne by each Officer, with the names of the four battles or sieges respectively inscribed thereupon ; and to be worn in substitution of the distinctions previously granted to such individuals.

'4th. Upon each occasion of a similar nature that may occur subsequently to the grant of a cross, the clasp shall again be issued to those who have a claim to the additional distinction, to be borne on the Ribbon to which the cross is suspended, in the same manner as described in No. 2 of these Regulations.

'His Royal Highness is further pleased to command, in the name and on the behalf of His Majesty, that the distribution of Medals, or Badges, for military services of distinguished merit, shall be regulated as follows, viz. :—

'1st. That no General, or other Officer, shall be considered entitled to receive them unless he has been personally and particularly engaged upon these occasions of great importance and peculiar brilliancy, in commemoration of which the Prince Regent, in the name and on the behalf of His Majesty, may be graciously pleased to bestow such marks of distinction.

'2nd. That no Officer shall be considered a Candidate for the Medal, or Badge, except under the special selection and report of the Commander of the Forces upon the spot, as having merited the distinction, by conspicuous services.

'3rd. That the Commander of the Forces shall transmit to the Commander-in-Chief returns signed by himself, specifying the names and ranks of those Officers whom he shall have selected as particularly deserving.

'4th. The Commander of the Forces, in making the selection, will restrict his choice to the undermentioned ranks, viz. :—

General Officers.
Commanding Officers of Brigades.
Commanding Officers of Artillery, or Engineers.
Adjutant-General and Quarter-Master-General.
Deputies of ditto, and ditto, having the rank of Field Officers.
Assistants—Adjutant and Quarter-Master-General, having the rank of Field Officers, and being at the head of the Staff, with a detached corps, or distinct division of the Army.
Military Secretary, having the rank of Field Officer.
Commanding Officers of Battalions, or corps equivalent thereto; and Officers who may have succeeded to the actual command during the engagement in consequence of the death or removal of the original Commanding Officer.

'The Prince Regent is therefore graciously pleased to command, in the name and on the behalf of His Majesty, that, in commemoration of the brilliant victories obtained by His Majesty's arms in the battles of Roleia and Vimiera, Corunna, Talavera de la Reyna, Busaco, Barossa, Fuentes de Onor, Albuhera, and Salamanca, and in the assaults and captures of Ciudad Rodrigo and Badajoz, the undermentioned Officers of the Army, present on those occasions, shall enjoy the privilege of bearing badges of distinction; and His Royal Highness having approved of the Crosses, Medals, and Clasps which have been prepared, is pleased to command that they shall be worn by the General Officers, suspended by a Ribbon of the colour of the Sash, with a blue edge, round the neck; and by the Commanding Officers of Battalions, or Corps equivalent thereto, and Officers who may have succeeded to the actual command during the engagement, the Chiefs of Military Departments and their Deputies and Assistants (having the rank of Field Officers), and such other Officers as may be specially recommended, attached by a ribbon of the same description to the button hole of their uniform.

'The Prince Regent is also pleased to command, in the name and on the behalf of His Majesty, that those badges which would have been conferred upon the Officers who have fallen at, or died since, the above-named battles and sieges shall, as a token of respect for their memories, be transmitted to their respective families.

. . . . . .

[Here follow the names of 318 Officers.]

'By command of His Royal Highness the Prince Regent.

'FREDERICK,
Commander-in-Chief.

'H. TORRENS,
Colonel and Military Secretary.'

(*London Gazette*, 9th October, 1813, p. 1985.)

'HORSE GUARDS, *28th March*, 1814.

'The Prince Regent has been graciously pleased, in the name and on behalf of His Majesty, to command that, in commemoration of the brilliant victory obtained over the enemy by the army under the orders of the Marquess of Wellington, in the battle of Vittoria on 21st June, 1813, the undermentioned Officers, present upon that memorable occasion, shall enjoy the privilege of bearing badges of distinction, in conformity with the regulations published on 7th October last.

[Here follow the names of

Field-Marshal the Marquess of Wellington, K.G., Commander of the Forces.
10 Lieutenant-Generals.
31 Major-Generals.
5 Brigadier-Generals.
28 Colonels.
97 Lieutenant-Colonels.
27 Majors.
11 Captains.]

'The Prince Regent has also been pleased to command, in the name and on behalf of His Majesty, that those badges which would have been conferred upon the Officers who fell in, or have died since, the battle of Vittoria shall, as a token of respect to their memories, be transmitted to their respective families.

'By command of H.R.H. the Prince Regent.

'FREDERICK,
Commander-in-Chief.

'H. TORRENS,
Military Secretary.'

(*London Gazette*, 19th April, 1814, p. 835.)

'HORSE GUARDS, *25th May*, 1814.

'The Prince Regent has been graciously pleased to command, in the name and on the behalf of His Majesty, that in consideration of the distinguished services of the troops engaged at the capture of the island of Java, in August and September, 1811, the undermentioned officers of His Majesty's and the Honourable the East India Company's army, present upon that memorable occasion, shall enjoy the privilege of bearing a Medal, in conformity to the regulations published on 7th October last, viz. :—

[Lieutenant-General Sir Samuel Auchmuty, K.B., Commander of the Forces, and thirty general and other officers.]

'The Prince Regent has also been pleased to command that those Medals which would have been conferred upon such of the officers above named who fell in, or have died since, the capture of Java shall, as a token of respect for their memories, be transmitted to their respective families.

'By command of His Royal Highness the Prince Regent.

'FREDERICK,
Commander-in-Chief.

'H. TORRENS,
Military Secretary.'

(*London Gazette*, 27th August, 1814, p. 1730.)

'HORSE GUARDS, *1st June*, 1814.

'The Prince Regent has been graciously pleased, in the name and on the behalf of His Majesty, to command that, in consideration of the distinguished services of the troops engaged in the battles in the Pyrenees, from 28th July to 2nd August, 1813; of the Nivelle, on 10th November, 1813; and at the siege and capture of St. Sebastian, in August and September, 1813, the undermentioned officers present upon those memorable occasions shall enjoy the privilege of bearing badges of distinction, in conformity to the regulations published on 7th October last, viz. :—

'BATTLES IN THE PYRENEES.

[Here follow the names of Field-Marshal the Duke of Wellington and of one hundred and five general and other officers.]

'BATTLE OF THE NIVELLE.

[The Duke of Wellington and one hundred and twenty-eight general and other officers.]

'SIEGE AND CAPTURE OF ST. SEBASTIAN.

[Lieutenant-General Lord Lynedock, K.B., and forty-eight general and other officers.]

'The Prince Regent has also been pleased to command, in the name and on the behalf of His Majesty, that the following officers who were present in the former battles and sieges in the Peninsula shall receive appropriate badges in commemoration of their services upon those occasions, viz.:—

Battles of Roleia and Vimiera. Two Officers.
Battle of Corunna. Two Officers.
Battle of Talavera de la Reyna. Two Officers.
Battle of Busaco. Fourteen Officers.
Battle of Fuentes de Onor. Twelve Officers.
Battle of Barossa. One Officer.
Battle of Albuhera. Four Officers.
Assault and capture of Ciudad Rodrigo. Three Officers.
Assault and capture of Badajoz. Five Officers.
Battle of Salamanca. Six Officers.
Battle of Vittoria. Two Officers.

'The Prince Regent has further been pleased to command, in the name and on the behalf of His Majesty, that those badges which would have been conferred upon such of the Officers abovenamed who fell in, or have died since, the said battles and sieges shall, as a token of respect for their memories, be transmitted to their respective families.

'By command of His Royal Highness the Prince Regent.

'FREDERICK,
Commander-in-Chief.

'H. TORRENS,
Major-General and Military Secretary.'

(*London Gazette*, 13th September, 1814, p. 1850.)

'HORSE GUARDS, *28th January*, 1814.

'SIR,

His Royal Highness the Prince Regent having observed with great satisfaction the successful exertions made by the Detachment of the British Army serving in the Canadas, against very superior numbers of the enemy, has been graciously pleased to signify his commands to me, through the Secretary of State, that the Officers who have been most distinguished in the two last campaigns in that quarter shall receive an honorary mark of approbation in commemoration of the events in which they have been distinguished. I have therefore to transmit, for your information and guidance, a copy of the Regulations published in the *Gazette* of 9th October last, respecting the grant of Medals and other Badges of Distinction, and to desire that you will immediately transmit me a list of the names of such Officers of the regular Army under your command as you may be induced to recommend, according to the principle contained in these regulations.

'The actions which are considered by His Royal Highness as giving a just claim to such distinctions on the part of the officers engaged, are :—

'1st. The capture of Detroit, and of the American Army under the command of General Hull, on 16th August, 1812.

'2ndly. The defeat of the American Army under the command of General Hampton, at Chateauguay, on 26th October, 1813.

'3rdly. The defeat of the American Army under General Wilkinson, at Chrystler's Farm, on 11th November, 1813.

'I am, Sir,
Yours,
'FREDERICK,
Commander-in-Chief.

'Lieut.-General SIR GEORGE PREVOST, Bart.,
(or Officer) Commanding the Forces in British North America.'

'HEAD QUARTERS, MONTREAL,
24th April, 1814.

GENERAL ORDERS.

'His Excellency the Governor-in-Chief and Commander of the Forces has great satisfaction in communicating to the Troops in British North America, a letter from H.R.H. the Commander-in-Chief (dated 28th January, 1814).

'His Excellency feels confident, that the Officers of this Army, deeply impressed with a grateful sense of the distinguished notice which H.R.H. the Prince Regent has been graciously pleased to confer upon their services, will zealously continue to exert their most devoted energies to merit the approbation of their Prince, and to establish their undoubted lineage with the great mass of their brave comrades, whose intrepid valour, and unshaken discipline, has immortalised the British Arms in Spain, Portugal, and in France.

'His Excellency the Governor-in-Chief and Commander of the Forces has also received, through the Right Honorable the Earl of Bathurst, the commands of H.R.H. the Prince Regent, to recommend for this mark of honorable distinction such Officers of the Militia as have, by their valour and exemplary conduct in the field, merited such reward. These Officers are to be selected under similar restrictions to those specified for His Majesty's Regular Forces.

'His Excellency directs the General Order of 7th October, 1813, to be published for the information of the Troops.

'EDWARD BAYNES,
Adjutant-General, N.A.'

No notice of the grant of the medal for services in Canada appears in the *London Gazette* for 1814 or 1815—that is to say, the grant is not mentioned in the Indices of the *Gazette* for those years. But the Indices are very often defective: *e.g.* the notice of the grant of the Maida medal is not recorded in the Index for 1808, although it appeared in the *Gazette* of 23rd February of that year.

GENERAL ORDER BY THE COMMANDER-IN-CHIEF, MADRAS,
25th August, 1819.

'The Commander-in-Chief has much gratification in publishing a letter from Major-General Sir Henry Torrens, K.C.B., Military Secretary to His Royal Highness the Duke of York, and his Excellency has consequently directed a letter to be addressed to every officer who served under his personal command on the 21st December, 1817, and whose name was submitted to His Royal Highness, to receive the honorary distinction of a medal.

'"HORSE GUARDS, *October* 15, 1818.

'"I have the Commander-in-chief's commands to acknowledge the receipt of your dispatch of the 7th January last, addressed to the Adjutant-General, transmitting a return of officers personally and particularly engaged in the battle of Mahidpore, whom under an idea of the continued existence of a system of granting medals of distinction, you consider worthy of bearing badges commemorating that glorious event.

'"I have His Royal Highness's commands to assure you, that he appreciates in the highest degree the bravery and discipline which so signally distinguished Sir John Malcolm and all the officers under your command in the battle of Mahidpore, as well as the valour, ability, and promptitude with which you directed their zeal in leading the troops to the accomplishment of a splendid achievement, which has mainly served to the overthrow of a confederacy that aimed at the subversion of the British power in India; but it is incumbent upon His Royal Highness to acquaint you, that when the military Order of the Bath was extended, His Majesty's Government thought proper to decide, for reasons which it is unnecessary here to detail, that the system of granting medals of distinction should be abolished, and under these circumstances His Royal Highness is reluctantly compelled to explain the impossibility of his giving effect to the wishes you have expressed in regard to the officers whose names you have transmitted.

'"You will find, however, that the Order of the Bath, as far as its statutes and regulations could permit His Royal Highness and the President of the Board of Control to recommend the grant of it, has been conferred on the officers of the King's and Honourable Company's Service, who have been principally distinguished under your command, and, should the circumstance of your having recommended the grant of medals of distinction have been made known to the army, His Royal Highness trusts that you will give such explanation to the officers who were under your command at Mahidpore, as may convince them that this kind of distinction is withheld in compliance with general regulations, and not from any failure in the due appreciation of their distinguished conduct.

'"Lt.-Genl. SIR THOS. HISLOP, Bart., G.C.B."'

The following extracts from the *Wellington Despatches* supply information on various points in reference to the medals and crosses:—

'To Lieut.-Colonel TORRENS,[1]
Military Secretary to the Commander-in-Chief.

'CARTAXO, *11th December*, 1810.

. . . .

'Some of the General Officers have applied to me to know whether, upon ordinary occasions, they might not wear the riband of the Medal at the button-hole,

---

[1] *Wellington Despatches* (Gurwood, 1838), vol. vii. p. 40.

instead of round the neck. This would be a more convenient way of wearing it, and they would wear it consequently more frequently, which would be desirable; and I shall be obliged if you will let me know whether there is any objection to what is proposed.

'WELLINGTON.'

'*CIRCULAR*[1]

'*To the General Officers who have lately received the Medal.*

'CARTAXO, *3rd February*, 1811.

'GENTLEMEN,

Having made a reference to the Commander-in-Chief, respecting the mode in which the General Officers should wear the distinction with which His Majesty has recently honored them by his orders of 30th September, I have received an answer from Lieut.-Colonel Torrens, stating "that the General Officers should wear the riband of the Medal at their button-hole, the same as the Field Officers, in undress; but when the Medal is worn itself, it should be round the neck."

'I have, etc.,

'WELLINGTON.'

The following despatch is of importance as indicating the views of the Duke of Wellington on the general question of the grant of medals. It will be seen that the Duke was in favour of the principle of selection without reference to rank. He could not agree that the principle which governed the grant of medals to admirals and captains in the Navy was applicable to officers of the Army.

'To the EARL OF LIVERPOOL,[2]
Secretary of State.

'QUINTA DE ST. JOÃO, *11th July*, 1811.

'MY LORD,

I have had the honour of receiving your Lordship's letter of 22nd June, in which your Lordship desires to have my opinion as to the restrictions which it may be expedient to put upon the grant of Medals to British Officers, for distinguished merit displayed upon such occasions as the battles of Vimeira, Coruña, Talavera and Barossa.

'My opinion has always been that the grant of a Medal to an individual officer ought to have been founded originally, partly on the importance of the occasion or action which it was intended to commemorate, and partly on the share which the individual officer had had in the action to be commemorated; and that Medals should have been granted for important actions only, and to those engaged in them in a conspicuous manner, whatever might be their rank in the service.

'It was decided, however, that Medals should be granted on the same principle only, but following strictly the example of the grant of Medals to the Navy, notwithstanding that an action on shore is very different from an action at sea; and the merits of the different classes of individuals are likewise entirely different. At the same time, this principle was departed from in some of the grants made.

'If the principle adopted in the grant of Medals to the Navy is adhered to in the

---

[1] *Wellington Despatches* (Gurwood, 1838), vol. vii. p. 225.

[2] *Ibid.* vol. viii. p. 94.

grant of Medals to Officers in the Army, and that Medals are to be granted to General Officers, and Lieut.-Colonels commanding Regiments, on an occasion to be commemorated, because, on a similar occasion, they would be granted to Admirals and Captains of ships of the line, it is difficult to restrict the grant, or to make a selection of Officers to whom they should be granted, to commemorate the battles at Busaco and Fuentes de Oñoro, if Govt. determine that these actions should be commemorated in that manner. If, however, that principle is departed from, it is not difficult to make out a list of the names of Officers already reported to your Lordship, who were at the head of Corps or detachments upon these occasions, and who had a conspicuous share in the event which it is the intention of the Govt. to commemorate in this manner. It is not probable, however, that the adoption of this principle will decrease the number of those to whom the honor would be granted; but as I have already represented to your Lordship, I do not think this important: that which is important in the establishment of the principle on which the grant of this honor should be made is, that every Officer should feel that he shall receive the mark or distinction, if he should be in the place to distinguish himself, and should act in the manner to deserve to be distinguished, whatever may be his military rank. It may be contended by me that the Officers of the British Army do not require an honor of this description to stimulate their exertions, and that the grant of the Medal is therefore useless; but, however, those who contend for this principle must admit that a selection of those who have had an opportunity of distinguishing themselves in an action is a less objectionable mode of granting it than the grant of it by classes, whether the individuals composing those classes have distinguished themselves or not.

'I have now the honor to enclose lists of the names of the Officers who, on the principle of selection, ought, in my opinion, to receive Medals for the battles of Busaco and Fuentes de Oñoro, if Govt. think proper to distinguish these battles by Medals.

'In respect of the battle of Albuera, I was not there, and I am not able to give an opinion upon it. One brigade of the 4th Division of Infantry, however, was not in the action, nor Brigadier-General Madden's brigade of cavalry. The brunt of the action was on the right; but some of the corps of infantry, I believe, and certainly General Otway's brigade of cavalry, on the left, were not engaged. At all events, these troops were not engaged, as far as I understand, in a greater degree than the whole army were at Busaco, and every corps on the field at Fuentes de Oñoro.

'I mention these circumstances only to point out to your Lordship, that, in every action on shore, however severe, there must be some to whose lot it does not fall to have an opportunity to distinguish themselves; and that the principle of selection, without reference to ranks, ought to be adopted in every instance of the grant of Medals to the Army.

'I have, etc.,

'WELLINGTON.'

'To the EARL OF LIVERPOOL,[1]
Secretary of State.

'RICHOSO, *1st October*, 1811.

'MY DEAR LORD,

Adverting to your Lordship's despatch of 3rd September, regarding the grant of Medals to the Officers of the Army, it occurs to me that an improvement might still be made in the system; for instance, many officers in the course of service become entitled to two, or three, or more medals. In my opinion they

[1] *Wellington Despatches* (Gurwood, 1838), vol. viii. p. 315.

should receive but one; but for every additional action deemed worthy of the medal, in which any officer having a medal should be present, he should be warranted to have the name of that action engraved on his medal, and that in that case the fresh medal for that action should be given to the officer next in command in the regiment, who was present, and distinguished in the action.

'Believe me, etc.,

'WELLINGTON.'

'To EARL BATHURST.[1]

'FRENEDA, *16th March*, 1813.

'MY DEAR LORD,

I have received your letter of 24th February, in regard to the Medals, and I concur entirely with you regarding all the improvements you propose on the subject. You have provided a remedy for a difficulty which I could never get over in a way at all satisfactory to myself.

'I likewise agree with you in the propriety of having a Cross with eight bars, or a Star with eight points, for those who are entitled to more than seven distinctions.

'I am not certain that it would not be best that all General Officers, as well as others, should wear the Medal or Cross at the button-hole till they should receive the last distinction. It is very awkward to ride in round the neck.

'According to the new principle, I believe that General Alava and General O'Lalor ought to have the Cross instead of a Medal, and I shall be obliged to your Lordship if you will so arrange it.

'Believe me, etc.,

'WELLINGTON.'

'To EARL BATHURST.[2]

'FRENEDA, *20th April*, 1813.

'I have received your letter of the 7th.

. . . .

'We must have the orders of the Secretary of State for any alteration in the mode of wearing the medal by the General Officers. It may do very well for an Admiral to wear his medal round his neck on his quarter deck, but we on horseback ought to wear it always at our button-hole. Indeed, this is the common practice in all distributions of this description, and was the rule at first on the grant of the medal for the battle of Maida; and I do not know why it was altered.

'WELLINGTON.'

'To Marshal SIR W. C. BERESFORD, K.B.[3]

'VERA, *6th Novr.*, 1813.

. . . .

'In regard to the medals, I have always been of opinion that Govt. should have extended the principle more than they did; and in executing their orders I believe it will be found that, whenever a medal could be given to an individual under the orders of Govt., I have inserted his name in the return. However, my decision in this or any other subject is not final; and if anybody doubts, I wish he would apply to superior authority.'

'WELLINGTON.'

---

[1] *Wellington Despatches* (Gurwood, 1838), vol. x. p. 179.

[2] *Ibid.* vol. x. p. 307.

[3] *Ibid.* vol. xi. p. 256.

'To Lieut.-General SIR S. COTTON, Bart., K.B.[1]

'ST. PÉ, *16th Novr.*, 1813. 4½ P.M.

'MY DEAR COTTON,

I have just received your letter of the 15th in regard to medals; and if you had spoken to me upon the subject before you wrote it, I could have shewn you, in the clearest manner, that I have nothing to say to the grant of medals, excepting to send the lists, under the orders of Government.

'For instance, the Secretary of State acquaints me that it is His Majesty's intention to grant a medal for a particular action, as for Busaco, and desires me to send lists of the officers to receive them, according to the orders and rules upon that subject. I send the lists accordingly. One of the rules is, that an officer shall receive a medal only for a particular action, in which the corps to which he belongs has been engaged with musketry. This was not the case with the cavalry at Busaco, nor with much of the infantry; and the action not having been a general one, only those of the infantry are in the list whose corps were engaged with musketry.

'It would be impossible, as long as the order remains as it is, and the order being for the battle of Busaco, to return the cavalry for the battle of Busaco, however meritorious their conduct might have been, both before and afterwards.

'In the same manner, the Badajoz medal is for those engaged in the siege and storm of that place; and, in obeying the orders of Government, I could not return the cavalry for their conduct at Slerena, however meritorious; nor any of the covering army. So far for the medals to which you advert.

'In regard to the other points, viz. the grant of a medal for the services of the cavalry in 1810 and 1812, I will forward your letter, if you think proper, to the Secretary of State; but I confess that I do not think it will be successful in attaining your object; and it will rest with you to determine whether you wish the letter to go.

'In no one instance has it ever occurred to me to apply for a medal for any service by the troops. I report the services which they perform, in what I think the clearest and the fairest manner to all concerned; and it rests with Government, and not with me, to notice them as they may think proper.

'Believe me, etc.,

'WELLINGTON.

'If you will advert to the lists for the battle of Fuentes de Oñoro, you will find those only returned who were engaged with musketry. In that battle there was a very heavy cannonade upon the troops, in which many were lost; but the officers of no corps were returned in the list for medals, whose corps had not been engaged with musketry with the enemy. That is the rule, and I cannot depart from it.'

'To Colonel TORRENS,[2]
Military Secretary, Horse Guards.

'ST. JEAN DE LUZ, *28th Novr.*, 1813.

'SIR,

I enclose two letters which I have received from Lieut.-General Sir William Stewart, in which he claims the medal for the battle of Busaco.

'I confess that I did not understand, from the first of the two letters, that the Lieut.-General wished that the subject should be referred to H.R.H. the Commander-in-Chief; and I made him acquainted with the principles on which I had ordered that the lists should be made out for each medal, for which I had received directions from the Secretary of State to send returns.

---

[1] *Wellington Despatches* (Gurwood, 1838), vol. xi. p. 294.

[2] *Ibid.* vol. xi. p. 331.

'In answer to this information I received the second letter, and a copy of one which the Lieut.-General had already written to His Royal Highness, of 19th November, from which I observe that he had already referred the subject for H.R.H.'s decision, notwithstanding the second article of the orders of H.R.H. of 1st October, 1813, which accompanied the medals recently transmitted to the officers.

'It certainly cannot be meant by that General Order that the decision of any Commander of the Forces shall be final on the claim of any officer to this mark of distinction, and I can feel no objection to the revision by H.R.H. of my decision on this or any other subject.

'It remains then for me only to state the principles on which I acted, in making the returns for the Busaco medal, which I believe will be found strictly conformable to the subsequent instructions of the Secretary of State, the Earl of Liverpool, of 3rd Sept., 1811, and H.R.H.'s orders of 1st Oct., 1813.

'I have always conceived that by the words ***personally and particularly engaged***, it was meant for the infantry that they should be at least engaged with musketry ***in general***; and so I have applied them. There certainly may be instances in which troops may be engaged in a cannonade, in which their conduct may be so conspicuously gallant as to induce a Commander of the Forces to use his discretion, and return the officers for a medal ordered for such an occasion; but I have not yet seen such a cannonade, and I have always considered that to be engaged at least with musketry was necessary.

'Now it happened that in the battle of Busaco the second division of infantry were not engaged "personally or particularly," or in any other manner, and I do not believe received a single shot of any description. The medal was not given for marches previous to, or during, or after the battle of Busaco, but to those "personally and particularly" engaged in the battle; and I therefore did not return Lieut.-General Sir Rowland Hill, who commanded, and has not made a claim, or Lieut.-General Sir William Stewart, or any other of the officers of that division.

'I would beg H.R.H. likewise to observe that there are other divisions in the same predicament, the whole army having been in the field on that day, and some even having lost men by cannonade, and even by the effect of distant musketry, whose officers are not returned.

'None of the cavalry, or of the 1st, 2nd, and 4th divisions of infantry were returned, excepting a few of the light infantry of the 1st division, nor the officers of a large part of the Portuguese army not engaged; but if Lieut.-General Sir W. Stewart's claim be admitted, it will be necessary to revise the list, not only for this battle, but for all the others for which medals have been granted.

'I have received many claims for medals since the publication of the orders upon the subject, some of which, in my opinion, are founded; and I propose hereafter to transmit them to be laid before H.R.H., with my opinion of the grounds on which they ought to be granted. For others there is no foundation whatever, under the instructions and general orders; and I beg to know whether it is H.R.H.'s wish that the whole should be transmitted to him, or that I shall forward only those for which there appears to me to be a fair foundation, rejecting the others.

'I have, etc.,

'WELLINGTON.'

'To His Excellency SIR CHARLES STUART, K.B.[1]

'ST. JEAN DE LUZ, 30*th Novr.*, 1813.

'SIR,

I have had the honor of receiving your letter of 21st Novr.; and I beg to acquaint you that, in the usual course, the officers of the Portuguese nation, to

[1] *Wellington Despatches* (Gurwood, 1838), vol. xi. p. 337.

whom medals have been granted, ought to apply for leave from their own Government to accept the mark of distinction.

'I have, etc.,

'WELLINGTON.'

'To Colonel TORRENS.[1]

'SEYSSES, *1st April*, 1814.

'MY DEAR TORRENS,

I have received your letter of 16th March, regarding the recommendations for the medals for the battle of Vitoria. I make a distinction between a general action in which we pursue the enemy from the ground, and one in a defensive position. This distinction is fairly deducible from the different nature of the operations.

'In the former it is very difficult to tell who is, and who is not, engaged in musketry. All are at times, to a certain degree, exposed to it; and I perfectly recollect seeing the Household Brigade at one time in a situation in the pursuit in which they were so. In an action in a defensive position, there are always some troops so situated as to have no share whatever in the action; some may be at the distance of miles from it, and in those cases I apply the rule strictly. In actions such as Salamanca and Vitoria, I do not.

'Believe me, etc.,

'WELLINGTON.'

To an OFFICER.[2]

'VIENNA, *5th February*, 1815.

. . . .

'The Government fixed the occasions on which medals should be granted to the army, and framed the rules according to which I was bound to make the lists of those to whom they were to be granted; and not having received their orders to recommend for medals for the service at Arroyo Molinos, Alba de Tormes, or at Beja, or at Aire, or at Arriverete, it was impossible for me to recommend you for a medal for your services on those occasions; neither was it possible for me to recommend you for a medal at Fuentes de Onoro, or in the Pyrenees, according to the rules by which I was ordered and bound to make out the lists of those I recommended.

. . . .

'WELLINGTON.'

No. 156.

GOLD MEDALS AND CROSSES PROPOSED TO BE GIVEN BY THE EAST INDIA COMPANY, 1816.

In 1816 the Court of Directors of the East Indian Company, with the view of placing officers performing distinguished services in India on an equality, in respect to decorative rewards, with officers in the Royal service distinguishing themselves elsewhere,

---

[1] *Wellington Despatches* (Gurwood, 1838), vol. xi. p. 620.

[2] *Ibid.* vol. xii. p. 260.

determined to institute medals and crosses under Regulations similar to those published in the *London Gazette* of 9th October, 1813, by the Horse Guards, in reference to officers of the Royal service.

Officers who had taken part in the then recent campaign in Nepal would have been the earliest recipients of the new medal.

It may be presumed that the Company's medals and crosses would have borne a general resemblance to those issued by the Crown, and, consequently, that they would have been made of gold.

No medals were, however, issued, and no further action was ever taken in the matter. The reason for this was that the Order of the Bath, as recently enlarged, afforded the means of rewarding officers of the ranks which had previously received the Gold Medal and Cross.

AT A GENERAL COURT OF THE EAST INDIA COMPANY,
11th December, 1816.

'The Chairman acquainted the Court that the Court of Directors being desirous of conferring every mark of distinction upon the Army serving in India and of commemorating the services of those officers who signalised themselves by exemplary zeal, valor and conduct in the field, has determined to grant Medals and Badges for distinguished services, and had come to sundry Resolutions in consequence thereof.

'The said Resolutions were then communicated to the Court.'

AT A COURT OF DIRECTORS, held on Friday, 6th December, 1816.

'*Resolved unanimously*: That the East India Company being desirous of conferring every mark of distinction upon the Army serving in India, and of commemorating the services of those officers who signalised themselves by exemplary zeal, valor and conduct in the field, the Court of Directors has determined to grant Medals and Badges for military services of distinguished merit, and that in the grant and distribution of such marks of distinction the following Regulations shall be strictly observed, and that they shall be extended to the officers of His Majesty's Service, provided it shall meet with the sanction of His Royal Highness the Prince Regent, and that the Right Honorable the Commissioners for the Affairs of India be requested to obtain His Royal Highness's sanction—

'1st. That one Medal only shall be borne by each Officer for such distinction.

'2nd. That for the second and third events which may be subsequently commemorated in like manner, each individual recommended to bear the distinction shall carry a Gold Clasp attached to the Ribbon to which the Medal is suspended, and inscribed with the name of the Battle or Siege to which it relates.

'3rd. That upon a claim being admitted to a fourth mark of distinction, a Cross shall be borne by each Officer, with the names of the four Battles or Sieges respectively inscribed thereupon, and to be worn in substitution of the distinction previously granted to such individual.

'4th. Upon each occasion of a similar nature that may occur, the Clasp again be issued to those who have a claim to the additional distinction, to be borne on the Ribbon to which the Cross is suspended, in the same manner as described in No. 2 of these Regulations.

'The Court of Directors resolves that the distribution of Medals or Badges for Military Services of distinguished merit shall be regulated as follows: viz.

'1st. That no General Officer or other Officer shall be considered entitled to receive them unless he has been personally and particularly engaged upon those occasions of great importance, in commemoration of which such marks of distinction shall be bestowed.

'2nd. That no Officer shall be considered a Candidate for the Medal or Badge, except under the special selection and report of the Commander of the Forces on the spot, as having merited the distinction by conspicuous services.

'3rd. That the Commander of the Forces shall transmit to the Commander-in-Chief returns signed by himself, specifying the names and ranks of those officers whom he shall have selected as particularly deserving.

'The Court of Directors resolve that in commemoration of the successful termination of the war against Nepaul, and of the services of those officers who, present in action, have been specially mentioned by name in Despatches published in the *Gazettes* as having distinguished themselves, or in General Orders published by the Commander-in-Chief or the Govt. in India, shall enjoy the privilege of bearing Badges of distinction, which shall be worn by the General Officers suspended by a Ribbon of the colour of the Sash with a blue edge round the neck, and by such other officers as may have been specially recommended, attached by a Ribbon of the same description to the button-hole of their Uniform.

'The Court of Directors resolve that these Badges which would have been conferred upon the Officers who fell or have died since of their wounds shall, as a token of respect for their memories, be transmitted to their respective families.'

No. 157.

WATERLOO, 1815.

PLATE 22.

Obv. Bust of the Prince Regent, laureated, *l.* *Leg.* GEORGE P. REGENT.

Below. T. WYON . JUN : S :

Rev. Figure of Victory seated; in her right hand, a palm branch; in her left, an olive branch. Above, WELLINGTON; below, WATERLOO . JUNE 18 . 1815.

Mainly copied from the *reverse* of a coin of Elis, B.C. 480-400. See *British Museum Catalogue.*

Circular, 1·4 inch. Silver.
Artist. T. Wyon.
Struck at the Royal Mint.
Dies at the Royal Mint.
Mounting. Steel ring, one inch in diameter.
Ribbon. 1½ inch. Crimson, with blue borders.
Worn on left breast.

In a despatch to H.R.H. the Duke of York, dated Orvillé, 28th June, 1815, the Duke of Wellington, after expressing his high gratification at His Royal Highness's approbation, suggested the expediency of giving a medal to the non-commissioned officers and soldiers engaged in the battle of Waterloo. His Grace added he was convinced it would have the best effect in the army, and that if the battle 'should settle our concerns, they will well deserve it.'

In a debate in the House of Commons on 29th June, 1815, on Lord Castlereagh's motion for an address to the Prince Regent on the subject of a national monument to commemorate the battle of Waterloo, and the fame of the officers and soldiers of the British Army who fell in the campaign, the Right Hon. William Watkins Wynn expressed his cordial concurrence in the motion, but at the same time hoped the intended monument would not be erected in any particular church, on which Lord Castlereagh said it was proposed to erect a triumphal arch or other architectural monument suitable to the magnificence of the nation, and which would not be confined within the walls of a church. Mr. Wynn at the same time suggested that medals should be struck in commemoration of the battle, and distributed to the survivors; and likewise that the medals should be of the same materials for officers and men, so that they who had been fellows in danger might bear the same badge of honour. (*Quarterly Review*, July, 1815.)

There were thus two suggestions made almost simultaneously in respect to the grant of a medal for Waterloo.

Although the Duke of Wellington appears to have originally contemplated giving the medal to the rank and file only, he subsequently wrote to Earl Bathurst, 17th September, 1815, recommending that all ranks should have 'the same medal, hung to the same ribbon as that now used with the medals,' *i.e.* red with blue borders. The Duke's views as to both medal and ribbon were thus adopted.

The grant of the medal was announced to the Army in a Memorandum by H.R.H. the Commander-in-Chief, dated 10th March, 1816.

'To H.R.H. the DUKE OF YORK.[1]

'ORVILLÉ, *28th June*, 1815.

'SIR,

I have had the honor of receiving your Royal Highness's letter of 23rd Instant, and I am highly flattered by your Royal Highness's approbation, and gratified by your attention to this army.

[1] *Wellington Despatches* (Gurwood, 1838), vol. xii. p. 520.

'Your Royal Highness will see, from what happens every day, that our victory is decisive, and I hope we shall bring the concerns of this country to a satisfactory close without striking another blow.

. . . .

'I confess that I do not concur in the limitation of the Order (of the Bath) to field officers. Many captains in the army conduct themselves in a very meritorious manner, and deserve it; and I never could see the reason for excluding them either from the Order or the Medal.

'I would likewise beg leave to suggest to your Royal Highness the expediency of giving to the non-commissioned officers and soldiers engaged in the battle of Waterloo, a Medal. I am convinced it would have the best effect in the army; and, if that battle should settle our concerns, they will well deserve it.

'I have, etc.,

'WELLINGTON.'

'To EARL BATHURST.[1]

'PARIS, *17th Sept.*, 1815.

'MY DEAR LORD,

I am very much obliged to you for appointing General Alava an extra Commander of the Bath.

'I have long intended to write to you about the Medal for Waterloo. I recommend that we should all have the same Medal, hung to the same ribband as that now used with the Medals.

'Believe me, etc.,

'WELLINGTON.'

MEMORANDUM.

'HORSE GUARDS, *March 10th*, 1816.

'The Prince Regent has been graciously pleased, in the name and on the behalf of His Majesty, to command, that in commemoration of the brilliant and decisive victory of Waterloo, a medal should be conferred on every officer, non-commissioned officer, and soldier of the British Army, present upon that memorable occasion.

'His Royal Highness has further been pleased to command that the ribband, issued with the medal, shall never be worn but with the medal suspended to it.

'By command of His Royal Highness the Prince Regent,

'FREDERICK,
Commander-in-Chief.'

'H. TORRENS, *Major-General and Military Secretary.*'

(*London Gazette*, 23rd April, 1816.)

No. 158.

DUKE OF WELLINGTON.

GOLD COLLAR AND CROSS.

PLATE 1. *FRONTISPIECE.*

The collar is composed of alternate gold lions and oval tablets showing the Union badge in enamel, bordered by a wreath of oak leaves. Across each tablet, on the horizontal bar of the Union, is the name of a battle or siege, the tablet bearing

[1] *Wellington Despatches* (Gurwood, 1838), vol. xii. p. 636.

'Waterloo' being at the bottom. Below the 'Waterloo' tablet hangs a Royal crown to which is suspended a gold cross, generally similar in design to the Gold Cross, No. 155, but much larger, and having a figure of Victory on one side, and a lion on the other. The collar is held together by two chains of long links attached above and below to the lions and tablets. The lions and tablets are each about two inches in length. The names on the tablets are as follow (*right*):—

CIUDAD RODRIGO.
BADAJOZ.
SALAMANCA.
VITTORIA.
TOULOUSE.
PYRENEES.
NIVELLE.
ORTHES.
NEIVE.
WATERLOO.

The cross is a Maltese one, 2½ inches across, with ornamental borders; on one side is a figure of Victory, and on the other, a lion. On the four limbs of the cross, on the side bearing the figure of Victory, are the names of the following actions:—

ROLEIA & VIMIERA.
TALAVERA.
BUSACO.
FUENTES DE ONOR.

These, together with those named on the collar, are the actions at which the Duke was present.

On the edges of the two sides and bottom of the cross is the inscription, 'Field Marshal Arthur Duke of Wellington.'

The collar is amongst the Wellington heirlooms preserved at Apsley House. The following is the entry in the Heirloom Catalogue regarding it:—

'Massy gold and enameled Triumphant collar, composed of alternate Lions and Medallions (each of the latter having the name of a battle inscribed on it), with badge or cross appended to it. Presented to His Grace by His Majesty King George the 4th, when Prince Regent, shortly after the Battle of Waterloo.'

Sir Albert W. Woods, Garter King of Arms, has, however, in his possession a memorandum relative to the collar drawn up by Sir George Nayler, Garter, for Sir William Knighton, Bart., Keeper of the Privy Purse to George IV. The memorandum is undated, but it was evidently not written until after the death of the Duke of York (5th January, 1827). It states that in the year 1814, in obedience to the commands of His Majesty, then Prince Regent, drawings were prepared, under Sir George's direction, of a collar intended to be presented to the Duke of Wellington, in commemoration of the glorious victories *personally* achieved by His Grace in the Peninsula; and His Majesty having been pleased to approve of a collar composed of Lions of England and the Union badge of the United Kingdom (which badge had been before granted by His Majesty as an augmentation to the Duke's arms), having in the centre of the Cross of St. George the names of ten of those battles inscribed, as worn by His Grace on gold clasps, the collar was duly made. To the collar was afterwards added, in pursuance of His Majesty's pleasure, a cross pendant, inscribed with the names of the other four battles on the military gold cross worn by His Grace, having in the centre, on one side, a figure of Victory, and on the other side, a British Lion. In the present memorandum Sir George Nayler submits the collar and cross to the King, with a humble request for His Majesty's gracious commands in regard to them.

There is thus no doubt that the idea of the collar originated before the battle of Waterloo, though for some reason it did not take effect until more than ten years after that battle.

The collar should therefore have been described as having been presented to the Duke of Wellington by George IV., and not by the Prince Regent as stated on Plate I. But the information derived from Sir G. Nayler's memorandum was not at the author's disposal before the Plate was printed.

Sir Albert Woods possesses also a detailed coloured drawing of the collar and cross, together with a rough pen-and-ink sketch of them made by Sir G. Nayler, showing that in all probability he was the designer of the whole decoration.

It is understood that the collar was made for the King by Messrs. Rundell and Bridge, of London.

The illustration, Plate I, was executed by the kind permission of His Grace, the present Duke of Wellington.

No 159.

MARSHAL VISCOUNT BERESFORD.

COLLAR AND CROSS.

This collar is composed of alternate lions and oval tablets bearing the Union badge bordered with laurel; in the centre, a crown, pendent from which is a cross similar to the Gold Cross (No. 155). The collar is held together by two chains of long links running above and below, and attached to the lions and tablets. The lions and tablets are about two inches in length. The lions are similar to the Royal crest of England.

This collar is shown on a bust of Viscount Beresford which was exhibited at the Royal Military Exhibition at Chelsea in 1890 (*Catalogue*, No. 815). What is the history of the collar we have not hitherto been able to discover, nor have we been able to learn whether it is now in existence.

From the above description it will be seen that this collar bears a general resemblance to that given to the Duke of Wellington by George IV. (No. 158).

William Carr, Viscount Beresford, died 8th Jany., 1854.

No. 160.

FIRST BURMESE WAR, 1824-6.

AVA, ASSAM, AND ARRACAN.

PLATE 23, *No.* 1.

Obv. Representation of the storming of the great Pagoda at Rangoon. On the left, the river, with steamer and boats.

Exergue, in Persian:—'The Standard of the victorious Army of England upon Ava.'

W. WYON, in left corner.

Rev. The White Elephant bowing down before the British Lion. Behind are the British and Burmese Flags.

Exergue, in Persian:—'The elephant of Ava submits to the lion of England, year 1826.'

W. DANIELL, R.A., DEL., in left corner.

Circular, 1.5 inch.
Gold, for officers. Silver, for other ranks.
Artists. Designed by W. Daniell, R.A., executed by W. Wyon.
Struck under the superintendence of Mr. Wyon.
Dies at the Royal Mint.
Mounting. Steel clip and ring, one inch in diameter.
Ribbon. Red, with blue borders. For the Madras troops.
Worn on left breast.

This medal was given to the native officers and soldiers who served in the first Burmese War, 1824-6. The grant was announced in a General Order by the Governor-General, dated 22nd April, 1826.

In reporting the grant to the Court of Directors, the Government of India requested that steps might be taken for the preparation of the medals in England. From this it may, perhaps, be inferred that they were not altogether satisfied with the performances of their own Mint on previous occasions.

The idea of the design is similar to that of the Seringapatam Medal. On the *obverse* is a representation of one of the chief exploits of the war, the storming of the great Pagoda at Rangoon; and on the *reverse* is the emblematic beast of Burmah bowing before that of England.

The number of medals struck were:—

	Gold	Silver
For the Bengal troops	308	13,108
For the Madras ,,	450	20,025

From a communication received from the late Mr. S. W. Wyon, the weight of the gold medal appears to have been 1 oz. 10 dwt. 5 grs.

No native officer or soldier who served in the first Burmese War, and received this medal, was permitted to claim the 'India, 1799-1826' medal which, with clasp for 'Ava,' was given in 1850 to the European officers and soldiers of the Royal and Company's Armies who served in it.

Of the medals for the Madras troops not more than half appear to have been claimed, since in the year 1840 the Government of Madras reported to the Court of Directors that 197 of the gold and 9022 of the silver medals remained unappropriated, and suggested that officers might be allowed to purchase the medals at their intrinsic value. The Court directed, however, that ten of the gold, and one hundred of the silver medals should be retained to meet any claims that might be made by native officers or soldiers, for whom alone[1] the medals were struck, and that the remainder should be sent to the Mint as bullion.

In connection with this medal we for the first time meet with mention of a ribbon for an Indian medal; and likewise with directions as to the manner in which medals should be worn.

In 1831 the Commander-in-Chief at Madras proposed that a red ribbon with blue edges should be issued with this medal for the purpose of ensuring uniformity, and to avoid putting the

---

[1] In an obituary of General Sir Archibald Campbell which appeared in the *United Service Magazine* for 1843, pp. 441-3, it is stated that the East India Company, in addition to the grant of a pension of £1000 a year for his services in Burmah, presented him with a handsome gold medal, possibly this one.

owners to expense. The Government consented to provide ribbon, but stipulated that the pattern should bear no resemblance to the Waterloo ribbon. They subsequently, however, waived this objection, and permitted the use of the ribbon in question. By a circular, dated 22nd November, 1831, the Commander-in-Chief directed that the medal should be worn perfectly square upon the centre of the left breast.

GENERAL ORDER BY THE GOVERNOR-GENERAL, 22nd April, 1826.

'In testimony of the brilliant services achieved by the Army under the command of Major-Genl. Sir Archibald Campbell, the Governor-General in Council is pleased to resolve that all the Corps, European and Native, in the Service of the Hon. East India Company, who have been employed in the Burman Country, including the Corps which were detached by that Officer from his more immediate command, for the conquest of the enemy's possessions of Cheduba, Negrais and Bassein on the one side, and Martaban, Ye, Tavoy and Mergui on the other, shall bear on their Regimental Colours the word "Ava" with the words "Rangoon," "Donabew," "Prome," "Malloon," and "Pagham," as they may have been respectively present at one or more of the actions at those places. With respect to the King's Regiments, the Governor-Genl. in Council will recommend to His Majesty through the proper channel, to grant the same distinction to them.

'Medals also, bearing a suitable device, are to be distributed to all the Native Troops which at any period during the War were employed under the command of Major-Genl. Sir Archibald Campbell, including the Officers and men of the Flotilla and Gun Boats serving in the Irrawaddy.

. . . .

'In testimony of the high sense entertained by Govt. of the services of the Troops, by whom the Provinces of Assam and Arracan were conquered, the Governor-General in Council is pleased to order that the several Native Corps who were employed in those countries, shall respectively bear on their Colours the words "Assam" and "Arracan" as the case may be, and His Majesty will be solicited to grant to the 44th and 54th Regiments the same distinction.

'In further proof of the approbation with which the Govt. regards the meritorious conduct of its Native Troops serving in foreign countries, Medals with an appropriate device shall be presented to the Troops which assisted at the conquest of Assam and Arracan.' (Page 158.)

GENERAL ORDER BY THE COMMANDER-IN-CHIEF, CALCUTTA, 22nd May, 1826.

'With reference to Govt. General Orders of 11th April last (published on 22nd April), the Commander-in-Chief directs that Rolls with figured abstracts, in the form prescribed by General Order of 13th May, 1811,[1] of all the Native Commissioned, Non-Commissioned Officers, Sepoys, Golundauze and Gun Lascars, belonging to Corps of the Bengal Establishment, who are entitled to Medals for their services in Assam, Arracan, and Ava, be prepared immediately and transmitted to the Adjutant-General's Office, by the officers commanding the several Corps and Establishments to which the

---

[1] Henley's *Military Code*, p. 257. Carroll's *Military Code*, Chap. xlvi;

persons so entitled may now belong, in order that the Medals authorised by Govt. in the orders alluded to may be furnished to them accordingly.

'Corps entitled to bear on their Regimental Colours any of the honorary distinctions conferred by Govt. in the same Orders are likewise to be reported by the several Commanding Officers to the Adjutant-General of the Army.' (Page 196.)

BENGAL MILITARY CONSULTATIONS. 12th May, 1826.

PROCEEDINGS OF THE GOVERNOR-GENERAL IN COUNCIL, SECRET DEPT.
5th May, 1826.

Letter to the Hon. the Secret Committee, dated 11th April, 1826.

'6. In the General Orders issued this day we have endeavored to express our sense of the merits of Major-General Sir Archibald Campbell, and the Officers and Troops who have been engaged in the contest. We earnestly hope that the sentiments and resolutions contained in those General Orders will receive the approbation and confirmation of your Hon. Committee, and that you will be pleased to adopt the necessary measures for giving them full effect, by causing Medals with a suitable device to be prepared, and by making application to the King's Govt. for leave to be granted to H.M.'s Regiments to carry on their Colours the words proposed. The necessary Returns of the numbers of Troops for whom medals are required, and other particulars will be forwarded to the Hon. the Court of Directors from the Military Dept.

'*Ordered*, that an Extract from the foregoing letter to the Honorable the Secret Committee be sent to the Military Dept. for information and any orders that may be necessary.'

FROM THE GOVERNMENT OF BENGAL TO THE COURT OF DIRECTORS.

20th Feb., 1827.

'47. Consultation No. 53 of 22nd April last is a General Order issued in the Secret Dept. on the 11th of the same month, in which Order we endeavoured to express our sense of the merits of Major-General Sir Archibald Campbell, and the Officers and men engaged in the Army in Ava, during the progress of the contest with the Burmese. We at the same time resolved that the necessary returns of the number of Troops, for which Medals with a suitable device might be required, should be forwarded to your Honorable Court from the Military Dept.

'48. In the General Order issued from the Secret Dept. we had directed that, in addition to the word "Ava," each Regiment should bear on its Colours the names of the several engagements in which it might have been present; but learning afterwards from Lord Combermere that such particular distinctions were seldom or never indiscriminately conferred on the entire force by which a victory was gained, but only on those Regiments whose good fortune might have afforded them opportunities during the action of displaying peculiar valour, we determined to limit the Honorary distinction to be borne on the Colours to the word "Ava." We have authorised the Troop and Company of Bengal Horse and Foot Artillery employed in Ava to bear upon their appointments the requisite honorary inscription.

'49. The Govt. of Fort St. George have been requested to transmit to your Hon. Court the necessary abstract Returns for the Medals for that Presidency; and so soon as H.E. the Commander-in-Chief has favored us with the abstracts of the number of individuals of this Presidency entitled to Medals, the documents shall be forwarded to you without delay.'

FROM THE GOVERNMENT OF BENGAL TO THE COURT OF DIRECTORS.

13th June, 1828—Military.

Paras. 16 to 19. Forward Return of Native Troops entitled to Medals for Ava, Arracan, Assam.

Artillery, . . .	1,158
Infantry, . . .	11,368
Cavalry, . . .	890
Total,	13,416

FROM THE COURT OF DIRECTORS TO THE GOVERNMENT OF BENGAL.

11th August, 1830. No. 78—Military.

Reply to Paras. 16 and 19 of Letter dated 13th June, 1828.

'1. Having caused a Medal to be struck for distribution to the Native Troops which served in Ava, Assam, and Arracan during the Burman War, agreeably to the intention announced by you in General Orders, the requisite number will be sent by an early opportunity.

'2. The supply which has been prepared is limited to fighting men, and the heirs of such as are dead, agreeably to the Returns forwarded by you, and amounts for your Presidency to

308[1] Gold, and
13,108 Silver.

FROM THE COURT OF DIRECTORS TO THE GOVERNMENT OF MADRAS.

11th August, 1830. No. 54—Military.

'1. Having caused a Medal to be struck for distribution to the Native Troops which served in Ava, Assam, and Arracan during the Burman War, agreeably to the intention announced by you in General Orders, the requisite number will be sent by an early opportunity.

'2. The supply which has been prepared amounts for your Presidency to

450 Gold, and
20,025 Silver.

'3. These are the totals contained in the Adjutant-General's Statement of 24th May, 1828, exclusive of Bheesties and Native Doctors, to whom Medals are not to be issued.'

---

[1]

Infantry, ...	256
Body Guard, ...	13
Irregular Horse, ...	27
Foot Artillery, ...	3
Gun Lascars, ...	9
	308

MADRAS MILITARY PROCEEDINGS, *12th July*, 1831.

'To the SECRETARY TO GOVERNMENT
in the Military Dept.

'No. 12. No. 3758.

'SIR,

Adverting to the Medals received for the Native Officers and Soldiers that were employed in the Birman Empire, I am directed by the Commander-in-Chief to submit the accompanying pattern of Ribbon that he considers should be issued with the Medals to each of those Officers and Soldiers now on the effective strength of the Army or attached to Veteran Corps, to insure uniformity in wearing them, without subjecting the individual to any expense, which His Excellency believes neither the Govt. nor the Court of Directors desire should be the case.

'In the event of the Commander-in-Chief's suggestion receiving the approval of Govt., he desires me to request you will express to the Right Hon. the Governor in Council his recommendation that the Clothing Board should be instructed to issue upon Indents countersigned in this Dept., one quarter of a yard of Ribbon to each Native Officer and Soldier entitled to receive Medals, that may now be employed in the service.

'The expense that will be incurred by Govt., should it adopt the Commander-in-Chief's recommendation, will be less than three annas for each person.

'I have, etc.,

'T. H. S. CONWAY,
Adjutant-General of the Army.

'ADJT.-GENL.'S OFFICE,
'FORT ST. GEORGE, *23rd June*, 1831.'

'*Ordered*, that the following reply be despatched to the Commander-in-Chief:—

'To H.E. Lt.-Genl. the Hon. SIR R. W. O'CALLAGHAN, K.C.B.,
Commander-in-Chief.

'SIR,

I am directed to acknowledge the receipt of a letter from the Adjutant-Genl. of the Army, dated 23rd ult. No. 3758.

'The Right Hon. the Governor in Council sanctioned the supply of a quarter of a yard of Ribbon to each Native Officer and Soldier on the effective strength of the Army, or attached to the Veteran Battalion who is entitled to an Ava Medal, but is of opinion that the pattern of the Ribbon should bear no resemblance to that by which Waterloo Medals are suspended.

'The Clothing Board will be instructed to comply with Indents from the Adjutant-Genl.'s Office for any other pattern Ribbon which your Excellency may be pleased to select.

'I have, etc.,

'R. CLERK,
Secretary to Govt.

'FORT ST. GEORGE, *12th July*, 1831.'

'No. 14. *Ordered also* that copies of the foregoing letters be transmitted to the Clothing Board, the Military Auditor-Genl., and the Accountant-General.

MADRAS MILITARY PROCEEDINGS, 9th August, 1831. Nos. 19 and 20.

'To the SECRETARY TO GOVT.
in the Military Dept.

'SIR,

I am directed by the Commander-in-Chief to acknowledge the receipt of your letter of 12th July. The Ribbon which the Commander-in-Chief would propose for the Ava Medal is Red with Blue edges, this being common to all Medals granted by His Majesty in modern times, and now considered to be the Medal Ribbon of England. The Medals of Seringapatam and Java[1] are both suspended from it, and both are so worn with the sanction of His Majesty.

'I have, etc.,

'J. H. S. CONWAY,
Adjt.-Genl. of the Army.

'ADJUTANT-GENL.'S OFFICE,
FORT ST. GEORGE, *5th Aug.*, 1831.'

RESOLUTION THEREON.

'Under the explanation afforded in the foregoing letter, the Right Hon. the Governor in Council permits the supply of a Red ribbon with blue edges for the suspension of the Ava Medals about to be issued to the Native Troops employed in the late Expedition.'

No. 6973. *CIRCULAR.*

'To the OFFICERS COMMANDING
European and Native Regiments.

'SIR,

I am directed to inform you that with the Ava Medals about to be despatched for the Regiment under your command, there will also be received Ribbon in the proportion of one quarter of a yard for each individual now upon the strength, to whom a Medal may be issued. One eighth of a yard is for present use—the remainder is to be held in reserve, in the Regimental Stores, under charge of the Quarter-Master, and to be issued as may be directed by the Commanding Officer. No further issue will be made by Govt.

'The Medal is to be worn perfectly square upon the centre of the left breast, the upper edge of the Ribbon being even with the first button for ranks wearing Sword Belts only, and even with the second button for ranks wearing Cross Belts.

'I am, etc.,

'B. R. HITCHINS,
Acting Adjutant-General.

'ADJUTANT-GENERAL'S OFFICE,
FORT ST. GEORGE, *22nd November*, 1831.

'*N.B.*—This letter is to be entered in the Regimental Order Book of the Corps under your command.'

FROM THE GOVERNMENT OF MADRAS TO THE COURT OF DIRECTORS.

6th March, 1832. No. 6—Military.

'16. At the recommendation of the Commander-in-Chief, we have sanctioned the supply of a quarter of a yard of red ribband with blue edges to each Native Officer and Soldier in the Army who is entitled to receive an Ava Medal.'

---

[1] *i.e.* the Gold War Medal (No. 155).

FROM THE GOVERNMENT OF MADRAS TO THE COURT OF DIRECTORS.

10th July, 1840. No. 20—Military.

'Deposited in the General Treasury at Fort St. George—

197 Gold } Ava Medals.
9022 Silver }

'37. We take advantage of the present opportunity to bring to the notice of your Hon. Court that the Ava Medals described in the margin remain unappropriated. We have caused them to be transferred from the Arsenal to the General Treasury. We beg to suggest for the favourable consideration of your Hon. Court, that the Officers of H.M.'s and the Indian Army may be allowed to obtain these Medals at their intrinsic value, and that the priority of claim to purchase be given to Officers who served in Ava. It is not probable that any more of the Medals will ever be required for issue to the Native Officers and Sepoys.'

FROM THE COURT OF DIRECTORS TO THE GOVERNMENT OF MADRAS.

16th June, 1841. No. 45—Military.

Letter dated 10th July, 1840, No. 20.

'34 to 37. Forward a list of articles found on a recent examination, surplus and deficient in the Arsenal of Fort St. George. A suggestion relative to the disposal of Ava Medals which remain unappropriated submitted for the favourable consideration of the Court.'

'18. You will be pleased to retain for the present ten of the Gold, and one hundred of the Silver, Ava Medals, to meet claims which may still possibly be made by Native Officers and Soldiers, for whose use alone they were struck. The remainder you will send to the Mint to be appropriated as Bullion.'

FROM THE GOVERNMENT OF MADRAS TO THE COURT OF DIRECTORS.

21st Dec., 1841. No. 57—Military.

Cons. 8th Sept., 1841, No. 348.
Cons. 12th Oct., 1841.

'Court's Letter, No. 45, dated 16th June, 1841. P. 18. Directs that for the present, 10 Gold and 100 Silver Ava Medals be retained to meet any claims, and that the rest be sent to the Mint to be appropriated as Bullion.

'21. In accordance with the recommendation of the Major-General Commanding the Forces, we have announced in General Orders that no applications for Ava Medals will be admitted after 31st Dec., 1841, and these remaining in store after that date will, agreeably to the instructions of your Hon. Court, be delivered to the Mint Master to be appropriated as Bullion.'

No. 161.

BURMESE CHIEFS, 1825-6.

PLATE 23, *No.* 2.

Obv. The sea-shore with hills. On the top of one on the right is a pagoda with a palm-tree. The setting sun. On the left, two steamers. In the foreground, two English soldiers, one holding a flag in his hand, and eight natives.

Rev. Arms, crest and motto of the East India College, Haileybury. The motto (Auspicio Regis et Senatus Angliæ) is rendered very incorrectly, thus :—

AUS⊏⊐CIO KEGE ET SPNATUS AN--IA.

On a scroll above, REWARD OF MERIT.

On a scroll below, an inscription in Burmese, 'Moung Myat Phyoo,' the name of the recipient.

The arms and the two scrolls are in three pieces, the former being riveted, and the latter soldered on to the medal.

Circular, 2.2 inches. Gold.

The following letter from the late Lieut.-General Sir Arthur P. Phayre, G.C.M.G., formerly Chief Commissioner of British Burmah, gives all the information we have been able to obtain as to this medal. A rubbing of it had been sent to him by Colonel Laurie, with a request that he would translate the inscription on the *obverse.*

'EAST INDIA UNITED SERVICE CLUB, 16*th May*, 1879.

'MY DEAR LAURIE,

I think there were some half dozen of these Medals struck to give to the Talaing Chiefs who joined the British Army in the war of 1825-26.

'The Burmese letters form the name of the recipient of this one, "Moung Myat Phyoo." Old Moung H. Fanlay, who joined me in Rangoon in 1852, had one of them presented to him as a young man, being a Talaing of ancient family.

'Ever yours sincerely,

'A. P. PHAYRE.

'To Colonel W. F. B. LAURIE.'

The medal is of peculiar formation, being composed apparently of two plates secured together by a gold rim. The devices on the *obverse* are kept in position by solder and rivets; the *reverse* is from a die.

Why the arms of the East India College should have been used instead of those of the East India Company is difficult to understand. It is singular that such a mistake should have occurred, because the arms of the Company were well known, and in general use in India, whereas those of the College were not in use at all; but the following may be the explanation.

At Haileybury College there used to be given as prizes a certain number of gold medals, some of which bore on one side the College arms; and on a comparison of one of these with the Burmese medal, it is at once manifest that the design on the latter is a copy of the former. It may consequently be conjectured that, it being desired that the Burmese Medal should bear the Company's arms, and a difficulty having arisen in regard to a suitable model to guide the engraver, some member of the Civil Service who happened to possess a prize medal lent it as a pattern, overlooking the fact that the arms thereon displayed, although in some respects similar to, were by no means the same as the Company's. The College arms were then copied by a native artist to the best of his ability, his skill not sufficing, however, for a correct imitation of the Latin motto. The medal was not manufactured at the Calcutta Mint.

The medal, of which an illustration is given, was bought at a sale of pledges by Mr. E. B. Partridge, of 24 New Street, Covent Garden, by whom it was, in May, 1879, sold to Colonel Murray, of Polmaise, who kindly allowed a cast of it to be taken for the purposes of this book.

No. 162.

COORG, 1837.

PLATE 23, *No.* 3.

Obv. A Coorg, his right hand upraised holding a Coorg knife, ready to strike; his left hand grasping a matchlock.

Leg. In Canarese:—'Mark of favor given for loyalty to the Company's Government, in suppressing rebellion in the months of April and May 1837.'

Rev. Trophy of Coorg arms and ornaments encircled by a wreath of laurel.

Leg. FOR DISTINGUISHED CONDUCT AND LOYALTY TO THE BRITISH GOVERNMENT COORG APRIL 1837.

Circular, 2 inches. Gold. Silver.
Struck at the Calcutta Mint.
Dies at the Calcutta Mint.
Worn suspended round the neck.
With some of the gold medals gold chains were given.

On the conclusion of the insurrection in Coorg in 1837, the Government desired to mark their sense of the courage and fidelity of such of the Coorgs as had assisted the local authorities in quelling it, and called on Colonel Cubbon, the Commissioner for Coorg, to submit suggestions on the subject.

One of Colonel Cubbon's recommendations was that gold and silver medals (fourteen of the former with chains), should be presented to the chiefs and subordinate leaders of the loyal Coorgs. Government approved, and Colonel Cubbon submitted a design for the medal, which was entrusted to the Calcutta Mint for execution.

The gold medals were, as proposed by the Commissioner, made of three values, weighing nine, seven, and four tolas respectively. In regard, however, to the silver medals, the Mint authorities represented that the proposed weight of ten tolas would be inconveniently heavy for the wearers, and the weight was in consequence reduced by about one-fourth.

The Government duly sanctioned the proposal to give gold chains with the first and second classes of the gold medals. These were probably obtained locally. The fact of their having been proposed indicates that it was intended the medals should be suspended round the neck, in the fashion in which probably all the earlier Indian medals were worn.

In the *Manual of Coorg*, by the Rev. G. Richter, Inspector of the Coorg Schools, published at Mangalore in 1870, there is an account of the revolt of 1837, and a lithograph of a Coorg with a medal hanging round his neck.

This medal was not given to any regular or irregular troops of the Indian Government.

The correspondence relative to the grant and preparation of the medal will be found in the Appendix.

OUTLINE OF PARTICULARS RESPECTING MEDALS AWARDED TO THE DEWANS POUNAPAP AND BAPOO, AND COORGS SERVING UNDER THEM, FOR SUPPRESSING THE INSURRECTION IN CANARA IN 1837.

'Letter from Lt.-Col. Mark Cubbon, Commissioner for Coorg,[1] acknowledging receipt of letters dated 22nd May and 5th June, in which the Governor-General in Council asks him to suggest what appears to him to be the best mode of strongly marking, by suitable distinctions, the sentiments of high appreciation entertained by Government in respect to the "zeal, devotion, and fidelity of that high-minded people on the above occasions," and authorising him "to distribute among the Coorgs the treasure captured by them from the Pretender in such manner as" (he) "may deem most proper."'—*India Political Cons.*, 28th Aug., 1837, No. 80.

[1] Dated 4th Aug., 1837.

'In this reply the Commissioner details at considerable length the circumstances of the case, and also forwards letters from Captain Le Hardy, Superintendent of Coorg,[1] in which the merits of individuals are, as far as practicable, particularised; in which it is stated in respect of the Dewans, that "it is impossible to appreciate too highly the exertions of those two excellent old men, for to them may in a great measure be ascribed the tranquillity which has so speedily been restored below as well as above the Ghauts."

'The officers commanding parties, "also all of whom joined . . . on the first outbreak of the insurrection, has been all along such as to call for the highest terms of praise."

'The inferior leaders also "made themselves conspicuous" for the zeal and gallantry displayed ". . . in the execution of the duties confided to them."

'The Moonshies "Timmapath and Nunyapah rendered" services only inferior "in importance" to "the Dewans and other most influential Chiefs." The Ryots behaved with a great deal "of gallantry" on occasions mentioned; and indeed the whole Coorg people are warmly commended for "noble conduct." "Their deeds speak for themselves." "A small number of ignorant Ryots" deluded by the artifices of certain Brahmins, "wavered for a couple of days in their allegiance, but were without difficulty brought to a sense of their duty by their own countrymen, and they were afterwards the foremost in the different attacks made upon the Insurgents." "Generally," the Superintendent concludes, "the fidelity of the people has been put to the severest tests, and no more willing, no more faithful, no more devoted subjects of the British Govt. than the real Coorgs are to be found in India." He encloses documents, translations, from the Dewans and other Coorgs interested in the Prize-money ordered to be distributed, embodying their deliberations on the subject and the result to which they arrive.

'The whole story reads like romance: "We might have reasonably accepted the money," they write, "had we taken it as spoil from a foreign country or had it belonged to the leader of the insurgents. It was not however obtained in either of these ways. Both the Coorg country and the Canara Zillah being Company's territory, some wicked persons meditating evil having rebelled against the Company's Circar (whose glory reaches to the sky), we thinking that if we suppressed the insurrection which had thus been raised in the Company's territory adjoining our country, Coorg, not only would our country be preserved from ill-fame, but moreover a high reputation would be gained for it, and being likewise desirous that glory should redound to our country, we led forth the Ryots according to the order of the Company's Circar, suppressed the insurrection, recovered the money of the Company which had been carried off and concealed by the leader of the Insurgents, and delivered it to the Circar. Under the influence of these motives and not in the hope of getting money, we have acted in this way."

'The Commissioner in his letter to the Governor-General writes: "His Lordship in Council after the many proofs already given of the noble disinterestedness of these brave mountaineers, will perhaps be prepared for the announcement that the Coorgs respectfully solicit permission to decline accepting any part of the captured treasure, while they express themselves deeply sensible of the high approbation of their conduct which the Order of Govt. assigning it to them has conveyed."

'The recommendations of the Commissioner include—

'2 Gold Medals and Chains for the two Dewans, valued at Rs. 400 each.
'12 do. and Chains at half that value (Rs. 200) for the Subadars and principal Chiefs.
'20 do. without Chains for the Parpattigars and others of Rs. 120 in value.

---

[1] Dated Mercara, 14th June and 20th May, 1837.

'10 Gold Medals of Rs. 50 in value for Ryots who specially distinguished themselves; and

'200 Silver Medals, without Chains, for inferior leaders and distinguished Ryots, of the value of Rs. 10 each,

together with grants of land and presents of Pegu ponies, fowling-pieces, shawls, clothes, Turbans, etc., and "a special plea for the Coorg Subadar, Mornien, who, though near 70 years of age, led on his men in one of the first attacks made on the rebels . . . and slew his antagonist in single combat, but being inconsolable for the loss on this occasion of a sword which had been given to him by the great Rajah Veerajunder," the Commissioner had "ventured in anticipation of His Lordship's sanction to promise him another in the name of the Governor-General."

'The whole of the recommendations of the Commissioner were approved and sanction conveyed in a letter dated 28th August, 1837.

'The Medals were ordered to be struck at the Calcutta Mint, and the Govt. of India's approval of the design was conveyed to the Commissioner of Coorg under date 30th May, 1838.

'The Medals were to be two inches in diameter, the thickness being gradually reduced to equal the weights specified.'[1]

'TORQUAY, *18th Dec.*, 1873.

'MY DEAR SIR,

It is most likely the Coorg Medal was struck in the Calcutta Mint, but I am not sure of the fact.

. . . . . .

'The Gold Medals which were given to the Coorg Headmen are greatly prized. I have a good Photograph of a group, several members of which have the Medal on, but as it is a large portfolio, I am sorry that I cannot send it for your inspection.

'L. B. BOWRING,
Late Bengal C. S. and Commissioner of Mysore.

'K. STEWART-MACKENZIE, Esq.'

'TORQUAY, *23rd Jan.*, 1874.

'MY DEAR SIR,

The accompanying lithographs will show you how the Coorg Medal is worn (No. 1), and the appearance of the Picha Katti or Waist Knife and the Odii Katti, or broad wood knife, worn on the back (No. 2).

'The Medals were in gold and silver, the principal Coorgs receiving the former, of which their descendants are very proud. They are worn you will see suspended round the neck attached to a chain. I do not think that any ribbon was given.

. . . . . .

'L. B. BOWRING.

'K. STEWART-MACKENZIE, Esq.'

'22 PRINCE OF WALES TERRACE,
KENSINGTON PALACE, *26th May*, 1874.

'MY DEAR SIR,

I am very much obliged to you for the two excellent Photographs which you have kindly sent to me.

'The Canarese legend on the obverse side strangely enough does not mention Coorg, but says that the "mark of favor" is given for loyalty to the Company's Govt. in suppressing rebellion in the months of April and May, 1837. The phrase

---

[1] Communicated by Mr. H. Smith, 2nd February, 1874.

used for suppressing rebellion, namely "sharàratû dabáyisuva" is pure Hindusthani put into Canarese characters and terminology. There is no word for Medal in the Indian languages except "takma" which is Arabic, so "nishani" which means a sign or mark, and is Persian, has been used to express it.

'The warrior represented, though he wields the broad Coorg knife, which is characteristic of these mountaineers, savours much of the Classic type, from which I infer that the medal was struck at Calcutta, where no Coorg had ever been seen. Had it been struck at Madras, the peculiar Coorg dress would probably have been more accurately delineated.

'A very good account of Coorg (out of which I took two Prints which I sent to you) was published about 4 years ago by the Revd. G. Richter, Director of Public Instruction in the Province. It contains some notice of military operations in Coorg in 1834 and in 1837, and I shall be happy to send you my copy for perusal, if you wish, on my return to Torquay in about a month. All the other accounts which I have seen were official papers.

'I do not remember ever having seen or heard of a Medal for Plassy.

'Believe me, etc.,

'L. B. BOWRING.

'To

'KEITH STEWART-MACKENZIE, Esq.
of Seaforth.'

No. 163.

GHUZNEE, 1839.

PLATE 24.

Obv. Representation of the gateway of the fortress of Ghuznee.
Below, GHUZNEE.

Rev. Within a wreath of laurel, a mural crown; above, 23^D JULY; below, 1839.
A space in the centre for the name of the recipient.

Circular, 1·5 inch. Silver.
Artist. Designed by a Committee.
Struck at the Calcutta Mint.
Dies at the Calcutta Mint.
Mounting. A plain silver bar.
Ribbon. 1¼ inch wide. Particolored, yellow and green; also, crimson and green.
Worn on left breast.

In a General Order issued by Lieutenant-General Sir John Keane, Commander-in-Chief of the Army of the Indus, dated 30th August, 1839, His Excellency announced that His Majesty Shah Shooja-ool-Moolk had intimated his intention of conferring medals on the troops engaged in the capture of Ghuznee, as a mark of the high estimation in which he held their gallantry and discipline.

In January, 1841, the Government of India reported to the Court of Directors that they did not feel themselves competent to authorise the issue of this medal, but that a die for it was in preparation, and that they would be glad of instructions. The action taken on this by the Court resulted in the sanction of Her Majesty being given for officers and soldiers to wear the medal.

From correspondence forwarded by the Government of India, it appears that the medals were to be made at the Calcutta Mint at the expense of the Indian Government; that they were all to be of silver, and mounted with proper clasps; and that they were to be worn with a green and yellow ribbon.

The fall of Shah Shooja had taken place before the medals were completed. The Governor-General, Lord Ellenborough, did not, however, consider that this should interfere with the presentation of the medals; and he accordingly issued a General Order, dated 23rd November, 1842, stating that it would not be just that, in consequence of the death of the Shah, the glorious achievement of the capture of Ghuznee should remain without due commemoration, and directing that the medals which had been prepared should be given 'in the name of the Government of India.' Writing at the same time to the Court of Directors, his lordship observed that 'to give a medal now in the name of Shah Shooja would be absurd, whatever may have been the supposed policy of so giving it in 1841.'

Although, therefore, the medal was originated by Shah Shooja, it was really made and presented by the Government of India, and it should consequently not be classified as a medal conferred by a foreign power.

This is the first Indian medal with a bar mounting affixed to it.

In a letter written by direction of the Government of India to the Calcutta Mint Committee on 18th May, 1842, it is stated that the Ghuznee medals 'are to be suspended by a green and yellow ribbon.' This ribbon was undoubtedly worn by some persons.[1] It was, however, superseded by one coloured green and crimson; but why this change was made cannot be traced in the official records.

There was some official correspondence between England and India in 1844, relative to some Ghuznee Medals which had been prepared by Messrs. Hunt and Roskell of London, to the

[1] In a portrait of General Sir Thomas Willshire, who was present at Ghuznee, the medal is shown suspended by a green and yellow ribbon. This portrait was in the Victorian Exhibition held in London in 1892.

order of the Adjutant-General of the Bombay Army, 'of a description different from those distributed by the authority of Government.' These, it afterwards appeared, were miniature medals.

GENERAL ORDER BY HIS EXCELLENCY THE COMMANDER-IN-CHIEF OF THE ARMY OF THE INDUS.

'CAMP NEAR CABUL, 30*th August*, 1839.

'His Majesty Shah Shoojah-ool-Moolk having intimated his intention, should Her Britannic Majesty be graciously pleased to permit them to be worn, to confer Medals on the Troops employed in the operations before Ghuznee, as a mark of the high estimation in which he holds their gallantry and discipline, H.E. the Commander-in-Chief is pleased to direct a nominal roll of all officers, European and Native, and a numerical return of all non-commissioned officers and privates, who were actually present with their Corps or Detachments on 21st or 23rd July last, to be prepared and forwarded in triplicate to the Deputy Adjutant-General of the Army of the Presidency to which they belong.'

FROM THE GOVERNMENT OF BENGAL TO THE COURT OF DIRECTORS, 25*th January*, 1841. No. 10—Military.

Cons. 20th June, 1841, Nos. 58 and 59.

'1. We do ourselves the honor to transmit for the consideration of your Honorable Court, a communication from H.E. the Commander-in-Chief in India, submitting a letter from Major G. Thomson, C.B., of Engineers, relative to the Medals proposed to be granted by His Majesty Shah Shoojah-ool-Moolk to the Officers and Soldiers who served at the capture of Ghuznee.

'2. We do not feel ourselves competent to authorise the distribution of the Medals in question to the Officers and Soldiers of the Hon. Company's Service, much less to those of the Royal Army. But a die for the Medals is now in a forward state of preparation, and we only await instructions from your Honorable Court to take the necessary measures for their distribution.'

'To the SECRETARY TO GOVT.,
Military Dept.

'HEAD QUARTERS, CALCUTTA,
'4*th January*, 1841.

'SIR,

I have the honor, by direction of H.E. the Commander-in-Chief, to forward for the consideration and orders of the Right Hon. the Governor-General of India in Council copies of a letter to my address from Major George Thomson, late Chief Engineer to the Army of the Indus, dated 30th ultimo, and of its annexments, on the subject of the Medal proposed by His Majesty Shah Shoojah-ool-Moolk, to be presented to the troops engaged at the capture of Ghuznee.

'His Excellency, with reference to Major Thomson's request, desires me to observe that there are at present in Calcutta several soldiers, both of Her Majesty's and of the Hon. Company's Service, on their way to Europe for the purpose of being discharged, who were present at the assault of Ghuznee, and that unless the Medals be now delivered to them it will be impossible to give effect to the wishes of the Shah, as indicated in the General Order adverted to in Major Thomson's letter, an extract of which is annexed.

'I have, etc.,

'J. R. LUMLEY, *Major-Genl.*,
'*Adjutant-Genl. of the Army.*'

LETTER FROM MAJOR G. THOMSON, BENGAL ENGINEERS, TO THE ADJUTANT-GENERAL OF THE BENGAL ARMY,
30th Dec., 1840.

'With reference to the annexed General Order (dated 30th Aug., 1839) by H.E. Lord Keane, and extract from a letter addressed to his Lordship by Sir William Woods, King-of-Arms, regarding the Medal intended for the Troops present at the capture of Ghuznee, I have the honor respectfully to solicit that H.E. the Commander-in-Chief will be so kind as to move the Govt. to permit this decoration being worn.

'I make this request as I am leaving India, and most anxious to obtain this distinction before I go. The European Sergeants of the Sappers who accompanied the explosion party to the Cabul Gate, are also very desirous to have the Medal granted, there is no other means of rewarding them, and they are naturally very anxious on the subject, as they see all the Sepoys of the party decorated with the "Order of Merit" for their conduct on that occasion.'

LETTER FROM SIR A. W. WOODS, GARTER KING-OF-ARMS, TO LIEUT.-GENERAL LORD KEANE, October, 1840.

'I have not been able to elicit any further information relative to the Medal. Has the Medal been struck, and if so has His Majesty sent them to the officers and men under your Lordship's command? Mr. Lindsay of the Commander-in-Chief's Office told me that the proper mode to proceed in this matter was for the Medal to be struck, and then for a list of the officers' names to be forwarded to the Horse Guards.'

(No. 59.)

'To
'Major-Genl. J. R. LUMLEY,
'Adjutant-Genl. of the Army.

'COUNCIL CHAMBER, CALCUTTA,
'*20th January*, 1841.

'SIR,
With reference to your letter No. 22 dated 4th instant, I am directed to state for the information of H.E. the Commander-in-Chief, that a communication will be made to the Hon. the Court of Directors on the subject of the Medals proposed to be granted by His Majesty Shah Shoojah-ool-Moolk to the Officers and Soldiers who served at the capture of Ghuznee.

'The Right Hon. the Governor-Genl. of India in Council has not the power of issuing any orders on the subject without previous reference to the Home Authorities.

'I have, etc.,
'J. STUART, *Lieut.-Colonel,*
'*Secretary to the Govt. of India, Military Dept.*'

FROM THE COURT OF DIRECTORS TO THE GOVERNOR-GENERAL, 31st March, 1841. No. 5—Military.

'We have the satisfaction to forward to you the copy of a letter from the Secretary of State for the Home Dept., announcing that Her Majesty has been graciously pleased to permit the officers and soldiers who were engaged in the assault and capture of the Fortress of Ghuznee, to wear the Medal which has been conferred upon them by the Shah Shoojah-ool-Moolk, in approbation of their services on that occasion.'

A similar despatch was addressed to the Government of Bombay, No. 21.

'INDIA BOARD, *23rd March*, 1841.

'GENTLEMEN,

I have the pleasure to transmit to you copy of a letter from the Secretary of State for the Home Dept., announcing that Her Majesty has been graciously pleased to permit the officers and soldiers who were engaged in the capture of the Fortress of Ghuznee to wear the Medal which has been conferred upon them by Shah Shooja-ool-Moolk, the King of Affghanistan, in approbation of their services on that occasion.

'I request that a Despatch may be prepared for the purpose of making this acceptable announcement to the Army of India.

'I am, etc.,
'JOHN HOBHOUSE.

'The Chairman and Deputy Chairman,
'East India House.'

'HOME OFFICE, WHITEHALL,
'*22nd March*, 1841.

'SIR,

'The Shah Shooja-ool-Moolk, King of Affghanistan, having conferred a Medal upon the officers and soldiers engaged in the assault and capture of the Fortress of Ghuznee on 21st and 23rd July, 1839, in approbation of their services on that occasion, I have the honor to acquaint you that Her Majesty has been graciously pleased to permit those officers and soldiers to accept and wear the Medal in question.

'I have, etc.,
'NORMANBY.

'The Right Honourable
'Sir JOHN HOBHOUSE,
'President of the India Board.'

FROM THE GOVERNMENT OF BENGAL TO THE COURT OF DIRECTORS, 29th Sept., 1841. No. 131—Military.

Answer to Letter No. 5, *dated* 31*st March*, 1841.

'Forwarding copy of a letter from the Secretary of State for the Home Dept. announcing that Her Majesty has permitted the Officers and Soldiers who were engaged in the assault and capture of Ghuznee, to wear the Medal conferred upon them by Shah Shooja-ool-Moolk.

'6. We beg to acquaint your Hon. Court that a Committee has been appointed by His Excellency the Commander-in-Chief, for the purpose of fixing on a Design, etc., for a Medal to be presented to the Troops engaged in the assault and capture of Ghuznee. *Vide* No. 94 to 96 of Consultation, 26th May, 1841, of which a copy annexed.'

BENGAL MILITARY PROCEEDINGS, 26th May, 1841. Nos. 94 to 96.

'To Lieut.-Colonel J. STUART,
'Secretary to the Govt. of India, Military Dept.

'HEAD QUARTERS, CALCUTTA, 21*st May*, 1841.

'SIR,

I have the honor, by direction of H. E. the Commander-in-Chief, to request that you will solicit the sanction of the Right Hon. the Governor-Genl. of India in Council to Major W. N. Forbes, Mint Master, being joined in Committee with other officers, to fix on a design for a Medal contemplated to be given to the Troops employed at Ghuznee.

'I have, etc.,

'P. CRAIGIE, *Major,*
'*Acting Adjutant-Genl. of the Army.*'

'*Ordered*, that the following letters be written to Major Forbes, and to the Acting Adjutant-General of the Army, in reply.

'To Major W. N. FORBES, Mint Master.

'COUNCIL CHAMBER, CALCUTTA,
'*26th May*, 1841.

'SIR,

I am directed to request that you will associate yourself with other Officers appointed by H.E. the Commander-in-Chief, in a Committee to design a Medal for presentation to the Troops who served at Ghuznee.

'I have, etc.,

'J. STUART, *Lieut.-Colonel,*
'*Secretary to the Govt. of India,*
Military Dept.'

'To Major P. CRAIGIE, Acting Adjutant-General of the Army.

'COUNCIL CHAMBER, CALCUTTA,
'*26th May*, 1841.

'SIR,

In reply to your letter No. 632 dated 21st Instant, I am directed to inform you that the Right Hon. the Governor-General of India in Council has caused Major W. N. Forbes, Mint Master, to be instructed to join himself in committee with other Officers to design a Medal for presentation to the Troops who served at Ghuznee.

'I am, etc.,

'J. STUART, *Lieut.-Colonel,*
'*Secretary to the Govt. of India,*
Military Dept.'

BENGAL MILITARY PROCEEDINGS, *27th May*, 1842. Nos. 151 and 152.

'To the Mint Committee.

'GENTLEMEN,

I am directed to inform you that the Hon. the President in Council has determined to have the Medals to be given to the Troops present on 23rd July, 1839, at the siege and capture of the Fortress of Ghuznee in Affghanistan, executed at the Calcutta Mint, and to desire that you will instruct the Mint Master to lose no time in preparing the die for the purpose.

'2. The enclosed paper E represents the Design approved by His Honor in Council for the Ghuznee Medals, having the Gate of the Fortress, with the word "Ghuznee," for the device on the obverse of the Medal: and on the reverse, a Mural Crown encircled by a wreath, with the date of the capture, a sufficient space being left for an inscription of the name of the owner in the blank place above the Crown.

'3. The Medals are to be all alike of silver, and are to be given to the Troops only who were actually present at the siege.

'4. The number required will be ascertained from the Military Dept. for the information and guidance of the Mint Master.

'5. The Medals are to be mounted with proper clasps, and to be suspended by a green and yellow riband. The President in Council requests that the Mint Master will undertake the whole of this preparation, and have the Ghuznee Medals out of hand at as early a period as practicable.

'6. Major Forbes will send in a Bill to be passed in this Dept. for the cost of these Medals.

'7. The Sub-Treasurer will be authorised to pay the amount of the expenses already incurred in procuring Dies and Specimens from the Houses named in the margin on the presentation of their respective Bills countersigned by Major Forbes. The Vouchers accompany.

Vouchers—A.			
Due to Messrs. Hamilton & Co., . . Rs.	143	4	0
B.			
Do. Messrs. Piller & Co., . .	103	8	0
C.			
Do. Messrs. Pillar, Lattey, & Co., .	248	0	0
	494	12	0

'8. I am directed to forward specimens consisting of one Gold Medal and 4 Silver Medals, and to desire that they may be melted and the value carried to public account.

'I have, etc.,

'G. A. BUSHBY.

'FORT WILLIAM, 18*th May*, 1842.'

No. 428.

'To Major-Genl. J. R. LUMLEY,
Adjutant-Genl. of the Army.

'FORT WILLIAM, 27*th May*, 1842.

'SIR,

I am directed by the Honorable the President in Council to request that you will move H.E. the Commander-in-Chief to cause early information to be furnished to Govt. as to the number of Medals required for distribution to the Force present at the siege and capture of the Fortress of Ghuznee in Affghanistan on 23rd July, 1839.

'I have, etc.,

'W. M. U. STURT, *Major,*
'*Offg. Secretary to the Govt. of India,*
Military Dept.'

BENGAL MILITARY PROCEEDINGS, 1*st July*, 1842. Nos. 76 to 78.

'To

'Major W. M. U. STURT, Offg. Secretary to the Govt. of India,
Military Dept.

'ADJUTANT-GENERAL'S OFFICE,
CALCUTTA, 23*rd June*, 1842.

'SIR,

Under instructions from H.E. the Commander-in-Chief, I have the honor to transmit to you a Return of the number of Medals required for distribution to the Forces present at the siege and capture of the Fortress of Ghuznee in Affghanistan on 23rd July, 1839.

'Numerical Roll of Officers and Men belonging to the Bengal Column of the Army of the Indus and in the service of His Majesty Shah Shoojah Ool Moolk, who were present at the investment, and the assault and capture of the Fortress of Ghuznee on 21st and 23rd July, 1839, and for whom Medals are required to be prepared:—

'European Commissioned Officers, ...	239
Native do., ...	153
European Warrant Officers, ...	6
Sergeants and Havildars, ...	456
Rank and file, ...	7,467
Sundry, ...	50
Total,	8,371

'I have, etc.,

'J. WELCHMAN, *Captain*,
'*Asst. Adjutant-General*.'

GENERAL ORDER BY THE GOVERNOR-GENERAL, *Camp*, *Buddee*, 23*rd Novr.*, 1842.

'The Governor-General being informed that the Medals once intended to be given, in the name of the late Shah Shooja, to the Officers and Soldiers engaged in the capture of Ghuznee in 1839, have been manufactured in the Govt. Mint at Calcutta, and considering that it is not just that, in consequence of the death of Shah Shooja, the glorious achievement of the capture by assault of Ghuznee should remain without due commemoration by the conferring of a personal decoration upon those engaged therein, is pleased to direct that the Medals prepared shall be given, in the name of the Govt. of India, to the Officers and Men entitled thereto for such service: and the several Officers commanding the Regiments and Corps employed at Ghuznee on 23rd July, 1839, will transmit to the Govr.-Genl. nominal lists of the Officers and Men then present, and now living.'

MILITARY DEPARTMENT (Separate), 23*rd Novr.*, 1842.

'To the Hon. the COURT OF DIRECTORS
of the EAST INDIA COMPANY.

'HON. SIRS,
I was recently informed that the Medals intended for the Officers and Soldiers engaged in the assault and capture of Ghuznee in 1839 were ready for distribution, and at the same time I received a copy of the Letter addressed by the Secretary of State to the President of the India Board on 22nd March, 1841, announcing that Her Majesty had been graciously pleased to permit those Officers and Soldiers to accept and wear the Medal which appears to have been made in Calcutta, but which was nominally to be conferred by Shah Shooja.

'2. To give a Medal now in the name of Shah Shooja would be absurd, whatever may have been the supposed policy of so giving it in 1841, and I have therefore issued the enclosed General Order, of which I trust your Hon. Court will approve.

'3. But it may be necessary to obtain anew Her Majesty's gracious permission that this Medal may be accepted and worn by Her Majesty's Officers and Soldiers, as Her Majesty's permission, granted in 1841, referred to a Medal to be at least nominally conferred by Shah Shoojah, and the Medal will now be given by the Govt. of India in its own name to its own Officers and Soldiers, and to Her Majesty's Officers and Soldiers employed in its service at Ghuznee.

'4. I shall distribute the Medals, as soon as I receive them, to Her Majesty's Officers and Soldiers and to those of the Govt. of India, without distinction; and I hope those who served at Ghuznee may, like those who served at Jellalabad, cross the Sutlej, bearing this well-merited decoration which has been earned by them in the field.

'I have, etc.,

'ELLENBOROUGH.

'CAMP, BUDDEE,
23rd Novr., 1842.'

FROM THE COURT OF DIRECTORS TO THE GOVERNMENT OF INDIA, *26th Sept.*, 1843. No. 59—Military.

'41. We approve of the determination to present the Medals commemorative of the Storm of Ghuznee to the Officers and Soldiers for whom it was struck. Should any additional permission be required from the Queen to allow of Her Majesty's Officers to accept and wear, and of our Officers to wear, these Medals, the requisite application will be made for that purpose.'

FROM THE COURT OF DIRECTORS TO THE GOVERNMENT OF BOMBAY, *31st July*, 1844. No. 43—Military.

'1. We forward the copy of a letter from the Deputy Secretary at War, informing us that it has incidentally appeared from communications from Officers of the Royal Mint, that Messrs. Hunt and Roskell of Bond Street have, by an order from Major Hagart of your Army, manufactured a quantity of Ghuznee Medals, of a description different from those distributed by the authority of Government.

'We desire that you will ascertain and report to us, under what circumstances these Medals have been ordered to be made.'

FROM THE GOVERNMENT OF BOMBAY TO THE COURT OF DIRECTORS, *30th Sept.*, 1844. No. 102—Military.

'With reference to your Hon. Court's Despatch, dated 31st July last, No. 43, we have the honor to transmit the accompanying copy of a letter from Lt.-Colonel Hagart, Adjutant-Genl. of the Army, dated 19th Inst., in explanation of his having ordered a number of Ghuznee Medals to be manufactured by Messrs. Hunt & Roskell.'

FROM THE COURT OF DIRECTORS TO THE GOVERNMENT OF BOMBAY, *22nd January*, 1845. No. 4—Military.

'Letter dated 30th Sept., 1844, No. 102. With reference to Court's letter, 31st July, 1844, No. 43, transmit letter from Lt.-Col. Hagart, Adjutant-Genl. of the Army, in explanation of his having ordered a number of miniature Ghuznee Medals to be manufactured by Messrs. Hunt & Roskell.

'13. This explanation has been forwarded for the information of Her Majesty's Secretary at War.'

FROM THE SECRETARY OF STATE FOR INDIA TO THE GOVERNMENT OF INDIA, *21st July*, 1881. No. 242—Military.

'13. In the proceedings of the Government of India in the Military Department of 27th May, 1842, Nos. 151-2, there is recorded a letter, dated 18th May, 1842, from the Secretary to Government to the Mint Committee at Calcutta, containing directions regarding the preparation of the medal for the capture of Ghuznee in 1839. In paragraph 5 of this letter it is intimated that the medals "are to be suspended by a green and yellow ribbon." This ribbon does not appear, however, to have been eventually adopted, but one coloured green and crimson. I request you will cause me to be informed under what circumstances the colour crimson was substituted for yellow.'

FROM THE GOVERNMENT OF INDIA TO THE SECRETARY OF STATE FOR INDIA, 9*th January*, 1882. No. 4—Military.

'18. With reference to para. 13 of Military despatch No. 242, dated India Office, the 21st July, 1881, asking for information regarding the circumstances under which the color of the ribbon for the Ghazni medal was changed from green and yellow to green and crimson, we beg to state that, after careful enquiry, nothing can be traced to shew why the original intention was departed from.'

No. 164.

JELLALABAD, 1842.

FIRST MEDAL.

PLATE 25.

Obv. A mural crown; above, JELLALABAD

Rev. VII APRIL 1842.

Circular, 1·5 inch. Silver.
Struck at the Calcutta Mint.
Dies at the Calcutta Mint.
Mounting. Plain straight bar.
Ribbon. 1¾ inch wide. The Military Ribbon of India, crimson, yellow, and blue.
Worn on left breast.

JELLALABAD, 1842.

SECOND MEDAL.

PLATE 25.

Obv. Head of Queen Victoria, diademed, *l.* *Leg.* VICTORIA VINDEX

Rev. Figure of Victory flying, holding in her right hand two wreaths, and in her left, the British flag. Beneath, the town of Jellalabad. Above, JELLALABAD VII APRIL *Exergue*, MDCCCXLII

Circular, 1·4 inch. Silver.
Artist. W. Wyon, R.A.
Dies at the Royal Mint and at the Calcutta Mint.
Mounting. Plain plated bar.
Ribbon. Military Ribbon of India.
Worn on left breast.

The Governor-General of India, Lord Ellenborough, in a General Order, dated 30th April, 1842, directed that a silver medal should be made for every officer and soldier, European and native, who belonged to the garrison of Jellalabad on 7th April, 1842: 'Such medals to be all similar, and to bear on one side a mural crown superscribed "Jellalabad"; and on the other side the words, "April 7, 1842."'

The action of the Governor-General having been approved by the Court of Directors, and the Royal sanction for the officers and soldiers of the British Army to wear the medal obtained, a General Order, under date 24th October, 1842, was issued, in which it was said that 'thus the European General in Her Majesty's Army, and the Native Sepoy in the Army of the East India Company, . . . will have the same decoration, commemorative of their common service in the field of danger and of glory.'

The preparation of the medals was entrusted to the Calcutta Mint, and Lord Ellenborough, in a despatch dated 5th October, 1842, stated that he had already forwarded some to Jellalabad, and that the rest would be ready before the troops crossed the Sutlej. The medals were distributed shortly before the triumphal reception of Sir Robert Sale and the 'illustrious garrison' by the Governor-General and the Commander-in-Chief at Ferozepore, on 17th December, 1842.

The total number of medals issued was 2596, the troops entitled being as under:—

Detachments:—Bengal Artillery,
5th Bengal Light Cavalry,
Anderson's Horse,
Sappers and Miners.

H.M.'s 13th Foot.

35th Bengal N. I.

Lord Ellenborough was not satisfied with the medal executed at the Calcutta Mint, and he suggested that a new die should be made in England, and that the requisite number of medals should be sent to India to be exchanged for those already distributed. A new medal was accordingly ordered by the Court of Directors, the artist employed being Mr. William Wyon.

A supply of the new medals was sent to Calcutta, and it was duly announced in General Orders (C.-in-C., 13th March, 1845), that commanding officers, on returning the medals already issued to their corps, would receive a like number of the English-made medals in their stead. How many were exchanged is not known. There is at the India Office a list of the officers and men of the 13th Foot entitled to exchange. Few, however, of these ever applied to do so, and it may therefore be inferred that, notwithstanding its inferior execution, they placed a higher value on the medal first presented to them.

In a despatch dated 5th October, 1842, Lord Ellenborough wrote:—'I will not ask the Honorable Court to bear the expense of the ribbon to be presented with the Jellalabad medals; that is my present to the brave garrison.' The Court considered, however, that in all cases the ribbon as well as the medal should be given by Government, and the cost of the ribbon was accordingly refunded to his Lordship.

The ribbon is shaded in three colours—crimson, yellow, and blue. It is popularly, although erroneously, styled the 'rainbow' ribbon. It did not, however, owe its origin to the idea of a rainbow. On this point we have the authority of Lord Ellenborough himself who, in a despatch dated 24th February, 1843, after observing that the ribbon, although very beautiful, soon faded, said: 'Perhaps a ribbon might be manufactured with colors more decided and more lasting; the idea being still preserved of representing the color of the eastern sky when the sun rises without a cloud, crimson falling into yellow, and yellow into blue.'

What led to this idea we do not know: possibly the dawn of a day of triumphant peace after a night of disastrous war. Or did his Lordship think to suggest that the British rule in India in some degree realised the ideal comprised in the last words of King David?—'He that ruleth over men must be just, ruling in the fear of God. And he shall be as the light of the morning, when the sun riseth, even a morning without clouds.' (2 Samuel xxiii. 3, 4.)

It was Lord Ellenborough's intention, as expressed in his General Order of 4th October, 1842, that this ribbon should thenceforward be the 'Military Ribbon of India'; and it was worn with all the medals granted for service in Afghanistan in 1842; with those for Sinde in the following year; and it was used also with the bronze Stars for Maharajpore and Punniar. It was revived on the issue of the Kabul-Kandahar Star of 1880.

GENERAL ORDER BY THE GOVERNOR-GENERAL, ALLAHABAD, 30th April, 1842.

(Published with G.O.C.C. 16th May, 1842.)

'The Governor-Genl. is further pleased to direct that a Silver Medal be made for every Officer, Non-Commissioned Officer and Private, European and Native, who belonged to the Garrison of Jellalabad on 7th April, 1842; such Medals to be all similar, and to bear on one side a Mural Crown superscribed "Jellalabad," and on the other side the words "April 7, 1842."

'The Govt. of India will present such Medal to every Officer, N.-C. Officer and Private, European and Native, belonging to their service, and will request the Home Authorities to lay before Her Majesty their most humble prayer, that Her Majesty will be graciously pleased to permit the Major-General Commanding, and the Officers, N.-C. Officers and Privates in H.M.'s Service, who formed part of the Garrison of Jellalabad, to receive and wear a Medal similar to that which will be so presented to their brothers in arms.'

FROM THE GOVERNOR-GENERAL TO THE COURT OF DIRECTORS, 19th October, 1842. No. 14—Political.

'I am much dissatisfied with the execution of the Medal which has been made at the Mint in Calcutta for the Garrison of Jellalabad, and I doubt the competence of the Mint there to execute at all in a creditable manner the Medals I have by my General Orders, recently published, resolved to bestow for the services performed by the Army of India in Affghanistan and China.

'2. I should be glad if your Hon. Court would give the necessary directions in England for the preparation of the dies for these Medals and send them to India by the overland mail.

'3. Despatch is, as your Hon. Court must feel, very desirable in this matter.

'4. It is a frequent subject of remark that the Medals promised for the first capture of Ghuznee are not yet distributed.

'5. I send a sample of the Jellalabad Medal for the inspection of your Hon. Court.

'6. I think it would be desirable that the new Medals should be as nearly as possible of the size of those given for the victory of Waterloo, that is, rather smaller in circumference, and rather thicker, than the sample I transmit of the Jellalabad Medal.'

GENERAL ORDER BY THE GOVERNOR-GENERAL, SECRET DEPARTMENT, Simla, 24th Oct., 1842.

(Published with G.O.C.C., 27th Oct., 1842.)

'The Govr-Genl. has the highest gratification in communicating to the Army, that Her Majesty has been graciously pleased to permit H.M. 13th Regt. of Light Infantry to receive and wear the Medal which he has ordered to be presented to every Officer, N.-C. Officer and Private, European and Native, who belonged to the Garrison of Jellalabad on 7th April, 1842.

'Thus the European General in H.M. Army and the Native Sepoy in the Army of the E. I. Co., and all the intermediate ranks of both armies and of both nations, will have the same decoration, commemorative of their common service in the field of danger and of glory.

'The Govr.-Genl. feels assured that he may in the name of the whole Army, as well as in that of the Govt. of India, lay at Her Majesty's feet his most humble acknowledgments of this boon, proceeding no less from H.M.'s enlightened wisdom than from H.M.'s gracious favor: a boon of all others the most grateful to men who justly feel that the first of all professions is that of a soldier, and that the first of all rewards is military honor.'

'WAR OFFICE, *26th August*, 1842.

'In consideration of the distinguished gallantry displayed by the 13th Light Infantry during the campaigns in the Burmese Empire and in Affghanistan, Her

Majesty has been graciously pleased to approve of that Regt. assuming the title of the 13th or Prince Albert's Regt. of Light Infantry, and of its facings being changed from yellow to blue.

'Her Majesty has also been pleased to authorise the 13th Regt. of Light Infantry being permitted to bear on its colors and appointments a Mural Crown superscribed Jellalabad, as a memorial of the fortitude, perseverance, and enterprise evinced by that Regt. and the several Corps which served during the blockade of Jellalabad.

'Her Majesty has been likewise pleased to permit the 13th Regt. to receive and wear a silver Medal, which has been directed by the Govr.-Genl. of India to be distributed to every Officer, N.-C. Officer and Private, European and Native, who belonged to the Garrison of Jellalabad on 7th April, 1842, such Medal to bear on one side a Mural Crown superscribed "Jellalabad" and on the other side "7 April 1842."'

NOTIFICATION BY THE RIGHT HON. THE GOVERNOR-GENERAL OF INDIA, Camp, Ferozepore, 17th Dec., 1842.

(At page 795 of G.O.C.C., 1842.)

'This day Major-Genl. Sir Robert Sale, G.C.B., passed the Sutlej at the head of all the Troops which composed the Garrison of Jellalabad.

'The Major-General was received at the foot of the Bridge by the Governor-Genl. and H.E. the Commander-in-Chief.

'The Army of Reserve, formed in one line extending two miles and a half, received the Major-General and the Garrison of Jellalabad in review order with presented arms.

'A salute of 19 guns was fired as the Major-General passed the centre of the line.

'Capt. Somerset, Military Secretary, and Capt. Colville, A.D.C. to the Govr.-Genl., had on 14th Instant conveyed the Medals granted to the Garrison of Jellalabad, under an Escort of the Body Guard, to the Camp of the Major-General, and all the Officers and Soldiers of the Garrison passed the Bridge of the Sutlej, wearing the honor they have so justly won.

'The following are the names of the surviving Officers to whom the Medal has been presented.

'Major-General Sir Robert Sale, G.C.B.

Artillery.

Major A. Abbot, C.B.
,, J. B. Backhouse.
,, G. H. Macgregor, C.B.
Lieut. M. Dawes.
Asst.-Surgeon E. Hare.

5th Light Cavalry.

Major C. E. T. Oldfield, C.B.
Lieut. E. W. C. Plowden.
,, A. Wrench.

Anderson's Horse.

Lieut. W. Mayne.

13th (Prince Albert's) Light Infantry.

Lieut.-Colonel R. Pattison.
Major H. Havelock, C.B.
,, A. P. J. Wilkinson.

Major H. C. Wade.
,, J. H. Fenwick.
Captain P. R. Jennings.
,, A. E. F. Holcombe.
Lieut. G. King.
,, W. A. Sinclair.
,, Hon. E. J. W. Forester.
,, D. Rattray.
,, G. Wade.
,, J. W. Cox.
,, F. Van Straubenzee.
,, T. B. Speedy.
,, G. G. C. Stapylton.
,, R. S. Parker.
,, A. Oakes.
,, G. Talbot.
Adjutant J. S. Wood—Lieutenant.
Asst.-Surgeon J. Robertson, M.D.
,, G. W. Barnes, M.D.
Lieut. William Williams, 54th Foot—doing duty with H.M. 13th L. I.

35th Regt. Light Infantry, N. I.

Colonel T. Monteath, C.B.
Major T. Seaton.
,, A. G. F. J. Younghusband.
Captain T. M. E. Moorhouse.
Lieut. J. Towgood.
,, M. U. Coombs.
,, E. J. Boileau.
,, R. B. Norton.

Doing duty with 35th N. I.

Major J. Fraser, C.B., 11th L. C.
,, H. P. Burn, 1st N. I.
Capt. J. G. Gerrard, 1st European L. I.
,, R. Dowson, 5th N. I.
Lieut. W. R. Hillersdon, 53th N. I.

Broadfoot's Sappers and Miners.

Major G. Broadfoot, C.B., 34th Madras N. I.
Lieut. J. G. G. Orr.
,, F. Cunningham.
Surgeon J. Forsyth.
Asst.-Surgeon W. Brydon.

Commissariat.

Major E. R. Mainwaring, 16th Bengal Grenadiers.

'The Govr.-Genl. will transmit the Medal to the mother of the late Colonel Dennie, C.B., who fell in the Battle of 7th April, and to the relatives of the officers and soldiers of the Garrison who have died since that day.

'By Order of the Rt. Hon. the Govr-Genl. of India.

'T. H. MADDOCK,
'Secretary to the Govt. of India with the Govr.-Genl.'

FROM THE COURT OF DIRECTORS TO THE GOVERNMENT OF BENGAL, *26th Sept.*, 1843. No. 60—Military.

Reply to Governor-Genl.'s Letter of 24th Feb., 1843,

On the subject of Medals for the Troops lately serving in Affghanistan and offering suggestions for the manufacture in England of a new die for the Jellalabad Medal, and a new Ribbon with colors more decided and lasting than those of the Ribbon already sent out.

'17. Referring to our communication of 30th May, 1843, No. 8, we have now to state that in compliance with the Govr.-Genl.'s request, the Medals for Jellalabad shall be struck in this country and forwarded to you to be exchanged for those already distributed.

'18. Having furnished a sufficient supply of Ribbon for the Medals to be issued to the Troops, we think it quite unnecessary to make any additional supply at present.'

GENERAL ORDER BY THE COMMANDER-IN-CHIEF IN INDIA, *13th March*, 1845.

'A supply of Medals of English manufacture having been received from Govt. for distribution to the Troops employed in the defence of Jellalabad in 1842, Officers commanding the Corps and Detachments that served there will, on returning the Medals already issued to the Officers and men under their command to the Asst. Adjutant-Genl. of the Army at the Presidency, receive a like number of the new English-made Medals in their stead.'

FROM THE COURT OF DIRECTORS TO THE GOVERNMENT OF BENGAL, *14th July*, 1847. No. 74—Military.

'1. We forward a number in the Packet a nominal roll of the officers and men of H.M.'s 13th Foot, on whose behalf application has been made to us, to have the Medal for Jellalabad, as first issued, exchanged for the one prepared in this country and sent out to your Govt., and we request that the Medals now applied for be accordingly returned to us.

'2. We would at the same time call your particular attention to our Letter in this Dept. of 19th March, 1844, No. 26, and we now desire that unclaimed Medals or Stars for Europeans, whether for parties deceased, or for those who may have left our Service, be immediately sent to us.'

FROM THE COURT OF DIRECTORS TO THE GOVERNMENT OF BENGAL, *19th January*, 1853. No. 6—Military.

Para. 12, in reply to p. 2 and 3 of Letter No. 194 of 1852, states that on a reference to the Secretary at War it appears that only five persons belonging to the 13th L. I. have applied for the new Jellalabad Medals.

Some other references to this Medal will be found in the Appendix amongst the Afghanistan papers, 1842.

No. 165.

KELAT–I–GHILZIE, 1842.

AFGHANISTAN.

PLATE 24.

Obv. A Shield inscribed KELAT I GHILZIE encircled by a wreath of laurel, and surmounted by a mural crown.

Rev. A military trophy. Beneath, on a tablet, INVICTA MDCCCXLII

Circular, 1·4 inch. Silver.
Artist. W. Wyon, R.A.
Dies at the Royal Mint.
Mounting. A steel bar.
Ribbon. 1⅜ inch wide. Military Ribbon of India.
Worn on left breast.

The Governor-General in a General Order, dated 4th October, 1842, notified that to every officer and soldier present, forming part of the garrison of Kelat-i-Ghilzie during the recent investment of that Fort, would be presented a silver medal bearing a mural crown superscribed 'Kelat-i-Ghilzie' on one side, and on the other, 'Invicta, 1842.'

It was apparently intended that the design of this medal should be very similar to that of the original Jellalabad Medal; but the artist imported variety by placing the name Kelat-i-Ghilzie on a shield surrounded by a wreath below the mural crown, and by introducing a military trophy above the inscription on the *reverse.*

In reward for its gallant behaviour during the investment and assault of Kelat-i-Ghilzie, the Government of India ordered that the regiment of Bengal Irregular Infantry, lately known as the 3rd Infantry, Shah Shooja's Force, should continue embodied, and be brought on the strength of the Bengal Army as an extra regiment, to be denominated the 'Regiment of Kelat-i-Ghilzie'; and that its Regimental Colours should be composed of the three colours of the Military Ribbon of India, having in the centre the name 'Kelat-i-Ghilzie.' The three colours were arranged horizontally, after the fashion of the Dutch flag.[1]

[1] The authorities in reference to the grant of the medal for Kelat-i-Ghilzie will be found amongst the Afghanistan, 1842, Medal papers; see Appendix.

No. 166.

AFGHANISTAN, 1842.

FOUR MEDALS.

PLATE 26.

Obv. Head of Queen Victoria, diademed, *l.* *Leg.* VICTORIA VINDEX

Rev. No. 1. CANDAHAR 1842 within a wreath of laurel; above, a crown.

No. 2. GHUZNEE CABUL each within a wreath of laurel; above, a crown; below, 1842.

No. 3. CANDAHAR GHUZNEE CABUL 1842 all within a wreath of laurel; above, a crown.

No. 4. CABUL 1842 within a wreath of laurel; above, a crown.[1]

Circular, 1·4 inch. Silver.
Artist. W. Wyon, R.A.
Dies. Nos. 2, 3, and 4 at the Royal Mint.
Nos. 1, 2, 3, and 4 at the Calcutta Mint.
Mounting. A steel bar.
Ribbon. 1¾ inch wide. Military Ribbon of India.
Worn on left breast.

These four medals were given for the operations in Afghanistan in 1842. The authority for them is the General Order of the Governor-General, dated 4th October, 1842, announcing that to every officer and soldier present in action with the enemy in the vicinity of Candahar would be presented a silver medal inscribed 'Candahar, 1842.'

To those present with the army under Major-General Nott, in the operations leading to the capture of Ghuznee and the occupation of Cabul, a similar medal inscribed 'Ghuznee—Cabool, 1842.'

To those entitled to both the above distinctions a medal inscribed 'Candahar, Ghuznee, Cabool, 1842.'

To those present with the army under Major-General Pollock, in the operations leading to the occupation of Cabul, a medal inscribed 'Cabool, 1842.'

These inscriptions were to be on one side of the medals. The other side was to bear in each case the words 'Victoria Vindex.' The General Order directed that the medals were to be worn suspended to a ribbon similar to that given with the

---

[1] The original die for this *reverse* had the word thus: 'CABVL'; but it was not adopted. It was in the possession of the late Mr. L. C. Wyon.

Jellalabad Medal, which was thenceforth to be the 'Military Ribbon of India.'

In reporting his proceedings to the Court of Directors, 5th October, 1842, the Governor-General stated his intention of giving immediate orders for making the medals so soon as he should learn the numbers required. A few days later, however, he wrote in a Despatch of 19th October, 1842, that he was dissatisfied with the execution of the medal made at the Calcutta Mint for the Jellalabad garrison, and that he doubted the competence of that establishment to execute, at all in a creditable manner, the medals for the services performed by the Army of India in Afghanistan and China. He therefore requested the Court to have the dies prepared in England, and to send them to India by the overland mail. He added that he thought it would be desirable the new medals should be as nearly as possible of the size of the Waterloo Medal—*i.e.* rather smaller in circumference, and thicker than the Jellalabad Medal.

The Court thereupon instructed Mr. W. Wyon, R.A., Chief Engraver to the Royal Mint, to prepare the requisite dies, and drawings of the medals were sent to India. But Lord Ellenborough still doubted the capabilities of the Calcutta Mint, and he expressed the opinion that the medals had better be made in England. This course was accordingly adopted.

GENERAL ORDER BY THE GOVERNOR-GENERAL OF INDIA,
Simla, 4th October, 1842.

'The Governor-General, earnestly desirous of evincing the gratitude of the Govt. of India towards the General Officers, Officers, and Non-Comd. Officers and Privates, engaged in the operations of the present campaign in Affghanistan, is pleased, after communicating with H.E. the Commander-in-Chief, to declare the following resolutions :—

. . . .

'7. To every General Officer, Officer, N.-C. Officer, and Private, present on the occasions above mentioned in action with the enemy in the vicinity of Candahar, will be presented a Silver Medal inscribed

'CANDAHAR
1842.

And to every General Officer, Officer, N.-C. Officer and Private present with the Army under Major-General Nott, in the operations leading to the capture of Ghuznee and the occupation of Cabool, will be presented a similar Silver Medal inscribed

'GHUZNEE
CABOOL
1842.

'Where the same person shall be entitled to both distinctions, one Medal only will be presented, and such Medal will be inscribed

'CANDAHAR
GHUZNEE
CABOOL
1842.

'Major-General Nott will transmit to the Governor-General nominal Lists of the several General Officers, Officers, N.-C. Officers and Privates so entitled respectively.

'8. Major-General Pollock will transmit to the Governor-General a nominal List of the General Officers, Officers, N.-C. Officers and Privates, present in action with the Enemy in the several operations of his Army leading to the occupation of Cabool, and to every person named in such List a Silver Medal will be presented inscribed

'CABOOL
1842.

'On the reverse of these several Medals will be inscribed the words

'VICTORIA
VINDEX.

'9. To every Officer, N.-C. Officer and Private present within Khelat-i-Ghilzie, and forming part of the Garrison thereof during the late investment and blockade of that Fort, will be presented a Silver Medal, bearing a Mural Crown with the superscription of "Khelat-i-Ghilzie," and on the *reverse* the word—

'INVICTA
1842.

'Capt. J. H. Craigie, late Commandant of the Fort of Khelat-i-Ghilzie, will transmit to Major-Genl. Nott a nominal List of the Officers, N.-C. Officers and Privates so present in Khelat-i-Ghilzie, and so entitled to the Medal above granted, and to every person named in such List, when sanctioned by Major-Genl. Nott, the Medal will be given.

'10. All the Medals above mentioned are to be worn suspended to a ribbon similar to that which will be given with the Jellalabad Medal, which ribbon will be henceforth the Military Ribbon of India.

'11. The Regimental Colours of the Regiment of Khelat-i-Ghilzie will be composed of the three colours of the Military Ribbon of India, and in the centre thereof will be inscribed the word "Khelat-i-Ghilzie."

'12. The Governor-General will, after communication with, and in conjunction with H.E. the Commander-in-Chief, represent to the authorities in England the high services rendered by the Officers of Her Majesty's and of the Indian Army, in the operations of the present campaign in Affghanistan, in order that they may be duly submitted to the gracious consideration of Her Majesty.

Numerical Rolls of those entitled to these Medals are with separate Letter from the Govr.-Genl., dated 24th Feb., 1843.

'13. Medals similar to those presented to the General Officers, Officers, Non-Commissioned Officers and Privates of the Indian Army, will be prepared for the General Officers, Officers, Non-Commissioned Officers and Privates of H.M.'s Army, having respectively similar claims to the honor of wearing such Medals; but the authority to wear such Medals depends upon Her Majesty's most gracious pleasure.'

FROM THE GOVERNOR-GENERAL TO THE COURT OF DIRECTORS, 5th October, 1842. No. 13—Political.

'1. I transmit a copy of the General Order I have issued to the armies engaged in the present campaign in Affghanistan.

'2. I can entertain no doubt of your giving your hearty sanction to the Resolutions so communicated to the Troops which have done such eminent service.

'3. I enclose a sample of the Jellalabad Ribbon, of which 14,000 yards will be required for presentation to the Officers and Soldiers with their Medals, and I request you will give directions for the early supply of this Ribbon.

'4. The Ribbon to be given to the Garrison of Jellalabad with their Medals was ordered by me on 21st April, made at Coventry, and received by me overland on 19th August. I have ordered an additional quantity to that first sent, the number of Officers and Soldiers entitled to the Jellalabad Medal being greater than I supposed when I sent the first order to England.

'5. I do not ask the Honble. Court to bear the expense of the Ribbon to be presented with the Jellalabad Medals; that is my present to that brave Garrison.

'6. I have the satisfaction to inform your Honble. Court that I have already forwarded to Jellalabad a few of the Medals, the rest will be ready before the Troops reach the Sutlej, and every man will pass the Sutlej with the decoration he has nobly won.

'7. I shall give immediately orders for the making of the Medals granted in the enclosed General Order as soon as I am informed of the number of persons entitled to the several Medals respectively.

'ELLENBOROUGH.'

FROM THE GOVERNMENT OF BENGAL TO THE COURT OF DIRECTORS, 17th Novr., 1842. No. 110—Military.

Cons. 21st Oct., 1842, Nos. 5 to 10.

'We have the honour to transmit for the information of your Hon. Court copy of General Orders by the Right Hon. the Governor-General of India, dated Simla, 4th Oct., 1842, containing certain Resolutions to the following effect.

'1st. A Donation of six months' Batta payable on 1st Jan., 1843, to be granted to the whole of the Troops serving under the command of Major-Generals Pollock, Nott, and England, between Attock and Ali Musjeed, and in and above the Khyber and Bolan Passes on 8th Sept., 1841.

'2nd. In commemoration of their distinguished services, the 2nd and 16th Regiments N. I., to be hereafter Regiments of Grenadiers, and the 38th, 42nd, and 43rd Regts. Bengal N. I. to be Regiments of Light Infantry.

'3rd. The Regiment of Bengal Irregular Infantry, lately known as the 3rd Infantry Regt., Shah Shoojah's Force, to continue embodied under its present Commandant, and be brought on the strength of the Bengal Army as an extra Regiment, and to be denominated the "Regiment of Khelat-i-Ghilzie."

'4th. The names of certain places in Affghanistan to be borne on the Colours and Appointments of such Corps as are entitled thereto, and Silver Medals to be presented to the General Officers, Officers, Non-Commissioned Officers and Privates, present in action with the Enemy in the several operations of the Army leading to the re-occupation of Cabool. Similar Medals to be prepared for the General Officers, Officers, Non-Commissioned Officers and Privates of Her Majesty's Army, having respectively similar claims to the honour of wearing them. The authority to wear such Medals, however, depending upon Her Majesty's pleasure.

'5th. Silver Medals to be likewise presented to every Officer, etc., forming part of the Garrison of Khelat-i-Ghilzie, during the late investment and blockade of that Fort.

'6th. The Regiment of Khelat-i-Ghilzie to be completed to 800 Privates by Drafts from the other Corps of the late Shah Shoojah's Force, as detailed in No. 8 of the marginal papers: the European Commissioned Officers and Staff Sergeants now serving with it to continue to hold their present appointments, and the Native Officers and Non-Commissioned Officers their present rank.'

FROM THE COURT OF DIRECTORS TO THE GOVERNOR-GENERAL OF INDIA, 30th Nov., 1842. No. 16—Military.

Reply to letter from Govr.-Gen. in Political Dept., 5th Oct., 1842.

'1. The momentous events which have just occurred in Affghanistan, their great importance to the interests of the British Empire in India, and the distinguished gallantry, perseverance, and discipline which have marked the conduct of the European and Native Troops engaged in their accomplishment, fully justify the resolution taken by the Governor-General after communication with the Commander-in-Chief, to confer on the East India Company's Troops Medals in commemoration of the particular services in which they have been engaged.

'2. We therefore cordially approve of the Resolutions to grant Medals to the Company's Troops engaged in the defence of Jellalabad during its memorable siege: to those engaged at Candahar and in the gallant defence of Khelat-i-Ghilzie: and to the Forces by which Ghuznee and Cabul have been again occupied.

'3. We also fully approve and confirm the other measures taken for perpetuating the recollection of these important services as announced in the G. O. by the Govr.-Genl., dated 4th Oct., 1842.

'4. We have already in our Letter of 2nd Novr., 1842, had the gratification of announcing to you the Honors which Her Majesty has been graciously pleased to bestow upon Officers of our Army for their services at Jellalabad and in the operations under Major.Genl. Sir Robert Sale before and after the siege of that place. The grant of further honors is at present under consideration and the result will be announced in an early Despatch.

'5. The Donation of 6 months' full Batta to the Troops specified in para. 1 of the same G. O. has our entire approbation.

'6. We will adopt immediate measures for supplying the Ribbon required for the Medals granted to the Troops, and as we consider that in all cases the Ribbon as well as the Medal should proceed from the Govt. of India, we have given directions for the payment from the Public Treasury of the cost of all the Ribbon, including that for Jellalabad.'

FROM THE SECRETARY OF STATE FOR WAR AND THE COLONIES TO FIELD-MARSHAL HIS GRACE THE DUKE OF WELLINGTON, COMMANDER-IN-CHIEF.

'DOWNING STREET, *3rd December*, 1842.

'MY LORD DUKE,

It appears by a General Order dated Simla, October 4th, 1842, extract of which is herewith transmitted to your Grace, that the Governor-General of India has seen fit to direct that Medals should be struck and issued to every officer, non-commissioned officer and private of the Indian Army, serving in the Corps, and on the occasions therein set forth. These Medals are to be worn suspended to a riband, similar to that which will be given with a Medal conferred in like manner by the Governor-General on those who were engaged in the defence of Jellalabad,

'The Governor-General having further expressed in the same G. O. his earnest desire that the regiments in the service of Her Majesty, which were employed on the same occasions under the orders of the Governor-General, should be permitted to receive and wear similar decorations, I have submitted the question to the Queen, for the signification of Her Majesty's pleasure, and I have the honor to acquaint Your Grace that Her Majesty has been graciously pleased to permit such of the officers, non-commissioned officers and privates, of Her Majesty's Army, as were engaged in any of the operations above referred to, to receive respectively Medals similar to those issued by the Governor-General to the Indian Army, in commemoration of the same services, and to wear such Medals, suspended by the Indian riband, in all parts of Her Majesty's dominions.

'I have, etc.,

'STANLEY.'

'INDIA BOARD,
6th Dec., 1842.

'GENTLEMEN,

I have the pleasure to transmit to you a copy of a letter from the Secretary of State announcing that the Queen has been graciously pleased to permit the Officers of the East India Company's Army to wear, in this country, the Medals which have been conferred upon them by the Govt. of India for services in Affghanistan.

'I have, etc.,

'FITZGERALD AND VESCI.

'The Chairman and Deputy Chairman
of the East India Company.'

(ENCLOSURE.)

'DOWNING STREET,
5th Dec., 1842.

'MY LORD,

I have the honor to acknowledge the receipt of your Lordship's letter of 5th Inst. together with its enclosure requesting that Her Majesty's gracious permission may be obtained for the officers of the East India Company's Army, who have participated in the late glorious successes in Affghanistan, to wear in this country the Medals which have been granted to them in the General Orders issued by the Governor-General of India: and I have to inform you in reply, that Her Majesty has been graciously pleased to signify her approval of that indulgence being extended to the officers in question.

'I have, etc.,

'STANLEY.

'The LORD FITZGERALD AND VESCI,
India Board.'

FROM THE COURT OF DIRECTORS TO THE GOVERNOR-GENERAL OF INDIA, *14th Dec.*, 1842. No. 17—Military.

'2. We have also, with reference to our Military Despatch of 30th ult., the satisfaction to enclose to you copies of further letters from the Right Hon. Lord Stanley, announcing that Her Majesty has been pleased to permit such of the Officers, N.-C. Officers and Privates of H.M.'s Army, as were engaged in the recent operations in Affghanistan, to wear the Medals which, for similar services, have been conferred by the Govt. of India upon the Soldiers of the East India Company's Army, and also to permit the Officers of that Army to wear in this country the Medals conferred upon them for services in Affghanistan.'

FROM THE COURT OF DIRECTORS TO THE GOVERNMENT OF BENGAL, 23rd Dec., 1842. No. 128—Military.

Cons. 27th May, 1842, Nos. 151 and 152; *Cons.* 1st July, 1842, Nos. 76 and 78.

'75. The Papers recorded in the margin relate to the preparation of Silver Medals and contain a return of the number required for distribution to the Force present at the siege and capture of the Fortress of Ghuznee in Affghanistan, on 23rd July, 1839, with reference to para. 6 of our General Letter, No. 131, dated 29th Sept., 1841.'

Cons. 20th May, 1842, Nos. 51 and 55; *Cons.* 8th July, 1842, Nos. 1 and 7.

'76. The marginal papers relate to the various honors and rewards, including Silver Medals, which we have accorded to the Officers, Non-Commissioned Officers and Privates, European and Native, who composed the Garrison of Jellalabad on 7th April, 1842, including the grant of honorary bearings upon their Standards, Colors, and Appointments, to the 35th Regt. N.I., to a Squadron of the 5th Cavalry, and to the 2nd Company of the 6th Battalion of Foot Artillery, in consideration of their distinguished merits during the blockade of the above Garrison.

'77. In conformity with the recommendation of H.E. the Commander-in-Chief, with a view to give additional and lasting honors to the 35th Regt. N.I., we have directed that Corps to be hereafter made a Light Infantry Regiment.'

FROM THE COURT OF DIRECTORS TO THE GOVERNOR-GENERAL OF INDIA, 4th January, 1843. No. 1—Military.

Reply to Letter in the Political Department, dated 19*th Oct.*, 1842, *No.* 14.

'The Govr.-Genl. being dissatisfied with the execution in India of the Medals for Jellalabad, requests that Dies for the Medals to be granted for services performed by the Army of India in Affghanistan and China may be prepared in England and sent by the overland Mail.

'1. On the receipt of this Letter instructions were given to Wm. Wyon, Esq., R.A., the Chief Engraver at the Queen's Mint, to prepare the requisite number of Dies of the several Medals required for the Forces in Affghanistan. We enclose in the Packet Drawings of the Medals upon the engraving of which Mr. Wyon is now actively employed. The Dies will be forwarded by the Overland Mail in succession as delivered to us.

'2. The Govr.-Genl. in his present letter notices the delay which has taken place in distributing the Medals promised by His late Majesty Shah Shooja for the first capture of Ghuznee. We have no information of the measures which may have been taken for procuring these Medals beyond the appointment by the Commander-in-Chief of a Committee for the purpose of fixing on a Design, as reported in para. 6 of your Military Letter of 29th Sept., 1841.'

GENERAL ORDER BY THE GOVERNOR-GENERAL, Kurnaul, 25th January, 1843,

Publishing the Despatch of the Court of Directors dated 14th December, 1842, No. 17; the letters of the Secretary of State for War and the Colonies to the Commander-in-Chief, and President of the India Board, dated respectively 3rd and 5th December, 1842.

This General Order is the authority for the British Army to accept and wear, and to the Indian Army to wear, out of India, the medals granted by the Government of India for services in Afghanistan.

GENERAL ORDER BY THE GOVERNOR-GENERAL,
Kurnaul, 27th January, 1843,

Publishing the Despatch of the Court of Directors dated 30th November, 1842, No. 16, approving of the grant by the Government of India of the various medals for services in Afghanistan.

This General Order is the 'Indian' authority for the use of the medals.

FROM THE COURT OF DIRECTORS TO THE GOVERNMENT OF BENGAL, 1st Feb., 1843. No. 3—Military.

'Referring to our Letter of 4th ultimo, No. 1, we have now to apprise you that a Box is forwarded by the present despatch containing Dies for Medals, as specified in a Letter from Mr. Wyon, of which a copy is enclosed. We also forward (a No. in the Packet) three Proofs of the Medals.'

FROM THE GOVERNOR-GENERAL OF INDIA TO THE COURT OF DIRECTORS, Camp, Baminee Khera, 24th Feb., 1843—Military.

'1. I have to acknowledge the receipt of the Drawings of Medals for the services rendered in Affghanistan, and of a most beautiful specimen of the Medal for "Cabul."

'2. I greatly fear that the Calcutta Mint will be unable to execute the work of making the Medals with the requisite correctness when the Dies are received, and I rather incline to the opinion that it wd. be better to make the Medals in England.

'3. The Medals made from the Dies to be sent out will be so very superior to the Jellalabad Medal made at Calcutta, that I would suggest that a new Die should be made in England for the Jellalabad Medal, and that the requisite number of new Jellalabad Medals should be sent out to India to be exchanged here for those already distributed.

'4. With a view to enable your Hon. Court at once to adopt the course I have suggested, I have enclosed a Statement[1] of the number of Medals required.

'5. I should mention with respect to the Jellalabad Ribbon, that although it is very beautiful it certainly fades very soon, and rain takes out the Colors.

'6. Perhaps a Ribbon might be manufactured with Colors more decided and more lasting; the idea being still preserved of representing the Color of the Eastern sky when the Sun rises without a cloud, Crimson falling into yellow, and yellow into Blue.

'7. The Flag given to the Khelat-i-Ghilzie Regt. has the three colors distinct as in the Flags of France and Holland, and is very beautiful.

'I have, etc.,

'ELLENBOROUGH.

'Numerical Returns of those entitled to the Medals for
Khelat-i-Ghilzie
Cabool (G. O. Simla, 4th Oct., 1842.)
Candahar
are annexed to this Despatch.'

---

[1] Total number of Medals required for the Jellalabad Garrison, 2596.

FROM THE COURT OF DIRECTORS TO THE GOVERNOR-GENERAL OF INDIA, 30*th May*, 1843. No. 8—Military.

Reply to Letter from the Governor-General, dated 24*th February*, 1843.

'A trial will be made at the Calcutta Mint to strike Medals equal to the samples sent from England. Should it fail, they are requested to be struck in England as before suggested. Dies for the Jellalabad Medal are requested to be sent out to be exchanged for those made at the Calcutta Mint. Another sample of the Clasp also requested.

'1. We await your further communication as to the means possessed by the Calcutta Mint to strike Medals from the Dies sent to you.

'2. Agreeably with the Governor-General's request we will cause Dies for the Jellalabad Medal, with an appropriate Device, to be prepared and transmitted to you.

'3. You will have learnt from our Secretary's Letter of 29th April last that Clips for the Medals have been sent from this country.'

'INDIA BOARD,
5*th August*, 1843.

'GENTLEMEN,

I have the honor to inform you with reference to the letter from Lord Stanley of 18th July, a copy of which I transmitted to you on the 20th of the same month, that I pointed out to his Lordship that the permission granted by Her Majesty for the Officers, Non-Commissioned Officers and Soldiers of the East India Company's Army, on whom a Medal might be conferred for services in Sinde, to wear such Medal in all parts of Her Majesty's Dominions, embraced other classes than those included in the permission granted for services rendered in Affghanistan.

'And I have now the pleasure to acquaint you that the Queen has been graciously pleased to allow all ranks of the East India Company's Army to wear the Affghanistan Medals in all parts of Her Majesty's Dominions.

'I have, etc.,

'RIPON.

'The Chairman and Deputy-Chairman
of the East India Company.'

FROM THE COURT OF DIRECTORS TO THE GOVERNOR-GENERAL IN COUNCIL, 1*st May*, 1884. No. 8—Military.

'We forward a No. in the Packet, copy of a Letter from Lieut.-General Lord Fitzroy Somerset, K.C.B., and of its enclosure, communicating by desire of Field-Marshal the Commander-in-Chief the remarks of the Secretary at War in regard to the omission of not placing on the Medals, to be granted to H.M.'s Troops employed at Ghuznee and Jellalabad, the name and rank of the Soldier, and the Regt. to which he belongs. We also send copy of our reply: and in pursuance of the intention therein expressed, we now desire that previously to the issue of the Jellalabad Medals (which will be forwarded to you by an early Despatch) measures may be taken for having the names, rank, and Regt. of those entitled to receive them engraved on their respective Medals. You will also take such measures as may be in your power for having the same particulars engraved on the Medals for Ghuznee, and for other services in Affghanistan, which have been already issued.'

FROM THE GOVERNMENT OF BENGAL TO THE COURT OF DIRECTORS, 18th Sept., 1844. No. 113—Military.

Paras. 10 to 12, in reply to Court's Despatch, No. 8, of 1st May, 1844, on the omission to inscribe the names of soldiers on the Ghuznee and Jellalabad Medals, state course proposed to be followed.

'54 HAMILTON TERRACE,
30th Nov., 1876.

'SIR,

With reference to your letters numbered 3745 and 3747, I regret to say that there is no Die for a Candahar Medal. One only has been required (in 1858) since the India Medal Dies came into my possession in 1851, and I wrote to the Military Secretary to the East India Company at the time to state this. As it was considered not worth while to make a Die for a single Medal, I was instructed to strike a Candahar-Ghuznee-Cabul Medal, and to erase Ghuznee and Cabul from it. The appearance was of course far from satisfactory, as "Candahar" was not in the centre of the Medal, and the marks of the erasure were very evident; but there was no other course to adopt except to make a Die for the purpose. Will you be so good as to inform me what I am to do in this matter?

'The Dies for this Campaign are:—

1	2	3
Candahar.[1]	Ghuznee.	Cabul.
Ghuznee.	Cabul.	
Cabul.		

. . . . . .

'I am, etc.,

'L. C. WYON.

'The Under Secretary of State,
India Office.'

No. 167.

POLLOCK MEDALS.

PLATE 27.

No. 1.

Obv. Bust of Major-General Sir George Pollock, *l.*, in the uniform of a General Officer, and wearing the Ribbon and Star of a Grand Cross of the Bath; also, the medal for Cabul, 1842; surrounded by the following three legends:—

Inner. MAJOR GENERAL SIR GEORGE POLLOCK G.C.B. BENGAL ARTILLERY

Intermediate. TREACHERY AVENGED – BRITISH HONOR VINDICATED – DISASTERS RETRIEVED – BRITISH CAPTIVES DELIVERED · KYBER PASS FORCED – JELALLABAD RELIEVED – VICTORIES OF MAMOO KHAIL – JUGDULLUCK – TEZEEN – ISTALIF ·

Outer. TO COMMEMORATE EMINENT SERVICES CABUL 1842

Rev. Leg. MILITARY SEMINARY [or COLLEGE] ADDISCOMBE POLLOCK PRIZE[2]

---

1 There is a 'Candahar' die at the Calcutta Mint.

2 By a Resolution of the Court of Directors, dated 30th January, 1856, the designation was altered from 'Military Seminary' to 'Military College.' The first sixteen of the Medals bore, therefore, the former designation.

Ins. PRESENTED BY THE BRITISH INHABITANTS OF CALCUTTA AND AWARDED BY THE COURT OF DIRECTORS OF THE EAST INDIA COMPANY TO THE MOST DISTINGUISHED CADET OF THE SEASON

Circular, 2.3 inches. Gold.
Artist. B. Wyon.
Dies with Messrs. Wyon, Regent Street.

No. 2.

Obv. Same as No. 1.

Rev. Leg. MILITARY COLLEGE ADDISCOMBE POLLOCK PRIZE

Ins. PRESENTED BY THE BRITISH INHABITANTS OF CALCUTTA AND AWARDED BY THE SECRETARY OF STATE FOR INDIA TO THE MOST DISTINGUISHED CADET OF THE SEASON

Circular, 2.3 inches. Gold.

No. 3.

Obv. Bust of Sir George Pollock, as in No. 1.
Leg. POLLOCK CABUL 1842

Rev. Leg. POLLOCK PRIZE · ROYAL MILITARY ACADEMY ·

Ins. FOUNDED BY THE BRITISH INHABITANTS OF CALCUTTA TO COMMEMORATE THE EMINENT SERVICES OF MAJOR GENERAL SIR GEORGE POLLOCK G.C.B. AND AWARDED TO THE MOST DISTINGUISHED CADET OF THE SEASON.

Circular, 1.8 inch. Gold.

This, not being a decorative medal, does not come strictly within the scope of this work. As, however, it is the only instance of a prize medal given in the British Military Colleges, it has been decided to include it.

The Pollock Prize at the East India Company's Military Seminary at Addiscombe was the outcome of a fund subscribed by the inhabitants of Calcutta to mark their high sense of the military services of Sir George Pollock, and as a means of stimulating young Indian officers to follow his example. The Court of Directors consented to become trustees of the fund, and decided that a gold medal should be presented at each half-yearly examination to the cadet who ranked highest in the scale of general merit, and who was also reported by the Lieutenant-Governor as being worthy by his conduct to receive it. The medal was presented for the first time on 9th June, 1848.

The cost of the preparation of the dies for the medal appears to have been £85, 12s. 6d., and that of each medal, £17, 1s. 6d.

When the Court of Directors became the trustees of the fund they called for information as to the amount of income derived from it; and the Government of India stated that the fund, after deducting the cost which had been incurred in England in respect of the medals, amounted to Rs. 6200, invested in Indian Government Securities, the interest being Rs. 269 per annum, equal, at 2s. the Rupee, to £26, 18s.

The cost of the medals being £17, 1s. 6d. each, the charge for two a year was £34, 3s., or £7, 5s. in excess of the income of the fund, and this deficit appears to have been borne by Indian revenues until 1861, when it was decided by the Secretary of State for India that the medal should be reduced in size. Dies for a reduced medal were accordingly prepared by Mr. B. Wyon at a cost of forty guineas, the price of the medals struck from them being £12, 12s.

The Pollock Medal was given at Addiscombe until 1861, when, in consequence of the transfer of the Government of India to the Crown, the College was abolished, and the prize made over to the Royal Military Academy at Woolwich.

The following is a list of the recipients of the medal. It shows that few but Engineer officers have ever received it, the most distinguished cadets having almost invariably elected for the Engineers.

LIST OF POLLOCK MEDALLISTS.

INSCRIBED ON THE WALLS OF THE GREAT DINING HALL, ROYAL MILITARY ACADEMY, WOOLWICH.

Printed at pp. 184–188 of *Addiscombe: its Heroes and Men of Note*, by Colonel H. M. Vibart. 1894.

PRESENTED AT ADDISCOMBE.

Year	Month	Name	Corps
1848.	June.	Edward C. S. Williams,	Bengal Engineers.
	Dec.	James J. M'Leod Innes,	do.
1849.	June.	Thomas G. Montgomerie,	do.
	Dec.	George A. Craster,	do.
1850.	June.	Patrick Stewart,	do.
	Dec.	Frederick S. Stanton,	do.
1851.	June.	Henry Goodwyn,	do.
	Dec.	James P. Bassevi,	do.
1852.	June.	Arthur M. Lang,	do.
	Dec.	Salisbury T. Trevor,	do.
1853.	June.	John U. Champain,	do.
	Dec.	E. B. Holland,	Bombay Engineers.
1854.	June.	W. Jeffreys,	Bengal Engineers.
	Dec.	Æneas R. R. Macdonald,	H.E.I.C. Engineers.[1]
1855.	June.	Charles H. Luard,	Bengal Engineers.
	Dec.	John Eckford,	do.

[1] On this occasion the Engineer Cadets were not posted to Presidencies until after the examination.

1856.	June.	John M. M'Neile, ...	Bengal Engineers.
	Dec.	John Herschell, ...	do.
1857.	June.	Keith A. Jopp, ...	Bombay Engineers.
	Dec.	Lewis Conway Gordon, . .	Bengal Engineers.
1858.	June.	William Maxwell Campbell, . .	Bombay Engineers.
	Dec.	William H. Pierson, . . .	Bengal Engineers.
1859.	June.	A. W. Elliot, ...	Not appointed.
	Dec.	W. Shepherd, ...	Bengal Engineers.
1860.	June.	A. J. C. Cunninghame, . .	do.
	Dec.	Kellen C. Pye, ...	do.
1861.	June.	W. J. Williamson, . . .	Bengal Infantry.

PRESENTED AT WOOLWICH.

1861.	Dec.	Clayton S. Beauchamp, . .	Royal Engineers.
1862.	June.	Thomas Fraser, ...	do.
	Dec.	Valentine F. Rowe, . . .	do.
1863.	June.	Herbert P. Knocker, . . .	do.
	Dec.	Francis Mascall, ...	do.
1864.	June.	Henry R. G. Georges, . . .	do.
	Dec.	William G. Nicholson, . . .	do.
1865.	June.	Sydney L. Jacob, ...	do.
	Dec.	Charles M. Watson, . . .	do.
1866.	June.	John E. Broadbent, . . .	do.
	Dec.	Harry M. Chambers, . . .	do.
1867.	June.	Felicien R. de Wolski, . . .	do.
	Dec.	Francis J. Day, ...	do.
1868.	June.	George Sydenham Clarke, . .	do.
	Dec.	Henry H. L. Cunninghame, . .	do.
1869.	June.	Henry J. Harman, . . .	do.
	Dec.	Richard de Villamil, . . .	do.
1870.	June.	Herbert C. Chirnside, . . .	do.
	Dec.	Philip Cardew, ...	do.
1871.	July.	Henry G. Kunhardt, . . .	do.
1872.	Feb.	Henry E. M'Callum, . . .	do.
	June.	John C. Addison, ...	do.
	Oct.	William C. Godsal, . . .	do.
1873.	Feb.	Henry D. Love, ...	do.
	June.	John C. Campbell, . . .	do.
	Oct.	Matthew H. P. R. Sankey, . .	do.
1874.	Feb.	Charles J. Hadden, . . .	Royal Artillery.
	July.	Hugh M. Sinclair, . . .	Royal Engineers.
1875.	Feb.	Maurice A. Cameron, . . .	do.
	July.	H. J. Folster, ...	do.
1876.	Feb.	V. H. P. Caillard, . . .	do.
	July.	J. H. Cowan, ...	do.
1877.	Feb.	W. H. Turton, ...	do.
	July.	A. P. Codd, ...	do.
	Dec.	H. D. Laffan, ...	do.
1878.	April.	E. Agar, ...	do.
	July.	A. M. Mantell, ...	do.
	Dec.	S. Davidson, ...	do.
1879.	April.	J. Winn, ...	do.
	July.	J. Dallas, ...	do.

1880.	Feb.	E. H. Hemming, ...	Royal Engineers.
	May.	M. Nathan, ...	do.
	July.	W. F. H. S. Kincaid, . . .	do.
1881.	Feb.	C. Hill, ...	do.
	July.	J. E. Edmonds, ...	do.
1882.	Feb.	J. R. L. Macdonald, . . .	do.
	July.	R. J. H. Mackenzie, . . .	do.
1883.	Feb.	G. A. S. Stone, ...	do.
	July.	W. G. Lawrie, ...	do.
1884.	Feb.	J. H. L. E. Johnstone, . . .	do.
	July.	C. F. Close, ...	do.
	Dec.	E. A. Edgell, ...	do.
1885.	April.	H. B. Williams, ...	do.
	Sept.	G. P. Lenox-Conyngham, . .	do.
1886.	Feb.	H. M. St. A. Wade, . . .	do.
	July.	C. H. Versturme, ...	do.
1887.	Feb.	T. E. Naish, ...	do.
	July.	R. F. G. Bond, ...	do.
1888.	Feb.	E. G. Godfrey-Faussett, . .	do.
	July.	W. M. Coldstream, . . .	do.
1889.	Feb.	B. H. Rooke, ...	do.
	July.	J. M. E. Colvin, ...	do.
1890.	Feb.	J. F. W. Johnson, . . .	do.
	July.	E. H. M. Leggett, . . .	do.
1891.	Feb.	S. G. Faber, ...	do.
	July.	R. Polwhele, ...	do.
1892.	Feb.	A. H. W. Grubb, ...	do.
	July.	C. E. Vickers, ...	do.
1893	Feb.	W. C. Symon, ...	Royal Artillery.
	July.	E. T. Rich, ...	Royal Engineers.
1894.	Feb.	J. B. Corry, ...	do.
	Aug.	A. Ff. Garrett, ...	do.
1895.	Mar.	H. O. Mance, ...	do.
	Aug.	L. C. Jackson, ...	do.
	Dec.	H. de L. Pollard-Hardy, . .	do.

It will be observed that the only medal represented on the breast of Sir George Pollock is that for 'Cabul, 1842,' to which alone, at the time the Prize was founded, he was entitled. On the issue in 1850 of the India General Service Medal, 1803-1826, Sir George received the decoration with clasps for battle of Deig, capture of Deig, Nepal, and Ava.

FROM THE COURT OF DIRECTORS TO THE GOVERNMENT OF BENGAL, 19th July, 1848. No. 50—Military.

'1. We have to apprise you that we have consented to become Trustees to a Fund subscribed by the inhabitants of Calcutta, for the purpose of presenting prizes to the most distinguished Cadet of the season at Addiscombe, as a mark of the high sense entertained by the subscribers of the great and successful military services and private worth of Major-Genl. Sir George Pollock, G.C.B., and to stimulate young Indian Soldiers to follow his distinguished example.

'2. The first Prize conferred in execution of this Trust, viz. a Gold Medal, designated the "Pollock Medal," was presented by our Chairman to the most distinguished Cadet who passed his public examination at the Military Seminary on 9th ultimo.

'3. We have paid expenses on account of the Medal amounting to £102, 14s., which you will cause to be debited to the Trust account.

'4. We are now desirous of being informed of the amount of income derived from the Trust Fund, in order that the same may be appropriated to the purposes agreed upon by us, viz. a Gold Medal at each Public Examination, and the surplus, if any, in suitable Books, to be presented in addition to the Medal.'

FROM THE GOVERNMENT OF BENGAL TO THE COURT OF DIRECTORS, *14th Oct.*, 1848. No. 151—Military.

Cons. 23rd Sept., 1848, No. 4.
Letter from Mr. Rogers, 30th Sept., 1848.
Letter to Offg. Acct. Mil. Dep., No. 109, of 7th Oct., 1848.

'1. With reference to your Despatch No. 50, of 19th July, 1848, to this Presidency, we have the honor to transmit for the information of your Honorable Court copy of the correspondence marginally recorded, from which it will be perceived that the amount of "the Pollock Medal and Prize Fund," which is stated to exceed Eight thousand Rupees (Rs. 8000) is to be immediately deposited in Company's Paper in the General Treasury for the purposes of the Fund, and that we have issued instructions for the sum of £102, 14s. paid by you for the Gold Medal presented to the most distinguished Cadet who passed his public examination at Addiscombe on 9th June last, to be debited to the Trust Account.

'2. We shall apprise your Hon. Court of the exact amount of income derivable from the Fund as soon as it has been accurately ascertained.'

FROM THE GOVERNMENT OF BENGAL TO THE COURT OF DIRECTORS, *28th July*, 1849. No. 148—Military.

Cons. 21st July, 1849.

'In continuation of our Separate Letter No. 151, dated 14th Oct., 1848, we have the honor to transmit the accompanying Report of the Officiating Accountant, Military Dept., on the subject of the Pollock Medal and Prize Fund, and to solicit the attention of your Hon. Court to the remarks of the Officiating Accountant regarding the necessity which appears to exist for reducing the cost of the annual prizes derivable from the interest thereof.'

FROM THE COURT OF DIRECTORS TO THE GOVERNMENT OF BENGAL, *21st Nov.*, 1849. No. 107—Military.

Reply to Letter 28th July, 1849, *No.* 148.

'In continuation of No. 151 of 1848 we forward a letter from Offg. Acct., Military Dept., regarding the Pollock Medal and Prize Fund, and the necessity which exists for reducing the cost of the annual prizes derivable from the interest thereof.

'12. We learn from these papers that the amount deposited in your Treasury on account of the Pollock Medal and Prize Fund is Rs. 7817.8, and that there are subscriptions still unrealised,

'13. From this amount you will deduct the expenses incurred by us on account of the Fund, as specified in the margin, and inform us of the amount of the interest on the residue.

'Sum specified in Statement sent with Military Letter 19th July, 1848, ...	£102 14 0
Medal presented 6th Dec., 1848, . . .	17 1 6
Do. 8th June, 1849, . . .	17 1 6
	£136 17 0'

FROM THE GOVERNMENT OF BENGAL TO THE COURT OF DIRECTORS, 22nd June, 1850. No. 105—Military.

'1. With reference to paras. 12 and 13 of your Military Letter to Bengal No. 107, dated 21st Novr., 1849, we have the honor to transmit the accompanying copy of a Despatch from the Accountant, Military Dept., on the subject of the Pollock Medal and Prize Fund, together with an account current shewing the present state thereof.

'2. From these papers it will be seen that the amount of the above Fund, after liquidation of expenditure incurred in England, is Rs. 6200, and that the interest annually accruing thereto amounts to Rs. 269.'

FROM THE COURT OF DIRECTORS TO THE GOVERNMENT OF BENGAL, 23rd Oct., 1850. No. 117—Military.

'Letter dated 22nd June, 1850, No. 105.

'With reference to Court's letter No. 107 of 1849, paras. 12 and 13, transmit papers on the subject of the Pollock Medal and Prize Fund, with an Account Current shewing its present state.

'7. From the Statement here sent to us it appears that the principal money of the Fund is Rs. 6200, and that the annual interest is Rs. 269. There are, however, subscriptions still unrecovered from Mr. A. Rogers.'

FROM THE GOVERNMENT OF BENGAL TO THE COURT OF DIRECTORS, 24th June, 1851. No. 94—Military.

'With reference to the 7th para. of your Hon. Court's Military Letter to the Governor of the Presidency of Fort William, No. 117, of 23rd Oct., 1850, we have the honour to transmit copy of a communication from the Accountant, Military Dept., from which your Hon. Court will observe that no further payments have been made by Mr. Rogers on account of the Pollock Fund, and that any additional recovery is considered hopeless.'

No. 168.

CHINA, 1842.

PLATE 28.

Obv. Head of Queen Victoria, diademed, *l.* *Leg.* VICTORIA REGINA

Rev. Military and Naval trophy. In the front, a shield of the Royal arms. Behind, a palm-tree. Above, ARMIS EXPOSCERE PACEM. In the *exergue*, CHINA 1842 [1]

Circular, 1.4 inch. Silver.
Artist. W. Wyon, R.A.
Struck at the Royal Mint.
Dies at the Royal Mint.
Mounting. Plain straight german silver bar.
Ribbon. 1½ inch wide, red with yellow borders.
Worn on left breast.

The idea of giving a medal for the China War of 1842 appears to have originated with the Governor-General of India, Lord Ellenborough, who, in a General Order dated 14th October, 1842, announced that the Government of India would present silver medals to the officers and soldiers of the Army of India who had served in China under Lieut.-General Sir Hugh Gough.

This intention was not, however, carried into effect, because on 5th January, 1843, Lord Stanley, Secretary of State for War, informed the Duke of Wellington, the Commander-in-Chief, that the Queen had directed the preparation of a medal to commemorate the 'signal successes of Her Majesty's Naval and Military Forces upon the coast and in the interior of the Empire of China,' which medal would be bestowed upon the officers and men of the Navy and Army, including those in the East India Company's service, who had served with distinction in any of the following operations:—

In the Canton river, in the operations of 1841.
At Chusan, in 1841 and 1842.
At Amoy, at Ningpo, at Chinpae, at Tsekee, Chapoo, in the river Woosung, in the Yangtse-Kiang, and in the assault of Ching-Kiang-Foo.

In communicating this letter to the President of the India Board, Lord Stanley stated that it might be right to suggest to the Court of Directors how far the grant by the Queen of the medal to the Company's Forces as well as to Her Majesty's, might affect the intention expressed by the Governor-General in his General Order of 14th October, 1842, of bestowing medals on the former.

---

[1] It will be observed that the design described in Lord Ellenborough's General Order of 14th October, 1842, was not adopted. A *reverse* die had, however, been prepared by Mr. W. Wyon, showing the British lion, crowned, with his fore-feet firmly placed on the back of a dragon, whose body and tail are curved over the lion's back. Above is the motto, 'Armis exposcere pacem'; in the *exergue*, 'Nanking, 1842.' This die was in the possession of the late Mr. L. C. Wyon.

The President accordingly communicated with the Court, with the result that the latter informed the Governor-General that it was their wish that no further steps should be taken in regard to the General Order in question, since the Medal therein described, although a reward justly merited by those for whom it was intended, was superseded by that bestowed by Her Majesty.

The ribbon is red, the heraldic colour of England, bordered with yellow—the Chinese imperial or court colour.

GENERAL ORDER BY THE GOVERNOR-GENERAL, SECRET DEPARTMENT, Simla, 14th Oct., 1842.

'The Governor-General requests that H.E. Lieut.-General Sir Hugh Gough will have the goodness to transmit to him a nominal List of such Officers, Non-Commissioned Officers and Privates, of the several Corps of the Army of India, serving under H.E.'s command, in the present or in the previous campaigns, as he may deem to be justly entitled by their services before the enemy to the honor of wearing a Medal commemorative of such services: and to every Officer, Non-Commissioned Officer and Private named in such List the Govt. of India will present a Silver Medal, bearing on one side the head of Her Majesty, with the superscription "Pax Asiæ Victoriâ restituta," and the figures "1842" underneath, and on the *reverse*, a Dragon wearing an Imperial Crown.'

FROM THE COURT OF DIRECTORS TO THE GOVERNOR-GENERAL OF INDIA, 4th January, 1843. No. 2—Military.

'1. We have the gratification to forward to you a copy of a Letter from the President of the Board of Commrs. for the Affairs of India, conveying to the Chairman and Deputy Chairman of the East India Company a Letter addressed by the Right Hon. Lord Stanley, one of Her Majesty's Principal Secretaries of State, to Lord Fitzgerald and Vesci.

'2. By this letter we are apprised that, as a special mark of Her Majesty's gracious approbation of the services performed by the Forces, Naval and Military, of the East India Company, acting in concert with the Forces of Her Majesty, engaged in the late operations in China, Her Majesty has been graciously pleased to direct that a Medal, to be worn in commemoration of their services, should be conferred on the Naval and Military Forces of the East India Company, thus marking Her Majesty's sense of the importance of that co-operation, and granting the same honorable distinction to the Royal Forces and to those of the East India Company.

'3. It is therefore our wish that no further proceedings should be taken to carry into execution the G. O. of 14th Oct., 1842, for bestowing the Medal therein described, which, though a reward justly merited by those for whom it was intended, is now superseded by the distinction which Her Majesty destines for the united Forces of Her Majesty and the East India Company.

'4. On this subject Lord Stanley has also addressed a Despatch to His Grace the Comr.-in-Chief, of which a copy is annexed. We have to call your attention to the instructions under which the Medal is to be granted by order of Her Majesty, and we desire that you take measures for transmitting to us a nominal List prepared in conformity with the regulations which that Despatch prescribes.'

'INDIA BOARD,
5th January, 1843.

'GENTLEMEN,

I hasten to impart to you a letter which I have only now received from Her Majesty's Principal Secretary of State for the Department of War.

'I lose no time in conveying to you a communication which will, I am sure, prove most gratifying to you, to the Court of Directors, and to the distinguished members of your Naval and Military Services, for whom Her Majesty destines a signal mark of Her Majesty's especial favor.

'The letter addressed by Lord Stanley to His Grace the Commander-in-Chief, of which also I annex a copy, will explain to you the gracious intentions of the Queen.

'The Governor-General of India will, I am convinced, share with you and with me in the satisfaction which we feel that the reward, intended by the Govt. of India for the Naval and Military Forces of the Company serving with Her Majesty's Fleet and Army in China, is now to be derived from the highest fountain of honor; and I have to request that the Court will prepare the draft of a Despatch to the Governor-General, informing his Lordship of Her Majesty's most gracious pleasure.

'I have, etc.,

'FITZGERALD AND VESCI.

'The Chairman and Deputy-Chairman
of the East India Company.'

'DOWNING STREET,
5th January, 1843.

'MY LORD,

I do myself the honor to transmit herewith to your Lordship a copy of a letter which I have addressed to the Duke of Wellington, in explanation of the Queen's gracious intention to grant Medals in commemoration of the success of Her Majesty's Arms in China to the officers and men of the East India Company's Naval and Military Forces, without distinction, who took part in the more prominent events of the War now happily concluded. I have especial pleasure in conveying to your Lordship this mark of the high sense entertained by Her Majesty of the zealous and valuable co-operation of the Indian Navy, because your Lordship is aware that the peculiar position of that Arm did not enable Her Majesty, under existing regulations, to signify her approbation of its services by individual marks of distinction conferred upon any of its Officers: and I should deeply regret that any erroneous inference should be drawn from that circumstance on the part of persons unaware of the real state of the case, disparaging to a Service which has proved itself well worthy of co-operating with Her Majesty's Naval Forces.

'Your Lordship may perhaps think it right to suggest to the Directors of the East India Company, how far the grant by Her Majesty of similar Medals to Her own Forces and those of the Company may affect the instructions which they may be prepared to send to the Governor-General as to the Medals which, by his General Order of 14th Oct. last, he appears to have contemplated bestowing on the East India Company's Forces engaged in China.

'I have, etc.,

'STANLEY.

'The President of the
India Board.'

'DOWNING STREET,
5th January, 1843.

'MY LORD DUKE,

I am commanded by the Queen to acquaint your Grace that Her Majesty has been pleased to give directions that a Medal should be prepared for the purpose of commemorating the signal successes of Her Majesty's Naval and Military Forces upon the Coast and in the interior of the Empire of China.

'Although Her Majesty is of opinion that the award of a distinction of this nature should be reserved, as it has hitherto been, for very peculiar and special occasions, and that great evil would arise from the frequent and indiscriminate grant of Medals for the commemoration of Naval or Military exploits of an ordinary character, yet it appears to Her Majesty that in the instance of the recent events in China an exception can properly and safely be made from a rule which ought to be generally observed.

'The difficulties with which Her Majesty's Forces have had to contend by Sea and Land, from the absence of that local information which is accessible in respect to almost every other Country on the face of the Globe, have been very great, and have been surmounted with consummate skill. Wherever opportunities have been afforded (and they have not been wanting) for the display of courage and determination, Her Majesty's Naval and Military Forces have amply sustained the character of their respective services; but Her Majesty is happy in the belief that the great moral effect which has been produced upon the Chinese people, and to which Her Majesty mainly looks for the permanent advantage to be derived from these operations, results not more from the proofs which have been displayed of irresistible power, than from the moderation which has been shown in victory, the studious abstinence from an unnecessary aggravation of the horrors of war, the discipline which has prevailed in the excitement of success, and the good faith with which, on the first intimation of acquiescence to our demands, the further pressure of an irresistible force has been at once withdrawn. Above all it is to those successes, so honorable in every respect to the character of the services by which they have been achieved, that Her Majesty ascribes the accomplishment of that which has been the main object of Her Majesty's solicitude, the conclusion of an honorable peace with a great Empire, with which, from the countless numbers of its people, from their industrious habits, from their products, and their wants affording facilities for the most extended commerce with the subjects of Her Majesty, it is most important that peaceful and friendly relations should be maintained.

'On a consideration of all these circumstances, although in other exploits of Her Majesty's Arms there may have been more equality in the contending forces, more obstinate resistance may have been shewn, and more formidable obstacles surmounted, yet Her Majesty deems it fitting that the conclusion of a War, leading to such important results, should be commemorated by the issue of a Medal, to be granted to those, to whose skill and gallantry such results are mainly attributable. The Queen is well aware that in the course of that War, while all engaged have had an equal desire, all have not had equal opportunities, of distinguishing themselves; but Her Majesty, anxious that no invidious distinctions should appear to be drawn between Men, who, as occasions have offered, have performed their duties with equal zeal, has been pleased to order that the Medal, which Her Majesty has directed to be struck in commemoration of the recent great successes, should be bestowed upon each Admiral, General and other Officers of the Navy and Army, including the Officers, European and Native, of the service of the East India Company, Petty Officers, Seamen and Marines of the Navy of Her Majesty and of the East India Company, and the Non-Commissioned Officers and Soldiers of Her Majesty's Army, and of the East India Company, including the Native Non-Commissioned Officers and Soldiers, belonging to such Regiments, Corps, Ships and other Vessels as have served with distinction at any of the following operations:

'In the Canton River, in the operations of 1841.

At Chusan in 1841 and 1842.

At Amoy, at Ningpo, at Chinpae, at Tsekee, Chapoo, in the River Woosung, in the Yangtse Kiang, and at the Assault of Ching-Kiang Foo.

Her Majesty is pleased to direct that the above list should comprise the Officers serving on the Staff of the several Armies, including those of the Ordnance, the Medical and Commissariat Staff, and Her Majesty's Superintendent and the Officers employed under his direction.

'In order to enable me to give effect to Her Majesty's gracious intentions as above explained, I have to request that your Grace will call upon Lieut.-General Sir Hugh Gough to furnish a nominal list of the Officers, Non-Commissioned Officers and Privates of Her Majesty's Army, who may be entitled to receive Medals under the foregoing Instructions. Copies of this letter, accompanied by similar requests, will be transmitted to the Lords Commissioners of the Admiralty, to the Commissioners for the Affairs of India, and to Her Majesty's Superintendent; and on the receipt of the returns thus called for, immediate orders will be issued to the Master of Her Majesty's Mint for the preparation and distribution of the Medals.

'I have, etc.,

STANLEY.

'Field Marshal,
HIS GRACE THE DUKE OF WELLINGTON, K.G., etc.'

GENERAL ORDER BY THE GOVERNMENT OF INDIA, No. 49,
Fort William, 28th February, 1843.

'H.M.'s 26th and 49th regiments being about to return to England, the President of the Council of India in Council cannot permit them to leave the shores of India without some public acknowledgment of their gallant services.

. . . . . .

'In thus taking leave of a body of men, who, in conjunction with the rest of the forces serving in China, have rendered such signal services to their country, the President of the Council of India in Council has the satisfaction of assuring them, that those services have been most highly appreciated, not only by the Government of India, but by their Sovereign, who has been pleased to direct that Medals be granted to the officers and men of Her Majesty's and the East India Company's naval and military forces, without distinction, who took part in the more prominent events of the war, in commemoration of the success of Her Majesty's Arms in China, and in token of Her Majesty's high approbation.'

No. 169.

CHINA, 1857-60.

PLATE 28.

This medal is the same as that for the war of 1842, with the exception that in the *exergue* of the *reverse* there is no date. The dates of the services are borne on the clasps.

Mounting. A silver cusped bar.
Ribbon. 1¼ inch wide. Red with yellow borders.
Clasps. FATSHAN 1857
CANTON 1857
TAKU FORTS 1858
TAKU FORTS 1860
PEKIN 1860

FROM THE SECRETARY OF STATE FOR INDIA TO THE GOVERNOR-GENERAL, 28*th February*, 1861. No. 106—Military.

'1. Her Majesty has been pleased to give directions that a medal should be prepared to commemorate the successes of Her Majesty's British and Indian forces, naval and military, employed in the operations in China, which terminated in the capture of the city of Canton on the 29th of December, 1857, and also in the operations which have recently terminated in the capture of the city of Pekin, and the restoration of peace.

'2. Her Majesty has been pleased to command:

'1stly. That a clasp to be attached to the said medal, inscribed "Canton, 1857," be granted to such of Her Majesty's forces aforesaid, as were employed in the operations undertaken against the city of Canton.

'2ndly. That a clasp to be attached to the said medal, inscribed "Taku Forts, 1860," be granted to such of her Majesty's forces aforesaid as were employed in the capture of the Taku forts.

'And 3rdly. That a clasp to be attached to the said medal, inscribed "Pekin, 1860," be granted to such of Her Majesty's forces aforesaid as were employed in the capture of the city of Pekin.

'3. Her Majesty has further been pleased to command that the medal be the same as that already granted by Her Majesty, in commemoration of the operations formerly undertaken in China, omitting the date 1842 inscribed thereon, and that it be suspended from a ribbon of the same width and pattern as that worn with that medal; and that a clasp to be attached to the medal, inscribed "China, 1842," be granted in addition to the clasps already enumerated, to such of Her Majesty's forces aforesaid then employed in the service of Her Majesty and of the East India Company, who have received the medal granted by Her Majesty in commemoration of the former operations, and have served in the operations which have recently terminated, in order that they may not lose the reward and record of their former services.

'4. The requisite instructions will be issued by the General Commanding-in-Chief to officers commanding Her Majesty's forces in China, to enable H.R.H. to give effect to Her Majesty's gracious intentions, by the preparation of medal rolls.

'5. In the event, however, of any of the corps having returned to India before the receipt of such instructions, your Government should direct the preparation and transmission of the medal rolls of such corps.

'6. In the preparation of these rolls, care should be taken to particularize the officers and soldiers who may be in possession of the China Medal of 1842, as in such case clasps only are on the present occasion to be awarded.'

No. 170.

SINDE, 1843.

THREE MEDALS.

PLATE 29.

Obv. Head of Queen Victoria, diademed, *l.*

Leg. VICTORIA REGINA The same for all the medals.

Rev. No. 1. MEEANEE 1843
No. 2. HYDERABAD 1843
No. 3. MEEANEE HYDERABAD 1843

In each case the inscription is surrounded by a laurel wreath, and surmounted by a crown.

Circular, 1.4 inch. Silver.
Artist. W. Wyon, R.A.
Struck at the Royal Mint.
Dies at the Royal Mint.
Mounting. Silver bar for commissioned officers.
Steel bar for N.-C. officers and soldiers.
Ribbon. The 'Military Ribbon of India,' 1¾ inch wide.
Worn on left breast.

The first mention of a medal for Sir Charles Napier's conquest of Sinde is in a letter dated 18th July, 1843, addressed by the Secretary of State for War and the Colonies to the President of the India Board, announcing that the Queen had been graciously pleased to command that a medal, to resemble as nearly as possible that proposed for the troops employed in Afghanistan, should be conferred upon the officers and soldiers of Her Majesty's service who were engaged at the battles of Meeanee (17th February, 1843) and Hyderabad (24th March, 1843). It was added that Her Majesty would readily permit the officers and soldiers of the Indian Army, to whom the Court of Directors might grant medals for the same services, to wear such medals in all parts of Her Majesty's dominions.

On this letter being communicated to the Court of Directors, they addressed a despatch to the Government of India, intimating Her Majesty's intentions, and stating that in testimony of their high approbation of the services rendered at the two battles by the Company's troops, they had resolved to present a silver medal to those engaged. The Court's despatch was published to the army in India in a General Order of the Governor-General, dated 22nd September, 1843.

Sir Charles Napier, in a General Order announcing to his troops the grant of the medal, said: 'Let me then congratulate you all upon these glorious medals, the fruits of discipline and of those well wielded weapons, the matchless musket and bayonet, which pour a double death upon an enemy, death by fire and death by steel.'

This is the only instance of any medals for Indian service being paid for by the Crown. On the occasion of the grant of medals for the Sutlej campaign, Her Majesty's Government expressed the opinion that the cost of all medals for Indian services should be met from Indian revenues.

In a General Order from Agra, 5th March, 1843, the Governor-General congratulated Major-General Sir C. Napier, and the army under his command, on the victory of Meeanee, and specified the distinctions to be borne on colours and appointments.

It is added that 'the Governor-General will not further anticipate the measures which the home authorities, informed, before they can receive his despatches, of the victory which has been obtained, may think fit to adopt for the purpose of marking their high sense of the merits of those by whom so great a service has been performed.'

GENERAL ORDER BY THE GOVERNOR-GENERAL,
Agra, 13*th March*, 1843.

POLITICAL DEPARTMENT.

'The Governor-General requests Major-General Sir Charles Napier K.C.B. will, in the name of the Government of India, present to the Sinde Horse the Standard[1] they took from the enemy in the ever memorable battle of Meeanee, in which that regiment by its distinguished conduct acquired for itself the honor of being hereafter permanently attached to the Bombay Army.

'The Governor-General has given directions that other Standards of the three colors of the military ribbon of India, inscribed with the words "Hyderabad 1843," in the Persian, English and Hindu languages, shall be prepared for the Sinde Horse.'

'INDIA BOARD,
20*th July*, 1843.

GENTLEMEN,

I have the pleasure to transmit to you for the information of the Court of Directors of the East India Company a copy of a letter which has been addressed to me by the Secretary of State for the Dept. of War, announcing that the Queen has been graciously pleased to command that a Medal, to commemorate the victories gained by the Troops under Major-General Sir Charles Napier, should be conferred on the Officers and Private Soldiers of Her Majesty's Army engaged in the Battles of Meeanee and Hyderabad, and further signifying Her Majesty's readiness to permit the Officers and Private Soldiers of the East India Company's Troops who were present in those brilliant actions, to wear, in any part of Her Majesty's Dominions, such Medal as the Court of Directors may think it right to bestow, as a mark of the high sense entertained of the gallantry of that portion of the Company's Forces which contributed to the successes recently achieved in Sinde.

'I have, etc.,

'RIPON.

'The Chairman and Deputy Chairman
of the East India Company.'

(ENCLOSURE.)

'COLONIAL OFFICE, DOWNING STREET,
18*th July*, 1843.

'MY LORD,

I have the honor to acquaint your Lordships that the Queen, being desirous of commemorating the signal success obtained by the Force under the com-

[1] The Standard was presented to the regiment at Meerpoor, on 30th March, 1843, by Sir C. Napier in due form in the presence of the troops.

mand of Major-General Sir Charles Napier in Sinde, has been graciously pleased to command that a Medal, to resemble as nearly as possible that proposed for the Troops employed in Affghanistan, should be conferred upon the Officers, Non-Commissioned Officers and Soldiers in Her Majesty's Service, who were engaged in the Battles of Meeanee and Hyderabad.

'Without anticipating the course which the Court of Directors of the East India Company may propose to take for commemorating the success of the Company's Troops in Sinde, I think it nevertheless right to add that Her Majesty would readily permit the Officers, Non-Commissioned Officers and Soldiers of the Company's Army, to whom the Court of Directors might think proper to grant Medals in commemoration of the Battles of Meeanee and Hyderabad, to wear such Medals in all parts of Her Majesty's Dominions.

'I have, etc.,

'STANLEY.

'The President of the
India Board.'

GENERAL ORDER BY THE GOVERNOR-GENERAL, *22nd September*, 1843. No. 205.

'The Right Hon. the Governor-General of India in Council has great pleasure in publishing to the Army the following paragraphs of a Military Letter, No. 13, from the Hon. the Court of Directors to the Governor-General of India in Council, dated 2nd August, 1843.

'"1. We have great satisfaction in acquainting you that the Queen has been graciously pleased to command that a Medal, to commemorate the victories gained by the Troops under Major-Genl. Sir Charles Napier, shall be conferred on the Officers and Private Soldiers of Her Majesty's Army engaged in the Battles of Meeanee and Hyderabad.

'"2. We have also to announce that we have resolved in commemoration of these brilliant actions, and in testimony of our high approbation of the services rendered by the Troops, European and Native, to cause an appropriate Medal to be struck in silver, to be presented to all the Officers and soldiers of the East India Company's Army who were engaged upon these memorable occasions.

'"3. We have further the gratification to apprise you that we have received the announcement that the Queen will graciously permit the Officers, Non-Commissioned Officers and Soldiers of our Army, to whom we may grant the Medal, to wear the same in all parts of Her Majesty's Dominions.

'"4. We shall take immediate measures for the preparation and despatch of the requisite number of Medals."'

LETTER FROM THE GOVERNOR IN COUNCIL OF BOMBAY TO MAJOR-GENERAL SIR C. J. NAPIER, G.C.B., Governor of Sinde.

'BOMBAY, *5th October*, 1843.

'SIR,

We have the highest gratification in transmitting to your Excellency three copies of a reprint of the General Order issued by the Right Honorable the Governor-General of India in Council on 22nd ultimo, publishing to the Army extract of a letter from the Honorable the Court of Directors, dated 2nd August last, announcing that Her Majesty and the Honorable Court have resolved to confer Medals on the gallant troops who were engaged in the battles of Meeanee and Hyderabad.

'In forwarding this General Order, we gladly avail ourselves of the opportunity afforded to us of offering to your Excellency our warmest congratulations on the occasion of so gratifying a testimony being accorded by Her Majesty and the Honorable Court of Directors of the high approbation of the valuable services, principally rendered by the troops of this Presidency, on the above memorable occasions, and reflecting such lustre on the able and gallant commander under whom these glorious victories were won.

'G. W. ARTHUR.
G. W. ANDERSON.
J. H. CRAWFORD.'

(Published in G.O.C.C., Bombay, 28th Oct., 1843.)

GENERAL ORDER BY HIS EXCELLENCY MAJOR-GENERAL SIR CHARLES NAPIER, G.C.B., Governor of Sinde.

'HEAD QUARTERS, KURRACHEE, *17th Oct.*, 1843.

'The honors which the Queen and the Honorable Court of Directors have bestowed upon their faithful troops must animate us all with gratitude and with pride. To do our duty in a battle is a negative virtue, Cowards and Traitors alone desert their Colours. Her Majesty has a right to our best exertions without other reward than the glory which beams from Victory. But the Sovereign has been graciously pleased to mark Her approbation of the courage displayed by Her united troops, in attacking enemies at once so numerous and so hardy.

'Let me then congratulate you all upon these glorious Medals, the fruits of discipline and of those well wielded weapons, the matchless musket and bayonet, which pour a double death upon an enemy, death by fire and death by steel.

'It is when we receive honors and rewards, that we should recur to the *means* by which they have been won. Thus do our minds gather confidence from reflection, and if again we have the good fortune to meet an enemy, again we shall conquer.

'The above Order is to be most carefully translated and read and explained to each regiment and detachment at a special parade ordered for the purpose.'

FROM THE GOVERNMENT OF BENGAL TO THE COURT OF DIRECTORS, 19th November, 1845. No. 164—Military.

'164. We issued the necessary orders for the Medals being delivered to the parties entitled to them, previously getting their names engraved at the Mint, and on a representation made to us by the Officiating Assistant Adjutant-General of the Army, we have ordered Clasps to be made up and affixed to each Medal.' (*Vide* Nos. 2 to 4 A. *Cons.* of 8th Augt., 1845, and Nos. 68 to 70 of 19th Sept. of the same year.)

FROM THE GOVERNMENT OF BENGAL TO THE COURT OF DIRECTORS, 11th March, 1846. No. 27—Military.

'123. Para. 164 of our Despatch No. 164, dated 19th Novr. last, informed your Hon. Court of our having authorised the preparation of Steel clasps for the Meeanee Medals: we have now to state that Silver clasps have been ordered to be affixed to the Medals intended for the Commissioned Officers.' (*Consultations*, 3rd October, 1845, No. 236; 21st November, 1845, Nos. 223 to 226.)

No. 171.

GWALIOR CAMPAIGN, 1843.

BATTLES OF MAHARAJPOOR AND PUNNIAR.

PLATE 30.

A Bronze Star of six points, 2 inches in diameter, having in the centre a silver star inscribed, MAHARAJPOOR 29TH DECR 1843

or

PUNNIAR 29TH DECR 1843

The recipient's name was engraved on the back of the Star.

Made at the Calcutta Mint.
Dies at the Calcutta Mint.
Mounting. Various.
Ribbon. The Military Ribbon of India.
Worn on left breast.

The battles of Maharajpoor and Punniar were fought on the 29th December, 1843. On 4th January following the Governor-General announced, in General Orders, that to every officer and soldier engaged the Government of India would present 'an Indian Star of Bronze made out of the guns taken at those battles.' It was further announced that a triumphal monument commemorative of the campaign of Gwalior would be erected at Calcutta, and inscribed with the names of all who fell in the two battles. The Governor-General subsequently ordered that a plate of silver should be inserted in the centre of the Stars to serve for the inscription.

It appears to have been the original intention that these Stars should be worn without ribbon, since they were made with hooks on the back to attach to the coat like Stars of orders of knighthood. We do not know to what extent this intention was carried out, but many of the Stars were mounted like medals and suspended by the Military Ribbon of India. No general pattern for the mounting seems to have been prescribed by authority; the fancy of the recipients apparently ruled in the matter, and some of the mountings were of an elaborate character.

GENERAL ORDER BY THE GOVERNOR-GENERAL, Camp, Gwalior Residency, 4th January, 1844.

'The Govt. of India will, as a mark of its grateful sense of their distinguished merit, permit to every General and other Officer, and to every Soldier engaged in the Battles of Maharajpore and Punniar, an Indian Star of Bronze, made out of the Guns taken at those Battles: and all Officers and Soldiers in the service of the Govt. of India will be permitted to wear the Star with their uniforms.

'H.E. the Commander-in-Chief is requested to furnish the Governor-General with nominal Rolls of all the Officers and Soldiers engaged in the two Battles respectively, in order that the Star presented to each may be inscribed with the name of the Battle in which he was engaged.

'A triumphal Monument commemorative of the Campaign of Gwalior will be erected at Calcutta, and inscribed with the names of all who fell in the two Battles.'

BENGAL MILITARY PROCEEDINGS, 26th April, 1844. No. 268.

'COUNCIL CHAMBER, CALCUTTA,
20th April, 1844.

SIR,

I am directed to inform you that the Governor-General in Council has decided that a plate of silver shall be inserted in the centre of the Star of the Gwalior Medals, to serve for the inscription, and to request that orders may be given accordingly.

'I am, etc.,

'J. STUART, *Lieut.-Colonel,*
Secretary to the Govt. of India, Military Dept.

Lt.-Col. W. N. FORBES,
Mint Master.

'INDIA BOARD,
3rd July, 1844.

'GENTLEMEN,

I have the pleasure to transmit to you a copy of a letter, dated 26th ultimo, which I have received from His Grace the Commander-in-Chief, informing me that the Queen has been graciously pleased to permit Her Majesty's Troops, whose gallant conduct contributed so importantly to the successes obtained in Affghanistan, and in the territory of Gwalior, to wear honorary distinctions similar to those which have been conferred on the East India Company's Army, for bravery displayed in the same engagements.

'I have, etc.,

'RIPON.

'The Chairman and Deputy Chairman
of the East India Company.'

(ENCLOSURE.)

'HORSE GUARDS,
26th June, 1844.

'MY LORD,

I have had the honor to receive your Lordship's letter of 11th inst., transmitting a copy of a Despatch from the Governor-General of India in Council to the Secret Committee of the East India Company, recommending that certain honorary distinctions, which have been granted to the East India Company's Army for services in Affghanistan and the Gwalior territory, should also be conferred upon such of Her Majesty's Troops as were similarly engaged: and having in consequence, with the concurrence of the Secretary of State, submitted the matter for the Queen's pleasure, I have now the satisfaction to acquaint your Lordship, that Her Majesty has been graciously pleased to permit the 41st Regt. to wear on its Colors and appointments the words "Ghuznee" and "Cabool, 1842."

'The 3rd Light Dragoons and the 9th, 13th, and 31st Regiments of Infantry, the words "Cabool, 1842."

'The 16th Lancers, and the 39th and 40th Regts. of Infantry, the word "Maharajpore," and the 9th Lancers, and the 3rd and 50th Regiments of Infantry, the word "Punniar."

'I have at the same time the honor to inform your Lordship, that the Queen has further been pleased to grant General Sir Hugh Gough, Bart., Major-Genl. Sir John Grey, the Officers and Men of the 9th and 16th Lancers, and the 3rd, 39th, 40th, and 50th Regiments of Infantry, and the Officers of the Staff serving with the Troops who were present in the Battles of Maharajpore and Punniar respectively, Her Majesty's most gracious permission to wear a Bronze Star made from the captured Guns, which in testimony of their services on these occasions, is to be presented to them by the Govt. of India.

'I have, etc.,

'WELLINGTON.

'The Right Hon. the EARL OF RIPON,
India Board.'

FROM THE COURT OF DIRECTORS TO THE GOVERNOR-GENERAL OF INDIA, *3rd July*, 1844. No. 21—Military.

'We have the satisfaction to transmit to you a copy of a letter dated 26th ultimo, from His Grace the Commander-in-Chief to the President of the Board of Commissioners for the Affairs of India, stating that the Queen has been graciously pleased to permit Her Majesty's troops, who were engaged in Afghanistan and the Gwalior Territory, to bear honorary distinctions similar to those which have been conferred on the Company's troops for the same services.'

GENERAL ORDER BY THE GOVERNOR-GENERAL OF INDIA, *Fort William*, *23rd August*, 1844. No. 244.

'The Governor-General of India in Council has much pleasure in publishing to the Army the following Military Despatch, No. 21, from the Hon. the Court of Directors to the Governor-General of India in Council dated 3rd July, 1844,[1] stating that the Queen has been pleased to permit certain honorary distinctions to be borne by Her Majesty's Troops for services in Afghanistan and Gwalior.'

---

[1] See above.

FROM THE GOVERNMENT OF BENGAL TO THE COURT OF DIRECTORS, 21st April, 1845. No. 61—Military.

Cons. 1844, 26th April, No. 268; 21st June, No. 2; 28th June, No. 62 to 64; 9th Aug., No. 89 to 91; 23rd Aug., No. 3; 4th Oct., No. 19 to 22; 1st Nov., No. 19-20; 8th Nov., No. 30 to 33; 22nd Nov., No. 141-142.

'78. With reference to the 10th para. of the General Order by the late Governor-General of 4th Jan., 1844, issued from the Foreign Dept., intimating that an Indian Star of Bronze made out of the Guns taken at the Battles of Maharajpore and Punniar, would be presented to every Officer and Soldier engaged: in the papers marginally recorded will be found correspondence shewing the steps taken by us in view to the preparation and distribution of the Stars, and to the carrying into effect the wishes of your Hon. Court, as conveyed in your Despatch to the Govt. of India, No. 8, dated 1st May, 1844, in respect to the Affghanistan Medals and Gwalior Stars being inscribed with the names, rank, and corps of the parties for whom intended, in the cases of H.M.'s Regiments and your European Corps.'

79. Prescribes measures for inscribing Medals at Calcutta Mint and up-country.

No. 172.

SEPOY GOLAPAH, 1845.

MEDAL.

From the following despatch of the Court of Directors we learn that the inhabitants of Perth presented a medal to a Sepoy who had protected the body of a British officer, Lieut. A. P. Campbell, of the 2nd Bombay European Regiment, who was killed in action at Sassedroog, on 31st December, 1844.

This is the only instance of the kind we have met with, and it is noticed here as the medal was presented with the entire approbation of the Court of Directors.

FROM THE COURT OF DIRECTORS TO THE GOVERNMENT OF MADRAS, 2nd July, 1845. No. 57—Military.

'We forward copy of a letter from the Lord Provost and Chief Magistrates of the City of Perth, with its accompanying Medal, which the inhabitants of Perth are desirous should be presented to Golapah, Sepoy of the 16th Madras N. I., as a mark of their sense of his gallantry in protecting, and carrying off the body of the late Lieut. Alexander P. Campbell, 2nd Bombay E. R., who was killed in action in Decr. last. We have great satisfaction in forwarding this Medal, which you will convey to the Sepoy for whom it is intended.'[1]

---

[1] There does not appear to be any trace of the award of this medal among the Corporation Records at Perth.

No. 173.

SUTLEJ CAMPAIGN, 1845-6.

FOUR MEDALS.

PLATE 31.

Obv. Head of Queen Victoria, diademed, *l.*

Leg. VICTORIA REGINA

The same for the four medals.

Rev. Figure of Victory, standing, holding in her right hand a wreath, in her left palm branch. At her feet a pile of captured arms.

Leg. ARMY OF THE SUTLEJ.

The medals differ only in the inscriptions in the *exergues*, which are as follow :

No. 1. MOODKEE 1845
No. 2. FEROZESHUHUR 1845
No. 3. ALIWAL 1846
No. 4. SOBRAON 1846

Circular, 1.4 inch. Silver.
Artist. W. Wyon, R.A.
Struck at the Royal Mint.
Dies at the Royal Mint.
Mounting. Silver scroll bar.
Ribbon. 1¼ inch wide. Blue, with crimson borders.
Worn on left breast.
Clasps. FEROZESHUHUR, ALIWAL, SOBRAON.

In a General Order dated Ferozepore, 25th December, 1845, the Governor-General, Sir Henry Hardinge, announced the repulse of the Sikh forces in their attack on a portion of the British army near Moodkee, on the night of the 18th December, and the capture on the evening of the 21st, and morning of the 22nd, of their entrenched camp, with seventy pieces of cannon, defended by 60,000 men, near the village of Ferozeshah; and stated that he would rejoice in recording the gallant exploits of the victors, by decorating their breasts with a medal. A further General Order, issued on 30th December, notified that to every officer and soldier in the service of the Government of India, engaged in these battles, would be granted a medal with the word 'Ferozeshah' inscribed on it.

The battle of Aliwal was fought on 28th January, 1846, and on 2nd February another General Order announced that a medal would be presented to every officer and soldier of the East India Company's Service engaged therein.

On 10th February the battle of Sobraon took place, and to commemorate this important victory, the fourth obtained by the Army of the Sutlej, the Governor-General notified in a

General Order, dated the 14th February, that a medal, inscribed 'Sobraon,' would be presented to the troops of the East India Company.

A subsequent General Order, issued on 17th April, 1846, announced that a medal would be bestowed on every officer and soldier who fought in the battle of Moodkee. It likewise set forth the conditions under which the four medals, together with the clasps which were, in certain cases, to accompany them, would be granted.

On the question of clasps, then a new one in connection with Indian medals, the General Order stated that, if an individual were entitled to be decorated for two battles, he would receive one silver medal bearing the name of the first battle, and a clasp or bar, inscribed with the name of the second battle, such bar to be fixed on the ribbon immediately above the medal. If entitled to be decorated for a third battle, the name of that battle would be inscribed on a second bar: and if entitled for four battles, the name of the fourth battle would be inscribed on a third bar, the bars being fixed in the order in which the battles were fought.

This Order clearly lays down the rule that the clasp for the second battle was to be fixed 'immediately above the medal,' and subsequent clasps 'in the order in which the battles were fought'—that is to say, the second clasp *above* the first, and the third *above* the second, and so on.

Thus, the Moodkee medal might carry clasps for	Ferozeshuhur. Aliwal. Sobraon.
The Ferozeshuhur medal ,, ,,	Aliwal. Sobraon.
The Aliwal medal ,, ,,	Sobraon.

The Sobraon medal could carry no clasp.

This was the first instance of clasps being given with an Indian medal.

From the official correspondence which took place in this country relative to the grant of these medals, it appears that the President of the India Board recommended to the Secretary of State for War, that a similar mark of distinction should be conferred by the Queen on such of Her Majesty's troops as were engaged. The Secretary of State replied, however, that, although the Crown would bear the cost of the medals prepared for Her Majesty's soldiers present at the victories in Sinde, both he and the Lords of the Treasury were of opinion that any medals thereafter granted to the Royal army for services in India should be supplied at the charge of the revenues of that country. The President in consequence suggested that the Governor-General should be permitted to grant to Her Majesty's troops whatever marks of honour he might have conferred upon those of the East India Company. The result was that the Court of Directors authorised the Government of India to announce the grant of such marks of honour to Her Majesty's troops. The General Order of the Governor-General of 12th August, 1846, was issued accordingly.

GENERAL ORDER BY THE GOVERNOR-GENERAL,
Camp, Ferozepore, 25th Dec., 1845.

'The Right Honorable the Governor-General is pleased to direct the publication in General Orders of the following Notification in the Foreign Department.

'The Governor-General has the heartfelt satisfaction to announce to His Honor the President in Council, to the Army, and to the people of India, the repulse of the Sikh Forces, in their attack on a portion of the British Army near Moodkee, on the night of the 18th Instant; and the capture on the evening of the 21st, and morning of the 22nd, of their entrenched camp, with 70 pieces of cannon, defended by 60,000 men, near the village of Feroze Shah. Upwards of 90 pieces of the enemy's artillery have been taken in these two operations.

. . . .

'The Governor-General will rejoice in recording the gallant exploits of the Army during this important campaign, by decorating the breasts of the Victors with a Medal, as soon as the report of these operations shall be received from the Commander-in-Chief.'

GENERAL ORDER BY THE GOVERNOR-GENERAL,
Camp, Ferozepore, 30th Dec., 1845.

'The Governor-General having received from the Commander-in-Chief in India the Despatches of the dates which are noted in the margin,[1] directs that they be published for the information of the Army and the people of India.

'The first Despatch from His Excellency reports the operations of the Army on the evening of 18th inst., at Moodkee, where the enemy attempted to surprise the British camp, and were repulsed at all points with the loss of 17 guns.

'The second Despatch reports the glorious successes obtained by the Army under the immediate command of His Excellency on the evening of 21st, and the morning of 22nd, at Ferozeshah, where the British Army assaulted the entrenched camp of the Sikhs defended by 108 pieces of cannon, some of heavy calibre, and after driving the enemy from his position, captured 74 guns. Thus the enemy have been forced to relinquish to their victors on these occasions upwards of 90 pieces of artillery, with all the munitions of war in their camp.

---

[1] 19th Dec., 1845; 22nd Dec., 1845.

'The Government of India, as a tribute of their esteem for the meritorious conduct of the Troops engaged in the recent operations, will grant to every Officer and Soldier in the service of the Government of India, engaged in these battles, a Medal to be worn with their uniforms, on which the word "Ferozeshah" shall be inscribed, as denoting that they have served in this important campaign.

'The Commander-in-Chief will be so good as to furnish the Governor-General with Lists of all the Officers and Soldiers engaged in the operations of this campaign.

'The Governor-General is further pleased to order that the following corps be permitted to wear the word "Ferozeshah" upon their appointments, Standards and Colors, in perpetual commemoration of their gallant services.

1st and 3rd Brigades Horse Artillery.
2nd, 3rd and 4th Companies, 4 Battalion Artillery.
2nd and 4th ,, 6 ,,
2nd ,, 7 ,,
Governor-General's Body Guard.
4th, 5th, and 8th Regiments Light Cavalry.
3rd, 8th and 9th Regiments Irregular Cavalry.
1st European Light Infantry.
2nd, 12th, 14th, 16th, 24th, 26th, 33rd, 42nd, 44th, 45th, 47th, 48th, 54th and 73rd Regiments of Native Infantry.'

GENERAL ORDER BY THE GOVERNOR-GENERAL, *Camp, Ferozepore, 2nd February,* 1846.

'The Governor-General announces to the Army and the people of India, that he has received from H.E. the Commander-in-Chief of the Army a Report by Major-General Sir Harry Smith, K.C.B., dated 30th ultimo, giving the details of a complete victory gained by the troops under the immediate command of the Major-General, on the 28th January, over the Sikh Forces commanded by the Sirdar Runjoor Sing Mujeshea.

. . . .

'The Government of India, ever desirous to mark its grateful sense of the services of the Army, will cause a Medal to be presented to every Officer and Soldier of the East India Company's Service engaged in the Battle of Aliwal, and requests, through H.E. the Commander-in-Chief, that a nominal Roll may be furnished for that purpose.'

GENERAL ORDER BY THE GOVERNOR-GENERAL, Camp, Kussoor, 14th February, 1846—Foreign Department.

'The Governor-General, having received from H.E. the Commander-in-Chief the Despatch annexed to this paper, announces to the Army and people of India, for the fourth time during this campaign, a most important and memorable victory obtained by the Army of the Sutlej over the Sikh Forces at Sobraon, on the 10th inst.

. . . .

'To commemorate this great victory, the Governor-General will cause a Medal to be struck, with "Sobraon" engraved upon it, to be presented to the victorious army in the service of the East India Company, and requests H.E. the Commander-in-Chief to forward the Lists usually furnished of those engaged.'

FROM THE COURT OF DIRECTORS TO THE GOVERNMENT OF INDIA, 3rd March, 1846. No. 2—Military.

'1. We have perused with the highest gratification the tribute of applause rendered by the Governor-General in the General Orders of 30th Dec., 1845, to the Forces engaged in the late military operations at Moodkee and Ferozeshah.

'2. The Resolutions of the Government of India, as announced in those Orders, to grant to every Officer and Soldier in the service of the Government of India engaged in these battles a Medal on which the name "Ferozeshah" shall be inscribed, as denoting that they have served in this important campaign, and directing that the Corps therein named shall be permitted to wear the same on their appointments, Standards and Colours, in perpetual commemoration of their gallant services, have our most cordial approval.

'3. As a special mark of our high approbation of the zeal, energy and indomitable courage displayed by the Troops in these arduous conflicts, and of the perseverance and fortitude with which they overcame the extraordinary difficulties to which they were exposed, we have resolved that a Donation of 6 months' full Batta shall be presented to all the Generals and other Officers, Non-commissioned Officers and Privates engaged in the Battles of Moodkee and Ferozeshah.'

GENERAL ORDER BY THE GOVERNOR-GENERAL, Simla, 17th April, 1846—Foreign Department.

'In reference to the Governor-General's Orders granting Decorations to the Officers and Soldiers of the Army of the Sutlej, who were present at the Battles of Ferozeshah, Aliwal and Sobraon, the Governor-General is pleased to direct that a similar Decoration shall be bestowed upon every Officer and Soldier who fought in the Battle of Moodkee.

'H.E. the Commander-in-Chief will cause the List of Claimants to be made out and decided according to the following Rules.

'All Officers and Soldiers fit for duty, who were at Moodkee on 18th Dec. (1845) whether engaged in the field, or employed in guarding the Camp, will be entitled to receive a Medal for Moodkee.

'All Officers and Soldiers fit for duty, who were ordered to remain at Moodkee in performance of the important duty of protecting the wounded and the camp on 21st Dec., will receive a Decoration for the Battle of Ferozeshah.

'All Officers and Soldiers fit for duty, who in obedience to the orders of Major-General Sir John Littler, K.C.B., remained at their posts in defence of the Fort and Cantonments of Ferozepore on 21st Dec., will be entitled to be decorated for the Battle of Ferozeshah.

'All Officers and Soldiers fit for duty, who in obedience to the orders they received from Major-General Sir Harry Smith, K.C.B., remained in defence of the Forts of Loodianah and Buddowal on 28th January, will receive a Decoration for the Battle of Aliwal.

'All Officers and Soldiers fit for duty, who in obedience to the orders of the Commander-in-Chief remained in defence of the post of Rhodawalla and the Camp of the Commander-in-Chief on 10th Feb. (1846) will be decorated for the Battle of Sobraon.

'Officers and Soldiers not included under the preceding Rules will not be entitled to be decorated.

'If the individual is entitled to be decorated for two Battles he will receive one Silver Medal bearing the name of the first Battle in which he was engaged, and a clasp or bar on which will be inscribed the name of the second Battle. This Bar will be fixed on the Ribband immediately above the Medal.

'If entitled to be decorated for a third Battle, the name of that Battle will be inscribed on the 2nd Bar: and if entitled to be decorated for four Battles, the name of the fourth Battle shall be inscribed on the 3rd Bar, the Bars being fixed in the order in which the Battles were fought.'

'INDIA BOARD,
27th May, 1846.

'GENTLEMEN,

'As soon as the Court of Directors of the East India Company had expressed their cordial approbation of the Orders issued by the Governor-General of India, granting a Medal to such of the Company's Troops as were engaged in the Battles of Moodkee and Ferozeshah, I recommended to the Secretary of State for the Department of War that the same mark of distinction should be conferred by the Queen upon that portion of Her Majesty's Army which was similarly employed.

'I have been informed in reply that though the Crown, as intimated to the Court in Lord Jocelyn's letter of 31st March, will pay the expense of the Medals prepared for Her Majesty's Soldiers who were present at the Victories in Sinde, yet the Secretary of State and the Lords Commissioners of the Treasury are of opinion that any Medals, hereafter granted to the Royal Army for services performed in India, should be supplied at the charge of the Revenues of India, subject however to the authority and consent of the Sovereign.

'Under these circumstances I have the honor to request that you will move the Court to propose that the Governor-General in Council should be permitted to grant to H.M.'s Troops whatever marks of honor may have been conferred by that authority upon the East India Company's Army engaged in the recent brilliant campaign on the banks of the Sutlej.

'I have, etc.

'RIPON.

'The Chairman and Deputy Chairman
of the East India Company.'

'EAST INDIA HOUSE,
3rd June, 1846.

'MY LORD,

'We have the honor to acknowledge the receipt of your Lordship's Letter of 27th ult., conveying the gratifying announcement that the Court of Directors are at liberty to propose that the Governor-General in Council may be permitted to grant to Her Majesty's Troops whatever marks of honor may have been conferred by that authority upon the East India Company's Army engaged in the late brilliant campaign on the banks of the Sutlej.

'We have now the satisfaction, at the request of the Court of Directors, to state that the Draft of a Despatch to the Government of India is this day forwarded through the usual channel, for the approval of the Board of Commissioners, conveying the requisite authority for the grant of honorary Medals to all the General Officers, Officers and Soldiers of Her Majesty's Service, who were engaged respectively in the Battles of Moodkee, Ferozeshah, Aliwal and Sobraon: and for the grant of permission to wear those distinctive names upon their Standards and Colours, in perpetual commemoration of their gallant services.

'We have, etc.,

'J. W. HOGG.
HENRY ST. G. TUCKER.

'The Right Hon.
THE EARL OF RIPON,
India Board.'

FROM THE COURT OF DIRECTORS TO THE GOVERNMENT OF INDIA, 3rd June, 1846. No. 16—Military.

'1. In our Military Letter of 3rd March, 1846, we communicated to you our most cordial approval of the Resolutions of your Government, as announced in General Orders, to grant to every Officer and Soldier in the service of the Government of India engaged in the Battles of Moodkee and Ferozeshah a Medal on which the name of "Ferozeshah" should be inscribed, and directing that the Corps specified in the General Orders should be permitted to wear the same name on their Colours and appointments.

'2. The grant of similar honorary distinctions to the officers and men, and to the several corps of our Service who were engaged in the Battles of Aliwal and Sobraon, as announced in General Orders of 2nd and 14th Feby., 1846, have also our most cordial approval.

'3. We have now the gratification to announce to you that, in pursuance of permission to that effect given to us by H.M.'s Government, your Government is hereby authorised to grant H.M.'s Troops the same marks of honor as have been conferred by you on the East India Company's Army engaged in the recent brilliant campaign on the banks of the Sutlej.

'4. Appropriate Dies will be prepared, and the requisite Medals struck at the Royal Mint, so soon as we shall receive from you intimation of your wish that the Medals should be prepared in this country.'

FROM THE GOVERNOR-GENERAL TO THE COURT OF DIRECTORS, 21st July, 1846—Military.

'1. I have the honor to acknowledge the receipt of your Hon. Court's letter to the Government of India, of 3rd June last, No. 16, conveying to me your cordial approbation of the measures of this Government, in granting Medals and honorary distinctions for the four Battles fought on the banks of the Sutlege, and I participate in the gratification expressed by your Hon. Court, that the Queen has been pleased to authorise H.M.'s Troops to receive the same marks of honour as those conferred on the East India Company's Army.

'2. I strongly recommend that appropriate Dies should be prepared for the medals in H.M.'s Mint, in accordance with the description transmitted to England at the same time with the Government G. O.

'3. It affords me much satisfaction that your Hon. Court should approve of the Government G. O. of 22nd Feb., 1846, conferring on the Army of the Sutlege a donation of 12 months' Batta as a testimony of the approbation of the Government of India of their bravery, discipline and soldierlike bearing.

'4. I hope to be able to transmit to your Hon. Court by this mail a List from the Adjutant-General's Office, specifying the number of Medals and Bars required and the name of the Battle on each, trusting that your Hon. Court will excuse my impatience in requesting that the utmost expedition be used, in order that the Soldiers may be decorated with these honorable badges of their valor at the earliest possible period.

'HARDINGE.

'*P.S.*—The proper name of the place where the second Battle was fought is Ferozeshuhur, and I would recommend that this orthography be adopted on the Medal, and in all future official references.'

FROM THE GOVERNOR-GENERAL TO THE COURT OF DIRECTORS, Simla, 12th August, 1846. No. 4—Foreign.

'1. I reported to your Hon. Court by the last mail, in the Military Department, that I had received your Despatch of 3rd June, No. 16, and I have now the honour to transmit the General Order which I have published, relating to the Medals and honorary distinctions for Her Majesty's and the East India Company's Armies.

'2. I also transmit copy of a Memorandum shewing the mode in which the different arms of both Services now wear the honors conferred upon them, and if H.M.'s Government should think proper to issue any Regulations by which the present want of uniformity may be corrected, I propose to recommend to your Honorable Court that the system which may be decided upon for the Royal Army, should be adopted by your Army.

'3. I have sent a copy of the Memorandum[1] to the Horse Guards.

'HARDINGE.'

GENERAL ORDER BY THE GOVERNOR-GENERAL, Simla, 12th August, 1846—Foreign Department.

'The Governor-General has the satisfaction to announce to the Army that he has received a Despatch from the Court of Directors, conveying their cordial approval of the several Resolutions and Orders of the Government of India in granting Medals to every Officer and Soldier in the service of the East India Company engaged in the Battles of Moodkee, Ferozeshah, Aliwal and Sobraon.

'The Court also express their gratification in apprizing the Governor-General that, "in pursuance of permission given by Her Majesty, the Government of India is authorised to grant to H.M.'s Troops the same Medals and marks of honor as have been conferred by the Governor-General on the East India Company's Army engaged in the recent brilliant campaigns on the banks of the Sutlege."

'H.E. the Commander-in-Chief is requested to furnish the Governor-General with the nominal Rolls of all the Officers and Soldiers engaged in the four Battles of the Sutlege, in order that the Court of Directors may cause the required number of Medals to be struck at the Mint to be presented to H.M.'s Troops by the East India Company.

'The Governor-General authorises the several Regiments Troops and Companies of H.M.'s and the East India Company's Armies, actually engaged in these Battles, and named in the annexed Return, to bear upon their Colours, Standards and appointments, in the usual manner, the words "Moodkee," "Ferozeshah," "Aliwal" and "Sobraon."

'On every occasion during the late operations the European and Native Troops of the Army of the Sutledge, animated by the same spirit and united together by mutual esteem, have nobly emulated each other in their exertions.

'It is a source of much gratification to the Governor-General that the honors commemorative of the campaign are by H.M.'s permission to be the same for the European and Native Troops.'

(Return follows.)

---

[1] The memorandum above referred to relates to the manner of wearing distinctions on colours, appointments, etc.

FROM THE COURT OF DIRECTORS TO THE GOVERNMENT OF INDIA, 18*th Nov.*, 1846. No. 26—Militaiy.

Letter from the Governor-General, 21*st July*, 1846.

'In reply to Court's letter of 3rd June, 1846, No. 16, on the subject of the Medals to be granted for the actions on the Sutlej, the Governor-General recommends that appropriate Dies should be prepared in England, and forwards a List of the Medals and Bars required. The proper name of the place at which the second battle was fought is *Ferozeshuhur*.

'11. We have given orders for the immediate preparation of Dies for the Medals for the Battles fought on the banks of the Sutlej. When these are ready, we will cause the required number of Medals and Bars to be struck at the Royal Mint and forwarded to you for distribution.'

END OF VOLUME I.